UNREMITTING

UNREMITTING

THE MARINE "BASTARD" BATTALION AND THE SAVAGE BATTLE THAT MARKED THE TRUE START OF AMERICA'S WAR IN IRAQ

GREGG ZOROYA

GRAND CENTRAL

New York   Boston

Copyright © 2025 by Gregg Zoroya

Jacket design by Rodrigo Corral. Jacket copyright © 2025 by Hachette Book Group, Inc.

Hachette Book Group supports the right to free expression and the value of copyright. The purpose of copyright is to encourage writers and artists to produce the creative works that enrich our culture.

The scanning, uploading, and distribution of this book without permission is a theft of the author's intellectual property. If you would like permission to use material from the book (other than for review purposes), please contact permissions@hbgusa.com. Thank you for your support of the author's rights.

Grand Central Publishing
Hachette Book Group
1290 Avenue of the Americas, New York, NY 10104
grandcentralpublishing.com
@grandcentralpub

First Edition: June 2025

Grand Central Publishing is a division of Hachette Book Group, Inc.
The Grand Central Publishing name and logo is a registered trademark of Hachette Book Group, Inc.

The publisher is not responsible for websites (or their content) that are not owned by the publisher.

The Hachette Speakers Bureau provides a wide range of authors for speaking events. To find out more, go to hachettespeakersbureau.com or email HachetteSpeakers@hbgusa.com.

Grand Central Publishing books may be purchased in bulk for business, educational, or promotional use. For information, please contact your local bookseller or the Hachette Book Group Special Markets Department at special.markets@hbgusa.com.

Select insert photos from *The Philadelphia Inquirer.* © 2025 Philadelphia Inquirer, LLC. All rights reserved. Used under license.

Print book interior design by Bart Dawson.

Library of Congress Control Number: 2025934020

ISBNs: 978-0-306-83302-1 (hardcover); 978-0-306-83304-5 (ebook)

Printed in Canada

MRQ-T

10 9 8 7 6 5 4 3 2 1

TO FAYE

For her love, her laugh, her spirit,
her decision to choose me

unremitting adj. Of an activity, condition, process, etc.;
continuing without pause or reduction in intensity;
continuous, constant, incessant.

—*Oxford English Dictionary*

CONTENTS

LIST OF MAPS	ix
FOREWORD BY GENERAL JOE DUNFORD, US MARINE CORPS (RET.)	xi
PROLOGUE	1
1 BASTARDS	11
2 CITY	28
3 PRELUDE	45
4 EVE OF BATTLE	72
5 BATTLE, DAY 1: CITY CENTER	91
6 BATTLE, DAY 1: SOFIA DISTRICT	120
7 BATTLE, DAY 1: THE AMBUSH	155
8 BATTLE, DAY 2	195
9 BATTLE, DAY 3	212
10 LUNACY	240
11 PERSEVERANCE	253
12 MISTAKES	272
13 WICKEDNESS	286
14 EXIT	317
EPILOGUE	339
ACKNOWLEDGMENTS	379
NOTES	383
INDEX	395
ABOUT THE AUTHOR	417

LIST OF MAPS

1	Iraq	xiv
2	Ramadi City Center	27
3	April 6 Ambushes of Golf Company Squads	90
4	April 6 Ambush of First Squad	97
5	April 6 Attacks on Echo Company Marines	113
6	April 6 Echo Company Movements Prior to Gypsum/Nova Ambush	146
7	April 6 Ambush at Gysum/Nova Intersection	171
8	April 10 Echo Company Fighting	211

FOREWORD

by General Joe Dunford, US Marine Corps (Ret.)

I WAS A colonel leading the 5th Marine Regiment during the invasion of Iraq in early 2003. I handed over command of that storied unit in May of that year and remained in Iraq serving as chief of staff for the 1st Marine Division.

When the division finally went home, I was on the last plane out in October, learning soon after that we would return early the next year. We arrived in March 2004 for what was originally thought to be a security-and-stability operation.

Earning trust and cooperation were the orders of the day, along with reestablishing basic services from electrical power to trash collection and continuing the task of building back Iraqi security forces for the anticipated handover of power to a new Iraqi government.

If the level of violence had gradually increased since the previous summer, precipitating the return of the Marine 1st Division so soon after the invasion, it was still thought to be only from remnants of the Baathist party that ruled Iraq under Saddam Hussein.

But that was post-invasion thinking. We were on the eve of something far more sinister and organized. Within a few weeks, Division leadership realized it was facing a Salafist and Sunni insurgency in Al Anbar Province.

We didn't yet know the breadth and depth of it. Nor could anyone have predicted that its most organized attack would be in the provincial capital of Ramadi aimed directly at 2nd Battalion, 4th Marines, known as "The Magnificent Bastards."

It literally unfolded in the front yard of 1st Marine Division headquarters in a palace located on the north shore of the Euphrates River just across from Ramadi.

The Marine Corps is demographically a young service with enlisted ranks made up of men and women who often join right out of high school. But 2nd Battalion, 4th Marines was disproportionately younger when it fought in Ramadi. The year before, the unit had returned from extended duty in the Western Pacific that included months where careers were frozen by stop-loss. When the battalion finally returned to California and prepared for duty in Iraq, so many Marines were cycling out that the unit was far below allotted strength. It had to be rebuilt in large part with brand-new Marines.

Almost as soon as the battalion took over combat operations in central Ramadi in March, enemy activity ensued and increased until reaching a crescendo in early April, particularly April 6. Twelve battalion members were killed that day. Insurgent attacks were spreading across Iraq, but the degree of enemy coordination, violence, and success in Ramadi was remarkable. Some of the worst actors within the Iraq insurgency were in Ramadi.

The Marines and sailors of 2/4 were tested as few have been since the Vietnam War. They were operating in an urban environment where the enemy was 360 degrees. There is no secure rear area. You're fighting at times in confined, uncertain spaces. There are improvised explosive devices in the streets. There are people shooting at you. Returning fire can be difficult because of the presence of unarmed civilians. I can't imagine more difficult circumstances.

I knew the battalion well, as it was part of 5th Regiment that I had commanded. I had served in combat with their senior leaders.

FOREWORD

Had promoted some of them. Knew their spouses. These were my guys.

What I saw in Ramadi made me proud of the leadership and the courage of Marines fighting at the lower tactical level. Despite the dangers, they went out there every day knowing there was a chance they might be killed. No one said no.

Moreover, despite the loss of buddies to wounds or death, they still treated the people of Ramadi with decency. They retained their humanity in the face of so much violence.

This is their story.

General Joe Dunford, USMC (Ret.)
19th Chairman, Joint Chiefs of Staff
36th Commandant of the Marine Corps

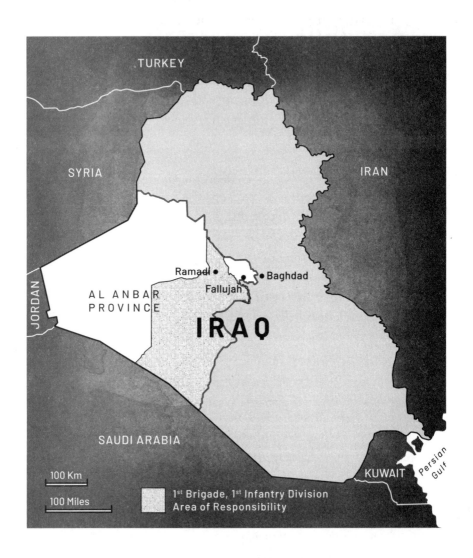

PROLOGUE

THEY WERE CHRISTENED "The Magnificent Bastards," yet they were warriors without a war. Kept stateside after 9/11 and left floating in the Pacific during the invasion of Iraq in 2003, the thousand men of 2nd Battalion, 4th Marines were told they were benchwarmers in a time of combat. America sent 21,000 other Marines to sweep across southern Iraq in March and April and achieve the longest sustained overland advance in Corps history as they drove toward the capital of Baghdad—and glory.[1] Two months later, George Bush rode a Navy jet to a cinematic touchdown on an aircraft carrier off San Diego and declared the war all but over. "Major combat operations in Iraq have ended," he told sailors against the backdrop of a "Mission Accomplished" banner. But war exploded less than a year later. The Bastard battalion found itself at the center of metastasizing attacks and violence across Iraq, fighting in the provincial capital of Ramadi. Enemy leaders designed a three-day offensive aimed at driving the Marines from the city of 450,000. What emerged was the kind of organized resistance that would characterize the Iraq War for years to come. During that Ramadi fight and throughout seven months of deployment, 2nd Battalion, 4th Marines suffered among the highest casualties of any other battalion. Many

PROLOGUE

soldiers from supporting forces died with them. The Marines responded with deadly proficiency, transforming hospitals and mosques into charnel houses, where the bodies of hundreds of Arab fighters were stacked. Yet much of the world's attention at that moment would be focused on an assault by several thousand other Marines on the smaller city of Fallujah, and what happened in Ramadi was nearly lost to history. James Mattis, Marine commander and later secretary of defense, would later testify before Congress that "for all you heard of Fallujah, Ramadi was the key terrain" and that Ramadi was "one of the toughest fights the Marine Corps has fought since Vietnam."

Their story has largely been untold.

KILL SHOTS

Years after the battle, Chris MacIntosh's memories would carry him back to that day he was trapped in a carport on the outskirts of Ramadi. Back to the kill shots he fired. And the tears would flow.

The recollections sometimes came to him when he was alone soaking in a tub of lukewarm water in his lake house home in East Bridgewater, Massachusetts. Flickering images always unspooled the same awful story: men with AK-47s charging around a corner, intent on killing him and a comrade Marine.

It was madness. Crouched beside him was a nineteen-year-old private first class barely out of high school and basic training. He and MacIntosh had raced into the courtyard of this house, fully aware that at least a half a dozen or more enemy gunmen were steps behind. The two had slipped around a corner into the carport and, at the front of a parked sedan, rifles at the ready, were ready to make a *last stand*.

So bodies piled up. First one, then two, then three, tumbling down in the carport, a dark red pool of blood oozing across the concrete floor. MacIntosh and Akey were firing almost point-blank. A

PROLOGUE

fourth fighter emerged, a man with a dark and angry look as if furious about whatever was going on. He pulled up short at the entrance, but the Marines shot him down, too.

Then MacIntosh, for good measure, put a bullet in each man's head to guard against a wounded enemy pulling a trigger or the pin on a hidden grenade.

Kill shots.

In that moment, MacIntosh found himself acting on instinct and training. If there was any emotion, it might have been anger— *How fucking dare you!* Days after the battle, there was pride in his ability to do what had been necessary. He'd proven himself a Marine: the consummate clearheaded warrior who could kill when called upon. No better friend, no worse enemy.

It was a stark contrast to MacIntosh's reputation as platoon class clown, the skinny goofball who drove officers nuts until they realized he had a gift for boosting morale when his fellow Marines were most in need. "He looked like a disheveled bag of ass," a former commander recalled with full-throated fondness. Nothing was sacrosanct, said Marine buddy Theophilus Tor. "He didn't only address the elephant in the room. He sat on the elephant. He fed the elephant peanuts."

But those nights—years after Ramadi and the Marine Corps— when MacIntosh soaked and wept, that unfettered spirit was gone. In its place was an ethereal web of harrowing, existential questions that stoked doubts.

What was that all about? Who exactly was the enemy? How could I have been granted such godlike power? And why does it feel, in the end, that I killed a bunch of people in their own backyard who were just defending their homes?

"I DID A HORRIBLE THING."

Grainy footage from an overhead security camera shows a middle-aged man in jeans and a hooded sweatshirt, unsteady from

PROLOGUE

too many drinks, slowly turning to grasp the back of a restaurant chair with both hands to use as a club.

The images are from the DarSalam Iraqi restaurant in Portland, Oregon, in April 2017. The man in the hooded sweatshirt is forty-year-old Marine Sergeant Major Damien Rodriguez, veteran of four combat deployments and recipient of the Bronze Star for valor during vicious fighting in Ramadi thirteen years before.

The video would bring his decorated military career to an end.

When Rodriguez arrived at the restaurant with a friend, a retired Marine, the two had already been drinking. They took a table where Rodriguez stared at scenes of the Iraqi countryside decorating the restaurant walls, glaring at employees, refusing to order food, loud and abusive. "Fuck your food. Fuck your restaurant," witnesses heard him say. "I have killed your people."

When a waiter told Rodriguez to be respectful, the video shows the Marine, now on his feet, turning to grab the chair. He pauses as if to steady himself, and then, leading with his left hip (witnesses hear him shout, "Fuck Iraqis"), he swings the chair so hard that he not only knocks down the waiter but loses his balance and goes sprawling to the floor. He comes up swinging, and a clutch of people restrain him.

The arrest that followed drew national headlines as prosecutors weighed whether to send Rodriguez to prison for a hate crime or consider leniency for a combat veteran who considerable evidence showed was afflicted with severe post-traumatic stress disorder.

A defense lawyer introduced in court health records proving Rodriguez's struggle with flashbacks and alcohol. Among the searing images from Ramadi haunting him was the fly-covered corpse of a Marine he found, another nineteen-year-old, who had been shot through the head. Rodriguez described in an after-action report how the young man was so terrified at the moment of death that he'd pissed his pants.

PROLOGUE

Prosecutors struck an agreement calling for probation and a fine, but no prison. "I did a horrible thing," Rodriguez said in court to victims of his crime. "The incident that took place in your restaurant breaks my heart. That is not the man and Marine I am."

"THE LAST THING YOU'RE EVER GOING TO FUCKING SEE."

The most magnificent of the Magnificent Bastards for the rank-and-file Marines who did the fighting and dying in Ramadi was Jim Booker.

He was the battalion sergeant major, a legend at age forty-two before the shooting even started. He had earned elite status as a Force Recon sniper trained to operate behind enemy lines, was awarded a Bronze Star for valor during combat in the Persian Gulf War, and fought in the 2003 Iraq invasion.

The slightest approbation from Booker was like a lifetime achievement award for the average Marine. The second time Brandon Lund was wounded in Ramadi, as he was carried down from a lookout post where a mortar round had just exploded, he spotted Booker and called out, "That's two, Sergeant Major."

"You're a fucking stud, Lund," Booker responded. The young Marine would never forget those words.

Within his portfolio of duties, Booker made a personal mission of overseeing the removal of dead Marines from Ramadi. When one of his men was decapitated by a rocket-propelled grenade round, Booker assumed the grim task of picking up the shards and slippery shreds left behind. And when others lay wounded in the Army medical facility across the canal, it was the sergeant major who bedded down nearby, a guardian angel while they slept.

When there was combat, Booker roamed the city with his big-caliber, nonregulation M14—a descendant of the World War II–era M1 Garand—and always seemed to show up when the fighting was at its most brutal. Hunkered-down Marines would glance over their shoulders, and there was Booker (often with the battalion commander, Lieutenant Colonel Paul Kennedy). "He was and still is to this day a badass motherfucker," Lance Corporal Jason Rosman would later write about Booker in a self-published memoir of his Ramadi experience he titled *I Should Have Gone to College*.[2]

The sergeant major once summarized the combat in Ramadi as "the biggest, widest, nastiest, downright gritty grunt fight I've ever seen." During those moments when he came face-to-face with the enemy, Booker was calm, efficient, and relentless. Marines and Navy corpsmen who had lost too many friends to a resourceful and illusive insurgency took note. He was their Ahab in a deadly pursuit of a faceless adversary.

He would enjoy a long and illustrious career, rising to regimental sergeant major, senior enlisted adviser to the allied command in Afghanistan, and finally earning his place on the shortest of candidate lists to become sergeant major of the entire Marine Corps. But the experience of Ramadi never left Booker. Even after retirement in 2015, a massive stroke months later, and the years of recovery that followed, Booker still drew pleasure from recounting feverish moments when he ran Arab fighters to ground.

Standing in the kitchen of his hilltop home northeast of Waco, Texas, in the spring of 2022, his arms raised as if still holding the M14, Booker described one emblematic moment during desperate fighting on April 10, 2004, when Marines and Army troops launched a counterattack on insurgent forces.

Booker had taken off after a black-clad enemy fighter who opened fire on him and other Marines with a light machine gun before turning to flee across a field. After a pursuit of several hundred yards, the gunman climbed up to the roof of a house and, with two other Iraqi insurgents, resumed firing away at the Americans. By the time Booker arrived there on foot, Marines had already charged up a set of stairs to reach the roof, only to be driven back down by automatic weapons fire that left three wounded. Among them was twenty-year-old Jose Texidor Jr., "Tex" to his friends, whose left leg was nearly severed at the knee by a round from the insurgent's machine gun. Blood spouted like a fountain as Tex was dragged downstairs so a corpsman could staunch the hemorrhaging.

Describing that event many years later, Booker remembered feeling rage at the sight of the mangled Texidor. "I thought he was dead." (In fact, the wounded Marine would survive.) The sergeant major quickly organized another assault up the stairs, this time first peppering the roof with grenades. Finally reaching the upper level, where two of the enemy fighters now lay dead, Booker found the gunman in black. The man was clearly dying from his wounds and struggling to suck in air. What Booker said to him would mirror the savage nature of what the battle of Ramadi had become.

"You motherfucker . . . you mujahideen motherfucker. You see my white, Christian face? It's the last thing you're ever going to fucking see."

"IF THE MEN DON'T SEE YOU SHARING THE SAME HARDSHIPS, THEY'RE NOT GOING TO LISTEN TO YOU."

Buck Connor knows the medication he takes to quell tremors from Parkinson's disease is no cure. It buys the retired Army colonel, who lives in the foothills of the Blue Ridge Mountains north of Atlanta, a few temperate hours when he feels closest to normal. Some days are better than others. But the brain disorder will never improve.

Ramadi is the cause of it.

In 2004, Connor commanded 1st Brigade of the Big Red One— the Army's vaunted 1st Infantry Division, the oldest continuously operated division in American history, organized in 1917. The brigade deployed to Iraq in August and September 2003 to provide security for an area of operations that was fifty thousand square miles of mostly southwestern Iraqi desert and scrubland. The biggest city, with nearly a half million people, was Ramadi, stretched out along the south bank of the Euphrates River. In a twist dictated by the exigencies of war planning, the Magnificent Bastards were attached to the Army 1st Brigade, led by Connor, and given the job of securing Ramadi. (That brigade, in turn, fell under the 1st Marine Division's area of operation in Iraq, resulting in a Marine battalion working for an Army brigade working for a Marine division.)

With his headquarters on the edge of Ramadi, Connor frequently ventured into the city and into combat with his security detail, sometimes fighting on foot with a pump-action, twelve-gauge shotgun loaded alternately with buckshot and slugs. Always with his distinctive bright yellow leather gloves. Marines caught in street fighting might look around to see an Army colonel in the thick of it with them. Connor had been a history student at West Point, and for anyone who thought his risk-taking unwise, he would explain that his inspiration was Union commanders during the Civil War who led from the front to inspire their troops and who didn't always survive.

"If the men don't see you sharing the same hardships, they're not going to listen to you," Connor would say. "If you're willing to do it, they're going to do it."

Eight times his command column was attacked by roadside bombs. The worst of it was May 26. Connor's Humvee was third in a five-vehicle convoy heading out of town at forty miles per hour when buried plastic explosives and a 155 mm artillery shell were detonated almost underneath where he was sitting. Soldiers in the vehicle behind saw debris fly two hundred feet into the air as the explosion appeared to engulf the colonel's Humvee. But much of the shrapnel went in the wrong direction. Connor seemed at first unscathed. The windshield blew out, and the Humvee was filled with dust and the smell of cordite as it rolled to a stop. Connor, who was forty-four at the time, felt an enormous pressure on his chest and body when the bomb went off, and lost consciousness. He collapsed after being pulled from the vehicle. When he came out of his haze, an Army doctor tried to quiz him. Connor said he was fine and then passed out, regaining consciousness in an Army aid station.

He refused to be evacuated to a higher level of medical care for a brain scan. Instead, with the help of a compliant brigade surgeon, Connor continued attending staff briefings, hiding his dizziness or vomiting until he left the meetings. All were strong signs of traumatic brain injury.

Two months later, on July 14, it happened again. Connor was riding in a fully armored Humvee when a bomb exploded in the heart of Ramadi. Once more, he seemed unharmed, before collapsing two steps out of the Humvee. Connor remained in command until the brigade went home.

Six years later, he was diagnosed with Parkinson's, a disorder to which scientists have drawn a direct line from traumatic brain injury.

1

BASTARDS

"YOU GO TO WAR WITH THE ARMY YOU HAVE."

THIRTY-THREE MARINES AND a sailor from 2nd Battalion, 4th Marines died in combat during seven months in Ramadi in 2004. That amounted to more than half the combat deaths inflicted on the entire reinforced combat brigade commanded by Buck Connor.

In all, 30 percent of 2/4's nearly 1,000 troops—or 289 Marines and sailors—were killed or wounded during the deployment. The battalion's hardest-hit company, Echo, had a casualty rate of 45 percent.

In response, they killed enemy fighters by the hundreds.

The Iraq War had started a year earlier in March 2003 when a US-led invasion swept across southern Iraq to overwhelm Iraqi forces and capture Baghdad in seven weeks. Casualties were relatively light. Bush all but declared victory on that aircraft carrier, and there were months of reasonable calm.

The kind of grinding insurgency that would define for Americans the next seven years in Iraq really began in 2004, and the epicenter was Ramadi.

That commencement carried with it more than just bloodier gunfights. The signature traumas that would bedevil US troops over the next decade or more of combat in Iraq and Afghanistan had roots in the violence of 2004. It was on these battlefields where traumatic brain injury from bomb blasts and post-traumatic stress disorder began afflicting troops in large numbers.

And the American military was utterly unprepared. Apart from a battalion chaplain making rounds, there were almost no uniformed therapists to counsel Marines troubled by any number of torments—the emotional trauma of heavy combat, the loss of close friends, the guilt of surviving, the toll of taking lives, and the ambiguity of a war with blurred distinctions between friend and foe where what constituted victory was a moral conundrum. A Pentagon policy to fully embrace and promote mental health care was still years away.

Nor did military medicine in 2004 understand the complexities of traumatic brain injury, particularly when it came to blast wave exposure and how that differs from a blow to the head. And it would be years before research showed that TBI, PTSD, and depression could be inextricably linked, with the injury from a bomb blast aggravating the emotional disorder from the experience of war.

It would, again, be years before scientists understood that simply being near an explosion, even in the absence of shrapnel wounds or loss of consciousness, could cause neural impairment. They would discover that repeated exposure, particularly within a few days, could cause permanent damage. And it would be even longer before battlefield protocols were in place requiring blast-exposed troops to be pulled from combat, thoroughly assessed, subjected to imaging scans, and allowed time for rest and healing.

Too many Marines who survived Ramadi would later succumb to the scourge of suicide, the rising occurrence of which— across America's military and veteran population—would shock

BASTARDS   13

the nation for years to come. Headlines would scream that twenty to twenty-two veterans were killing themselves *every day*. (VA methodology behind the numbers, it later turned out, was flawed and the actual rate was closer to sixteen per day, still far higher than nonveteran suicides.)

When the real war started in 2004, the American military was not even up to the task of providing adequate vehicle armor to guard against what was quickly becoming the enemy's weapon of choice—the roadside bomb, or IED (improvised explosive device), which debuted at scale on the streets where the Magnificent Bastards waged combat.

The staple of Army and Marine Corps troop transport up until that time was the Humvee, a squat, thinly protected truck ideal for cross-country mobility. But its body of aluminum, plastic, and fiberglass and its flat-bottom chassis were no match against powerful land mines. As early as the 1990s, the US military began looking at buying heavily armored vehicles with V-shaped hulls designed to deflect and mitigate blasts.

Both the US Army and Marine Corps had certain models in mind, already commercially available, that they wanted to start buying. But high costs and ossified procurement processes created delays and cancellations. It wasn't until 2007 that large numbers of what would be called MRAPs (mine-resistant ambush-protected vehicles) would be provided to troops in combat.

Meanwhile, the Pentagon ordered a newly produced brand of Humvee with a steel frame, and a stream of these began flowing overseas in February 2004. But by then, 2/4 was already in Kuwait, heading into Iraq. Marines were left to scrounge scrap metal to bolt onto the old aluminum/plastic/fiberglass models. "Hillbilly armor" they called it. Even with that, the Marines riding in open-backed troop carrier Humvees still had their shoulders and heads exposed. Steel plates were also bolted on the tall, cargo trucks that the Marines called "7-tons" because they were heavy enough to haul seven tons off-road. It was a Band-Aid solution that too many paid for with their lives. "There is no doubt in my mind some of the Marines that have been lost would be alive right now if we had the better vehicles," Gunnery Sergeant Bernard C. Coleman of Echo Company wrote in an after-action report halfway through the deployment.

Still, many Marines took the shoddy protective measures in stride in the tradition that the Corps always had to do more with less. But there were those like twenty-one-year-old Lance Corporal Roy Thomas of Echo Company—born on the Fourth of July, the son of a factory worker and a college cook, from central Michigan—who were shocked that the US government would send troops to war in thin-skinned vehicles. It made him feel like he was just a number on a "big government" tally sheet.

In December 2004, three months after the decimated battalion came home, Defense Secretary Donald Rumsfeld used a stopover in Kuwait to chat with a group of war-bound troops. A couple of soldiers in the audience asked questions about how the Pentagon had dropped the ball on protective vehicle armor. Rumsfeld's widely reported response was weak tea: "You go to war with the Army you have, not the Army you might want or wish you have at a later time."

He was tragically spot-on. When it came to shielding troops from the emotional and physical horrors of a new conflict, the Magnificent Bastards went to war with what little they had, and far less than what they needed.

"MY LIEUTENANTS AND I CHALLENGE ANYBODY WITH BALLS TO A THUNDERDOME."

They bitterly came to call themselves "No-War 2/4."

And who could blame them? They were a battalion nested within one of the most storied regiments in Marine Corps history, the Fighting Fifth out of Camp Pendleton, California. Yet when the time came for the invasion of Iraq, every other battalion in the regiment was sent into the fray except 2nd Battalion, 4th Marines. The Magnificent Bastards were left floating in the ocean. Quite literally.

Months before the invasion, the battalion had been cycled out to the western Pacific for a six-month deployment as part of a Marine expeditionary unit—an assemblage of infantry, aircraft, tanks, artillery, and amphibious landing vehicles pre-positioned on Okinawa or on Navy ships, and capable of being launched into trouble spots within six hours. It was a routine mission.

When there wasn't trouble, which was most of the time, they were training aboard ships, in the jungles of Okinawa, on frozen hilltops in South Korea, or on the beaches of the iconic World War II battle site of Iwo Jima. On leave, they drank themselves into oblivion.

It was a fighting unit with a strong heritage. The history of 2nd Battalion, 4th Marines dated back to some of the toughest fighting of the Vietnam War when then commander Joseph R. "Bull" Fisher—who was himself a legend in the Corps as recipient of two Silver Stars and a Navy Cross—chose the moniker "the Magnificent Bastards." The nom de guerre stuck and found its way onto the unit's official coat of arms.

But now, as the nation was preparing to invade Iraq, military planners decided in their haste to rearrange and redirect troop formations to just leave 2/4 in the Pacific for another six months.

The famous fighting bastards who had trained for war would have nothing to do with it.

Not only that, but the decision to keep them in the Pacific disrupted lives. Marines who were supposed to finish their tours of service—and made plans with their families to move on to new places and careers—were suddenly stop-lossed, their military status frozen in place. Marriages and relationships suffered. Colonel Joe Dunford, regimental commander, spent four and a half hours in a Camp Pendleton auditorium fielding angry questions from more than three hundred spouses anxious because homes had already been sold or base housing already vacated, or identification cards already expired.

Morale plummeted as 2/4 Marines watched their comrades on television fight their way to Baghdad and into Corps history. And it certainly didn't help when Marine Corps commandant Michael Hagee paid a visit in April 2003 and spoke to an assemblage of Marines in the hangar bay of the amphibious assault ship USS *Essex*. His remarks went over like a bad smell at a garden party, essentially telling them a nation at war needs a good B team waiting in the wings. "Every good team needs benchwarmers," Hagee said.

That was the last thing they needed to hear. Some actually started walking out. Others stood seething. "You got to be kidding me," platoon commander John "JD" Stephens was thinking. "I stood at attention for an hour and a half for this shit?" Echo Company Marine Brian Telinda was so roiled that when Hagee and his wife, Silke, began greeting several of the troops, the twenty-one-year-old Marine created a bit of a spectacle by refusing to shake hands with the commandant's wife. Snubbing Hagee would have been an infraction, but his wife, Telinda surmised, was fair game. That view wasn't shared by platoon Sergeant Damien Coan, who yanked the young Marine out of formation and delivered what is commonly referred to in the Corps as a "good ass-chewing."

The truth was that 2/4 Marines, despite being left at the altar by the war's architects, were so convinced of their neglected prowess as warriors that they were starting to exhibit their own brand of swagger, one that lived up to their nickname. They might not be as squared away or straitlaced or pretty as other Marine formations marching off to war and triumph. But they manifested a grit and moxie that said these Marines could do what was necessary. Floating on those ships out in the ocean, all they had time for was

BASTARDS

eating and lifting weights, and they were turning into bulked-up bruisers. Jim Booker, who took over as battalion sergeant major about the time the unit was coming home, thought they looked like they'd just gotten out of prison. He worried they might kick the shit out of anybody who crossed them. "We really were bastards," recalled Lucas Wells, a fifth-generation Texan and one of the battalion's few Annapolis graduates.

They thought all the fuss was over in Iraq with George Bush's announcement. They didn't know the brass ring—with all the horrors of war it promised—was still waiting for them.

More immediately, they got Lieutenant Colonel Paul Kennedy as a new battalion commander. He was a James Mattis protégé who served as the lead invasion planner for the 1st Marine Division commander when the fighting started in 2003. Before that, he had been among a select group of officers accepted into the Marine Corps School of Advanced Warfighting, a prestigious opportunity for rising officers to study history and travel to the world's most famous battlefields courtesy of the Corps.

Kennedy was ambitious and competitive. A woman reporter who embedded with his battalion in Ramadi described him as a handsome man with a derisively mocking side to his nature.

Kennedy arrived at 2/4 with orders to restore morale and rebuild discipline after a scandalous firing of a predecessor and a bitterness by Marines of having been shunted aside by the Corps. He thought he had at least six months to a year to turn things around.

A Boston University graduate and a native of Hartford, Connecticut, Kennedy, then forty, was the third of four children in an Irish Catholic family that believed displays of emotion were a sign of weakness. His grandmother O'Brien had emigrated from the same clan in Tipperary, Ireland, as the Kennedys of Hyannis Port, and there were thought to be ancient familial connections. (In fact, Paul Kennedy bears a passing resemblance, especially around the eyes.)

Military service within the family was almost a given. Paul Kennedy's grandfather was a submariner in the First World War, and his grandmother was among the first women allowed to join the Navy. The boy was weaned on stories of war from a father and three uncles who served during World War II. From his mother, Constance, who for forty years ran a throwaway advertiser called the *Yankee Flyer*, Kennedy learned toughness and to never back down from a challenge. From his father, he learned about the hidden costs of war. Richard Kennedy would lose the thread of a career as he sank into alcohol abuse. He was almost certainly afflicted with post-traumatic stress disorder from experiences at the Battle of the Bulge and the capture of the bridge at Remagen, Germany.

When Paul Kennedy took command of 2nd Battalion, 4th Marines in late May 2003, much of the officer upper echelon was rotating out. One exception was a rising captain in command of one of the battalion companies. Dave "JD" Harrill had been kicked out of his first year at the Naval Academy, only to immediately drive south to Auburn University and sign up for the ROTC program there, determined to fulfill a childhood dream of becoming a Marine Corps officer.

Kennedy thought Harrill showed considerable promise and, after Harrill's promotion to major, tapped him for the pivotal job of running operations and training for the battalion. Harrill would take center stage when 2/4 came under withering attacks in Ramadi, earning a Silver Star for heroism in combat.

One new battalion addition was Mike Wylie as executive officer, a native of South Carolina whose father had been a torpedoman on both attack and ballistic missile submarines, the so-called boomers. (Wylie, as a teenager, spent seven days aboard the USS *Newport News* as part of an ROTC summer program, and that quickly affirmed the boy's desire to join the Marine Corps.) As battalion intel officer, Kennedy chose Wyeth Towle, who shared with the commander the alma mater of Boston University.

BASTARDS

Towle was on the rowing team there. Raised in an upper-middle-class home in the Bay Area, he had been an Eagle Scout who devoured Tom Clancy novels. His father worked for a computer company in nearby Silicon Valley, and the decision to join the Marines was out of step with everything his parents wanted for him.

Apart from rebuilding battalion leadership, Kennedy had to deal with the wide-scale hemorrhaging of enlisted Marines as the unit finally returned from Okinawa. The usual attrition any battalion undergoes after six months deployed was made worse for 2/4 because of the additional six months overseas when all Marines were stop-lossed. After stop-loss was finally lifted, hundreds of Marines whose enlistments were up or who were looking for a transfer began streaming out of the battalion.

Added to this were orders for a deployment sooner rather than later. Kennedy was attending the Marine Corps birthday bash November 10 when Major General Mattis pulled him aside to tell him his Marines were finally heading to Iraq for seven months. (The general had a soft spot for the Magnificent Bastards because he had served as a platoon commander in 2/4 as a second lieutenant.) The Bush administration's early view of Iraq, promoted by Defense Secretary Donald Rumsfeld, that resistance in the country was fading and relegated to a few Ba'athist-regime "dead-enders," had been shown to be terribly wrong, and violence was increasing. The 1st Marine Division, which had just left Iraq a few months earlier, was going to be sent right back. This time, 2nd Battalion, 4th Marines would be part of the action. (Weeks earlier in October, then Colonel Joe Dunford, division chief of staff, was on the last plane leaving Iraq after the Marine invasion campaign. Mattis greeted him upon arrival at March Air Force Base east of Los Angeles and told him they were likely going right back.)

At the birthday ball, Kennedy asked Mattis how much time he had to prepare. The general told him to be ready by January.

The machine for making Marines kicked into high gear. In the next three months, the battalion received a series of "boot drops"—arriving batches of newly minted Marines just out of boot camp and the Corps School of Infantry. As ranks were replenished, 40 percent of the battalion's junior enlisted infantrymen were brand spanking new, 229 in all, an unusually high influx at such a late hour.

Almost half showed up in January, a few weeks before the battalion would head to Kuwait and then on to Iraq. And that was just newly arrived boots. There were more than a hundred other more senior enlisted and commissioned officers who'd arrived just a few months, weeks, or even days before heading to Iraq. Kennedy knew there wasn't enough time for the battalion to fully coalesce and integrate new members. It wasn't an ideal way to enter combat.

In years to come, he would say the Magnificent Bastards fought the war of 2004 with the high school graduating class of 2003. He wasn't far off.

They were the youngest of men with almost no life experience, rushing headlong into a violent and uncertain future. In a few cases, as their Marine brethren would learn from private barrack conversations, that included some who had never had sex. And tragically, as it turned out, never would.

They were teenagers, barely legal age. There was Marcus Cherry, just seventeen and already engaged to marry his high school sweetheart back in the Imperial Valley of California. Matthew Milczark and Moisés Langhorst, both eighteen, were friends who graduated from Moose Lake High School in Moose Lake, Minnesota—where Matt was homecoming king and Moisés was on the school's championship Knowledge Bowl team—before both enlisted in the Marines, reporting to the battalion the day before Thanksgiving 2003. There was Kyle Crowley, eighteen, from San Ramon, California, who enlisted over his father's objections. He showed up in December 2003 and wasted little time distinguishing himself. And there was Dean Cugliotta Jr., nicknamed "Marine Dean" at his tiny Michigan high school because he started shaving his head even before joining the Corps at seventeen, right after graduation.

One other "boot" who showed up in January just weeks before the battalion left for Iraq may have had the most tangible connection with the nation's war on terror than any other Marine in 2/4. Justin Weaver grew up in rural Pennsylvania not far from Shanksville and, with other students at Shade-Central High School in nearby Cairnbrook, had been sent home when the 9/11 attacks began. Walking to his house, he saw Flight 93 miles to the west, likely at the moment passengers were fighting to gain entry into the hijacked cockpit. He could see the wings rock back and forth. The aircraft crashed seconds later. Weaver graduated two years later, entered the Marine Corps, and reported to 2/4.

With the battalion, he and the other boots fell in with the more senior members they saw as experienced in all matters, though almost none had actually been to war. And that was a point of endless irritation for the older enlisteds, because too often it was brought to their attention that they had never heard a shot fired in anger. During a victory parade down the streets of Oceanside, California, in October, resplendent with dignitaries cheering thousands of Iraq War veterans marching past in desert tan uniforms, No-War 2/4 Marines were in formation wearing jungle green because they hadn't been anywhere near the desert. Sometimes, the jeers and the razzing by the combat-ribbon-wearing members of 5th Marines led to arguments and fistfights.

It boiled over on Valentine's Day 2004, in the finest tradition of drunken devil dog carousing just forty-eight hours before 2nd Battalion, 4th Marines finally went off to war.

The combustible spark was a directive from 5th Marine regimental commander Colonel Stewart Navarre for attendance at an

Officers' Field Mess, a kind of white-linen soirée with live music. It would be held, in this case, under a big tent on a bluff overlooking Camp Pendleton's famed Red Beach amphibious assault training area. The idea was for officers to assemble over dinner in a spirit of promoting unit cohesion and camaraderie—esprit de corps. They could leave their dress blues at home and wear utility fatigues. Navarre's wife, Yana, designed the table décor with vaulting flower arrangements accented with glass bowls stocked with goldfish.

To guard against inebriation, cocktail hour would close promptly with additional alcohol only by permission. And Navarre would enforce decorum with a gavel. He demanded everyone be there.

Officers of 3/5, the Darkhorse battalion, naturally intended to bring their unit mascot—a three-foot statue of an ugly little man with large genitalia, wearing a kilt. Carved out of some ancient, Asian wood, it dated back to the Vietnam War and by tradition was zealously guarded against anyone who might try to snatch it away, a prank that was also a part of tradition.

By contrast, officers of 2/4 brought a glowering disposition. They were furious at having to spend the Valentine's Day before their departure at this event, when they should be with wives and children, or girlfriends, or an excess amount of cold beer.

So they arrived with a plan. They muscled a keg of beer from a hapless lance corporal manning a delivery truck and stuffed it under their table. Then they slipped a sergeant at the wet bar a hundred dollars for two jugs of whiskey.

As the unauthorized liquor flowed well into the dining phase of the evening, a sloshed communications officer with the 2/4 battalion suddenly staggered to his feet to announce, "Ladies and gentlemen, comm is down!" and collapsed into his Caesar salad. That was only the beginning.

Moments later, the commander of 2/4's Headquarters and Service Company, Captain Wilson Leech III, stood up to issue a challenge. "You ain't shit," he called out, "until you drink the

BASTARDS

fish!" whereby he lifted the decorative fishbowl from his table and gulped down its occupants, wriggling fins and all. Not to be outdone, officers across the tent guzzled the carp contents of their own table centerpieces.

Then Rob Weiler, burly captain of 2/4's Weapons Company, ratcheted tension a notch higher by calling on all attendees to engage in—of all things—gladiator-style combat.

"My lieutenants and I challenge anybody with balls to a Thunderdome."

This was too far for Navarre, who began banging at the head table with his gavel and shouting, "Stand down!"

The band broke into a lively tune to fill the void. But a sourness had descended, and before too long, the colonel overheard that he was being lampooned about a rather heroic, Patton-esque portrait of himself he kept in his home on a brass easel. The source of the disparagements, unsurprisingly, was the Magnificent Bastards—specifically, Weapons Company executive officer Lucas "Duke" Wells.

Wells played safety for the Navy and was on the field in 1998 when a railing collapsed at Veterans Stadium, injuring Army cadets. The origin of his nickname was that his high crew cut bore a close resemblance to the boxed quaff of a video game hero named Duke Nukem. Duke, the Marine officer, was summoned to the commander's table to answer for himself at the Officers' Mess.

For some reason, he was accompanied by the newly appointed commander of 2/4's Echo Company, Kelly Royer. A onetime Air Force chauffeur, Royer transitioned from active duty to the California Air National Guard and, after a brief hiatus from the military, to the Marine Corps' officer candidate school. Blue-eyed and freckled, with jug-handle ears, Royer had a baritone voice that led him at one point in his career to contemplate becoming a military television or radio broadcaster.

Now, at thirty-six, he was a newly appointed commander of a rifle company heading off to war and thought it would be fun to prank the battalion to which he had once belonged—3/5.

Beside Royer, a drunken Wells stood before Navarre and congratulated him on a wonderful dinner. "I, for one, especially enjoyed the fish." This last remark fomented whooping and hollering from the 2/4 table that led the colonel once again to start banging his gavel and demanding civility. Royer used the moment to suddenly snatch 3/5's little wooden figurine from its guardian and hoist it over his head in triumph.

It was game on. Tables emptied as Darkhorse Marines rallied to their mascot's defense. Magnificent Bastards rose to retrieve Royer. And anyone else eager for action waded into a burgeoning donnybrook. Plates and wineglasses and floral centerpieces went airborne, tables were overturned, lights were momentarily extinguished. The mascot and a beaten-down Royer were finally recovered by their respective battalions. Weiler thought he might have punched out another unit's senior officer. A lieutenant came away with stitches. Royer was bloodied and left with a black eye. (Later that evening, he got trapped in a portable toilet by 3/5 Marines who'd flipped it over.)

Navarre capitulated and called an end to the evening, and officers slept the night off on the beach.

Within two days, 2/4 was no longer No-War. The battalion assembled at a staging area in northern Kuwait known as Camp Victory and used a precious few weeks to train its large crop of newbies basic techniques such as locating IEDs, clearing houses, and establishing vehicle checkpoints.

By early March, the bulk of 2nd Battalion, 4th Marines was shuttling into Ramadi.

"I'm a little scared," Private First Class Geoff Morris wrote in his diary the night before he left Camp Victory for Ramadi. The nineteen-year-old had graduated high school in Gurnee, Illinois, the previous summer and been with the battalion only four months. "I don't want to die. But who really wants to die? Not a whole lot of people if you're sane. It's okay though. I know God will protect me."

Others preparing to cross the border into Iraq felt like they

BASTARDS

were on the brink of a great adventure. "I'm starting to like this more and more," Private First Class Moisés Langhorst wrote in a letter home. He had turned nineteen in January. "I love the sun and the heat, playing with weapons and demo. I think time will fly once we get into 'the shit.'"

But tragedy would strike the battalion even before they all reached Iraq. It involved one of the new boots, Matthew Milczark, homecoming king from Kettle River, Minnesota. On one of the last nights at Camp Victory, on a trip to one of the camp's shower trailers, Milczark was spotted pocketing an electric shaver left behind by a soldier.

Milczark's platoon sergeant from Echo Company was Damien Coan, a short-tempered Marine with a reputation for never suffering fools. Coan, who was twenty-five, had grown up in the tiny hamlet of Frewsburg, New York. He was a scrawny kid who wrestled in high school in the ninety-eight-pound class and got himself suspended more than once for settling disputes with his fists.

At Camp Victory, he called Milczark out in front of the entire platoon for a severe dressing-down. "We're supposed to deploy to a combat zone and trust you. This [pilfering] is not honor and commitment," Coan said, listing two of the three (the third being courage) central Corps tenets. He ordered the young Marine to stand guard duty all night and draft an essay about integrity.

It was a common punishment handed down by a senior enlisted officer, the kind of justice dispensed almost daily in the US military. But this time, on the eve of going to war, something went terribly wrong.

The next morning, March 8, a female service member came running out of the chapel screaming. There was blood splattered on the inside of the tent ceiling and a dead Marine on the floor. Milczark had shot himself with his M16.

The teenager had left a note behind. "I compromised my integrity for the price of a $25 razor. I fear that where we're going, I won't be trusted."

The incident was a shattering experience for Echo Company. Word quickly spread through the rest of the battalion. Milczark's Moose Lake High School classmate, Langhorst, was with Golf Company and already in Ramadi when he received word. "I was totally shocked," he wrote to his parents. There was a quickly arranged memorial service at Camp Victory the next day conducted by the battalion's new chaplain, Navy Lieutenant Brian Weigelt, a minister with the Church of the Nazarene who was on his first deployment.

As the Marines filed out after the ceremony, Milczark's platoon's commander lagged behind. Lieutenant John Wroblewski had the classic chiseled features of what most people would think a young Marine officer looks like. He was trim, fit, and handsome and had chosen the Marine Corps out of sheer patriotism after the attacks on 9/11. A native of New Jersey and graduate of Rutgers University, Wroblewski, twenty-five, had married just the year before, and since taking command of Second Platoon, he had become totally devoted to the thirty-four men under his command. It was a good fit. They reciprocated with respect and affection and called him "Lieutenant Ski." But this terrible act of self-destruction over such a meager offense was emotionally devastating for the young officer. He laid his head on the chaplain's shoulder and began sobbing, unable to understand the unknowable.

It was less complicated for some of the other Marines. The implication of the suicide was simple: it had to be a bad omen for what lay ahead.

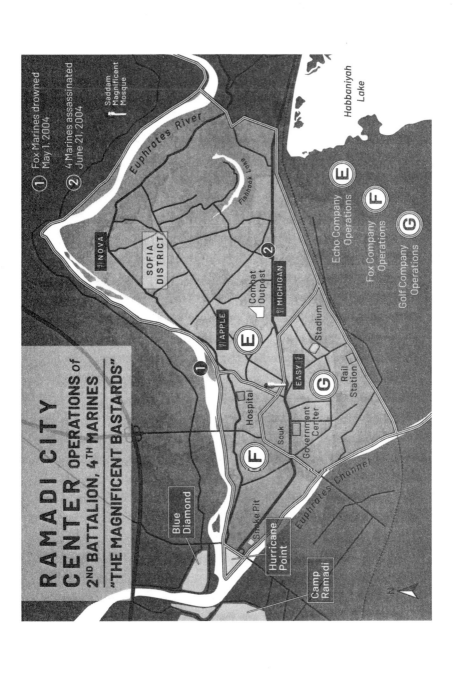

2

CITY

"YOU DON'T PICK AND CHOOSE WHEN YOU DIE IN COMBAT."

THE CRADLE OF Civilization, otherwise known as Mesopotamia, is a region that stretches north and northeast from the city of Ramadi, across the rich soil of what for centuries was known as the Fertile Crescent between the Euphrates River and the Tigris River to the east.

The waters of these biblical rivers flow southeast through the center of Iraq from the mountains of Turkey, irrigating a region that would otherwise be barren desert. And in fact, that is what lies to the southwest of Ramadi all the way to Syria, Jordan, and Saudi Arabia. This arid southwestern corner of Iraq is what constitutes the country's geographically largest province, an area of sixty-four thousand square miles (about the size of the land mass of Wisconsin) and home in 2004 to 1.5 million. Ramadi is the provincial capital, a city of about thirty-five square miles laid out along the southern bank of the Euphrates, sixty-eight miles west of Baghdad. (Fallujah, some twenty-five miles to the east, was by comparison about twelve square miles.)

It is not an ancient city. Founded by local rulers under the Ottoman Empire in the nineteenth century as a means of controlling local nomadic tribes, it was a departure point for overland trade and smuggling west across the desert to Amman and Damascus. (The same routes would become "ratlines" during the Iraq War, funneling foreign recruits east into the battlefields of Ramadi and Fallujah to fight Americans.) As such, Ramadi developed as a more secular city than nearby Fallujah, which earned the name "city of mosques." The tribes in and around Ramadi were always fiercely independent, even under Saddam Hussein, who managed to tame the city through a combination of coercion and patronage.

The population of Ramadi in 2004 was listed as 456,853 and was overwhelmingly Sunni Arab. Across the world's great religious divide that splits Islam between Sunni and Shia sects—because of centuries-old debates over succession of Islamic leadership—the Shia are the majority in only a few Muslim countries. Iraq is one of them. Yet the Sunni minority under Saddam's iron fist controlled the country for nearly thirty years before the US-led invasion drove him from power and instituted a semblance of democracy. Among the most respected institutions up until then was the Iraqi military. The most feared were the internal security intelligence services. All were dominated by Sunni Arabs, thousands of whom were from tribes in and around Ramadi. A neighborhood in the city's south-central area carried the name Mukhabarat, the Arabic word for *intelligence*, as in what spies gather. Ruling Ba'ath Party officials resided in Ramadi as well, as did many retired and active-duty members of the Iraqi special forces and the former paramilitary irregulars known as the Fedayeen Saddam, among the toughest combatants Iraq had. Many of the middle-aged males had combat experience in the Iraq-Iran War and the Persian Gulf War against the US. A good number of them lived privileged lives with Saddam buying loyalty with government cars, subsidized loans, extra rations, and access to the purchase of luxury goods.[1]

They grew up and retired in walled villas of the Sofia District of northeast Ramadi, a plush area of towering date palm trees where the Euphrates River winding along opposite sides of the neighborhood offered cooling cross breezes. Highway 10 bisected the city running east and west, and other military and security officials lived in villages to the east, such as Khalidiyah and Habbaniyah, a former resort area on the banks of the shallow, saline Habbaniyah Lake. There was even a vacation resort for the privileged Ba'athists on the south shore of the lake, with an amusement park, high-rise hotel, bungalows, and boat docks.

Just south of Habbaniyah was Al Taqaddum Air Base. Once home to Iraqi fighter and bomber squadrons, "TQ" became, after the 2003 invasion, a major air transit center for US troops and materiel flowing into Iraq.

So the reality for foreign troops deployed to this region was that much of Ramadi and nearby villages were essentially bedroom communities for the cream of Iraq's military and security services. A favorite observation by Kennedy's intel officer, Wyeth Towle, was that sending US troops to patrol there was like a foreign power trying to occupy North Carolina with its ample population of US military.

By the spring of 2003, the people of this Sunni region were in the throes of defeat and humiliation. Their armies had been vanquished, their regime erased, and their access to the levers of power stripped away. Salt into this wound came in the form of orders issued in May by Bush's viceroy to Iraq, Paul Bremer, head of the Coalition Provisional Authority (CPA). Bremer directed the de-Ba'athification of all government services and the disbandment of the Iraq military.

Suddenly, hundreds of thousands across Iraq were without careers or a sense of purpose. (The CPA in June would authorize pension-like payments about equal to military salaries.) History would judge Bremer's orders as among the Bush administration's biggest mistakes. Bush would later concede in a memoir that he didn't foresee the fallout. "Many Sunnis took [Bremer's orders] as a signal they would have no place in Iraq's future. This was especially dangerous in the case of the Army. Thousands of armed men had just been told they were not wanted. Instead of signing up for the new military, many joined the insurgency."

At the time, however, the American president not only seemed unconcerned about all of this, he all but dared dissident Iraqis to do something about it. "There are some who feel that the conditions are such that they can attack us there," Bush said on July 2. "My answer is: Bring 'em on. We've got the force necessary to deal with the security situation."

These were toxins brewing as fresh American troops flowed into the country to replace the divisions that had invaded Iraq. Among those arriving was the 1st Brigade, 1st Infantry Division, out of Fort Riley, Kansas, assigned specifically to Ramadi and much of Al Anbar Province.

They were attacked before they even arrived in Ramadi. As the rear guard of the brigade column, soldiers of the 1st Engineer Battalion, were paused near Fallujah, they were hit with mortars, rocket-propelled grenades, and rifle fire. The gunfight lasted forty-five minutes before enemy fighters dispersed.

The Devil Brigade was commanded by Colonel Arthur "Buck" Connor Jr., a six-foot-five Ohio native, who grew up fascinated by military history. During his studies at West Point, he concentrated on the lessons learned about small-unit combat from Korea and Vietnam. He later earned a master's degree in history from Temple University. The advent of war in Iraq offered Connor the rare chance for a student of military history to become part of it. But he was crushed to discover as armies were assembling for the invasion that he and his heavy armored brigade in Kansas would not be needed. He wrote in his journal in early January 2003 that he felt "like the homely nerd not invited to the high school graduation party."

That angst only grew worse as Connor watched televised images of US soldiers fighting their way into Iraq. He took it as a personal failure. Returning home from church on a Sunday morning, Connor slipped into a bathroom and wept uncontrollably.

But he only had to be patient. By early September, Connor was working out of an Iraqi military headquarters building on a large US military base in Iraq named Junction City in honor of the Kansas town that hosts Fort Riley. (It would later come to be known simply as Camp Ramadi.) It was situated on Ramadi's western edge just across a canal that fed Euphrates River waters miles to the southeast into Lake Habbaniyah.

Invasion operations had ended months before, so coalition forces across Iraq were focused on stabilization and the training of new Iraqi security personnel. As a result, Connor had to leave most of his heavy armored vehicles back in Kansas, managing only a limited number of M1 Abrams tanks and Bradley Fighting Vehicles, and a single battery of six 155 mm self-propelled Paladin howitzers. Many of his soldiers would have to patrol in boxy, tracked Vietnam-era personnel carriers made out of aluminum or Humvees with bolted-on steel plates.

Connor ordered that the brigade's overarching mission at the start would be reconnaissance of his entire area of operation. He wanted to know what he was up against. His area of operation extended 200 miles west of Fallujah and 247 miles south to the Saudi border. For the next three months, Connor wanted his soldiers to show themselves in every hamlet, drive down every street, and talk with every tribal leader. They worked off whatever intel could be gathered to capture enemy strategists and bomb makers, and seize munition caches. In a year's time, they dished out $23.8 million on civil affairs projects to build trust with the population, trained and equipped police, and organized a brigade of Iraqi National Guard. Improving civic operations seemed like low-hanging fruit given that public services had decayed under Saddam amid corruption and dealmaking with local tribal leaders to elicit support for the dictator.

Along the way, the brigade grappled with ways to de-escalate

CITY

tensions whenever they had to enter people's homes or search cars at vehicle checkpoints. There was always, for example, the thorny issue of how to deal with women and children. Women couldn't be touched, much less frisked for weapons by a male American soldier, and at vehicle checkpoints, they sometimes refused to leave the cars so the vehicles could be searched. These dramas escalated when Iraqi women grew upset, children turned hysterical, and men got angry—all while US troops stood by nervously with their weapons up.

It was a recipe for trouble, and in November, it became a late-night topic of discussion at the base mess hall for two of Connor's battalion commanders: Richard "Mike" Cabrey, thirty-nine, a Utah native who had wrestled at West Point and now commanded artillery; and William "Dave" Brinkley, forty-four, a Virginia Tech graduate who led the 1st Engineer Battalion.

About a hundred of Cabrey's artillery troops were being used to patrol southwest Ramadi. What he needed on these missions was a female soldier who could deal with the Iraqi women and children. Brinkley had female soldiers in his headquarters company (the commander, Captain Kate Pendry, was one of his best officers) and among the battalion's medics. Other women were serving as cooks, mechanics, truck drivers, supply personnel, and communications specialists.

But military regulations banned women from direct combat operations in the US military—a restriction that wouldn't be lifted for another ten years. The reality of these new insurgent wars, where there was no front line, was rendering that rule an anachronism. In Iraq or Afghanistan, a woman driving a supply truck—technically a noncombat job—was as much at risk of coming under fire or running across a roadside bomb as any infantryman on patrol. Indeed, during a coalition firefight with Iraqi militia in Karbala on October 17 that left three US soldiers dead, women who were members of an Army military police unit were directly involved in the combat.

Cabrey and Brinkley settled on the idea of setting up teams of two women to accompany missions. Twenty-six female soldiers volunteered, many of them excited about taking a more active role in the deployment. To foster esprit de corps, the two battalion commanders kicked around names like Iron Maidens (which the women hated) before hitting on calling them Lionesses. Kate Pendry was put in charge.

An Ohio native who grew up playing soccer, Pendry learned from a personality test in high school that she had an aptitude for the military, and her father, a Vietnam veteran, recommended she check out the academies. The Air Force accepted her first. But on a visit to West Point, Pendry fell in love with the historic campus on the Hudson River. The academy's ornate mess hall reminded her of the Hogwarts School from the *Harry Potter* series. She began classes at seventeen.

Her Lionesses started accompanying combat missions on October 11. It was an immediate success. Not only did their presence tamp down tensions during searches and vehicle stops, but in some instances when Iraqi women were frisked, team members found useful information in their clothing, such as identification papers or phone records, apparently hidden there with the assumption the women wouldn't be searched. Other times, Iraqi women were open to sharing information but only under the condition of speaking through an interpreter with another woman. They were fascinated with these soldiers who had blond hair and ponytails.

Even more importantly, community leaders told the Americans they appreciated this effort to be respectful. "Our people are much happier now that there are women that are out there," one religious leader said.

The Lionesses began doing missions with artillery troops on patrol, but other battalions soon started using them, as did the Marines when they arrived in March 2004. It was with Marines that these women would encounter their heaviest street fighting.

Adjustments such as the Lioness program in Ramadi, along

with the larger efforts to invest in municipal improvements and train new Iraqi security personnel, were part of broad preparations by the nearly 140,000 US troops and another 25,000 multinational forces across the country to eventually return Iraq to Iraqis. (The United Nations Security Council unanimously adopted a resolution calling for an interim Iraqi government to take over on June 30, 2004.)

The problem was that violence was trending in the wrong direction. Attacks were on the rise by the fall of 2003, and US military leaders were eager to quell this resistance quickly. When Lieutenant General Ricardo Sanchez, commander of coalition forces, arrived in Ramadi on October 8, 2003, for a brigade briefing, he interrupted as Connor was talking about efforts to chase down and capture anti-coalition fighters.

"Why aren't you killing them?" Sanchez asked. "I want you to kill them."

He would be in charge when Iraq was shaken by violent upheaval in 2004 and, two years later, would be forced into retirement because of investigative findings that showed dereliction of duty in the 2004 Abu Ghraib prisoner-abuse scandal.

To meet threats in his area of operation, Connor concentrated most of his battalions along the winding Euphrates River, principally in and around Ramadi. A National Guard unit from South Florida nicknamed the "Hurricane" battalion had already been conducting missions in the city center for months before the Devil Brigade arrived, and now under Connor's command, it continued doing so.

Elsewhere, a mechanized infantry battalion was assigned to patrol north of the Euphrates and west of Ramadi. Three of Connor's six artillery Paladin howitzers were placed at Camp Ramadi, the other three at a location in Habbaniyah, near Al Taqaddum Air Base.

The cannons were restricted from firing into congested areas of Ramadi. But targets on the fringes or in rural areas were fair game, particularly if enemy mortar or rocket emplacements were found there. The Army had radar systems that could track incoming rounds and calculate their points of origin, allowing howitzer crews to effectively shoot back. But Connor—who could be quick to anger, even launching a chair on occasion—nearly had a meltdown inside the brigade combat center when he saw that it took eight minutes for the counterfire process to work, more than enough time for enemy gunners to break down launchers and scamper away. The standard was three minutes.

"Look, you're majors. You're lieutenant colonels. You're captains. This has got to stop." He ordered the cannoneers to drill seven days a week, and over time, response fire was possible in less than ninety seconds. The enemy responded by setting up loaded mortar tubes wired to timers so when the rounds were fired, insurgents could be long gone.

With only six Paladins to fire, Connor turned a portion of his field artillery troops into infantry and had them patrol villages southwest of Ramadi where the University of Anbar was located, a hotbed of anti-American resentment and for insurgents a fertile recruitment zone. Cabrey's cannoneers had T-shirts made emblazoned with the phrase ANBAR U., HOME OF THE FIGHTING SUNNIS. Connor kept another unit out along the Saudi border. And he sent an armored battalion supplemented by a company of engineers to prowl the eastern approaches to Ramadi stretching nearly to Fallujah. The key towns there were Habbaniyah and Khalidiyah, home to ex–Iraqi military and intelligence troops.

It was here that the brigade encountered its first serious fight, a running gun battle on September 29, 2003, that went on for seven hours. After detonating an IED near Khalidiyah, fifty to one hundred insurgents fought with a surprising level of military discipline, shooting and moving as a force. As more Army resources entered the fray, the fight extended north of the Euphrates and ended when the last enemy holdouts retreated into two houses that were blasted apart by the main gun of an M1 tank. Later, when brigade intel officers described to higher command how organized the enemy appeared to be, their report was met with skepticism. A widely held view at the time was that attacks against US forces were either roadside bombs, snipers, or sporadic small engagements by either remnants of Saddam's military, criminals, or a few religious zealots.

A week after the Khalidiyah battle, General John Abizaid arrived for a briefing. The four-star general was head of Central Command, or CENTCOM, overseeing all US military forces from the Horn of Africa to Central Asia to include Iraq and Afghanistan. He was a realist, among the first in the Bush administration to have acknowledged that Iraq was still very much a war for the US. Always hungry for better intelligence, Abizaid wanted to know what was happening in the Sunni-rich area of Al Anbar Province and who was the opposition, telling Connor and his men that time was not on the side of the coalition and the insurgency had to be overcome soon.

What he learned was something new and disturbing. After two months in Iraq, Connor's intelligence team discovered through a growing network of informants, raids, and interrogations that there was a collaboration underway. Former senior government officials, ex-military, and former members of Saddam's much-feared Mukhabarat intelligence service were sitting down and planning attacks with religious extremists such as Wahhabis, who hold to a purist interpretation of Islam, and even terrorists linked with al-Qaeda. And some tribal leaders were at least tacitly approving.

"The Islamists are on the rise," brigade intel officer Kyle Teamey would write in his journal that fall. "If we don't offer an alternative, they will be running amok soon. I spoke with one twice. Friendly, intelligent guy. He's a nut though. I'm certain he would kill me given the right circumstances."

Exhibit A for the lethality of this new alliance between secular and religious militants was the Khalidiyah battle the week before

Abizaid's visit when the brigade suffered its first casualty killed in action. Christopher Cutchall, a thirty-year-old staff sergeant from Pennsylvania, died in the IED explosion that initiated the fight. He was riding a Humvee that offered no protection, and the blast tore off one arm and ripped open his chest. Medics couldn't save him.

Back in the United States, the deadliness of these bombs and the vulnerability of US troops had yet to sink in for political leaders. It would be well over a year before members of Congress demanded answers about why so many troops were killed just driving down the road in Iraq. Their belated ire was triggered by growing press coverage about roadside bombs, particularly a 2005 *New York Times* story about the IED destruction of 2/4 Marines fighting in Ramadi in 2004.

"How did we get ourselves in this situation?" Colorado Republican Joel Hefley asked a panel of military leaders at a committee hearing May 5, 2005. "Did we have no idea going in there that we would need armored vehicles?"

Brigadier General William Catto, head of Marine Corps acquisitions, responded that when Marines arrived in Ramadi in March 2004, IED threats were less of an issue. "They were at low level," he testified. "We did not have a lot of incidents of IEDs in that time frame." Moreover, Catto added, early generations of roadside bombs through March 2004 contained small munitions such as mortar rounds.

But none of that was true.

Cutchall's death in 2003 was just the first of at least twenty in Connor's area of operation between late September of that year and late March 2004, when the troops of 2nd Battalion, 4th Marines took the field. All but one of these soldiers died in explosions, four from suicide car bombers and sixteen from IEDs.

And what killed them were explosives that were certainly larger than a mortar shell. Beyond those twenty deaths, five other Devil Brigade soldiers who had been temporarily assigned to other units operating near Fallujah died in roadside bomb blasts. In one case, the explosion was so massive it killed three troopers riding in a Bradley Fighting Vehicle, a kind of small tank that doubled as a troop carrier. On November 8, they were patrolling Highway 10 east of Fallujah, trying to spot buried IEDs. They missed one. The explosion destroyed the Bradley, killing two of the soldiers outright. A third, Sergeant Ryan Young, twenty-one, of Corona, California, hung on for nearly a month before succumbing to his wounds at Walter Reed Army Medical Center in Washington, DC.

Across Iraq, from late September 2003 through March 2004, nearly a hundred US troops were killed by IEDs.

Most of those roadside bomb incidents for the Devil Brigade occurred in and around the difficult areas of Khalidiyah and Habbaniyah. The IEDs were often artillery shells detonated either by an electric charge sent through a long ground wire or by a short-distance radio frequency from a cell phone or even a garage-door opener. The attackers had to remain hidden, calm, and patient enough to time the detonation for just that second when a Humvee, traveling up to thirty-five miles per hour, passed directly over the roadside bomb.

West Point graduate Todd Bryant, twenty-three—who had gotten married just two weeks before the brigade deployed—was killed on Halloween when a 152 mm artillery shell buried in a road near the Khalidiyah Bridge was remotely detonated as his Humvee approached. The trigger man had been watching from across the Euphrates River, where he was hiding in shoreline reeds. He escaped.

Nor were lethal explosives always buried. On January 24, a car bomb was detonated as a suicide driver pulled up next to a Humvee near Khalidiyah carrying three soldiers from a cavalry unit on loan to the Devil Brigade. All three died, and seven other soldiers were wounded. It was a checkpoint, and Iraqi civilians sitting in vehicles nearby were also killed by the blast. The military, through its stilted nomenclature, would come to call these bombs *vehicle-borne IEDs*, or VBIEDs.

Three days after that suicide attack, the brigade held a memorial service for the dead cavalrymen at a military installation near Habbaniyah. Connor drove out from Camp Ramadi to attend, arriving in his usual convoy of several Humvees manned by a security detachment of more than two dozen soldiers. He often also traveled with the brigade surgeon.

Enemy radio intercepts would later reveal he was being watched.

Insurgents had already tried to kill him back in November, ambushing his convoy along Highway 10 with rifle fire and rocket-propelled grenades. Armed with a Mossberg 12-gauge pump-action shotgun that Connor always loaded alternately with buckshot and one-inch slugs, he left his Humvee and with other soldiers began advancing on three insurgents three hundred yards away as machine gunners on convoy trucks covered them. The enemy fighters managed to flee along the banks of the Euphrates.

In January, after the memorial service for the three cavalry soldiers ended, Connor lingered for a while to have lunch with a battalion commander. Meanwhile, another convoy left the base heading west toward Ramadi. Insurgents suspected this was the colonel on his return trip to Camp Ramadi.

Connor was only about a minute into lunch when he and others could feel and hear the rumble of a major explosion. The colonel and his security detail rushed to a scene of devastation along Highway 10. Medevac helicopters from the air base were already en route.

A truck and a bus were burning on the westbound lane beside a couple of damaged cars. In the eastbound lane was an obliterated Humvee. The huge explosion was from an IED buried in the highway median. It was a homemade device that worked much like a Claymore mine, throwing out a cloud of half-inch cubes of steel like a giant shotgun blast. The effect shredded the Humvee.

Medevac pilots landed their aircraft on the paved roadway near overhead power lines. When Connor arrived, he saw two soldiers on stretchers nearby and wondered why no medics were

CITY

attending them. As he approached, he understood why. One was a sergeant, his uniform covered in blood; the other was a sergeant first class, his face nearly gone. Both were clearly dead.

Someone said they were Army engineers and there were two others in a ditch nearby where medics were feverishly working. A medevac crew chief approached to say he wanted the dead soldiers placed aboard a waiting helicopter immediately. Four members of Connor's security detail picked up the sergeant's body. The brigade commander and three of his men lifted the sergeant first class.

Connor gripped a litter handle that was slick with blood, and the dead man's arm suddenly draped over the side of the stretcher, brushing blood against Connor's leg. The colonel gently lifted the soldier's arm back onto the litter, and as he and the other bearers paused while the body of the other slain soldier was placed on the helicopter, Connor forced himself to once more look into the face of the man he was carrying. Through the gore, familiar features began to emerge. It was James Hoffman, the senior enlisted adviser for Bravo Company, 1st Engineers. Connor had shaken Hoffman's hand less than an hour before at the memorial service and greeted the company commander, Captain Matt August.

They placed Hoffman's body on the helicopter as medics and others raced the two wounded men into the second aircraft. An officer walked up and handed Connor a piece of paper with four names on it—the casualties.

"I'm sorry, sir," he said.

August's name was there. He and Staff Sergeant Sean Landrus were both in critical condition. The other dead engineer besides Hoffman was a twenty-three-year-old sergeant named Travis Moothart.

As the helicopters lifted off, Connor directed his security detail to look for the trigger man, and just then, there were two explosions about 100 yards down the road near an M1 tank. More IEDs. No one was hurt, and the tank was undamaged. But a detonation wire was spotted. Connor and his troops followed the line for about 150 yards into a schoolyard from where the bombs were set off. The insurgent was gone, but there was a picture left stuck into a fence nearby—an image of Saddam Hussein. *They're taunting us*, Connor thought.

Minutes later, brigade command Sergeant Major Ron Riling walked up and whispered into Connor's ear that August, who was twenty-eight and yet another West Point graduate, had just died on a treatment table at a medical facility. Three metal chunks thrown out by the explosion had struck him in the side where there was no body armor protection. His wife, Maureen, would have to be notified. She was also an Army captain (they had met as students at the military academy) and serving in Iraq.

Connor was stunned. He took a few steps away and began to weep, overcome with the thought that August and the others were unintended victims of the attack. "That was supposed to be me," Connor said. Riling tried to offer solace. "Sir, you don't pick and choose when you die in combat." Connor's tall figure sank down on one knee and he began reciting the prayer of repentance from Psalm 51: "Have mercy upon me oh God. . . . Blot out my transgressions." Riling, a bear of a man just a few inches shorter than Connor and powerfully built, knelt beside him. Then he cautioned Connor that they needed to get out of there. Another enemy attack could come anytime.

The one soldier still alive following the IED explosion, Landrus, who was married and the father of a twelve-year-old girl, survived only another two days.

Attacks against US troops across Iraq had risen exponentially since the summer of 2003, tripling from ten to fifteen per day to more than forty per day by mid-November. In the latter half of that month, there was a dramatic spike as thirty-nine Army personnel were killed in a series of helicopter crashes caused by ground fire in Fallujah, Tikrit, and Mosul.

Yet in the midst of the growing carnage, the one place that seemed strangely quiescent was in the city of Ramadi itself. The deadliest attacks on brigade troops so far were in villages immediately east of the city. Inside Ramadi, the Florida National Guard unit deployed there had not suffered a single soldier killed in action. The 1st Battalion, 124th Infantry arrived in the city early in 2003 to conduct combat and security operations and, eventually, to train Iraqi police and develop working relationships with the local power structure of government officials and tribal leaders.

Kyle Teamey was particularly impressed with what he saw in Ramadi. Dozens of the citizen soldiers were police officers back in Florida. The commander, Lieutenant Colonel Hector Mirabile, was a major with the Miami Police Department.

The twenty-seven-year-old Teamey was an Ivy Leaguer from Klamath Falls, Oregon, who brigade staff viewed as a wunderkind on intel analysis. He had won an ROTC scholarship to Dartmouth College in New Hampshire and was handling human-intelligence collection as well as targeting and operational planning for the brigade. He thought the National Guard troops brought an interesting skill set to Ramadi with their experience dealing with gangs and drug dealers back home. They met regularly with local leaders over tea and negotiated for tamped-down violence in exchange for US Army funding of municipal improvements. The Hurricane battalion was assembling a list of crucial tribal contacts, most notably Sheikh Abdul Sattar Abu Risha, who, after several hard years to come, would help win the peace in Al Anbar Province and shake hands with the president of the United States before being assassinated by extremist holdouts.

The Florida soldiers' successes were a good-news story in an otherwise bleak Iraqi narrative and drew coverage from the *Washington Post*, *Wall Street Journal*, and *Guardian*. "Intelligence, intelligence, intelligence," Mirabile told *60 Minutes* correspondent Christiane Amanpour. "Everything is driven by the intelligence you gather."

The National Guard troops had begun reducing their presence in the city in the final weeks before heading home.

They left in February just as the Marines started to arrive. Before that, 1st Marine Division intel officers debriefed the National Guard commander and his staff on February 22 to provide Kennedy and his people a sense of what they were up against. Mirabile and his officers expressed confidence that the provincial capital was largely secure, even pacified. Stores were reopening. Businesses were starting up. Normalcy was returning.

The IED attacks were less effective than elsewhere, devices that were crudely and hastily assembled. Incoming mortar fire usually missed targets. Gunfights were sporadic, amounting to someone holding an AK-47 over a wall and spraying rounds before running away. Occasionally, there might be a sniper who could be readily dispatched with shoulder-mounted AT4 anti-tank rounds.

Less frequent were attacks by groups of fighters. They were dealt with swiftly because National Guard foot patrols never strayed far from a truck mounted with a .50-caliber machine gun or automatic grenade launcher.

On the whole, the enemy in Ramadi was unimpressive, the battalion leaders said: "Punks and thugs who want to see what we are made of to see if they can push us around." Their motivations were those of teenage boys, according to a summary of remarks by Mirabile and his staff. "It is a macho thing for local youths to fight the occupier. It helps them get chicks, and they often use drugs/alcohol to get their courage up."

The Florida soldiers said word had circulated fast throughout the city that they were leaving and that a Marine battalion—a "new Army"—was arriving as replacements. The Marines should expect to get tested a bit. But a company commander with the 1st Brigade who gave an orientation tour of the city to Chris Bronzi, a captain in charge of 2/4's Golf Company, told him their deployment would be a walk in the park. "Hey, man, you're not going to be doing much more than cutting ribbons and kissing babies."

3

PRELUDE

"HE SEES ME AS THE DEVIL."

> An Old Man, bent double with age and toil, was gathering sticks in a forest. At last he grew so tired and hopeless that he threw down the bundle of sticks, and cried out: "I cannot bear this life any longer. Death come and take me!" As he spoke, Death appeared.
>
> —Origin of "Be careful what you wish for,"
> *Aesop's Fables*

THE OPEN-BACKED HUMVEE ground to a halt in gravel outside the Army medical facility at Camp Ramadi late on a Saturday afternoon, and the first casualty pulled out of it was a brand-new Marine who had joined the battalion just fifty-five days earlier. Lance Corporal Patrick Zimmerman's military career had just begun and was now already over. His right eye was blown out and he was going home.

But it was the second wounded Marine in the back of the truck—conscious and sitting up, with a terrified look in his eyes—that stopped Jody Schroeder cold. Corporal Brian "Mack" McPherson's jaw was gone. The Navy corpsman with him looked terror-stricken. Medical airway support gear strewn across the back of the truck was testament to why. The sailor had tried every means he had to insert a tube so that Mack could breathe easier. Schroeder could see an endotracheal tube in the truck and a rubbery tube called a *nasopharyngeal airway device*. But with all the destruction to Mack's lower face, the corpsman hadn't been able to find a pathway. "Ma'am, I couldn't. There was nothing I could do," he said to Schroeder.

She tried to reassure. "No, you're good. It's okay. It's okay."

The corpsman had thought to keep Mack sitting upright in the truck. That almost certainly prevented him from suffocating in his own blood. He remained upright as Army medical personnel moved him into the treatment area on a litter. Paul Kennedy showed up with a plastic Meal, Ready to Eat, or MRE, bag containing Mack's jaw, which someone found at the blast site. Doctors said it was beyond salvageable. The battalion commander would never forget the sight of his Marine with his tongue hanging down on his chest.

Schroeder and Dr. Joel Reynolds, a kidney specialist who was with her, went to work. The first task was ministering to Mack's fear. Schroeder needed to calm him. She took a moment to look directly into his eyes.

"Hey, so here's the deal," she said with a sense of calm urgency. "You're not going to be able to breathe on your own much longer. We've got an IV started in you. We're going to give you this medication and you're going to start getting sleepy, and we're going to lay you down and we're going to secure your airway. And we're going to get you back to the States."

He held her gaze and nodded. As Mack slipped away, they laid him back on the gurney and started searching the terrible mess

PRELUDE

where his jaw had been ripped away for a certain guidepost to his airway—white, shiny vocal cords. Schroeder spotted them. "Hey, Joel, aim for that." Success.

Blond, blue-eyed, and five-foot-four, Army Captain Jodelle "Jody" Schroeder was a critical care nurse and the driving force behind the organization and delivery of trauma care at the Army medical facility at Camp Ramadi, known as Charlie Med. (C, or Charlie, Company is typically the medical unit of a forward Army support battalion.) She saw it as a calling. "These guys give up so much. These are days upon days where they are on mission after mission risking their lives," she wrote in her diary days before. "I believe that God put me here to do this very job." Schroeder had a gift for soothing the young men who arrived fighting for their lives. The twenty-nine-year-old officer could instinctively connect with someone in wretched condition, who was certain they were going to die, and tell them in clear, compassionate language that they would be saved. Marines who were brought to Charlie Med for anything from sick-call abscesses to gaping blast wounds would come to see her as their Florence Nightingale. One Marine bleeding from shrapnel wounds looked up from a stretcher, caught sight of Schroeder, and said, "Oh my God, you're gorgeous." She brushed it off. "You are just hallucinating. Let's get him some oxygen, guys."

Prior to the war, the Army medical department had grown accustomed to peacetime care of garrisoned soldiers. So there were shortages in war-related specialties when the fighting started, and Schroeder was the only trained trauma-care specialist in the brigade. It wasn't that the doctors on staff weren't capable or that the other nurses and physician assistants didn't quickly learn the art of life- or limb-threatening treatment. But they had deployed with disciplines from other areas—infectious diseases, family medicine, kidney disorders. Schroeder showed up already skilled in dealing with patients in agony, who arrived at a Charlie Med terrified, their bodies sundered and hemorrhaging, and their airways and heart rates constricted. And sometimes, beyond saving.

The Minnesota native, who had received an ROTC nursing scholarship from Marquette University in Milwaukee, Wisconsin, had long since become immune to something called *distracting trauma*, the clinical term for what happens when medical personnel are so shocked by the physical damage they see that they have a hard time doing their jobs.

It was an acquired skill. A dying Iraqi man was brought into the medical facility with horrible belly wounds from .50-caliber heavy machine gun rounds after a firefight with US soldiers. When he was rolled over, what seemed like his entire body contents spilled onto the ground, and a Medical Service Corps lieutenant standing nearby fainted and fell face-first into the dirt. Another attending officer grew so distraught by the assembly line of bloodied war fighters that she ran out of the building in tears and didn't come out of her room for days.

The one-story Charlie Med facility at Camp Ramadi offered the highest level of care in the brigade's area of operation. There was a smaller Army facility at Al Taqaddum Air Base, and 2nd Battalion, 4th Marines had two aid stations manned by Navy doctors. But the Camp Ramadi facility had x-ray capacity and laboratory testing. Still, for the sickest or most direly wounded, all the facilities were designed principally to stabilize patients until they could be medevacked by air transport to larger military hospitals, such as those in Baghdad and Balad, then if necessary on to the Army's Landstuhl Regional Medical Center in Germany, and finally for long-term care stateside at places such as Walter Reed Army Medical Center in Washington, DC, or the Bethesda Naval Hospital in Maryland.

It was in Bethesda where Mack McPherson came out of a coma ten days after he was blown up, his memory of what had happened wiped clean. His last recollection was the night before the attack, writing a letter to his father, Brian McPherson Sr., to say he was doing just fine so far on the deployment.

His father was bedside when Mack opened his eyes, and the

Marine's first thought was *Wow, that was one short deployment.* Then he saw his father's grim expression. *Oh shit, this is not good.* That's when the dad told his twenty-five-year-old son, "You cannot talk right now."

Mack's recovery would be years in the making.

He was wounded following a morning foot patrol by his fire team in western Ramadi. They were in a convoy of vehicles returning to Combat Outpost, heading east on the city's main thoroughfare, passing through an area of government buildings, and no one noticed the bicycle leaning against the curb on the south side of the highway. The force of the blast from explosives attached to the bicycle blew north, disabling the fourth vehicle in the convoy that carried McPherson and his men, and leaving four Marines and a soldier wounded.

It was March 13, 2004, the first day 2nd Battalion, 4th Marines took control of its battle space in the city of Ramadi.

The gruesome violence that maimed McPherson was not what 2/4 Marines expected, especially given the comparatively benign experience of the National Guard soldiers who preceded them.

Ramadi was supposed to be pacified. The Marines thought the extent of their combat deployment would be handing out to children candies that wouldn't readily melt in the Ramadi heat, such as Jolly Ranchers and Blow Pops, as well as soccer balls and school supplies, waving and smiling at the adults. What happened to Mack was a shocker.

"This place is serious," Corporal Joe Hayes wrote to his father the next day about his friend's appalling wound, urging the details be kept from his mom. "I don't want her to have to worry more."

Moisés Langhorst, in the same squad as Hayes, was becoming a prolific letter writer to his parents back home and asked them for prayers after McPherson's grievous wound. "There is no doubt that we are in the Valley of the Shadow of Death," he penned.

As James Mattis and his 1st Marine Division replaced the Army's 82nd Airborne Division in providing security for Iraq's

Sunni heartland, where anti-coalition resentment was extreme, the initial approach was decidedly less warlike. It would be a stability and security operation—known simply as SASO—aimed at easing the transition to self-government. Iraqi police and military would be developed and nurtured. Restless areas quieted. Aggressive threats quelled. Mattis emphasized the latter in an "All Hands" letter to troops: "We are going to destroy the enemy with precise firepower while diminishing the conditions that create adversarial relationships between us and the Iraqi people." He wanted to extend the hand of goodwill while making clear the consequences for violence. It was the premise from an ancient Roman general's creed he adopted as division motto: "No better friend, no worse enemy."

Earlier reconnaissance by his assistant division commander, Brigadier General John Kelly, offered insight into a way forward, including a sense that Army predecessors had too often been heavy-handed and disproportionate in responding to threats, too easily relying on heavy munitions that risked collateral damage and alienating Iraqi citizens.

Buck Connor was all too aware of this Marine bias about Army tactics, and while he had enormous respect for Mattis, he took pains to demonstrate that 1st Brigade did not operate this way. Still, there were times when his soldiers were indeed inclined to use a big gun to deal with a small menace. When a sniper took shots at Connor's convoy along Route Michigan in late December 2003, his people called in an air strike with a guided bomb, or JDAM—at a cost of $21,000 apiece—and leveled the two-story structure.

Marine leadership would demand far more restraint. The downside of this for Kennedy and his Marines was that in the event of a major firefight, particularly in the dense urban jungle of Ramadi, air strikes or artillery support were out of the question. Marines would have to fight it out largely on their own.

The first tranche of 2/4 Marines had arrived in Ramadi on February 26. The National Guard battalion that the Marines were

PRELUDE

replacing had gone home by then, so other Army elements of the Devil Brigade conducted the usual right-seat-left-seat orientation tour of the city. Many of the new arrivals would notice how the soldiers would point to areas of Ramadi and say, "We never go down there." That would change, the Marines were thinking.

The battle space for 2nd Battalion, 4th Marines was the center of the provincial capital, an area that was very nearly a peninsula. The northern flank was tucked up against the Euphrates as the river gently rolled eastward for a few miles before zigging north and then south again around the Sofia District that was the city's northeastern edge. Sofia was a floodplain of tall grasses and date palm forests that was so unexpectedly lush for a desert country that it reminded US troops of what South Vietnam must look like. The river detour on a map looked like a shark fin, and that's what Marines sometimes called it.

The western edge of their battle space was the Euphrates Channel, a broad canal that fed waters from the river to Habbaniyah Lake miles to the southeast. An east–west rail line marked the southern border. And the eastern approach into Ramadi bisected a narrow stretch of land between the lake and the Euphrates.

Anyone entering the city from the direction of Baghdad along Highway 10 would pass beneath a set of gateway arches and be struck first by a swath of brown that stretched as far as the eye could see, broken only by occasional stretches of dull green foliage. Barren fields were brown, cemeteries were brown, unpaved roadways were brown, college campuses were brown, buildings were brown. The color scheme varied slightly as Highway 10 became Ramadi's main, east–west thoroughfare, which Marines on their maps called Route Michigan. There was a light industrial area and then a densely congested district of markets—the souk—where streets would be clogged with vehicles, and sidewalks with shoppers, for the better part of each day. At a thriving black market, thirty dollars could buy an AK-47 rifle, fifteen to twenty dollars for a rocket-propelled grenade launcher.

What city skyline existed silhouetted modest high-rises alongside block after city block of provincial government structures or industrial warehouses. Farther north and south were expanding square blocks of densely packed residential homes along narrow streets crisscrossed by alleyways, where overhead tangles of power lines offered intermittent electricity. Residences were of a distinctive Middle Eastern layout and design that essentially made each home a mini-fortress—daunting real estate for urban warfare. They were one- or two-story structures of concrete or brick under a roof ringed by a parapet and on a space enclosed by eight-foot walls and iron gates.

Ramadi's most prominent landmarks included a huge soccer stadium to the southeast, a high-rise hospital near the river in the west, and a towering government office building along Michigan. Overshadowing all and dead center in Ramadi was the Saddam Magnificent Mosque with its Ottoman-style architecture, spiraling prayer tower, and massive dome covered in a mosaic of blue, red, and aqua inlays. It held sway over a central crossroads and was one of the largest mosques in all of Iraq. There were sixty-eight mosques in Ramadi, and Marines through interpreters kept track of those where imams preached virulent anti-American sermons on Friday holy days or any other day.

Among the hundred palaces and residences that Saddam Hussein had built across Iraq, two in Ramadi were used as US military installations. Portions of the structures had been bombed during the invasion but remained functional. One was at the northwest end of Ramadi inside a military base that the Florida troops had named Hurricane Point. Directly north of Hurricane Point across the Euphrates River was an opulent palace complex that Mattis and the 1st Marine Division took over as headquarters from the 82nd Airborne. That encampment carried the Marine division nickname, Blue Diamond. Connor and his brigade staff operated out of a former Iraqi military headquarters building at Camp Ramadi.

PRELUDE

(The premier structures built by the Saddam regime were often palaces in name only. While the lavish design was an attempt to evoke a sense of splendor, it was often only a veneer. Bombing damage would show that surfaces of marble or sandstone were a thin overlay on brick and mortar.)

Kennedy and his staff and two of his battalion companies—headquarters and service, and weapons—occupied Hurricane Point. A second military base about four hundred yards to the west along Route Michigan was called Snake Pit and was home to Fox Company. The remaining rifle companies, Golf and Echo, were located at Combat Outpost, an austere former Iraqi military maintenance facility along Route Michigan a bit more than a mile east of the Saddam Magnificent Mosque. All the bases were ringed by walls, razor wire, HESCO barriers (large, steel mesh baskets lined with heavy fabric and filled with dirt), and heavy machine gun positions.

Combat Outpost was the most isolated, located a dangerous urban drive from other fortified posts. Referenced sometimes with the acronym COP, it was visited in the summer of 2004 by Navy psychiatrist Bill Nash, who subsequently described it in a letter home:

> As an island of American troops in a very hostile urban sea, COP has almost no ability to sustain itself. No plumbing, no running water, no electricity except what can be produced by big diesel generators that they try to keep running around the clock. The only "hot" food available is what is brought in on the Log Train [a truck convoy], mostly twice a day. But this is very unreliable. They never know when (or if) the Log Train will show up, so mealtimes can never be planned. And the food that is brought out is awful! . . . The smelly, stale, and room-temperature slop that is brought out on the Log Train does not help morale much. (Thank you, Halliburton!) I saw some of

the Marines out there eating potato chips three meals a day (a mobile PX trailer comes out once a week to sell such stuff to them—the only place they can shop). Garbage is burned right there on the compound, so the acrid smell of burning plastic hangs constantly in the air.

The city was broken into thirds for each of three rifle companies. Northwest belonged to Fox. South-central to Golf—McPherson and his fire team were Golf Marines. And the largest by size, the northeast and the Sofia District, was for Echo. Weapons Company, with its disproportionate share of battalion vehicles and heavy weapons, acted as a quick-reaction force for the battalion, or what Kennedy liked to call a *mobile assault company*, able to respond rapidly when troops came under attack. They were firepower in a hurry, heavy weapon Humvees able to race across the city with *Mad Max* lethality wherever embattled Marines were in trouble. Their range extended to margins of the city east and south.

As Marines and corpsmen began venturing into the streets, what held the most wonder for them were the people of Ramadi. It was a culture so alien from anything these young men had seen before. The muezzin calls to prayer spoken from loudspeakers atop minarets were five times a day. Stoic women in their abayas or hijabs. Scowling men in their starched, white dishdashas, or Adidas tracksuits. And the laughing, begging, sometimes profane children. *Who are these people? What do they want? How do they see us? Are we a good thing, or are we a nuisance? Do they wish us dead or driven away?* The throngs filling the souk or crowding the streets with their Corollas and Opels and Toyota trucks and taxis were like the flickering wall images in Plato's allegory of the cave. What you were allowed to see wasn't necessarily what there was.

The Marine command used color-coded maps and categories to broadly make sense of it all. They sifted intel to ascertain which

Ramadi tribes were friendly, such as the Resha, Bu'Alwani, or Ali Jasm on the city's western fringe. Or which posed a threat, such as those in south-central Ramadi or out in Sofia, among them the Al Sueda, whom outgoing guardsmen described as "cutthroat smugglers and thieves," or the Etha and Khalifa, whose leadership gave lip service to supporting the Americans but whose younger members were eager to fight them.

Colored maps were also used to record fluctuating attitudes across neighborhoods over time, with areas shaded in green friendly, in yellow neutral, and in red hostile. There were crimson splotches in all the areas patrolled by the three rifle companies. And over time, no matter how much the battalion tried to expand and improve municipal programs, areas of red barely shifted. The largest swath was more than a square mile of densely populated neighborhoods south of Michigan and the Saddam Magnificent Mosque, known as the Malaab District, right in Golf Company's venue.

Yet all these inkblot efforts to define populations were of little use to a Marine heading out on patrol. It was impossible to understand the authenticity of one Iraqi man's smile or the sinister limits behind another's sullenness. Just how serious was that throat-slitting gesture? There was, after all, no enemy dressed in a uniform. Among a gaggle of people along the road could be someone who had just fired an AK-47 or an RPG, discarded the weapon, and blended in. They might just as well have vanished into thin air. Is another person with a cell phone calling his mother? Or is he alerting an ambush or preparing to set off an IED?

For Rob Weiler, the thirty-one-year-old Weapons Company captain who had thrown punches at the Valentine's Day brawl, the Ramadi experience resembled a college exam without answers. In any other test where a participant was challenged to choose correctly, they always learned in the end whether they were right or wrong. But in Ramadi, the answer to whether some citizen, government official, or police chief was friend or foe was never revealed until, in the latter instance, you had to kill them on the battlefield. Then, and only then, would you learn.

Children, at first blush, had to be a safe bet, universally innocent and lacking malevolence. When Americans approached, they ran into the street with squeals and extended hands, begging for giveaways. "Mister, mister, chocolate." "Mister, mister, football." Or when others could be seen playing in the dirt fields just north of Combat Outpost, it had to be a chance for Marines on guard duty to exhale, because they were watching the antithesis of war.

But then it would change on a dime. The same children in the street would later throw rocks at the Marines. And those frolicking in the field would, as if on cue, run away just before mortar rounds began falling inside the walls of the base.

The manner in which Ramadians could disassociate themselves from the storms of violence that would sweep through their city was a marvel to the Marines. They would observe men and women seemingly heedless of danger, as if the bullets flying overhead or IEDs that might indiscriminately explode were merely squalls that, given a few minutes, would pass. Their determination to carry on their lives undeterred by mayhem was striking.

Marines might temporarily shut down a street, only to see civilian drivers barreling right through, despite shouted warnings from Americans who were all too willing—because they didn't know this driver's intent—to gun them down (and sometimes did). Some looked to be drunk. Once, a bicyclist appeared insistent on pedaling his way right through a gunfight in the Sofia District. Marines under attack from two directions were transfixed by the guy's cluelessness. "Get the fuck out of here!" one of them yelled. The rider finally turned around and road off as if it were all just another annoyance.

The Americans became amateur anthropologists learning the rhythms of daily Ramadi life—housewives hanging laundry, parents disciplining children, butchers sectioning off freshly slaughtered animals, farmers grazing cattle, sheep, or goats, or irrigating

PRELUDE

plots of land. (The Florida troops were particularly impressed with the tomatoes and watermelons Ramadi fields yielded, fruit they found succulent and three times the size of anything in the States.)

And the people of Ramadi, in turn, became students of Marine behavior. They couldn't help it. These new Americans went everywhere and on foot, not concealed inside boxy armored vehicles but right out where you could see them sweat and read their faces and study how they slung their rifles and which ones offered smiles and waves. The Americans looked young and friendly and engaging and were even dressed differently from soldiers. The Marines' desert utilities displayed more pixelated beige markings that gave them a lighter appearance than Army troopers with the coffee-stain pattern of their desert camouflage fatigues. Some Iraqis thought they were Spanish troops.

For darker elements in the city, the way the Marines looked and behaved with their boyish faces and their smiles and pockets full of candy led militants to conclude that maybe this "new Army" could be intimidated. They came up with a disparagement that the Marines were—loosely translated—"soft cake." An obscene insult of President George Bush was even spray-painted on a donkey that was left tethered in front of Hurricane Point. (The Marines made it a kind of mascot. It took an hour for First Lieutenant Sean Schickel of Headquarters Company, working with other troops, to maneuver the stubborn equine into Hurricane Point.)

"They saw us showing up and waving at everybody, and they thought we were sissies," Captain Wyeth Towle, the battalion intel officer, told the author in 2004.

So as predicted by their National Guard predecessors, the enemy quickly started testing the Marines. The Tuesday after Mack was disfigured, two rocket-propelled grenades were shot at a Fox Company convoy almost right outside their base. No one got hurt, and the attackers got away. That same night, on the other side of town, an Echo Company squad that had set up an observation post along Michigan spotted three men, including one who seemed in the midst of planting an IED. As Lance Corporal Nathan Appel and a second Marine approached, Appel yelled out in Arabic for the man to stop. The Iraqi immediately spun around and opened fire with a light machine gun. Appel fired back and dropped him with a round into the man's right thigh—the first blood drawn by the battalion. The only downside was that in the confusion and darkness, two Marines and a corpsman fell into a marsh alongside the road and had to be fished out. One of them was the platoon commander, Second Lieutenant Vincent Valdes.

The wounded insurgent, who looked to be in his thirties, was loaded into the back of a seven-ton truck, and Private First Class Jose Texidor Jr. climbed in to watch him on the trip back to the base. Texidor was one of the many "boots" new to the battalion, having arrived in January, seven months after graduating high school. Like a surprising number of Marines, Texidor was small in stature, five foot six, 120 pounds. They called him "Tex," and he hated the name. He had never been to Texas. Didn't want to go to Texas. Didn't even like Texas. He was in fact the son of a bank teller from Passaic, New Jersey. But with his last name, it didn't matter. That night, riding in the truck, Tex and the wounded insurgent locked eyes, and the enemy wouldn't look away. The wounded man was in pain and groaning. But his eyes remained empty and black, filled with malevolence. *He sees me as the devil*, Texidor thought. *I guess I'm at war.*

Harrying attacks continued. The next day, a supply convoy was hit with a small IED, and two Marines suffered busted eardrums. A shepherd walking down the street nearby was blown to bits. Shortly after midnight March 18, three Marines from Weapons Company were hit by shrapnel from an IED exploding near their Humvee on Michigan just west of Combat Outpost. And twelve hours later, a few blocks south, Golf Company Marines jumped out of the way of an RPG skidding down the street, fired from near the anti-American Al Haq Mosque.

PRELUDE

It felt like the entire city was getting into the act. A four-vehicle Weapons Company convoy was headed east on Michigan near the Saddam Magnificent Mosque on Saturday, March 20—one week after McPherson was wounded—when a police officer waved the column through a traffic signal into a stretch of the highway where there were suddenly no vehicles in either direction. Another bicycle on the side of the road exploded, wounding three Marines, including Lance Corporal Clinton Warth, who had to be evacuated home with an eye injury. Iraqi university students standing nearby broke out in laughter as they watched the injured Marines taken away. A few hours later, rocket attacks on Blue Diamond and Hurricane Point wounded five Marines, a soldier, and a private contractor. Acquisition radar over at Camp Ramadi was pointed the wrong way, and artillery crews who might have shot back at the launchers had no idea where they were.

Two days later, the battalion suffered its first Marine killed in action. It was one of the most freakish occurrences anyone had ever seen. And because it occurred late at night—shortly before 1:00 a.m.—and the streets were dark except for the eerie glow of an occasional streetlamp, there was an illusory, bad-dream quality to what unfolded. A column of Humvees was returning to Snake Pit after picking up Marines who had been out on foot patrol. Everyone was tired and just wanted to get back to base.

At the wheel of the last vehicle was Lance Corporal Andrew Dang, a Marine engineer and twenty-year-old native of Central California's Bay Area. He was the son of a Vietnamese immigrant and very bright, having graduated from San Mateo High School with a 3.7 grade point average. Under his photo in the senior yearbook, Dang quoted British novelist Iris Murdoch: "We live in a fantasy world of illusion. The great task in life is to find reality."[1] Dang hated those periods when he was confined to Snake Pit and had worried that night he might get rotated off the team going out to fetch the foot patrol.

The open-backed Humvee he was driving was now loaded with Marines. Bouncing right behind Dang in the back of the vehicle was Private First Class Dean Cugliotta Jr., just eighteen. As the column moved down Michigan at forty miles per hour, they passed an ice cream shop, now closed, and were just about to turn into Snake Pit. There was a flash in an alleyway to their right.

The truck suddenly went into a hard spin and smashed into a concrete bus stop. The men in the back were violently slammed forward, Cugliotta thrown headfirst into the truck cab. The impact shattered his right arm and collarbone and left him unconscious for a few seconds. When he finally opened his eyes, he saw the body of Andrew Dang beside him in the driver's seat. Dang's head was sheared off above the middle of his face. "We're fucked," Cugliotta said.

An insurgent in the alleyway had unloosed a rocket-propelled grenade timed so well that it passed directly through the right window of the moving Humvee, its propellent temporarily blinding the Marine in the passenger seat, and the warhead decapitated Dang, causing the Humvee to spin out of control. There was no explosion. The grenade was either a dud or a dummy round. But one Marine was dead, five wounded, and the Humvee demolished.

Reinforcements converged. Fox Company First Sergeant Tim Weber took charge of the scene and with others loaded up Dang's body and two other Marines with the worst injuries—Cugliotta and Lance Corporal Simon Aguirre, whose right hand was crushed—for transport to Charlie Med at Camp Ramadi. Kennedy and Booker arrived. Weber could see some of his men were in shock, in part because they were faced with something their training never anticipated. There were bits and splatters of a man scattered throughout the interior of the Humvee and in the street, some of it glistening in the fractured glow of the streetlights. What's to be done? Do you try to clean it up? Do you linger and risk another attack? Do you simply mount up and go home? What's the mission?

Marines from Weapons Company came to haul the wrecked Humvee back to base. One of them, Lance Corporal Reagan Hodges, climbed into the front seat of the vehicle to help steer as it was being readied for towing and could see that the inside of the windshield was covered in what he began realizing were shreds of a human being. A wave of emotion flowed over him. He was thinking that there was a family somewhere back in the United States about to receive the worst and most unimaginable news about their loved one, and they didn't even know it.

Weber felt equally distraught as he accompanied Dang's remains to the Camp Ramadi medical facility. The first sergeant, just shy of his thirty-eighth birthday, had a distinctive look with a shaved head and scar on the left side of his face running down to his neck from surgery for tonsil cancer. He was from Ohio, married, and a father of five, with thirteen years in the Marine Corps, much of it in logistics. On promotion to first sergeant, he requested infantry and was sent to 2/4.

Now he could smell scorched flesh and fresh blood as he worked with a Marine sergeant to prepare Dang's remains for removal to a morgue. They worked on the floor trying to wrestle armored plates out of the dead Marines' vest, simultaneously holding the seated body upright. It seemed to take an eternity. Afterward, Weber started wiping up blood on the floor with paper towels and then didn't know whether to discard them. So he stuffed the soaked paper into his cargo pockets.

Jody Schroeder was part of the team that prepared Cugliotta and Aguirre for a medical evacuation that would ultimately take them back to the States. She was struck by how the Marines were already taking a beating so early into their tour.

The next morning, Dang's helmet with the RPG warhead still embedded, was found a hundred yards from the attack site. A bit of remains were still inside, enough to fill a small plastic bag. There was deliberation about what to do with that. Gunnery Sergeant Dirk Lens had a thought. He started a small blaze in a firepit on the far side of camp and, with Weber, said a prayer and burned what had been found. Weber did the same with the bloody paper towels.

They were improvising. The *Marine Corps Manual* doesn't speak to such things.

Just as McPherson's maiming had shaken Golf Company, Dang's decapitation rattled the men of Fox. Each rifle company would make a bloody sacrifice to this opening phase of Ramadi. The Florida troopers hadn't lost a single soldier in nearly a year, and now Marines were dying in their first weeks.

Still, the patrols continued. Echo, Fox, and Golf Companies cycled their men out into the streets every day and often every night. Marine and Navy corpsmen would circle through all areas of the city, setting up ambushes at night where there was suspected enemy activity or presence patrols by day. Platoons went out in what were called *satellite formations*, with squads moving independently from one another but still close enough to provide mutual support and security through overwatch positions as the platoon gradually moved through the city. Squads were supposed to stay within sight of one another. In theory, the practice allowed a platoon to cover a wider area while being able to provide flanking support should one squad come under fire. The British used the tactic with some success in Northern Ireland.

Most important of all the routine missions, however, was something called *route clearance*. It was a banal label for a terrifying experience: walking down a street that could blow up under you at any second, all the while scouring the ground strewn with trash and clutter, trying to spot a wire, a disturbance in pavement or earth, any anomaly that might betray a buried explosive. "Anything look weird about this?" All the while fully aware that a trigger man hidden in bushes or on a nearby rooftop could press a button on a detonator and make your world explode. Fox Company Marine Jonathan Schulze wrote to his father and stepmother about it. "I bet I easily pray over a dozen times a day and I always pray while I am on patrol as I am terrified of getting hit by an IED aka a bomb."[2] Lance Corporal Chris MacIntosh more than once wished he was back pumping gas in his hometown of Scituate, Massachusetts. Particularly scary were those days when women and children were off the streets—a tip-off something was in store. The Americans tried hard not to let thoughts of doom overtake their vigilant study of the terrain. Nineteen-year-old Jarad Cole would recite in his head lyrics of the Eric Clapton song "Layla" that somehow insanely fit the circumstances: *You've got me on my knees / I'm begging, darling, please.*

The skill of finding killer devices before they killed was acquired through attrition. "We learned how to do it by trial and error, where error was costing Marines' lives," a platoon commander later wrote in an after-action report. But it was the teeth-rattling tactic of choice to keep the main highways trafficked by coalition convoys free of IEDs as much as possible. Certainly, Route Michigan was a priority, as was Highway 1 to the north (which was Army responsibility). Around the Sofia area, there was a byway the Marines called Nova, a raised roadway that doubled as a dike to hold back Euphrates floodwaters. Squads of Marines out of Echo Company each day had to walk Nova, trekking a huge circle of more than ten miles around the district. There were interlacing roadways they had to cover as well. It was scary, repetitive, and exhausting work that blistered feet and broke down combat boots. Between the constant patrolling—along with other responsibilities such as guard duty at Combat Outpost or being on standby as part of a quick-reaction force—the Marines, particularly of Echo Company, were getting worn down from lack of sleep. Moreover, every patrol had to have a Navy corpsman along, and since there were too few of them, the sailors were treading the streets more often than Marines. Hospitalman Elias Monarez, a twenty-one-year-old native of West Covina, California, would catch himself drifting almost into a dream state as he shuffled the same steps down the same streets over and over.

Particularly at risk were Marine engineers who accompanied the infantry using mine detectors to find IEDs, getting a positive signal only when they were well within a blast radius. Other Marines were amazed by the sheer courage of these men.

One tactic for hunting IEDs was for a squad to patrol in a kind of reverse-V formation with outer prongs of the column walking ahead and some distance from the roadway to look for the trigger man or maybe spook him into giving his position away. This was effective, particularly if the bomb was wire detonated. But if triggered by a radio signal, the bomber could be too far away to spot.

Nor was the effort merely a straight-line mission. If an IED was located, protocol was to radio for an explosive ordnance disposal team to come out and use a robot device to set explosives near the roadside bomb and blow it up. (And at night, insurgents could just as easily return and replant an IED in the crater left behind by the bomb disposal team.) Only when the IED was neutralized could Marines resume their patrol. The result was that road clearance missions in the sprawling Echo Company sector could easily last from sunup to sundown. The pace was brutal, particularly in the opening months of the deployment, and bloody.

The day after Dang was killed, the executive officer for Echo Company nearly had his arm blown off by a roadside bomb. A company's second-in-command typically works out of headquarters. But First Lieutenant Benjamin Kaler, one of the battalion's few Annapolis graduates, got permission from his boss, Captain Kelly Royer, to go out on patrol. The route clearance mission was along Nova in the northern portion of the Sofia District. The severe blast damage to Kaler's left arm included a compound fracture.

Fifteen hours later, Private First Class Chris Yansky was shot through the right arm in a coordinated, nighttime ambush of a Golf Company platoon right outside Combat Outpost—another brand-new Marine heading home after only two months with the battalion.

PRELUDE

The morning after that incident, two more Marine recruits, both nineteen, were mangled by an IED explosion along Nova. Hospitalman Monarez reached the first, Private First Class Christopher Robins, who had a hole blown through his left wrist so large the sailor could see through it. The corpsman was bandaging up the limb when he heard another Marine yell out, "Oh, yo. It's got Carroll!" Monarez took off and located Private First Class Sean Carroll in a pile of debris where the explosion had thrown him like a rag doll. A more senior corpsman, Tyrynn (pronounced TIE-rin) Dennis, rushed over to take the lead. Carroll had been standing almost directly over the IED when it exploded, and the sailors were shocked by the physical destruction. The red-haired Carroll, who had enlisted right out of high school the year before, had burns over 60 percent of his body and his lower right leg remained connected by a few tortured ligaments. He was in shock and instinctively trying to stand up. Dennis held him down by the shoulders. "You can't get up. Stay down. We're working on it."

The twenty-three-year-old sailor had never seen anything like it before and wasn't sure at first where to begin. Dennis's mind was racing. His hands were slick with blood and sweat. Each time he struggled to pull on rubber gloves, they tore.

"Shit!"

He paused, took a deep breath, and thought, *I've got to start doing something.* He had Monarez put a tourniquet above the mass of torn flesh and bone that was Carroll's right leg. Dennis turned his attention to the shredded lower portion of that limb. Simply wrapping that mass seemed futile. So Dennis pulled out soft, absorbent rolls of gauze known as Kerlix bandage rolls, each about the size of a human fist, and began stuffing them into the massive wound one after the other to staunch the hemorrhaging. He saved just enough Kerlix to wrap what he'd done, all the while thinking, *He's not going to make it.*

His frantic improvising to save this Marine's life was so far removed from anything Dennis had ever imagined for himself when he joined the Navy four years before. Dennis was the oldest of three children raised by a widowed mother who moved the family repeatedly before settling in Phoenix. There, Tyrynn graduated high school and enrolled at an electronic engineering school, where he found that his partial color blindness made it impossible to repair color-coded electronic circuits. In the Navy, he became a hospitalman and had been serving with the Magnificent Bastards for more than three years.

His efforts that day on Route Nova paid off. A helicopter arrived to carry Carroll and Robins away. Carroll's decimated limb would be amputated, along with two fingers on his left hand. Military doctors would initially give the Colorado native scant chance of surviving. But after two months in a coma, he regained consciousness and began a long road of convalescence and rehabilitation.[3]

One other eye-opening insight for Tyrynn Dennis that day was how that kind of terrible event back home would bring daily life to a screeching halt, but here it was only a momentary pause in a day's mission. After feverish efforts to save a mangled comrade (easily the most traumatic event of the corpsman's life to that point), he and the others merely resumed the patrol. No time to decompress. No chance to reflect. No cleaning the blood soaking his uniform. *We push on*, he thought. War.

Blast injuries naturally varied depending on the distance from detonation. Twenty feet away from the blast that devastated Carroll and Robins, their team leader, Lance Corporal Chris MacIntosh, was knocked to the ground by the shock wave. He had no shrapnel wounds. But he had classic symptoms of what would become one of the war's signature wounds, traumatic brain injury—an intense headache and an inability to focus. Dozens of other Marines with the battalion would suffer the same wound during the deployment, as would an estimated 320,000 US troops serving in Iraq and Afghanistan over the next six years, largely as the result of the enemy's reliance on roadside bombs as a weapon

PRELUDE

of choice. Protocols would eventually be established requiring anyone exposed to a blast to be closely monitored for symptoms before returning to duty. (Most recover, but 5–15 percent suffer lasting brain damage.) None of this was known when 2/4 Marines fought in Ramadi. MacIntosh took a day off and then was back at work. He got a chance to use one of the few satellite phones to call his mother, Lauren MacIntosh, to let her know he was hurt but alive. She had long been terrified at the prospect of bad news from Ramadi, and this would not be the last phone call she would receive.

That same day, Jonathan Embrey, a twenty-one-year-old corporal from Springfield, Illinois, tracked mounting casualties in a journal. Embrey had earned the nickname in Golf Company of "Chaplain" or "Chaps" because he had a soft spot for Iraqi kids and because he didn't subscribe to the excessive yelling and hazing of new Marines and saw it as tiresome Marine caveman culture. In Ramadi, he figured the battalion was losing one man per day to death or severe wounds.

It was a casualty pace that was both terrifying and maddening because the enemy never seemed to pay a price for the butchery. Americans were getting killed or maimed by people who then simply disappeared. That finally changed the day after Robins and Carroll were wounded.

Echo Company Captain Kelly Royer was working with his men to put a stop to the enemy's diabolical schedule of mortaring Combat Outpost every Thursday night. Analysis indicated insurgents were using 60 mm mortars. Range rings drawn on a map narrowed a search for launch sites to three locations. On the night of Thursday, March 25, a day after turning twenty-nine, Sergeant Chuck Sheldon led a three-vehicle convoy of twenty Marines and a corpsman out the front gate of Combat Outpost and turned east on Michigan toward a field that was their first prospective launch site. The trucks missed a left turn and did a turnaround on a frontage road to head back west. Dust thrown up by the vehicles reduced visibility to near zero, even with night vision goggles. But at least one of the Marines spotted movement behind a short berm to the right, and the convoy halted. There was suddenly an explosion of gunfire from what would prove to be a cadre of nine insurgents tucked behind the berm just several feet away. The Americans had driven right up on the mortar team.

Every member of the convoy immediately returned fire, and the two groups of men blasted away at each other in the darkness, like opposing formations on a Civil War battlefield. With AK-47 rifles and machine guns, the insurgents raked the front of the lead Humvee, where Sheldon was in the passenger seat alongside the driver, Private First Class Justin Cussans, another of the battalion's new recruits. Enemy rounds shattered the Humvee windshield and disabled the engine, and bullets bored holes through the hillbilly armor on a vehicle door. Cussans took a minor bullet wound to his midsection and damage to one hand. Sheldon emptied a full magazine from his M16 rifle out the passenger-side window before he and Cussans climbed out of the Humvee under covering fire from other troops. Meanwhile, two Marines in a seven-ton truck right behind them were hit, the worst of it a leg wound for Private First Class David Lloyd that nicked his femoral artery. He was another boot who had joined the battalion in January. Lloyd had been firing an M240 medium machine gun from the truck's turret, and after he was hurt, hospitalman Miguel Escalera organized efforts to pull him out and carry him to an ad hoc casualty collection point the sailor set up behind the last vehicle. The torrent of opposing gunfire was deafening. Tracer rounds passed overhead. Rocket-propelled grenades swooshed close by and exploded.

But with Marines concentrating their shooting on whatever muzzle flashes they could see in the darkness, fire superiority quickly turned in their favor. In the meantime, Escalera seemed to be everywhere. After treating a wounded Marine in the back of

PRELUDE

the seven-ton who had suffered a through-and-through gunshot wound to his arm, he got Lloyd to safety and applied a tourniquet to his leg. Then he exposed himself to enemy fire to retrieve Cussans and did the same with the radioman, Lance Corporal Jose Bernardino, who had taken shelter behind the lead Humvee when that vehicle slipped out of gear and rolled backward, the rear tire running over Bernardino's leg.

There was a pause in the shooting as enemy fire suddenly let up. Under directions from Sheldon and team leaders, the Marines maneuvered to gain better fire advantage, and when some of the surviving insurgents began shooting again, the sergeant and his men opened up in unison and quickly ended the fight. All of it lasted only a few minutes, but it was an adrenaline-pumping exhilaration for the young Americans. Everything they had trained for had suddenly become real. And they'd won. Escalera would later be awarded a Bronze Star for valor.

Royer arrived with reinforcements from Combat Outpost, and his wounded men were evacuated. (Lloyd would have to be airlifted out of the war zone. Cussans was evacuated to a nearby medical facility and eventually returned to duty.) Machine guns, RPGs, mortar rounds, and a mortar were recovered, along with four dead or dying insurgents. Three others were captured, including an Iraqi policeman. The battalion daily log exulted over the first enemy killed in action: "4xEKIA!!!"

Royer with a translator tried questioning an enemy fighter who was mortally wounded. The company commander had his hand on the man's chest and could feel a last breath leave. His instant reaction to feeling that life pass away: "It bothered me not one fucking bit."

He felt intense pride for what he and his men had accomplished.

Royer had one of the most unusual backgrounds of any officer in the battalion. He was among the oldest at thirty-six, only a few years younger than Kennedy. Originally from Santa Clara, California, Royer was the product of what he liked to characterize as a "very rugged background." He was the child of a single mother and never met his biological father until he was an adult and a friend located him as a favor. Nor did Royer know until he was a teenager that a stepdad was not his biological father. His childhood was largely shaped by a mother who was constantly leaving a bad situation. She was married seven times, most of them abusive relationships, and Royer once calculated he had moved an astonishing seventy-seven times by age seventeen. (He noted this in his bio/résumé.) It was a cycle of government housing, foster homes, and battered women's shelters from California to Oregon to Texas. The boy was always an outsider in a new place, and he finally left home at sixteen to finish high school in Salem, Oregon, where Kelly worked nights at a deli and rented a room from the restaurant manager. The next year, 1986, he enlisted in the Air Force, where he served nearly six years. With his baritone voice, Royer contemplated military broadcasting but instead became a vehicle operator and, for a time, a military chauffeur for VIPs while stationed in England. All the while, he earned college credits and received an undergraduate degree in 1992 with the hope of one day becoming an officer. He left the Air Force and served a little more than two years in the California Air National Guard. After another two years as a civilian, Royer finally enrolled in Officer Candidates School with the Marines and earned a commission in 1996.

He was chosen as commander of Headquarters and Service Company for 2nd Battalion, 4th Marines in late 2003. When the commander of Echo asked to be relieved for personal reasons on the eve of deploying to Iraq, Royer was shifted over to take his place. It was a few days later that he grabbed another battalion's mascot at the Valentine's Day Officers' Mess, triggering a brouhaha.

A lot of the Marines, including the battalion sergeant major, Jim Booker, were impressed with Royer's chutzpah that night and the black eye they saw as kind of a badge of honor. But there were

PRELUDE 71

also a few things about the guy that rubbed people the wrong way. He could sometimes come across as abrasive. When Booker had an introductory conversation with the newly arrived captain, he was surprised when Royer acted as if he were interviewing Booker for a job. What could the sergeant major offer Royer? How much experience did Booker have in the Corps? What was his tactical background?

Kennedy, in particular, was also finding Royer off-putting. He flat-out told the captain that he was getting Echo command *despite* his behavior. "You wire-brush everybody you come in contact with," Kennedy said to him.

When it came time to choose call signs for each company, Kennedy picked "Porcupine" for Echo because of what he saw as Royer's prickly demeanor. It got shortened to "Porky," and the Marines of Echo grew to hate it.

Kennedy chose "Joker" for Golf Company because its commander, Chris Bronzi, had an explosively loud laugh. A visiting reporter described it as "one piercing, explosive 'Ha!' head thrown back, followed by a staccato of smaller notes."[4]

For the command element's call sign, Kennedy elected to choose "Bastard," as irreverent as it sounded. He himself was "Bastard 6," with the number six typically designating commander.

But the mission to find and destroy the mortar crew on the night of March 25 was a victory for Royer. He snapped photographs of his Marines standing or crouched next to the dead bodies: men in dark clothing and running shoes with gaping wounds in their heads and torsos. In one photograph, a Marine gestures with a thumbs-up.

4

EVE OF BATTLE

"DAWG, THIS IS WHAT MARINES DO."

As MARCH DREW to a close, the pace of events in Ramadi and across Iraq began to speed up. At 1st Marine Division headquarters in Blue Diamond, the 2nd Intelligence Battalion had established what was known as the Tactical Fusion Center, where information from division-wide down to the company level was collected and collated; it was beginning to show results.

As he monitored the new intel information coming in, Colonel Joe Dunford, division chief of staff, could see that whatever enemy was out there was coalescing into something far more daunting than a few fellows planting IEDs. There was increasing evidence of coordinated attacks by groups of six to ten people acting as a combat unit, like a squad of troops. They were Sunni Arab, the same people who had been defeated and humiliated by the US-led invasion the year before. They had succeeded during the intervening months in a resurrection of sorts, building a network of training, weapon resources, and planning, all of it largely conducted outside of what the coalition could see. The Marine leadership believed

EVE OF BATTLE

there was an organized enemy force in the making, though they didn't precisely understand its command structure. Something was coming that was far more than what the division expected when it arrived with its security and stability plans. Insurgent elements didn't want to merely disrupt any transition to a new Iraqi government. They wanted the Americans gone. "To them, we were an antibody in the Iraq ecosystem," Dunford was thinking. "What do they want to do? They want to get rid of it."

Insurgents in Fallujah launched a series of coordinated ambushes on March 26 using mortar and rifle fire against two companies of Marines trying to enter a portion of the city. During the midday sermon at the Al Haq Mosque in eastern Ramadi, members of Golf Company could hear the imam preaching violence in the wake of the insurgents killed the night before by Royer's Marines, and God's help in achieving victory: "The mujahideen are not dead but martyrs in paradise. Do not deal with the US. But fight them. Allah will grant an afterlife."

Two crucial events unfolded one week later. One, on March 30, would rock Echo Company. The other, on March 31, would rock the world.

MARCH 30

For Echo Company, it began another game of Russian roulette in the never-ending search for IEDs. This time, the foot patrol was along Route Michigan by members of Third Platoon humping the same highway where buried artillery rounds had been found just the day before. Key to the operation was Lance Corporal William Wiscowiche, "Whiskey" to the other men, a combat engineer equipped with a mine detector. The twenty-year-old from Victorville, California, was a rare commodity in the battalion, being one of the few on a second combat tour to Iraq. He had fought with 1st Marine Division in its sweep into Baghdad in 2003 and watched the iconic image of Saddam's statue being pulled down before a cheering crowd. He felt he'd seen his share of combat and had no immediate desire for more. Wiscowiche had married his high school girlfriend during what proved to be only a brief reprieve from war. The couple had a daughter born during Whiskey's first Iraq deployment. Now he was called back to serve in Ramadi, where the missions were getting even more dangerous, particularly these treacherous efforts to find buried explosives before a trigger man detonated them. The day before the mission, Wiscowiche had called his father, Joseph, whom he idolized. The elder Wiscowiche was a Vietnam veteran, and the son had adopted his father's "Whiskey" nickname from the military as his own in the Marines. During the phone call, William Wiscowiche told his father he was scared. Joseph told his son to stay focused and rely on his training.

As the young engineer and other Marines carefully walked west along Route Michigan—one line of them along the highway's north edge, another along the median—a ten-vehicle convoy flowed past going in the same direction. Seconds later, there was an explosion so massive it could be felt back at Combat Outpost a mile away.

Between forty and fifty pounds of plastic explosive stuffed into a propane tank had been buried about sixteen inches deep in the median, and the site was hidden under scrub brush. Lance Corporal Jason Murray was about three feet from stepping on the device when a trigger man detonated it. The direction of the blast was southward, or to Murray's right, and the massive force of it nearly sheared off that side of his face. His right forehead was crushed. His right eye was destroyed and his left eye blinded. Shrapnel hit him in the chest and arms and through his right eye into his brain.

To Murray's right—and almost directly in the path of the blast force—was Wiscowiche. There was speculation later that the engineer was carrying a supply of plastic explosives to be used to blow up IEDs and that the huge blast caused that bomb material to also detonate.

The result was that the top half of Wiscowiche's body above his belly button was cleanly severed and vaulted into the air. His lower half was blown to pieces. Where his upper body landed, the young Marine was tragically still breathing. As the others looked on in horror, the engineer gave no conscious reaction, as if he was already gone but his heart and respiration wouldn't give up. His last breaths left his body seconds after a quick-reaction force arrived from Combat Outpost. Most of the Marines present were ordered to set up security to guard against a follow-on attack but also to keep them from seeing the carnage. A suspected trigger man was found and detained. He was carrying a possible trigger device—a knob power switch from an electric fan, something you could activate with a simple twist with your thumb and forefinger.

A medevac helicopter landed in a field south of the highway to evacuate Murray. The upper-body remains of Wiscowiche were placed in a body bag. An extra bag was thrown into the helicopter because it was thought there was no way Murray would survive. (Miraculously, like Carroll before him, he did, if sightless.) And the Marines were left, once again, with the grim task of locating pieces of a friend. Soldiers from the convoy showed up to assist them.

The squad leader for the quick-reaction Marine force that arrived was Corporal Eric Smith of Second Platoon, the twenty-one-year-old son of a state game warden from Waxahachie, Texas. It took only a few seconds for Smith to assess what he was facing and order most of his men to join perimeter defense. They didn't need to see this. He kept with him one of his most seasoned Marines and a good friend, Lance Corporal Jason L. Birmelin, and a corpsman, Sergio Gutierrez, and the three went about their terrible recovery task. What they had to use—and what would be a key element of the post-traumatic stress disorder haunting Smith in the years to some—was a trash bag. *They had to place bits of their comrade into a trash bag.* It was all they had, and the job needed to get done. Gutierrez, for one, didn't want anything left behind for feral dogs to find, as happened with remains of enemy suicide bombers. While they worked, Birmelin saw that Eric seemed determined to find one thing and not leave until he had it. Smith knew Wiscowiche had married a month before the deployment. They finally found the wedding band on a finger.

As the disfigurement of Mack McPherson shocked Golf Company and decapitation of Andrew Dang stunned Fox Company, so the demolishment of William Wiscowiche sent shock waves through Echo Company. It was a flashing neon warning about the horrors lurking outside the gates of their combat bases. And yet platoon commander Tom Cogan marveled at how his young Marines persevered through these barbarities, assembling each morning for another mission. What they were seeing, the bloody results of it, had to have an emotional impact, Cogan thought. Yet these men—so many of them Kennedy's high schoolers serving beside others only a few years older—just sucked it up and pushed on. Cogan couldn't help but be impressed. They, in turn, respected him for his quiet proficiency and courage under fire. "He wanted the job done and wanted it done efficiently," one of his team leaders, Corporal Evan Null, would later say. The twenty-three-year-old second lieutenant was also one of the most natural-born fighters in the battalion. Cogan was raised in the Lower Northeast section of Philadelphia, a cluster of tough, blue-collar neighborhoods. His father managed a Burger King before becoming a public school teacher. His mother was a secretary. Tom, their only son of three children, loved physical action and used the same word to describe fistfights, his beloved sport of ice hockey (football was too slow), and combat: *fun.* At the beach melee before the battalion departed, Cogan happily waded into the fray. The Marine Corps was a perfect fit for him.

The young lieutenants who led the platoons were a curiosity to the enlisted Marines and sailors. First, they weren't a whole lot older, and yet they'd been to college, had been commissioned, and were in charge. Some seemed particularly accessible, like John Wroblewski in Echo Company. Some were quiet and a little harder

EVE OF BATTLE

to read, like Cogan, although his men noticed that he brightened and chatted if someone mentioned hockey.

As they took the measure of their commander, he did the same with them. When Cogan joined the battalion in November 2003, one task he took on was sitting down with each of his men to learn their motivations and goals. After watching how they weathered the destruction of one of their own and the blinding of another, his understanding of them deepened.

It was small surprise that many of the men took up the practice of drafting death letters. Some had begun this ritual even before arriving in Ramadi. They would write a letter or inscribe a photograph, typically to a girlfriend, and then entrust it to another Marine for delivery in the event that the worst happened. Escalera, the corpsman who received a Bronze Star for valor during fighting on March 25, saw his young Marines in Echo Company's Third Platoon doing this and hated it. He thought it was bad luck. Their well-being was his responsibility, and Escalera didn't like them dwelling on death.

"Don't do that, Downing. You're jinxing yourself," Escalera said to Ryan Downing, a twenty-year-old Iowa Marine who had exchanged last letters with one of his best friends in his squad, Californian Travis Layfield, nineteen.

"Dawg, this is what Marines do," Downing said.

MARCH 31

It was never clear why four Blackwater USA contractors who were providing security for a convoy of flatbed trucks decided to drive through Fallujah the morning of Wednesday, March 31. Marines had taken over patrolling the city from 82nd Airborne soldiers just days before, and violence was increasing. The city should have been closed to such traffic. One theory was that the men, all former members of the US military, didn't have proper maps and were merely following the most direct route through Fallujah. Thomas

E. Ricks, in his book *Fiasco: The American Military Adventure in Iraq*, wrote that word of the mission had leaked, and insurgents had carefully prepared an ambush.[1] Whatever the case, the convoy became slowed by heavy traffic and then roadblocks. Gunmen opened fire, and all four Blackwater personnel were killed. A raucous crowd gathered, and at least two of the bodies were burned, dismembered, and hung from a trestle bridge over the Euphrates. Gruesome images were relayed around the world through video and photographs. The bodies had been dragged through the streets, much as a dead US soldier was dragged through the streets of Mogadishu, Somalia, in 1993, in a battle that precipitated US withdrawal of troops from that country.

Fallujah was an opening salvo. The next seventy-two hours would be fraught with debate in Washington over how to respond. Marine leadership in Iraq counseled caution. Lieutenant General James Conway, commander of the 1st Marine Expeditionary Force and the top Marine officer in Iraq, pleaded with higher command not to overreact.[2] Mattis quickly drew up a plan for steady-as-she-goes patrol operations continuing across the region while investigations deconstructed what happened.

This would allow time for ringleaders to be identified and then killed or captured in raids conducted at a time of the Marine command's choosing. It could avoid inciting the population and upending the broader plan for support and stabilization across the Sunni region. "Going overly kinetic at this juncture plays into the hands of the opposition," wrote Brigadier General John Kelly, Mattis's assistant division commander, in a daily note. "We should not fall victim to their hopes for a vengeful response."

But back home, it was an election year, there were concerns about showing weakness, and the Bush administration wanted blood. "We've got to pound these guys," Defense Secretary Donald Rumsfeld said, and he ordered that plans be drawn up for an immediate assault on the city of 250,000–300,000. Army Lieutenant General Ricardo Sanchez, overall commander of coalition

EVE OF BATTLE 79

forces in Iraq, agreed. His deputy director of operations, Brigadier General Mark Kimmett, promised a response. "It will be overwhelming. . . . We will pacify that city."[3]

A few hours before the contractors were killed, Connor's brigade suffered what would be its worst single-day loss of soldiers during the entire deployment. Five Army engineers were killed in a single, massive explosion of an IED. The tragedy was little more than a footnote in the maelstrom of news coverage over the Fallujah killings.

The two events were about twelve miles apart. A platoon of engineers in armored personnel carriers had been heading north from the Euphrates when what was later determined to be a 220-pound warhead for a surface-to-air missile was remotely detonated as the platoon leader's boxy APC drove over it. The tracked vehicle was obliterated, as were the five men inside. A distraught Buck Connor arrived and assisted in collecting the scattered pieces of his men. During that recovery effort, small red flags were planted marking anything resembling human remains. When Dave Brinkley, the engineer battalion commander, arrived, the expanse of red across a field looked like poppies in bloom.

Leading the platoon was First Lieutenant Doyle Hufstedler III, twenty-five, a Texas Aggie from Abilene whose wife would give birth to his daughter five weeks later. Hufstedler had called home three days earlier to ask that members of his church pray for him because the missions were growing more dangerous. The others killed were Specialist Sean Robert Mitchell, twenty-four, of Youngsville, Pennsylvania, who was six foot four and known to his friends as "the gentle giant"; Specialist Michael G. Karr Jr., twenty-three, of San Antonio, who left college to become an Army medic; Private First Class Cleston Raney, twenty, of Rupert, Idaho; and Private Brandon Lee Davis, twenty, of Cumberland, Maryland. What parts of each soldier could be positively identified were presented to families for individual burial. The remainder were commingled inside a steel casket and buried at Arlington National Cemetery under a headstone bearing their names.

"SIR, THERE'S SOME EVIL SHIT OUT THERE."

Hours after the soldiers were killed and miles to the west, the Marines in Ramadi were trying to unlock the mystery of who was leading attacks in the area. Paul Kennedy and his command staff convoyed across Ramadi to the Government Center and dinner with the police chief, Ja'ardon Mohammed Habeisi, and his entourage. The police commander was a burly fellow with receding white hair and a thick, gray mustache. His officers wore blue and carried AK-47s, and many often wore traditional red-and-white kaffiyeh headdresses. They didn't always feel like allies. During one visit to a police station, a Marine officer turned to Sergeant Major Booker and asked, "Is it me or is it scarier in here?" "It's straight up scarier in here," Booker responded. The Florida soldiers had believed Habeisi to be as corrupt as any Iraqi official but also a tough man who was committed to supporting the coalition. The Marines thought he might be too dangerous. That night, the plan, over flatbread and chicken, was to collaborate in identifying locations where weapons and insurgent leaders could be ferreted out. Habeisi's men could make this easy by simply going to a house that insurgent leaders were suspected of using, and obtaining the map coordinates by operating a Global Position Lightweight GPS receiver, known colloquially as a plugger. But they didn't seem to be able to do that—or didn't want to. So Booker came up with an extraordinary idea.

He essentially volunteered to go behind enemy lines. It was small surprise given that the forty-two-year-old Marine was a veteran of the Corps's most elite groups of fighters. He was sent to sniper school two years after enlistment in 1985, and two years after that, he was accepted into Force Reconnaissance, or Force Recon for short. The decades-old institution is delegated the most dangerous combat missions of obtaining information deep behind enemy lines. They undergo training similar to that of Navy SEALs. As a Force Recon staff sergeant and platoon sergeant, Booker engaged in some of the most intense, close-up combat of the Persian Gulf War. He and his Marines served as a trip wire force on January 21, 1991, along the Saudi Arabian border with Kuwait. They first came under artillery fire and then successfully defeated an attack by more than one hundred Iraqi troops. At one point, Booker ran across open bullet-swept terrain to link with and retrieve a small outpost of his Marines with whom he'd lost contact. He was awarded the Bronze Star for Valor for that and also discovered he could remain calm and high functioning under fire.

What Booker was proposing to Kennedy and the others was that he be allowed to go with a couple of Habeisi's men to the target locations and learn enemy whereabouts for future raids. "I'm going to wear one of those dishdashas. I have a grenade. I'll have a walkie-talkie and I'll have a pistol. Put me in the car and I'll go thumb the thing . . . and get the GPS."

Kennedy had platoons ready to respond if events went south. He told Booker to go for it. The sergeant major slipped on a dishdasha over his fatigues, climbed into the back seat of a sedan with a 9 mm and a small radio, and, with two Iraqi men in the front seat, he began heading deep into the city where there were enemy checkpoints manned by men with AK-47s standing over trash can fires. Booker thought it looked like scenes from the movie *Escape from New York*. He got his coordinates, and they returned to the government.

"Sir, there's some evil shit out there," he told Kennedy.

The convoy started back to Hurricane Point. But the night wasn't nearly over. The four Humvees were just over half a mile out from their base along Route Michigan when they were ambushed by enemy fighters using light machine guns and rocket-propelled grenades. There were explosions on both ends of the four-vehicle convoy. The trucks ground to a halt, and Kennedy told Booker he wanted to counterattack. "Let's get out of here and kill these motherfuckers." Major JD Harrill, the battalion operations officer riding in the second vehicle, called out, "Ambush right!" over the radio and then repeated it as he got out of the truck. This was a chance for the command element to personally practice what they had demanded of their Marines—aggressively, immediately turning in to any attack. Booker and Harrill were leading the others to a dark alleyway as green tracers from an enemy light machine gun laced the night. Both men opened fire, Booker with his M14, a nonregulation sniper rifle for the Marine Corps, that fired a heavier-caliber round at a higher muzzle velocity than an M16. They both took off down the alleyway running after retreating enemy fighters. Booker spotted the silhouette of a man with an RPG launcher taking direct aim at him, and he fired first. The man dropped into the street. A blood trail on the pavement led Booker, Harrill, and Kennedy to a ramp into a garage, where the fighter— a heavyset man wearing a dark windbreaker—had bled to death on the floor. Booker had shot him through the throat. There were eight people in the house, all suspected of being part of an insurgent cell, and all were taken into custody. One of them was the brother of a police official.

The sergeant major wanted very much to believe he had killed the man responsible for the death of Marine engineer Andrew Dang, who was decapitated. "Most people don't get that satisfaction," he later told a documentary filmmaker.

The swift counterattack by the battalion command officers that night was a small action, really no more than a skirmish. But it encapsulated doctrinal elements Kennedy endorsed and Harrill, as operations officer, worked to instill at the platoon and squad level—this notion that Marines must act instinctively to punish any enemy who dares to attack them. It must be immediate, deadly, and make them pay a price for shooting at Americans. "We're going to lead with our chin," Kennedy had told his senior leaders and noncommissioned officers even before they left Camp Pendleton. It didn't mean being reckless or needlessly exposing oneself to enemy fire. But it meant swift, aggressive, smart engagement and relentless pursuit. It would be so automatic that officers, rather than being consumed with urging troops forward, could concentrate on marshaling air or ground support. Foundational to that approach were schoolhouse classics such as those promoted by Prussian military theorist Carl von Clausewitz and his mentor, military reformist Gerhard von Scharnhorst, who espoused that the element of chance in warfare—in the instance of Ramadi, the ever-present threat of an ambush—demands a creative response. It mirrored a famous argument of legendary German general Erwin Rommel that when in battle and in doubt, attack. The doctrine, in simplest terms, was to react in such a uniformly belligerent manner that an enemy fighter who wanted to take a shot at a Marine was gambling with his life. Kennedy wanted his people to be feared.

To achieve his goals, the battalion commander emphasized the primacy of small-unit leaders—the sergeants and corporals who led squads. Kennedy felt strongly that if they weren't imbued with an air of confidence and authority, they wouldn't take the initiative when necessary, and they wouldn't act in lieu of direct orders. That was why he ordered all the portraits of previous battalion commanders taken down on the quarterdeck of the main battalion offices and replaced with portraits of the battalion's twenty-seven squad leaders. It was why when he conducted his Socratic war-gaming discussions, those same squad leaders were seated right up front while commissioned officers were in the back.

Harrill believed that creativity also meant abandoning rigid concepts that never really made sense. The Marines were required, for example, to police black market sales of gasoline—vendors hawking it from jugs along the road—upending livelihoods for poor people in a war-ravaged economy. Harrill wanted to ignore that order. He also quickly lost patience with what he saw as the deadly and shortsighted practice of walking highways to find buried IEDs, "exposing Marines to a long walk of death." Company commanders were required to keep main arteries free of roadside bombs, but how they did it was their choice. Creative thought.

Some of this was happening elsewhere in the brigade's areas of operation. There were two primary east–west arteries linking Baghdad and much of Iraq with points west. One was Highway 10, which the Marines called Route Michigan, as it passed through Ramadi. The other was Highway 1 that ran parallel to Highway 10, but north of the Euphrates River and outside Ramadi. Army Captain Nicholas Ayers controlled that stretch of Highway 1 with his armored company of tanks and Bradley Fighting Vehicles, and he was grappling with the same IED issues that were bedeviling commanders and killing Marines and soldiers in and around Ramadi. Ayers, a twenty-eight-year-old West Point graduate from Southern California, had also lost soldiers to a roadside bomb. To maximize flexibility, he experimented in ways he could use his 125 troopers, either with tanks in combination with Bradleys or with armored personnel carriers, or up-armored Humvees. Then he decided to simply position his men along the highway overpasses twenty-four hours a day with eyes on the highway. They could still pull away for missions or, in some cases, to reinforce the Marines south of the river. It worked. He shut down the planting of IEDs along the highway.

Probably the most creative concept for dealing with buried roadside bombs sprang from a contest held within the 1st Engineer Battalion, where the soldiers were urged to get innovative. Someone came up with rigging phony surveillance cameras to power poles throughout the city so the enemy would think the Americans were constantly watching. What they built for a few dollars each were basically boxes made to look like cameras, complete with blinking lights powered by a couple of batteries. The insurgents were clearly impressed. They kept trying to blow up the power poles where the "cameras" were attached.

For the Marine company commanders, Harrill counseled a reliance on a combination of alternatives to dangerous foot patrols: random observation posts and setting up ambushes to surprise bomb planters. He grew increasingly impatient when Echo commander

Captain Kelly Royer persisted with hours-long foot-patrol missions, blowing up at him during a face-to-face at Combat Outpost. "This is not making sense, and you don't need to be doing this."

Meanwhile, small attacks across the city continued. The Golf Company commander, Captain Chris Bronzi, caught a piece of shrapnel in his thigh from a grenade someone threw over a wall at his command group outside a police station on the afternoon of April 1. The thirty-year-old officer saw the bomb land and bounce and tried to shout a warning, but his voice was muffled by the explosion. The next night, Golf Company Gunnery Sergeant Winston Jaugan and two other Marines caught some shrapnel from an IED explosion near the Saddam Magnificent Mosque.

Twenty-four hours later, on the night of April 3, First Lieutenant JD Stephens took his Weapons Platoon out on a nighttime mission of establishing observation posts to spot enemy activity. After dinner at the Army chow hall at Camp Ramadi, the platoon riding in six Humvees headed into the streets, splitting into two groups to observe different sectors of the city. Half the platoon positioned their vehicles near a water tower just east of the Saddam Magnificent Mosque, where Iraqi police were working on a vehicle checkpoint. With the Marines at this position was Stephens, a twenty-five-year-old Texan who grew up in San Antonio and graduated from Texas Tech. Streetlights were out to the east, and the idea was that insurgents using the darkness to set up IEDs might be spotted with thermal sights the Americans had mounted on their trucks. But no one saw a man with a rocket-propelled grenade launcher fire from the edge of the shadows at about 10:45 p.m. He was aiming at Stephens's Humvee where it was parked. A young Marine manning the .50-caliber on that truck had just climbed out of the turret and was standing where the rocket struck. It was Geoff Morris, the Illinois teenager who had told his diary he was a little scared but felt God would protect him. Morris caught the full impact of the RPG explosion in his lower back, likely sparing two Marines who were nearby, one of whom suffered minor wounds.

The Americans opened fire as a truck peeled off, possibly with the enemy attacker on board.

Morris was rushed to an aid station at Combat Outpost, where Navy doctor Colin Crickard worked feverishly to stabilize the horribly wounded Marine in preparation for a helicopter medevac.

"What are his chances?" Morris's previous squad leader, Sergeant Shane Nylin, asked Crickard when he arrived at Combat Outpost.

"Well, the human body is an amazing thing. He is still alive now and he is still breathing on his own," Crickard told him before starting to equivocate. "If he makes it through the night, he will probably be okay. But don't expect it."

They shook hands. The helicopter arrived to carry a bundled-up Morris away. He died hours later on Palm Sunday—the battalion's third fatal casualty in as many weeks.

Stephens and his men returned to the water tower area the next day to scour buildings, businesses, and cars, and question citizens, seeking any information about the attackers. That night, another platoon arrived to try to draw out the enemy, all to no avail. "We will continue to taunt them and hunt them until they come out of hiding," Stephens wrote in a letter to Morris's father.

The day Morris was fatally wounded, Lieutenant General Sanchez had issued orders for an attack to commence on Fallujah, designed to wipe out insurgent strongholds and bring to justice those responsible for killing and desecrating the four American contractors. Mattis chose to launch operations in the early hours of April 5 using the two Marine battalions he had outside the city, supported by a handful of tanks, along with C-130 gunships and Cobra helicopters. Two more battalions would be diverted from other missions to supplement the attack. The first two phases would involve setting up blocking positions in the city and vehicle checkpoints to prevent enemy fighters from escaping while raids were conducted to kill or capture key enemy leaders. The final two phases would involve seizing hostile areas of the city. The battle

EVE OF BATTLE

could last days. "We will fight smart," Mattis wrote in a statement on April 3. "We do not have to be loved at the end of the day, this is a goal that is no longer achievable in Fallujah, but we must avoid turning more young men into terrorists."[4]

As open warfare broke out between Marine battalions and Arab fighters in Fallujah, militia fighters from the nation's Shia population simultaneously launched attacks on Palm Sunday in Baghdad and cities throughout the southeast—Najaf, Amara, and Nasiriyah. The violence was led by Muqtada al-Sadr, a junior cleric and twenty-nine-year-old son of a popular Shia leader who had been assassinated under the Saddam regime. The militant son had fiercely opposed the presence of coalition troops after the invasion and drew power from a growing resentment among Iraq's majority Shia population over mounting poverty and unemployment. The trigger for violence was likely moves that Iraq administrator Paul Bremer ordered—the shuttering on March 28 of a Sadr newspaper, an event that triggered demonstrations where protestors were killed—and the capture on April 3 of a leading Sadr deputy.

The worst of the Shia attacks by Sadr's Mahdi Army was April 4 in Baghdad slums known as Sadr City, where two million lived. A platoon of eighteen soldiers with the 1st Armored Cavalry Division was returning to base when it was ambushed, and soldiers were forced to retreat down an alley into a house. Two companies of troopers fought their way into Sadr City to rescue the trapped platoon. In all, eight soldiers died and sixty were wounded.[5] Mahdi Army clashes would continue every day for more than two months.

The coalition was now suddenly fighting a two-front war against militants from Iraq's Sunni and Shia Islamic sects.

For the Marines in Ramadi, there was a sense that something big was coming their way. With Fallujah under assault, it was expected that enemy fighters could "squirt" west into the provincial capital. Posters had gone up in the city from dissident groups promising a coordinated resistance. But such threats had been seen before and always proved empty. Still, there was a choice piece of new intel that the brigade hoped would undercut an organized insurgency in Ramadi.

One of the major underground leaders Army officials had been trying to capture for almost a year was believed to be relocating operations from Khalidiyah to Ramadi. Adnan Hassan Farhan had been a lieutenant colonel in Saddam's elite Republican Guard, had an alleged history of war crimes, and had claimed responsibility for attacks against coalition forces from Baghdad to Fallujah to Khalidiyah. Most of the Devil Brigade soldiers killed in action had died in Khalidiyah. Kyle Teamey, the Dartmouth graduate who led targeting operations for Buck Connor's intel section, helped draw up plans for Operation Wildbunch that would rely, in part, on Booker's undercover work from March 31 and the new information about Farhan's arrival in the city. Raids against potential targets or to seize weapons caches were launched nearly every week by 2/4 Marines and often turned out to be dry holes because the so-called intel was bad, dated, or some tipster's way of punishing a rival.

But this information on Farhan looked strong. Marines from Weapons Company headed into the streets in the wee hours of Tuesday, April 6, to establish a cordon around city blocks in south Ramadi where the two target houses were located in one of the city's nicer neighborhoods. One house turned out to be a bust. But the other was strangely full of about twenty women, and one of the platoon commanders, First Lieutenant Dan Crawford, thought it suspicious enough that he and his Marines kept poking around until they found a hidden entrance in the backyard for a tunnel leading to an adjacent house. Crawford immediately led a search of that building and hit pay dirt. Not only did they find Farhan but his brother Majeed Abdullah Farhan, another wanted man, and eight other people, including Jihadist ringleaders, further evidence that former regime dissidents were collaborating with Islamic extremists.

Farhan and the others were flex-cuffed and taken away. Teamey would do some initial questioning and concluded that the former Republican Guard officer was definitely a hard case. With a muscled build and an intense look in the eyes, he reminded Teamey of the actor Dwayne "the Rock" Johnson, only with hair and a beard.

Shortly before that interrogation, as Farhan and the others were being brought to Hurricane Point he was being guarded by one of the most intimidating Marines in Weapons Company. Lance Corporal Reagan Hodges was the "old man" of the unit at twenty-eight. He'd left the Marine Corps and then couldn't resist coming back in—and at six foot one, 230 pounds, he was physically imposing and often used that to his advantage. Hodges, who had assisted at the scene where Lance Corporal Andrew Dang was killed two weeks earlier, was a true "field Marine." He was a Devil Dog who had problems in garrison but was peerless on the battlefield. His platoon commander, David Dobb, had to run interference for him with the battalion's upper echelon after Hodges thrashed a guy he found sleeping with his wife. To hear Hodges tell the story, everything would have been fine when he first walked into his apartment and the guy got up to leave. Hodges was behaving himself. But it was a passing remark the man uttered when he walked by Hodges—"Well, dude, shit happens"—that landed him in the hospital. Hodges spent two weeks in jail.

On the night of the big capture in Ramadi, Hodges tried to scare some answers out of Farhan, but the insurgent showed him nothing. *There's not many people I can't make scared of me,* Hodges thought. *Not this guy. You have to respect that.*

Duke Wells, the executive officer for Weapons Company, had been in charge of handling the detainees, and the work ran well into the morning. Wells, who had thrown one of the first punches in the infamous Valentine's Day melee back at Pendleton, was feeling good about what they'd accomplished, believing they might have put a major dent in enemy operations. *Maybe this is a little like what victory feels like,* Wells thought as he finally bedded down.

It was fleeting. Within a few minutes, he could hear the radio erupt with news of gunfights breaking out all over the city. The battalion was under attack.

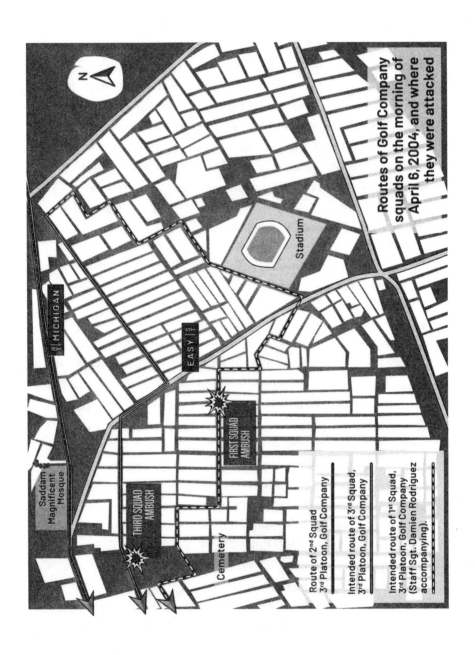

5

BATTLE, DAY 1: CITY CENTER

As THE MARINES of the Magnificent Bastards headed off to war in early 2004, a college sophomore named Mark Zuckerberg launched what became known as Facebook from his dormitory bedroom at Harvard, a social media phenom that would eventually draw 2.9 billion active monthly users. The New England Patriots won the Super Bowl as a record 144.4 million watched. The Passion of the Christ was the hottest movie at the box office. John Kerry became the presumptive Democratic nominee for president (only to lose the election in November). And Martha Stewart was convicted of insider trading.

The first week of March, "Yeah!" by Usher was No. 1 on the US Billboard Top 100; Entertainment Weekly found it "irresistibly crunked-out" for its shouted catchphrase. Kanye West declared "We at war / We at war with terrorism" with his popular gospel-rap "Jesus Walks." And a favorite country western song that week was John Michael Montgomery's ode to a soldier at

*war getting a letter from Mom: " I fold it up and put it in my shirt /
Pick up my gun and get back to work."*

"Shit hits the fan . . ."

—Diary entry for April 6, 2004,
Corporal Jonathan Embrey

EAST CEMETERY, CENTRAL RAMADI,
10:48 A.M., TUESDAY, APRIL 6

LANCE CORPORAL JEREMIAH Letterman carefully scanned the
street looking for trouble first this way, then that, mirroring other
Marines in his squad as they carefully walked in a column west
along a narrow residential roadway. Ahead just a few blocks was
a ten-acre rectangle of mausoleums, headstones, and tombs, a
city graveyard the Marines designated East Cemetery. Letterman
peered down an alleyway to his right when suddenly he heard the
squad leader, Corporal Eric Eggink, call out, "RPG! RPG! RPG!"
and the lance corporal turned his head just as the rocket hissed
past and exploded against a palm tree nearby, a piece of shrapnel
piercing his arm.

Gunmen suddenly appeared on rooftops and around corners
armed with AK-47s and opened fire. The dozen or so Marines were
all members of Third Squad of Golf Company's Third Platoon. It
had been an uneventful morning. Third Platoon was commanded
by Second Lieutenant Jonathan Hesener, a Naval Academy graduate and, of all things, a leukemia survivor. He had the Lord's
Prayer tattooed on his torso in Aramaic.

Hesener was tasked that day with taking his platoon from
Combat Outpost to the Government Center, a little over two miles
to the west, where it would replace another Golf Company platoon
in providing security. The lieutenant had sent out his three squads
from Combat Outpost in thirty-minute intervals beginning at

BATTLE, DAY 1: CITY CENTER

8:00 a.m. The weather was comfortable. Hesener was with Second Squad, the first to leave, riding in four Humvees, and they took the straightest route to the center complex of several buildings, driving directly along Michigan, arriving without incident. The other two squads traversed on foot through the broad Malaab District that extended east to west, south of Michigan. Third Squad took a route several hundred feet south of Route Michigan through narrow residential streets, and First Squad, accompanied by the platoon sergeant, twenty-seven-year-old Staff Sergeant Damien Rodriguez, hiked west along a route even farther to the south, walking through the Mukhabarat neighborhood and past the city's large soccer stadium in the southeastern edge of Ramadi.

About an hour into the patrol, a voice on loudspeakers from a nearby mosque ominously began calling out, "Jihad! Jihad!"

The Marines were operating in a conventional satellite-patrol formation designed to cover a broad area and allow each squad to mutually support one another. But the squads on this day were hundreds of feet apart. Marines in one squad couldn't see or keep track of Marines paralleling them in another squad. They were effectively isolated from one another. It was a battalion tactic that had worried the 1st Brigade commander, Army Colonel Buck Connor, during the previous week. He feared it left the Marines too vulnerable to attack. And now that was exactly what was about to happen to Hesener's platoon. In fact, scores of enemy fighters, supplemented by last-minute volunteers—ballooning to what would be an estimated insurgent force of five hundred people—had spread out across the city to observe, isolate, and destroy small numbers of Marines deemed targets of opportunity. It was a citywide offensive against the Magnificent Bastards. The enemy had watched the Americans for weeks, noting how they responded with their quick-reaction forces and what routes they took. Enemy commanders identified funnel points through which US reinforcements would likely flow and had set up complex ambushes designed to snare small numbers of Marines and then block larger numbers from coming to their aid. One particular trap established in the Sofia District was built around a dug-in, Soviet-era 12.7 mm DShK heavy machine gun, commonly known as a *dishka* and very similar to an American .50-caliber. The weapon was oriented down the axis of a frequently traveled route just waiting for the Marines to show up that day. Shop owners along the road were ordered that morning to vacate their premises by fighters who said, "Today, we are going to kill Americans."

The overall strategy behind this assault would never be fully understood, whether it was to take pressure off fellow enemy fighters under attack just then by Marine battalions in Fallujah, whether it was to drive Americans out of Ramadi, or whether it was both. Marine intel officers would later speculate that the enemy had planned a three-day offensive in Ramadi beginning April 7 but had moved up the start date to April 6 after the Farhan brothers were captured and they feared someone would talk.

Of course, US military commanders in Ramadi knew none of this when the attack started. Nor were they warned by anyone in the Iraqi community. Despite elaborate enemy preparations conducted across the city, not a single Iraqi police officer, soldier, government official, tribal leader, or traffic cop tipped off the Marines or the Army. All that Paul Kennedy heard and passed along to his men the night before was that more attacks were likely.

Golf Company commander Christopher J. Bronzi was at his headquarters in Combat Outpost when reports arrived about shots fired on one of Hesener's squads and Letterman suffering shrapnel wounds. Bronzi, thirty, was an officer of slim build with a relaxed demeanor who grew up in the tiny, bucolic hamlet of Poughquag, New York, in the Hudson River Valley. He was the third of seven children raised by a single parent, his mother, Mary, who supported the family as a bank teller and later as a school guidance counselor. As Bronzi grew to manhood and attended the

BATTLE, DAY 1: CITY CENTER

Naval Academy to become a Marine officer, Mary Bronzi would remain one of his lifelong heroes.

On that day in April, from company headquarters, Bronzi was trying to get a sense of what was happening. Over the previous three days, he had been meeting with police and officials of the ministry of health and education. Four additional meetings had been planned for April 5–6. But those were all unexpectedly canceled when the Iraqis simply didn't show.

Initial reports from Third Squad were that Letterman was only slightly wounded and still in the fight and Eggink's Marines were attacking forward. Bronzi elected not to send any reinforcements, although Hesener at the Government Center grabbed three Marines and a corpsman and moved east to link with Third Squad.

Meanwhile, Eggink's men were in the middle of a gunfight that was growing fiercer by the second and was bigger than anything they'd encountered before. The road they were on was lined on each side by houses, walls, and gated entrances. A few children in the street had been kicking around a soccer ball right before the shooting started, and Corporal Jonathan Embrey, whom everybody called "Chaps," and another Marine, Lance Corporal Nicholas Erwin, instinctively ran over to herd them into a courtyard and out of danger. About eighty yards ahead at the T intersection, there were enemy fighters on each corner peering around and firing their AK-47s at the Marines on full automatic setting. Embrey thought it was a miracle none of the children were wounded. The road was like a closed corridor. With nowhere else to go, Embrey, Erwin, Eggink, and the others did exactly what Kennedy and Harrill had trained them to do. They attacked straight ahead down the road, bounding as they went—one Marine unleashing rounds to force an enemy shooter to pull back as another Marine leapfrogged ahead to take up a position and do the same, and so on. For some of the men, it was the first time they had fired weapons in combat. Letterman had been bandaged up, and he joined the fighting, telling his comrades, "I'm still good to go." The insurgents retreated, leaving piles of brass shells at each corner.

Reaching the T intersection, the Marines kept moving west, working their way across 160 yards of open graveyard. They picked their way between tombs and markers, fighting to survive in a place of the dead, throwing themselves on the ground to fire from prone positions using headstones for cover. Insurgents to the rear of the squad started shooting, and Marines at the back of the column engaged them. Other enemy gunmen from rooftops bordering East Cemetery tried to pick off the Americans. Embrey carefully targeted one and shot him through the head. But what momentarily unnerved him was that the guy was wearing a helmet, and Embrey wondered briefly whether he'd shot an American until he realized that couldn't possibly be the case. He and the other Marines reached the far side of the cemetery as the platoon commander, Lieutenant Hesener, and his small group joined them. There was a pause in the gunfire as Embrey and Letterman spotted a crowd gathering to the west, and suddenly rounds started snapping overhead. "Oh shit!" Letterman called out. Embrey turned to see him trotting back to a street corner across from the cemetery, where he lowered himself to the ground with his back against a power pole. As Embrey approached him, Letterman looked up and, without emotion, said, "I think I got shot." Sure enough, on closer examination, there was a neat round hole near his navel and what looked like smoke wafting out of it.

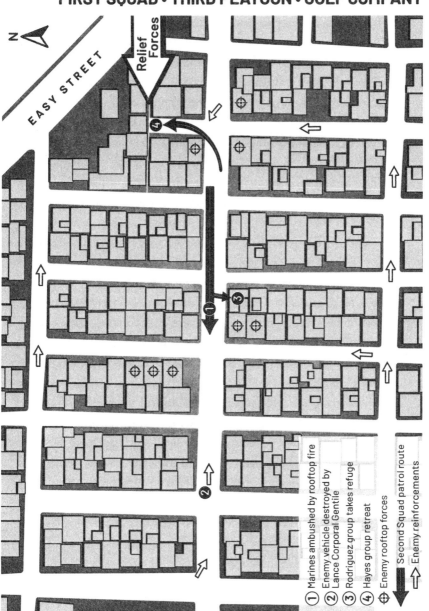

JUST WEST OF MUKHABARAT NEIGHBORHOOD, 11:15 A.M.

Staff Sergeant Rodriguez and the Marines of First Squad had been the last to leave Combat Outpost at 9:00 a.m. that morning for the mission to the Government Center. They took a circuitous route on foot to the south of Ramadi and then southwest along the city's large soccer stadium before reaching a major road running diagonally to the northeast that the Americans called Easy Street. The Mukhabarat neighborhood lay to the east and the Malaab District to the west.

The eleven Marines and a corpsman were walking up Easy Street when they heard over the radio that Third Squad was under attack, and they immediately started working their way west to lend support. For Rodriguez, it looked like they were traversing a ghetto, a ghost town ghetto. No one was on the streets. The squad radio operator, nineteen-year-old Private First Class Pete Flom, a six-foot-four midwesterner from Stillwater, Minnesota, thought he saw men with cell phones on rooftops. Before long, the Marines could actually hear Third Squad's gunfight, and they started getting excited. Combat, finally. Rodriguez started calling out to Corporal Joe Hayes—who had written to his father the previous month about Mack McPherson's terrible face wound, and who on this day was leading a fire team of three Marines—to speed it up.

Hayes, who had just turned twenty-one and bore a slight resemblance to a young Matt Damon, was the second of six children of a cement worker and his wife who lived in the mountain community of Tehachapi along the southeast rim of the San Joaquin valley in California. They were devout Christian Baptists, and the children were homeschooled until Joe's mother and a friend established a Christian school for their education. Like so many other members of 2/4, it was the striking image of a Marine decked out in the Corps's iconic dress uniform that first dazzled Joe about the service and led him to enlist. The blue dress coat with its high collar pinned with metal insignia of the Marine Corps—the Eagle,

Globe, and Anchor—gloriously fronted with gilded buttons bearing the same emblem. The white shirt, white gloves, and blue trousers with the distinctive red stripe. It was the only uniform in the US military reflecting all three colors of the American flag. Joe was only seven or eight when he saw a Marine in dress blues show up in church, and he would never forget it.

Now he, too, was a Marine and finally heading into a shooting war. The squad was stretched out about four to five blocks west of Easy Street when they first heard a smattering of rifle fire, and then enemy machine gun nests on rooftops in front and behind started shooting. As with Third Squad, there was little cover. Buildings and walled courtyards lined the street. There were a few parked cars. The Marines took a knee and tried to return fire, each focusing on a different quadrant. But acoustics and the rattling echo of rifles and machine guns made it almost impossible to tell where shots were coming from. Some enemy gunmen were firing from "mouse holes," positions inside second-story rooms back away from windows to hide muzzle flashes. Others were launching rocket-propelled grenades. Rodriguez radioed headquarters requesting a quick-reaction force as reinforcements.

Then they started carrying the fight to the enemy as best they could by entering and clearing the nearest buildings where there were threats. Rodriguez lobbed a grenade on the roof of one structure just to the south, where enemy gunmen had been firing. Then he and the squad leader, Sergeant Allen Holt, and twenty-year-old Lance Corporal Juan Ortiz and Private First Class Moisés Langhorst entered. Just the month before, Langhorst had lost his Minnesota high school classmate Matt Milczark to suicide back at Camp Victory. Inside the building, the Marines found two men and two women and empty shell casings on the roof, but no weapons. Back outside, the cycle was repeated on a second house. But it was like Whac-A-Mole. Every time they cleared a building, insurgents started firing from yet another house. Rodriguez saw a gunman jump down into a courtyard on a cross street to the north and fired a grenade at him with the M203 launcher on his rifle, killing him. More shots were coming from a machine gun on a rooftop a few blocks to the east, and Hayes and his fire team—Lance Corporal Juan Linares and Private First Class Deryk Hallal—moved in that direction to suppress it.

All the while, the Marines caught glimpses of armed men running to flank them along parallel roads to the north and south. Enemy fighters were climbing across rooftops to gain shooting advantage. Gunmen inside cars tucked back into cross streets were firing, and ambulances were circling to carry out dead or wounded enemy gunmen and drop off additional fighters. It all looked frightfully organized, and Rodriguez feared the enemy was gaining the initiative. Criers at three mosques in the surrounding area had been calling for jihad from their tower loudspeakers, and the rallying cry was having the desired effect. Rodriguez estimated there were more than a platoon-size number of enemy fighters when the shooting started, perhaps forty-five men. But with each passing minute, that number grew and was looking to be about a hundred. It felt like the entire neighborhood was out to kill the twelve Americans.

Hayes and his team advanced to the northeast corner of an intersection where they were treated to the bizarre sight of unarmed residents still walking the streets like it was just any other day. The Marines couldn't believe what they saw and yelled at the people to get inside. Suddenly, enemy riflemen appeared on balconies to their right and opened fire. Hallal went down with a wound to his right thigh.

Back to the west, two Marines served as point men in that direction, Langhorst and Lance Corporal James Gentile. Langhorst was armed with only a 9 mm pistol and a bazooka-like device called a Shoulder-Launched Multipurpose Assault Weapon, or SMAW, and carried only a single rocket. Gentile, by contrast, had a squad automatic weapon, or SAW, a light machine gun with hundreds of rounds of ammunition.

BATTLE, DAY 1: CITY CENTER

Gentile was twenty-one and grew up in the suburbs of Kansas City, Missouri. His father was an Air Force missileman who maintained nuclear intercontinental ballistic missiles hidden in silos. Jimmy wrestled in high school and was a big kid, and that was likely why he was assigned to carry the machine gun, although he still hated its heaviness with all the ammunition. It was a fully automatic weapon, and Marines were trained to fire in eight-to-ten-round bursts, long enough to recite in their thoughts *Die, motherfucker, die.* On this day, Rodriguez had Gentile watching for any threats coming from the west, and in fact, a car loaded with men was even then barreling down the road in their direction with gunmen firing out the windows. Gentile was down on one knee and opened up with his SAW raking the car with bullets and burning through an entire drum of two hundred rounds. The vehicle ground to a halt, and it looked like only one survivor managed to get out and flee north.

When Rodriguez and Holt got word that Hallal was down, Lance Corporal Ortiz, Private First Class Daniel Tapia—another of Kennedy's class-of-2003 high school grads—and the Navy corpsman were sent to assist.

Gentile, meanwhile, had reloaded and was firing south, where still more cars and gunmen on foot were approaching. He could hear Langhorst calling out to him from somewhere close by, asking where Gentile was, obviously wanting to link up. Gentile tried to yell back a description of where he was located and then started to turn to his left to find Langhorst, who he thought was in a courtyard on the south side of the street. Suddenly, it felt to Gentile like the right side of his face exploded. A bullet had struck just below his right ear and plowed through his jaw, destroying his teeth and blowing out a section of his face to the right of his nose. Rodriguez saw it all happen from several feet away and was shocked by the destruction the bullet caused. Gentile went down on one knee, blood pouring from his wounds. For a second or two, he thought he caught sight of Langhorst in that courtyard struck by the same volley of fire. But he was also stunned and terrified and felt exposed where he was. So Gentile got to his feet and, leaving his automatic weapon on the ground, staggered back in the direction of Rodriguez and the other Marines. As Private First Class Higinio Martinez provided cover fire, Holt and radio operator Flom assisted Gentile. The sergeant started bandaging him right there in the street. But enemy gunfire was intensifying, and all five Marines took refuge in a nearby house. Among the jumbled thoughts racing through Gentile's head just then was how he could feel with his tongue the smashed teeth from the bullet damage and recalled a childhood wearing braces. *All for nothing*, he thought.

Blocks to the east where Hallal lay wounded, the corpsman was bandaging his leg as Hallal used the sailor's 9 mm to return fire. "Hayes, don't let me die out here," he called out to his team leader. Hallal, six foot five and twenty-four, was from Indianapolis, where he had dropped out of computer training classes nine weeks before graduation to enlist in the Marine Corps. He had always wanted to make a difference after the 9/11 attacks, and working as a computer technician wasn't cutting it.[1]

After he was wounded, Hayes and other Marines opened fire on buildings across the street where they spotted enemy fighters. Linares managed to launch a high-explosive grenade from his M203 into a car carrying gunmen, and it exploded on target. For a moment, there was a pause in the gunfire. Hayes wanted to move all the men with him—Hallal, Linares, the corpsman, Tapia, and Ortiz—farther north on a side street that extended about fifty yards to a T intersection. There were no enemy fighters down that way, and Hayes hoped to avoid encirclement. Hallal got to his feet and, with Linares on one side and the corpsman on the other, started limping up the street. The leg wound was causing him considerable pain. The Marines could see enemy reinforcements arriving in cars to the south and taking up positions behind the vehicles to fire at the retreating Americans. Hayes grabbed an AT4 recoilless anti-tank weapon, a one-shot disposable launcher that looked a little like a bazooka, and was going to fire into those vehicles. But just then, an insurgent shot first, drilling a round into the back of Hallal's head. The big man let out a shriek and went down, his body twitching.

EAST CEMETERY, CENTRAL RAMADI, 11:30 A.M.

The bullet that struck Letterman in the stomach first smashed through the carry handle on his M16. Embrey saw the damaged rifle and tried to put Letterman at ease. "It's just a small little scratch. It looks like the bullet hit your rifle. I think you're fine."

"Are you sure, man? It feels funny."

The two made their way north to Hesener and the other Marines, where a corpsman tended Letterman's wound.

When Captain Chris Bronzi, the Golf Company commander back at Combat Outpost, got word that Letterman had been gutshot after previously being wounded by shrapnel, he finally requested that a battalion quick-reaction force respond. Weapons Company Gunnery Sergeant Anthony Crutcher, thirty-four, from St. Anne, Illinois, led thirty Marines of Third Platoon in a four-vehicle convoy out of Hurricane Point. Hesener had his men clear two buildings on the west side of the cemetery and establish firing positions on the roofs. Opposite them across the cemetery were about fifteen enemy fighters on rooftops to the east, northeast, and south of the cemetery. They and the Marines began shooting at one another. When five of the insurgents tried to maneuver across the rooftops, Hesener's men cut them down. Circling overhead were three helicopters—two Cobras and a Huey. Each Cobra had what amounted to a 20 mm Gatling gun mounted on a turret under the nose of the aircraft, along with rockets and missiles. Huey helicopters could carry medium or heavy machine guns and six-thousand-rounds-per-minute mini-guns set up in the doorways. But the pilots were often restricted from opening fire over

Ramadi and would instead make show-of-force passes to intimidate enemy fighters on the ground. It didn't work. The insurgents simply tried to shoot them down with rifles and rocket-propelled grenades. Crutcher's convoy showed up and retrieved Letterman. But with the battle growing, it would be a while before the wounded Marine would see a doctor.

Back at Combat Outpost, Bronzi ordered his First Platoon to prepare to go out receiving Rodriguez's call for assistance. The roughly three dozen troops of First Platoon were under the command of First Lieutenant Donovan Campbell, who had graduated with honors from Princeton. (When the young officer first joined the battalion, he mentioned being a Princeton graduate while meeting the executive officer, Major Mike Wylie. Wylie recommended Campbell not do the same around Kennedy, who was not particularly impressed with name-dropping.) First Platoon was out the front gate by 11:45 a.m., and Bronzi went with them. One problem was that Bronzi didn't know exactly where Rodriguez and his men were.

JUST WEST OF MUKHABARAT NEIGHBORHOOD, NOON

From where he lay on his stomach on the street with his rifle, Hayes could see the grenade almost as if it were moving in slow motion through the air, flying and then bouncing inexorably his way. The brown-and-yellow steel orb, thrown directly where he and Ortiz lay prone in the street, skipped down the pavement and rolled to a stop a dozen feet from the two Marines. Ortiz was closer, and Hayes instinctively threw his left arm over his buddy's head to help protect him. Then they put their heads down.

The explosion was a miasma of shock wave and shrapnel. Hayes felt like his body was struck by an earthquake. Both men were raked by clouds of steel.

Just moments before, Hallal had suffered what was clearly a mortal head wound. There was little that could be done. He was clearly struggling with his last breaths and was administered morphine. Tapia held his hand. The other Marines had dropped to the ground and started returning fire. Hayes's only communication with the outside world was a small device called a PRR—or personal role radio—attached to his flak jacket and connected to a headset he wore under his helmet. It could transmit only short distances. He informed Holt that Hallal was dead, and the squad leader, at first, didn't seem to grasp it. "Can you say that again?" Hayes repeated himself. "Hallal's dead!"

The news hit Pete Flom hard. Hallal was his best friend in the company. With Flom six foot four and Hallal an inch taller, the other Marines called them "the Twin Towers."

When the grenade landed near Hayes, the explosion left the team leader stunned and momentarily deafened. He saw his left hand covered in blood. Picking up his weapon and rising to his feet, Hayes stood dazed in the middle of the road in the middle of a gunfight. Then he turned and began walking north to the T intersection. The other Marines followed, Tapia finally relinquishing Hallal's hand. The grenade blast had shredded Ortiz's left hand and lacerated his leg. But he could still walk. A bone in Hayes's left hand was shattered—the limb immediately swelling up like a softball—and metal pieces had embedded into his upper left arm and left shoulder. As Hayes began regaining his senses, he realized his left hand was useless and asked a buddy to reload his rifle. Hayes's father had sent him bipod legs for his M16 as a gift from home, and now the Marine used those as he splayed himself across the ground and began firing. He and Linares and Tapia set up an Alamo-like defensive line at that T intersection, orienting fire south where the insurgents now occupied the intersection where Hallal was first wounded.

The corpsman, meanwhile, was an emotional casualty. With one Marine dead, two wounded, and a relentless enemy attack, the sailor had simply gone to pieces. He sobbed, curled up into a fetal position.

The reality was that First Squad of Golf Company's Second Platoon was disintegrating. One Marine was dead. Another, Langhorst, was missing and presumed dead. The survivors were split up and under separate assaults. Hayes and his men were fighting to stay alive at the end of a street. Rodriguez and his men, including the wounded Gentile, were holed up in a building around which a noose of enemy fighters was tightening.

A walled courtyard with an iron gate fronted the house. The family living there huddled in a back room, and the father insisted the Americans leave them alone. Rodriguez obliged, and to his surprise, the man later brought blankets that could be used as bandages, which the platoon sergeant thought was awesome given that the whole city seemed to want them dead. Holt concentrated on tending to Gentile, whose blood was soaking whatever was wrapped around his head. Flom guarded the front entrance, and the bespectacled Martinez, who was nineteen, was in the courtyard watching the roof with his light machine gun. It was unclear how many of the enemy realized exactly where the Marines were. One gunman simply started walking through the front entrance, his AK-47 dangling at his side. Flom gunned him down, firing over and over because the man simply didn't fall. Another insurgent came to drag the body away. Flom shot him, too. Martinez saw someone on the roof and opened fire with his SAW, killing the man.

Rodriguez's greatest fear was that they would run out of ammunition, and he cautioned his men to shoot sparingly and only when they had a clear target. He believed their chances would improve if they could link up with Hayes and the others. But Gentile clearly was in no shape to run through the streets. Flom believed with all his heart that time was running out and prayed that reinforcements would reach them soon.

A hundred and fifty yards away, Hayes tried to rally his men as best he could. "Every one of you had better start praying right now. Pray to God that he gets us out of here."

Over the sound of everyone shooting, including himself, Hayes led the prayer at the top of his lungs. "God deliver us! Help us to shoot straight! Help us to kill the enemy! Be our strength! Help us to get out of here! Deliver us, oh Lord!"

AL FAROUK WATER TOWER, SOUTH END OF EASY STREET, NOON

Relief forces were converging, even then, to deliver the embattled squad from its nightmare. But they were in the wrong place. Bronzi led First Platoon in the direction of what he thought was the last known position of Rodriguez and his men, a point not far from the Al Farouk water tower at the south end of Easy Street. They were actually about a half mile northwest of there. Ten minutes out of Combat Outpost, Bronzi and First Platoon arrived a few hundred yards east of the water tower, and the company commander chose to walk from there, leaving one squad to guard the vehicles. They moved west, and Bronzi learned over the radio that Gentile had been shot in the face. The situation was spiraling.

Weapons Gunnery Sergeant Crutcher and his troops, fresh from retrieving the wounded Letterman near East Cemetery, had quickly made their way to the same location where Bronzi was headed and drove right into an ambush. At the south end of Easy Street, insurgents had blocked out a kill zone with downed palm trees and rocks in the roadway and were sweeping the area with machine gun fire and rocket-propelled grenades. Crutcher's men responded with .50-caliber heavy machine guns and automatic grenade launchers and cleared the threat.

As Bronzi and his people approached the same area on foot from the southeast, one of the squads with him took a bad turn, walking way to the east around the large soccer stadium. Those roughly dozen Marines would be out of radio contact for the next hour or so. Still, Bronzi managed to link up with Crutcher but grew frustrated with himself, realizing he was in the wrong place for relieving Rodriguez and his men. They were somewhere deep in the neighborhoods to the northwest, where gunfire cracked in the distance.

Easy Street was turning into the next major battleground. The two-way highway extended diagonally nine-tenths of a mile from the soccer stadium in the city's southeast end to the Saddam Magnificent Mosque in the center of Ramadi. The enemy fighters were using it like a moat, setting up machine gun positions on rooftops along the west side, where their guns could sweep the roadway to block Marines from crossing. At the street level, insurgents were firing from around corners or as they zigzagged across Easy Street. All were trying to buy time for comrades to kill Rodriguez, Holt, Hayes, and the others trapped west of the avenue.

In response, Bronzi with Crutcher now had more than forty men backed up by mobilized heavy machine guns and grenade launchers, and began organizing a way to break through.

And more battalion reinforcements were on the way. A second Weapons Company platoon under the command of First Lieutenant Dave Dobb had left Hurricane Point to stage at the Government Center, as had Kennedy, Booker, Harrill, and their security detachment. Bronzi's Fourth Platoon was heading into the city. And at Camp Ramadi, Army Colonel Buck Connor and his security team were on their way. And he would ultimately call in an Army platoon of Bradley Fighting Vehicles.

All that would take time.

Meanwhile, Easy Street was growing chaotic. Cars speeding north and south were either panicked residents trying to flee the violence or insurgents bringing in reinforcements. One of those sedans screeched to a halt just a few feet from where Bronzi and his radioman crouched on the east side of Easy Street. The doors flew open, and armed insurgents poured out, the nearest one to Bronzi a man about his age carrying a grenade launcher. The captain shot him several times in the stomach, and the fighter crumpled to the ground as the others scattered. For a fleeting moment, Bronzi realized this was the first time he'd taken a life and acted without hesitation. *I can do this*, he thought.

Others were also killing for the first time. First Lieutenant Campbell was down to one squad. His Second Squad had taken a wrong turn, and his Third Squad was back with the vehicles. Half of First Squad was pinned down on the east side of Easy Street, and the other half was working with Campbell trying to destroy a machine gun nest. The enemy gunmen were in a second-story window on the west side of the street.

Gunfire was deafening as Campbell yelled instructions into a corporal's ear. "Okay, on the count of three, we're going to pop out and fire! Watch my tracers—they'll tell you where that gun is. Got it?"

"Got it, sir!" the corporal screamed back over the din.

"Okay, one, two, *three*." He and the Marine simultaneously stepped around a corner into the open and poured rifle fire into the second-story window. The machine gunner responded with a burst of gunfire and then fell silent. Campbell was certain they'd killed him and realized he felt nothing in response. His men crossed Easy. Bronzi and the other half of Campbell's squad were also on the other side, thanks to a well-thrown grenade onto a second-story balcony from where an insurgent was firing. Troops from Weapons Company had also breached the avenue.[2]

Near the front of the advance was a team led by Weapons Company Sergeant Kenneth Conde Jr., a twenty-two-year-old native of Orlando, Florida, who was one of the most beloved and respected members of the battalion. He was quiet, reflective, and fearless. The Weapons Company commander, Captain Rob Weiler, saw Conde as integral as a middle linebacker on a football team. Before leaving for Iraq, Conde had a long conversation for a night with his mother, Theresa, and told her he wasn't afraid to die. But he was fearful about making a mistake that might cause harm to any of his Marines. For him, their safety was uppermost, and they loved him for it.

On this day, he was in the second vehicle of the Weapons convoy turning off Easy Street. As they started taking fire, Conde dismounted and pushed ahead of the lead truck with Corporal Heath McKenzie and Lance Corporal Aaron Cox, both twenty-two, all three shooting and killing maybe seven enemy fighters in the streets and on rooftops. They bounded down a roadway, and when Conde suddenly turned left down an alley, his men were close behind. That's when he saw a red mist off his left shoulder—his own blood. He fell to the ground. Cox behind him opened fire, as did Conde, taking aim at three enemy insurgents who were trying to flee down the alley. All three were killed, including the one who had shot Conde through the left shoulder. Conde climbed to his feet only to be grabbed by the back of his flak jacket by McKenzie and pulled out of the alleyway. "Fuck, you're shot," he told Conde.

"It's hot. It's hot," the sergeant said of the sensation from the wound.

McKenzie and Cox accompanied the sergeant back to one of the trucks where he was bandaged up by a corpsman. And then, to the astonishment of everyone watching, he went back into the fray. In his mind, it was simple. He could function; therefore, he could fight. Bronzi, from nearby, watched it all. The ferocity in Conde's expression. The grimace as he put his flak vest back on over his bandaged shoulder and picked up his rifle. The captain felt certain he was witnessing the archetypal Marine combat leader.

HAYES POSITION, 1:30 P.M.

Joe Hayes was convinced the Cobras that arrived overhead were an absolute answer to prayer.

And as the minutes passed, and Hayes and the clutch of men with him could hear the staccato rhythm of .50-caliber machine gun fire and the clackety discharge from MK19, or Mark 19, automatic grenade launchers, the sound was music to their ears. Relief troops were getting closer. The only other concern, beyond running out of ammo, was that as Hayes and his men continued firing at enemy fighters to their south, they might be mistaken for insurgents by in-coming Marines and risk friendly fire.

The alleyway running east from their intersection led to Easy Street, and before long, Hayes and others could see reinforcements moving up along that highway from the south. They started calling out to them. Finally, First Platoon Marines reached them, and not far behind was Bronzi.

"Corporal Hayes, what's going on?"

Hayes gave him a rundown on the wounded. Then he said, "Sir, we got to get Hallal."

For a moment, Bronzi didn't quite understand. "Okay, where is he? Let's go get him."

"He's in the street. He's dead, sir," Hayes answered, and Bronzi felt like the wind had been knocked out of him. One of his Marines killed? The captain peered around the corner of a building and looked south to where he could see the big Marine's body lying on the road.

Suddenly behind him was Buck Connor, the brigade commander, who had just arrived with his command team. "Chris, what do you need?" The question was like a tonic for Bronzi. Not just because the Army was there with reinforcements. But Connor didn't show up to take over. He wasn't trying to push rank. He was just offering help. Bronzi asked for assistance with support fire and to handle the evacuation of the dead and wounded so he could concentrate on continuing his attack. For the imminent task of recovering Hallal's body, a team of soldiers and Marines was quickly organized to provide cover fire, and after a count of three, the troops charged south with guns blazing as Bronzi and Hayes moved out and retrieved the slain Marine.

The area was now overflowing with reinforcements. First Platoon Lieutenant Campbell's wayward Second Squad had finally linked up. An additional Weapons Company platoon was on scene. There were four Army Bradley Fighting Vehicles at the ready. Connor and his brigade command Sergeant Major Riling had twenty-five soldiers with them. And Paul Kennedy and his battalion command element of fewer than twenty people were just then on foot fighting their way north along a track of residential streets about 240 yards west of Bronzi and his men. Kennedy, Booker, and their Marines had come under occasional fire or had a grenade or two thrown at them. At one point, as they neared the area where Rodriguez and his men were barricaded, Kennedy, Booker, and another Marine cleared a house and, on the roof, found a helmet. The mystery of the missing Marine, Private First Class Moisés Langhorst, was about to be solved. But not before the enemy unleashed a second round of ambushes to the east that would prove to be even deadlier.

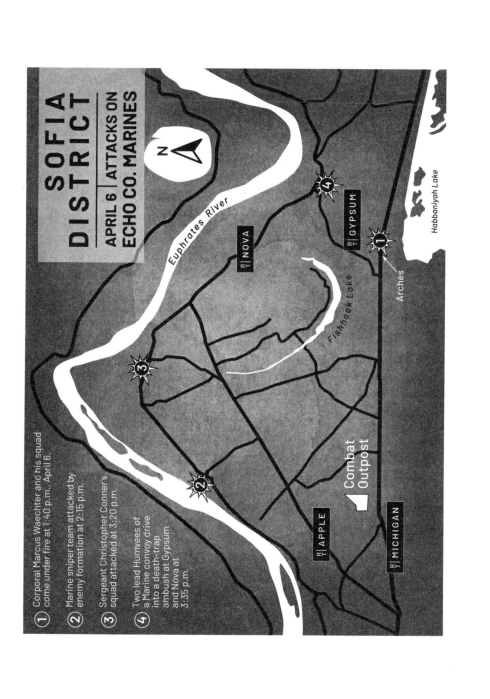

ARCHES, EASTERN GATEWAY TO RAMADI, 1:40 P.M.

It was a difference of night and day between the east entrance to the city and the dense warren of run-down residential homes in Ramadi's center where Golf Company had been fighting for hours. The ten Marines and one Navy corpsman who made up Third Squad of Echo Company's Third Platoon had left Combat Outpost nearly three hours earlier, patrolling on foot through the southeast area of the Sofia District, through dirt fields and clusters of large residential homes with walled courtyards. To the south across Route Michigan were scattered commercial buildings, a fuel station, and then a vast expanse of undulating brown gullies stretching for hundreds of yards. To the southeast was Habbaniyah Lake. It was a largely uneventful hike, actually at times pleasant. There were children around, and the Marines were handing out candy. That always put the Americans at ease, because they felt the enemy wouldn't attack with the young ones present. They were cutting through backyards and came to a gate where there was a man in a black dishdasha who told them in clear English that they couldn't go through. Something about the guy, who looked to be in his late thirties with a full beard and full head of hair, really bothered Lance Corporal Deshon Otey. The twenty-four-year-old native of Radcliffe, Kentucky, just south of Louisville, called out to the man, "You, Ali Baba"—an accusation that he was the enemy. The man stopped in his tracks, turned around, glanced at Otey, and smiled before walking back into a house. Before that, the Marine noticed that he seemed to be counting how many people were in the squad.

They continued their patrol east until they reached the gateway arches marking the city's east end, turned south, crossed Route Michigan, and headed down a dirt road that passed underneath an east–west rail line. That's when gunfire erupted from a house behind them on the north side of Michigan about 250 yards away. For most of the Marines, that was the first time they had

BATTLE, DAY 1: CITY CENTER 115

been shot at. They notified Echo Company headquarters back at Combat Outpost, and Captain Kelly Royer, given what was unfolding in the city with Golf Company, decided to flood the zone with troops just to be safe.

He had one quick-reaction force of fewer than twenty Marines and a corpsman already assembled and led by his Second Platoon commander, Second Lieutenant John Wroblewski, the tender-hearted officer who had wept when he learned back in early March that one of his men had died by suicide. Wroblewski had gathered his men in vehicles to go out and support Golf Company, but if there was action in Echo Company's area, the lieutenant wanted to be a part of it. "I want to get into the fight," he told Royer. "I can give them a hand right now." Royer agreed and diverted Wroblewski and his men to the gateway arches. Then Royer himself led a second force to the arches that was a mix of men from Echo Company's Weapons Platoon and its Third Platoon led by Second Lieutenant Tom Cogan, the tough Philly native who had lost two people a week earlier—one blown apart and another blinded in a roadside bomb attack. Royer would have sixty troops to deal with anything he might come up against.

The Echo Company commander already had two other groups of Marines out in the field that day, although in far different locations.

One was a four-man scout/sniper team permanently assigned to support his company. The four Marines had left Combat Outpost at dusk the evening before and worked their way north toward the Euphrates and then eventually northeast, skirting the berm-like roadway known as Route Nova. The team—their call sign was Headhunter 2—were to be out for more than thirty hours in classic sniper fashion, moving cautiously, slowly, and with infinite patience through the night to reach an overlook position among a pair of cinder block pump houses just off the bank of the river. The huts contained engines for pulling river water into irrigation ditches. The sniper nests were about eighty yards west of

Nova. Beyond that road, another 150 yards or so away, within a grove of towering date palms, was one of the area's most recognizable landmarks: a cluster of rusted, decommissioned Iraqi tanks, some of them disassembled. Marines called it "the tank graveyard."

The sniper mission had been utterly mundane through the night up until the last few hours when events started getting peculiar. And then terrifying.

The team leader was Sergeant Romeo Santiago, a muscular, five-foot-three native of the Philippines who grew up in the outskirts of Phoenix. The twenty-five-year-old Marine was the only member of his team certified as an official Hunter of Gunmen, or HOG. That meant Santiago had endured rigorous training and testing to earn a spot on a Corps sniper team, and then taken it up a notch by competing for, being accepted into, and graduating from the elite scout/sniper school. The Marines called him "Yago." There were three corporals on his team. California native Richard Stayskal, who was a week from turning twenty-three, was utterly unflappable. Ted Stanton, twenty-one, who sometimes seemed to have a chip on his shoulder, was the US-born son of Cambodian refugees. He had been adopted by an American human-rights activist couple with ties to the Cambodian community. And Cameron Ferguson was a twenty-one-year-old Pennsylvanian who, if you closed your eyes, sounded just like a surfer from California. They were a good team. What unnerved Santiago was the killing of the four contractors in Fallujah six days earlier. If the enemy could rally a force to slaughter a mobile four-man team so readily, what did the snipers risk moving around on foot? If anything happened, it would still take several minutes, if not longer, for a quick-reaction force to reach them.

What shattered their monotony that morning was something that happened shortly before noon. A young Iraqi boy came walking up Nova in their general direction. "Hey, there's a kid coming our way," Stayskal whispered. As he and Santiago watched, the boy left the road and cut across the field directly toward them, as if he knew precisely where the Marines were, until he was just several feet away and staring at the two men. For a second, Stayskal flashed on the idea that maybe they should shoot him since now they were dangerously compromised. But of course, that was out of the question. The child soon walked away, and the Marines debated what to do. It would be exceedingly dangerous for Americans to make their way back to Combat Outpost on foot in daylight, particularly through residential areas. Stayskal, however, was adamant that they should move. He was angry and thought it was crazy to stay one more minute in a place where people knew they were hiding. There was at least hope the child might keep the secret to himself. But within minutes, that evaporated when the snipers saw a man and woman approach. The couple walked right up on them, and the woman, clearly angry, began yelling in Arabic. The snipers had no idea what she was saying. But it obviously wasn't kind. The man finally pulled her back, and they turned and walked away. Word was spreading.

The other group of Marines out that morning were two squads from Echo Company's First Platoon. They had left the base and started another one of the long, foot-weary patrols around the entire Sofia District to locate buried IEDs, a walk of some ten miles. The combined squads were made up of twenty Marines and a Navy corpsman and were led by the First Platoon commander, Second Lieutenant Vincent Valdes, thirty, a graduate with honors from the University of New Mexico. A man of short stature who was a by-the-book officer, Valdes was also quiet and amenable but with a demeanor that suggested a certain complexity beneath the surface. Other patrol commanders liked him but thought he was a bit humorless, perhaps wound a little tight. On this day's patrol, most of his men were on foot. They had an opened-back Humvee with them, and they'd already found one buried bomb earlier in the day. At this point, they had worked their way up Nova, past where the sniper team was hidden across from the tank graveyard, and

RODRIGUEZ POSITION,
1:50 P.M.

After Joe Hayes and his men had been rescued, and the body of Deryk Hallal recovered, Marines and soldiers began working their way the last hundred yards or so through the streets toward where the other half of the embattled squad was barricaded in a house. Staff Sergeant Damien Rodriguez finally could see them approaching and, by radio, walked them to his position. Soon, the wounded Jimmy Gentile was taken away to a casualty collection point, repeatedly telling Rodriguez he was sorry for leaving his light machine gun and letting him down. Gentile joined two other wounded comrades, Joe Hayes and Juan Ortiz, and when he saw that Hayes didn't recognize him, Gentile realized how badly he must have been mauled by the round to his face. But suddenly, Hayes could make out his friend's prominent facial feature protruding from a mass of bandages—Gentile's "big Sicilian nose," Hayes called it. Now he knew who it was. As Hayes climbed into the front passenger seat, Ortiz and Gentile went in the back of the truck along with the body of Deryk Hallal and the wounded Jeremiah Letterman, still waiting to be delivered to doctors more than two hours after being shot in the stomach near the cemetery.

And there was still the question of the missing Moisés Langhorst. A member of First Platoon finally found his body just down the street to the west of where Rodriguez and his men had been holed up. The platoon sergeant and Holt immediately made their way there. The body appeared to be rolled up in a rug or tapestry. Langhorst's shoulder-fired rocket launcher and his 9 mm handgun were gone. There was a check for booby traps around the body, and then it was pulled out of the line of fire. Langhorst had been riddled by bullets, including one round through the right side of his face that almost certainly was fatal, according to an autopsy done later. The battalion command element soon arrived and took responsibility for evacuating the remains.

Exactly what happened to the teenage Marine would remain unclear. Gentile was certain that when he was shot in the face, Langhorst was killed in the same burst of fire. The autopsy seems to support that version. Langhorst was struck six times, none at close range. There remained the curious and unexplained issue of Kennedy and Booker finding Langhorst's helmet on the roof of a building nearby. Months later, an enemy recruitment video circulated on the internet showing footage of Langhorst's body laid out on the ground in an almost crucifixion-like posture, his face and name identification clearly visible.

For the moment, however, with trapped Marines now rescued, Bronzi was ready to keep pushing west with the troops he had on hand—two squads from Lieutenant Campbell's First Platoon along with remnants of the embattled squad with Staff Sergeant Rodriguez. Bronzi would soon be joined by a whole other Golf Company platoon, and the last of Campbell's three squads for a total force of well over eighty troops. The captain was eager to box in any remaining insurgents between his location and a blocking force established by the Golf Company Third Platoon commander, Second Lieutenant Hesener, who had Marines on rooftops about a half mile to the west on the far side of the cemetery. Bronzi would now be executing what his future Silver Star citation would describe as a "company-level hammer and anvil technique." The bottom line was that he wanted to throw as many people as he could into this fight against a suddenly more formidable enemy and overwhelm it with firepower and aggression.

6

BATTLE, DAY 1: SOFIA DISTRICT

HEADHUNTER 2 SNIPER TEAM, 2:15 P.M.

IT HAD BEEN nearly an hour since the screaming woman episode, and as the sun rose higher in the afternoon sky and the air grew warm, the team settled back into its routine of two men on and two men off. Stanton and Ferguson tried to close their eyes a bit while Santiago and Stayskal stood watch over Route Nova. The team leader was never satisfied they could see enough of the road and, leaving Stayskal behind, moved downriver to a second broken-down pump house, where he settled himself inside and kept the door ajar to watch the roadway. By this time, Santiago and Stayskal could hear gunfire from downtown Ramadi and even see helicopters over the city. The two chatted over their small radios about being at war and never seeing a shot fired in anger. When were *they* going to get some action? Stayskal couldn't agree more. As the sergeant continued his overwatch of Nova and relaxed with a languid breeze filtering through the slats in the pump house, his eyes grew heavy, and Santiago decided to head back to the team. But first he wanted to get a good look at what was beyond Route Nova. Because the road was essentially a berm, he needed to sneak up to the edge of the roadway and peer over it to see areas to the east. From there, he started scanning back and forth looking through the scope on his assault rifle. He and Stanton each carried a bolt-action sniper rifle and an M16, as well as a 9 mm in a holster worn on the hip. Ferguson and Stayskal each carried an M16. Ferguson's had an M203 grenade launcher attached to it. Santiago could see the tank graveyard, the palm grove, and houses farther to the east. The stillness of the panorama was suddenly broken by the figure of a man running out of an alley in the housing area and turning toward Nova. The Iraqi was carrying something in his hands, and Santiago at first thought he was a farmer with a shovel. Then another man appeared and headed the same way. They were 250 yards away. One of them stepped into a ray of sunlight shining through the palm fronds, and Santiago could see clearly that he had a rifle, an AK-47. As the Marine watched, more armed men emerged, twelve to fifteen of them, and then he stopped counting. (Later estimates would place the total number of the force at about thirty gunmen.) They lined up in formation, a single row of armed men stepping out in the direction of where the snipers were located. Santiago, who had spent the last several weeks watching average Ramadi residents move about the city, was stunned. These were men using classic infantry tactics. They were organized. *They're coming to get us*, he thought.

The sergeant turned and in a crouch quickly hurried back toward his team, cradling his handheld radio. "Hey, get your gear, get your gear on." Stayskal responded that he didn't understand. Ferguson was incredulous because Santiago was too reliable a jokester. "Are you serious? Are you really serious?" Santiago waited until he reached the men to say more. "Get your gear on. We're in trouble. We're about to get some right now. I count fifteen guys and more behind them, all with weapons, coming this way. We need to get ready. They're going to come over the road any minute."

Flak jackets and helmets were donned. Magazines were arranged on the ground in grabbing distance. They prepared to defend. Like so many of the Magnificent Bastards on this day, the snipers were sorely short of ammunition. They had been limited to six magazines each because no one expected prolonged combat. Ferguson carried a grenade launcher attached to his rifle, but only had three grenades. They had been demanding more ammunition before their missions and were repeatedly turned down. The prospect now of running out of bullets and grenades during a major attack was terrifying. The four arranged themselves around the two closely adjacent pump houses. There were trees and foliage behind them and then a slope that dropped off to the river's edge. Santiago pulled the bolt out of his sniper rifle and stuffed it in his pocket. He didn't want to leave a functional weapon to the enemy if it came to that. His mind was racing for contingencies, and he finally offered to the others, "We might have to swim for it." He tried to read the current of the Euphrates. The river was more than two hundred yards wide behind them. But they were outnumbered at least four to one, and the odds of fending off an attack by such a larger force were not good, he thought.

Ferguson balked at the idea. "You know I'll drown."

Santiago tried to work it out in his head. He'd hold the riverbank as long as possible, allowing his men to cover a good portion of distance across the Euphrates before beginning his own desperate swim.

But then Ferguson wanted to be the last man because of his fear of swimming the river. In any event, the idea soon faded without further discussion. The four Marines knew their only chance was to fight it out there and hope that help arrived. By radio, they made plain to Echo Company headquarters their predicament and the need for immediate assistance. Santiago never in a thousand years

BATTLE, DAY 1: SOFIA DISTRICT

thought his first war experience as a sniper would be close-quarters combat with an overwhelming force. That wasn't sniper work.

The four locked eyes on the raised asphalt of Route Nova, watching for the first sign of an approaching enemy.

What they didn't know was that help was already on its way and not too distant. A little less than a mile and a half up Nova to the northeast were two squads of Echo Company's First Platoon set up around an IED and waiting for an explosives-disposal team to show up. Their commander, Second Lieutenant Vincent Valdes, had already gotten word over the radio from headquarters that the snipers were in trouble. He took his Third Squad with eleven Marines and a corpsman, crammed them into their one Humvee, and, as Valdes would later write in his report, "hauled ass."

CHARLIE MED, CAMP RAMADI, 2:30 P.M.

The medical team at Charlie Med was first alerted at about 11:00 a.m. that a battle casualty was coming in. It was Jeremiah Letterman with a gunshot wound to the stomach. Medical personnel prepared to receive the wounded Marine and waited. And waited. New messages trickled in. There was a second casualty with a leg wound. And then that changed to a KIA. And finally, word arrived about three other wounded men. But everything was delayed, the doctors were told, because a battle was raging.

Finally, an open-backed Humvee pulled up to the south side of Charlie Med, where patients were received right in front of a broad canopied area that medical personnel called the Lanai, a fancy Hawaiian word for *veranda*.

It was an otherworldly sight that greeted the Army medical folks, four Marines wedged together in the back like pieces of a jigsaw puzzle. A mosaic of desert tan fatigues, medical equipment, bandages, and blood. One was dead. That was Deryk Hallal, his body covered by a poncho. What was striking about the three—Juan Ortiz, Jimmy Gentile, and Letterman—were their eyes, wide, egg white, and glazed over "as if they were seated in place with a clear paste," combat medic Colt Crutchfield was thinking. All were motionless except for Ortiz, who shifted a bit. They seemed in shock and were taken into the facility. Joe Hayes was in the front seat and was able to walk in, assisting Gentile along the way. Hayes was eventually brought to a back, overflow room for treatment, where he was administered intravenous fluids, his wounds irrigated, and he was ultimately x-rayed. He had arrived in moderate spirits, almost as if he were showing up for just another routine sick-call visit. After a while, an Army chaplain appeared and eased over to where Hayes was resting, striking up a quiet conversation. Suddenly and uncontrollably, Hayes began to cry, showing clear signs of an emotional wound just as plain and painful as any physical one. Crutchfield watched it unfold and had a sudden moment of clarity about war's impact. "We've seen so much blood, so many X-rays, so many things lost and far too many people die in that trauma room," Crutchfield wrote to his family days later. "Sometimes, I think we've lost touch with [emotional] stories behind the trauma story."

The body of Moisés Langhorst soon arrived. There would be more alerts from the field about new wounded and dead casualties on the way.

HEADHUNTER 2 SNIPER TEAM, 2:30 P.M.

Santiago studied the raised roadway of Nova some seventy yards away, panning back and forth with the scope on his M16. He and the other snipers hadn't heard or seen anything for some minutes, and a part of Santiago hoped nothing would happen, although his right brain doubted that seriously. Stayskal was covering the left flank and was still pissed off that they hadn't decided to hike their way out of there long ago. Just then, Santiago saw a man wearing

BATTLE, DAY 1: SOFIA DISTRICT

125

a red-and-white kaffiyeh around his head stand up from just the other side of the road and survey the riverfront left to right until he spotted the Marines. Santiago clicked the safety off on his rifle. He had the tiny red chevron reticle in his ACOG scope directly on the man's face and was thinking, *Should I pop this dude's head open?*

If an ACOG scope and rifle were properly adjusted for distance in advance, the red chevron performed like a weapon in a video game—place the marker on a target and all that was left was pulling the trigger.

But Santiago hesitated. *Maybe they won't actually attack. Maybe Marine reinforcements will suddenly appear and quell it. Maybe this will all go away.* The man dropped back down.

A rocket-propelled grenade suddenly came whooshing in the snipers' direction and exploded into the trees just behind them and above their heads. They could feel the heat from it on the backs of their necks. Ferguson was shocked by the sudden explosive violence and realized it was truly game on. Stayskal was knocked to the ground and instantly became a true believer in the life-passing-before-your-eyes axiom: middle school, high school, playing baseball, skateboarding, it was all there. Then there was another RPG. And more. Light machine gun fire opened up as did rifle shots and rounds were hitting inches from where the four snipers crouched in a half circle broken up by the pump houses. Ferguson and Santiago were in the center between the huts, with Stayskal left and Stanton on the right. "If they're trying to flank, watch out. Watch the flanks!" Santiago called out.

The team leader pushed forward a few feet to position behind a fifty-five-gallon drum. Santiago wanted to cover the road with gunfire as fully as possible to discourage the enemy from coming across. He wanted to buy time for the relief force to arrive. But he could hear Ferguson over the gunfire yelling at him, "Dude, they're shooting at you!" And Santiago realized they were focusing shots in his direction with bullets striking the drum and the cinder blocks near his head. He was on his knees and pulled back as rounds hit the ground in front of him. The sound was deafening. Stayskal was carrying the large team radio and was yelling into it that they're going to fucking die and needed help pronto. The chilling response: "Everybody's busy. The whole city is fighting right now."

Adding to their sense of abandonment was how radio communications were in disarray. Multiple voices from separate gunfights were talking over one another, with stronger signals stepping on weaker ones. It was little wonder that headquarters was struggling to grasp and fully understand the enormity of what was happening.

The snipers were twenty to twenty-five minutes into the gunfight and already running low on ammunition. Santiago had two magazines left. Meanwhile, Ferguson was struggling with his M203 grenade launcher. The first lobbed too far and the second too short. But the third was on target, exploding right on the other side of the road. Santiago yelled out his congratulations, with tips on how to make a slight adjustment the next time he fired a grenade.

"I don't have any more, goddamn it," Ferguson responded.

Amid the violence, there was rough choreography to how the snipers fought. They loaded their M16 magazines with the red tracer rounds at the bottom so that when those laced the field, they knew they were running low; and their fellow Marines, seeing the same tracers, would direct their fire to cover that sector until the sniper could reload.

Two enemy fighters tried to flank to the south. One was on the road, the other was across Nova and making his way down the slope. Stanton was on that flank and cut them both down. He didn't think for a moment about those being the first human beings he had ever killed. He simply acted on pure muscle memory. His thoughts were confined to the need to move on to the next

target to stay alive. There was foliage on the left flank, and Stayskal thought he saw movement there, someone trying to infiltrate
from that side. He riddled the area with gunfire, and the movement stopped.

For a moment, it seemed as if the enemy attack was stalled
at the road. But every one of the snipers was down to one or two
mags of ammo.

Just then, one of the most thrilling sights any of them had
ever seen approached from the northeast. A Humvee loaded with
Marines and a Navy corpsman ground to a halt on Nova, one
of the men on board blasting away at the enemy with an M240
medium machine gun affixed to the back of the truck.

Second Lieutenant Valdes had arrived with as many people
as could be crammed into the open-backed Humvee. Besides the
lieutenant, there were eleven enlisted Marines and a sailor. Like so
many squads in the battalion, nearly half of them were teenagers
who had been in high school just the year before. Among them was
Lance Corporal Marcus Cherry, eighteen; Lance Corporal Jarad
Cole, nineteen; Lance Corporal Kevin Gaeden, nineteen; and
Private First Class David Quetglas, nineteen.

At the rear of the truck was Lance Corporal Brian Telinda, the
twenty-two-year-old Marine who had refused to shake hands with
the commandant's wife when the battalion was out in the western Pacific the year before. Telinda's daughter, a baby girl named
Trinity, had been born just three weeks earlier. On this day, as
they were driving down to where the snipers were under attack,
Valdes reached over and grabbed the back of Telinda's flak jacket.
"When I tell you, you jump the fuck out of this truck, and you and
[Lance Corporal Michael] Hawn will lay down suppressive fire."
The truck stopped. Both jumped out. But then Valdes had the
Humvee driven farther down the road to get closer to the snipers.
Telinda and Hawn looked at each other in disbelief. They were
alone. The cover-fire plan immediately fell apart. Enemy rounds

skipped off the road, forcing both Marines to jump down the opposite side of Nova. Hawn, twenty-two, fired a few bursts from his light machine gun, and the pair ran down to link back up with the others.

The enemy assault force that had tried to storm the trapped snipers broke and ran as the Humvee approached. But there were more enemy gunmen hidden among the rusted hulks in the tank graveyard and in houses far beyond the palm grove. Included among those who had taken up positions behind the wrecked tanks was an insurgent dressed in black and armed with a Soviet-era Dragunov sniper rifle, a weapon with an effective range of more than 650 yards. Those insurgents who weren't retreating redirected their gunfire from the snipers to the newly arrived Humvee, raking the back of the vehicle where Marines were clambering to get out and attack. The truck had hillbilly armor bolted to the side, but so far as the troops were exposed above the plates as they started climbing out of the truck, they were targets. Three were wounded immediately. Rounds peppered the M240 medium machine gun that had a protective bullet shield and was mounted on a swivel base, and the gunner, Martinez, saw part of his left hand chewed up. Fragments from other rounds that hit the machine gun struck Lance Corporal Brandon Lund in his right hand and left shoulder, and he went down. This was his twenty-first birthday. Another enemy round hit Lance Corporal Benjamin Carman, twenty, in the arm and burrowed through his chest before exiting his back. The Iowa native slumped into the lap of the corpsman, Tyrynn Dennis, who immediately began looking for the wound. He noticed right away that Carman didn't appear to be breathing.

Meanwhile, those who managed to safely get out of the truck began firing at the enemy and one by one joined a charge led by Cherry, one of the youngest people in the battalion. "We have to rush 'em and drive 'em back!" he yelled with youthful bravado as he took off running.

It was in character for the teenager, who was already an up-and-comer. He had joined the battalion at seventeen only a few months earlier and had already risen to lance corporal and become a team leader. (Marine squads are typically broken down into three fire teams.) He had proudly written his mother, Genevieve King, about the promotion. "I'm picking up rather quickly because of my capabilities to handle responsibilities. I know the Marine Corps was the best decision for my life." Bernard Calvin Coleman, the hard-nosed gunnery sergeant for Echo Company both feared and admired by the young Marines, was impressed with Cherry. Beyond being a quick study, the teenager had charisma and was popular among his peers. His parents were divorced, and his mother, who worked as a prison guard, had raised four children on her own. Cherry's older brother, Andre, was also in the Marines and stationed, of all things, at nearby Al Taqaddum Air Base. Weeks earlier, Coleman had taken a group of Marines to the base to scavenge vehicle armor and brought Cherry along to see his brother, but not without first giving him the requisite shit for even asking to go. "What the fuck makes you so special? We're here to fight, not go see family." Coleman thought Cherry had the makings of a future sergeant major. But that would never happen.

As Cherry bolted forward, two of the other young Marines nearby, Cole and Gaeden, exchanged apprehensive looks until Gaeden said, "Let's do it," and they followed Cherry. An older Marine nearby, twenty-seven-year-old Lance Corporal Pedro Contreras, was already ahead of them. As Contreras and Cherry reached the tank graveyard, they shot and wounded one enemy fighter hiding among the wrecks. But they didn't see the one in black armed with a sniper rifle. That gunman put a bullet through Cherry's head, and he dropped to the ground.

Cole saw his body, and in a letter he later wrote to his father, he marveled at the hitting power of the sniper round that "went through his helmet like it was nothing."

ARCHES, EASTERN GATEWAY TO RAMADI, 2:45 P.M.

An hour earlier, at the site near the arches where fighting had first broken out in eastern Ramadi, the squad of Marines under fire notified headquarters and proceeded to counterattack. They were led by a twenty-one-year-old corporal, Marcus Waechter, from the Dallas suburb of McKinney. As the men moved north across Route Michigan and began closing in on a house from where they had seen muzzle flashes, enemy fire stopped as abruptly as it began. Squad members entered and searched the building, but the gunmen had either fled or the men inside had disposed of their weapons. It didn't occur to any of them that this event was a gambit by the enemy designed to lure them into a trap.

Soon thereafter, Echo Company Captain Kelly Royer and his reinforcements arrived in several trucks and Humvees. It was 2:15 p.m., and he ordered half his troops to surround a stretch of houses to the west while the other half surrounded houses to the east, and then Royer took several of his men and began searching the homes. Nothing was found, although three Iraqi men who tried to flee were detained and flex-cuffed.

Word from company headquarters arrived about a half hour later that the Headhunter 2 sniper team was under enemy assault. The problem for Royer was that the snipers were on the far northwest side of Sofia District from where Royer and his men were located, more than two and a half miles as the crow flies, and considerably longer for a convoy of vehicles because the interior of the area was marshland. A road trip would be circuitous, and it would take precious time to reassemble his men who were surrounding and searching homes. So Royer asked battalion headquarters to send a quick-reaction force from Weapons Company to aid the snipers.

Almost as soon as he finished that radio call, Royer and the men with him could hear gunfire to the northwest. He and Second Lieutenant Tom Cogan, who commanded Third Platoon, led about two dozen troops on foot in the direction of the gunfire. The remainder of Royer's force stayed with the eight vehicles, a mix of Humvees and seven-ton trucks. Those men left behind included Second Lieutenant John Wroblewski and a portion of his Marines from Second Platoon; Staff Sergeant Allan Walker, who was Cogan's platoon sergeant; and Waechter's squad. One of the Humvees was Royer's command vehicle with a company radio bolted to the dashboard. He left the radio for Wroblewski to use and took the lieutenant's radio operator. Royer wanted two radio operators with him, one to communicate with command elements and the other to communicate with potential air assets. Then Royer set off on foot to investigate the gunfire with Cogan and about two dozen Marines, a corpsman, and two civilian photojournalists who had embedded with the battalion. It would prove to be a wild-goose chase. For whatever acoustic reason, the gunfire they heard was likely from the battle Santiago's sniper team was waging much farther away. The sound had seemed closer. Royer and Cogan wouldn't figure this out until they'd hiked through backyards and across fields and palm groves for more than a third of a mile.

SNAKE PIT,
3:00 P.M.

Meanwhile, a platoon of Army engineers ready to respond to any Marines in trouble had been cooling their heels for hours back at Camp Ramadi. They were mounted up on five M113 armored personnel carriers armed with .50-caliber machine guns and automatic grenade launchers. Orders finally arrived directing them to the Marines' Snake Pit base on Ramadi's far west end. There, while fighting broke out across the city, they kept biding their time. No one was asking for their help.

There were twenty-nine soldiers on board, primarily members of Second Platoon, Charlie Company of the 1st Engineer Battalion, along with their company commander, Captain Tyler Faulk, a twenty-nine-year-old Denver native. The Army engineers were skilled at building things and blowing things up, but they had largely been used as infantry since arriving in Ramadi the previous September. Now, in addition to periodic patrol missions and conducting searches for weapons caches, the engineers were on call to assist the Marines whenever necessary. But it felt like they rarely sought help from the Army engineers. Since 11:00 a.m., the soldiers could hear massive gunfire spreading across the city. But they had spent the late morning and early afternoon simply waiting.

The armored personnel carriers they operated, or APCs, were basically throwbacks to Vietnam—big, square boxes on twin tracks. Their heavy weapons were mounted on turrets. Each tracked vehicle also had a cargo or troop hatch on the top that could be flipped open, allowing soldiers inside the vehicle to stand up in shooting positions. This afforded 360-degree fire coverage, and the vehicles looked like porcupines moving down the road with barrels poking out every which way. A drawback to the APC was that it was made out of aluminum, which worked against shrapnel and small arms fire but not so well against heavier machine guns or rocket-propelled grenades. So the engineers had stacked sandbags along the interior walls and around the rim of the skylight, transforming the vehicle into a rolling bunker.

Almost a stone's throw to the west of Snake Pit was Hurricane Point, which was 2/4 battalion headquarters and the base for Weapons Company, the vehicle-bound Marines whose platoons were the quick-reaction reinforcements for any battalion unit in trouble. As the engineers were pulling into Snake Pit, the Weapons Company commander, Captain Rob Weiler, was leaving Hurricane Point in a convoy with his Second Platoon under the command of First Lieutenant JD Stephens. It was just three days prior that Stephens had lost a man, Geoff Morris, to an RPG attack near the Saddam Magnificent Mosque. They headed east to the Sofia District and the relief of Headhunter 2 in response to Kelly Royer's call for assistance.

BATTLE, DAY 1: SOFIA DISTRICT

At battalion headquarters, the burden of making sense of the chaos enveloping the city fell on the shoulders of the 2/4 executive officer, Major Mike Wylie. At the operations center, Marines were working to track attacks and the movements of troops across the city on a large wall map. Calls about new enemy assaults and troop movements by friendly forces were tumbling across the airwaves, distorted by the sound of gunfire in the background and the agitated voices of excited radio operators. Before Wylie even arrived, the noncommissioned officer running the map was quickly becoming overwhelmed, and the major relieved him, ordering that his best operator be awakened and brought in. He'd been on night duty. At one point, for at least an hour while Kennedy, Harrill, and Booker were engaged in actual street combat, Wylie lost radio contact with them. He couldn't believe the battalion was under attack and he was unable to speak with its commander or, worse, didn't really know whether Kennedy was alive or dead. *This is the stuff of war movies, not real life*, Wylie thought.

There was similar confusion at the brigade command center across the Euphrates Channel to the west. It was by far the largest fight for the Devil Brigade in nine months of deployment, and like the Marine battalion headquarters at Hurricane Point, they found themselves slow to react to a series of blossoming crises. At the start, the brigade commander, Colonel Buck Connor, had quickly plunged into the fray with his security detail and Bradley Fighting Vehicles. But as the fight grew, it was hard to know who was where. That wasn't a problem so much with Army units, which had blue force tracking computer systems that were GPS-enabled, allowing headquarters to identify their precise locations. Still, that was new technology that extended only to company level and some of the platoons. By contrast, Marine squads on foot patrols had nothing of the sort, and their locations could only be guessed at based on radio transmissions. The result was that Army forces weren't sure where Marines were located and vice versa. As a precaution, soldiers were sent to choke points around Ramadi to block enemy reinforcements from getting in and killing enemy fighters trying to get out. Like their Marine counterparts, Army leaders were shocked that the enemy was showing such a high degree of sophistication in launching attacks. They estimated enemy forces had to be at least in the hundreds of fighters. To a limited degree, the Army could watch some of what was happening thanks to a drone flying overhead. They saw the enemy using ambulances or Toyota Hilux pickup trucks to circulate the battlefield, delivering ammunition and reinforcements and pulling out wounded. The troops at brigade headquarters had never seen that before. They witnessed considerable traffic concentrated on and around one of the expensive homes in the Sofia District. There even appeared to be an operations center of sorts in the backyard, where a dozen or so men sat facing one another on chairs in deep discussion or planning while others, evidently lower-level operators, came and went.

Captain Kyle Teamey, the brigade targeting operations officer who had spent the wee hours of the morning questioning the detained enemy leader Adnan Hassan Farhan, watched the unmanned-aerial-vehicle footage on this backyard group. He immediately proposed that coalition forces drop a guided bomb on them. But, particularly with Connor absent from the decision-making process, permission never came through.

EAST CEMETERY, CENTRAL RAMADI, 3:10 P.M.

After finally reaching Staff Sergeant Rodriguez, the wounded Corporal Hayes, and what was left of their squad, Bronzi and an assembled force of roughly eighty Marines and sailors continued to push through the narrow city streets west toward East Cemetery, where the whole battle had started that morning. Bronzi ordered his Third Platoon commander, Second Lieutenant Hesener, and some of his men to continue holding positions on rooftops along the west side of the cemetery and act as a blocking force for any enemy fighters fleeing west.

But while the insurgents grudgingly gave ground as Bronzi and his men advanced, they kept up a constant stream of fire from light machine guns, AK-47s, and rocket-propelled grenade launchers. As the Marines moved west, a few enemy fighters tried to cut them off as they'd done to Rodriguez and his men. Kennedy's security detail—which included his operations officer, Major Harrill, and his sergeant major, Jim Booker—was moving behind Bronzi by a few hundred yards. They watched as an enemy fighter with a light machine gun moved in between the Marine elements, set up his gun behind a berm, and began shooting into Kennedy's team, trying to break up the advance. Other insurgents in nearby buildings fired RPGs or threw hand grenades. Harrill watched this unfold in front of him, amazed that an enemy that had played hit and run for so long was now aggressively employing urban warfare tactics. While Booker had troops start clearing the houses, Harrill moved in a crouch with his M16 toward the machine gunner. The man was shooting too high to threaten him, and the officer managed to inch up and kill him from below the berm. But not before Booker yelled out to Harrill, "Don't shoot Bronzi!" who was moving down the street far beyond the machine gun.

Marine Corporal Heath McKenzie was amazed when he saw the brigade commander, Buck Connor, fighting like an infantryman alongside the Marines. "It was actually a full-bird colonel and a [brigade] sergeant major that was out there with us," McKenzie would tell a Marine Corps historian weeks later. At one point, Connor was crouched with his Mossberg shotgun firing down the street. He had the weapon rigged with a pistol grip. A door nearby opened, and an insurgent with an AK-47 stepped out to shoot the colonel. Ron Riling, the thirty-nine-year-old brigade command sergeant major, was directly behind his boss and told him to "stay still for one minute." Riling rested his M4 rifle on Connor's shoulder to steady his aim and put two rounds into the enemy fighter, killing him. Connor's hearing in that right ear was out for days. Riling was a powerfully built soldier at six foot two and two hundred pounds. At another point during the April 6 battle, he had moved forward to assist in clearing a house. Another soldier had tried and failed to knock open the steel door into the building's front courtyard. Riling told him to stand aside and, lowering his shoulder, smashed the door down off its hinges onto the ground. It fell with Riling on top and an enemy gunman mashed underneath. The man wasn't breathing. The brigade surgeon, Captain Randy Radmer, arrived to see what he could do for the insurgent, whose AK-47 lay nearby. Radmer guessed that his lungs might have been crushed or an artery severed. He looked dead. The surgeon was about to intubate him when civilian ambulance personnel showed up and took over.

Connor eventually got word of the sniper team under attack. He pulled his security detail and his Bradleys out of the inner-city battle and headed for the Sofia District.

Bronzi and his men finally linked up with Hesener's team. The Golf Company commander had the lieutenant move west to clear areas back to the Government Center. And then Bronzi took his men and began moving back east, seeking out any enemy still willing to put up a fight. The insurgents were on the run, abandoning their weapons and blending in with the citizenry. Others were captured. After hours of battling for this core inner-city part of Ramadi, Bronzi was willing to spend the night in these streets with his Marines rather than return to base and cede the ground back to the enemy. But he was ordered back to Combat Outpost.

ROUTE APPLE, SOFIA DISTRICT, 3:10 P.M.

The Weapons Company platoon heading out to rescue the Headhunter snipers was made up of twenty-five to thirty troops in assorted Humvees armed with medium and heavy weapons. They

BATTLE, DAY 1: SOFIA DISTRICT

had quickly traveled five miles across the north edge of Ramadi and jogged over to take a road the Americans called Route Apple. This would ultimately bring them behind the enemy force attacking the snipers. The trucks were flying down the road. It was a residential area, and women, children, and men scattered as the convoy barreled toward an intersection where they would turn north to reach the snipers. But once again, insurgents had anticipated what route a relief force would take, and Weiler and his troops drove right into an ambush. There were machine gun nests down almost every alley. Still, enemy fire was haphazard. Bursts were badly timed as Humvees drove past and rounds flew between rather than into the trucks as they drove along Apple. Stunningly, no Americans were hurt. Weiler and his men reached the intersection and turned their vehicles around, unleashing .50-caliber heavy machine guns and MK19 automatic grenade launchers. For the moment, Weiler chose to set aside reaching the snipers in favor of attacking and destroying an enemy close at hand. For weeks, insurgents had played hit-and-run, using roadside bombs, launching mortar rounds, or spraying gunfire and fleeing. Now they seemed willing to stand and fight, and it was too irresistible a target for Weiler and his men to ignore. *Here's the bad guy shooting*, JD Stephens was thinking. *I'm not going to leave.* Besides, it was payback for Geoff Morris.

TANK GRAVEYARD, 3:15 P.M.

Stayskal, who was covering the left flank of the snipers' defensive position, was the first to spot Valdes and his Marines. "Hey, there's a Humvee! There's a Humvee! QRF is here!"

Santiago came around to peer over Stayskal's shoulder and saw the truck and, best of all, Martinez firing the M240 machine gun. He had Stayskal throw a smoke grenade to mark their position.

"Get ready," Santiago called out to his team. "When the QRF gets closer, we're going across the road to assault through."[1]

This move carried enormous risks. Even with the reinforcements, the Marines were still potentially outnumbered (and, in fact, three in the truck were almost immediately taken out of action by enemy counterfire). Yet it was a chance to strike back, and Santiago, Stayskal, Stanton, and Ferguson took it.

Now it was the Marine snipers' turn to get into an attack formation. They raced through the smoke and across eighty yards to the roadway.

Years later, Santiago would wonder how that charge through the haze would have made a terrific Instagram post if someone had taken a photograph (and if the social networking site existed; it wouldn't be invented for another six years).

They reached the roadway and could see the enemy had fled, leaving behind a scatter of sandals, RPG rounds, and blood trails. Dozens of yards away, insurgents were running into the palm grove and tank graveyard. "We're winning this thing! We're winning!" Stanton called out. Beyond Nova, there was a plowed field and an irrigation ditch and then flat, hard ground beneath palm trees that soared fifty to seventy-five feet in the air around the hulks of dilapidated tanks. Some were dismantled with the turret and cannon barrel lying on the ground next to an undercarriage. A dirt road that Cherry had charged down ran along the north edge of the grove.

Behind one of the wrecks was the man with a Dragunov sniper rifle taking aim at the oncoming Marines. After the enemy sniper shot Cherry, Stayskal caught sight of him from a distance of about a hundred yards. He was tucked up against a tank, taking time to aim and fire. "I see him! He's right there! He's right there!" Stayskal, who was six foot two and more than two hundred pounds, was waving and pointing. The enemy sniper swung his rifle from right to left, aimed and fired. The round struck Stayskal in his left arm, blew out his shoulder blade, shattered his collarbone, drilled through his left lung, and exited near his spine, lodging on the inside of his ceramic bulletproof plate in his vest. (He would later

BATTLE, DAY 1: SOFIA DISTRICT

keep the slug as a souvenir.) Stayskal fell face-first into the dirt. The bullet impact was horrific, and for a moment, the Marine lost track of where he was. When his wits coalesced, his first thought was, *Oh shit, that's right. Here I am. I'm still in it.*

A hundred yards to the rear, where the platoon Humvee was located, Second Lieutenant Valdes threw himself over the side and started shooting at retreating insurgents. He saw that the M240 machine gun was down because the gunner, Martinez, had been wounded. So Valdes climbed behind it and opened fire, certain that he'd knocked down at least one or two enemy fighters. When the machine gun was empty of rounds, Valdes turned to help Dennis, the Navy corpsman, tend to Carman. They found a large exit wound in his back. Dennis felt certain the Marine was already gone. He couldn't feel a pulse, and there was no sign of breathing. His facial pallor was turning blue. And now there were others calling out for help. Lance Corporal Contreras had run all the way across the battlefield to fetch the corpsman for the wounded Stayskal. "Come on, we got to get over there," Contreras said. He knew Dennis's reputation as maybe not the fastest runner in the company and offered, with a grin, to carry the corpsman's body armor to lighten his load.

"I'm not taking off my vest," Dennis said, then headed across the plowed field. Meanwhile, Valdes had already reached the tank graveyard where the Marines were working to envelop what enemy remained hiding in the wrecks. Valdes's men were on the left flank, the four snipers on the right.

When Stayskal yelled out a warning about the enemy sniper before being felled by a gunshot, Sergeant Romeo Santiago had turned to see it all happen. This was just a minute or two after he had watched Cherry die. By that time, Valdes's squad appeared momentarily pinned down, and the snipers were trying to flank the enemy. Santiago knew he should continue his attack and end this threat that was killing and wounding his brethren. But instead, he feared Stayskal's wound was serious because the big man had stopped moving. Santiago ran to his teammate and found Stayskal moaning and complaining of harsh pain in his back. The sergeant took out his knife to start cutting off the wounded Marine's flak jacket but paused to turn and look where Stayskal had been pointing. Santiago could see the man in the distance, clothed in black, crouched where he had cover from Valdes's troops. Just then, Stanton fell with a gunshot wound from another direction that hit him in the back and passed through the fleshy part of his left shoulder. He was quick to get back up, and Santiago yelled at him to deal with Stayskal. Then Santiago turned to finally end the enemy sniper threat. In a crouching half run and keeping his ACOG chevron on the man with the Dragunov rifle, Santiago advanced in a quick step straight at him through the palms. Other Marines watched him run through their field of vision and checked their fire. Stanton, too, had been taking aim, and when Santiago suddenly stepped into his line of fire, the corporal pulled up at the last second and fired high.

Santiago kept moving across the football-field length, closing in on his target, firing a few rounds to at least keep the enemy sniper's head down. The Marine would duck behind a palm tree and head off again. As he drew closer, he could see the man in black, perhaps already wounded, sitting on the ground, propped against the tank, trying to pull up his rifle to once again take aim. Santiago was breathing hard and could see that his shots were hitting low. He adjusted and, after hitting the man in the thigh, put a bullet in his abdomen and a final round in his chest. The enemy sniper who had killed Cherry and wounded Stayskal slumped over dead.

NORTH END OF SOFIA DISTRICT, 3:20 P.M.

It had been over a half hour since Second Lieutenant Vincent Valdes took one of two squads of Marines and peeled off in a Humvee to reach the embattled Headhunter team nearly a mile and a half down Nova to the southwest. The men left behind were restless and growing angry, their animus largely directed at their squad leader, Sergeant Christopher Conner. The squad was maintaining security on an IED found buried in the roadway, but the sergeant had them so spread out that they could barely see one another.

It was the second roadside bomb they'd found that day. Shortly after Valdes's First and Third Squads left Combat Outpost that morning on what was supposed to be a routine route clearance mission along the entirety of Route Nova, one of their newest Marines, Private First Class Eric Akey, had walked right up on a buried IED with a yellow wire sticking out of the dirt. Lance Corporal Roy Thomas, one of the senior team leaders, watched as Akey froze and turned pale as a ghost. "Hey, are those wires?" Akey said to Lance Corporal Chris MacIntosh, his team leader standing close by. MacIntosh took one look and yelled for both of them to run, warning everyone else that they'd found an IED. The Marines followed the wire from the explosives to a hiding place in the bushes where the insurgent must have gotten nervous as the Americans approached on foot, and fled. They saw where he was smoking cigarettes and had taken a shit while biding his time.

The protocol was to summon bomb disposal technicians to remove IEDs. Those were people with robots and big, oversize bomb suits who could dismantle and remove explosives, particularly the most dangerous ones that were linked to a remote-control device. The IED found by Akey, however, was hardwired. An EOD team that came by said the Marine engineers with the patrol could simply blow up the artillery shells in place. They did so, and Valdes's men continued their long hike along Nova. They passed through the tank graveyard across from where a four-man sniper team was hidden and headed northeast following the road. Nova continued in a long arc across the northern end of Sofia District, flanked on one side by the Euphrates. The area was an expanse of fields and farmland crisscrossed with irrigation ditches, palm groves, and gated residential compounds. The

Marines eventually came across a second IED consisting of three artillery shells laid out in a so-called daisy-chain pattern. They were set to be detonated by remote radio command, so a cordon was set up around the site and EOD was summoned. It was only minutes later that Valdes got the call about the snipers and drove off in the patrol's only Humvee with one squad and the only corpsman.

The eleven men left behind could hear the gunfire down the road and felt vulnerable. They were spread out over three hundred yards. And, in fact, when shots rang out from the south side of Nova and the Marines realized they were now also under attack, the thin cordon quickly disintegrated. In the confusion that followed, small groups became isolated.

The exception was where Lance Corporal Thomas was located at the west end of the cordon. The Michigan native, who had been appalled that the US government would send troops to an IED-plagued war with thin-skinned Humvees, effectively took charge at his end. Far-flung squad members began assembling around him. He established a firing position on the north edge of Nova and began shooting at enemy gunmen to the south. Lance Corporal Adam Carter, the squad radioman, was there, as was Private First Class Justin Woodall. Both were new Marines who had just joined the battalion.

Woodall, nineteen, had shown up in January. He was a native of Macon, Georgia, who had been enthralled with military service since he was a little boy. No one in his working-class family had served. His father was a lifelong welder. But the boy had been mesmerized by a popular recruitment commercial that depicted a young man slaying a dragon with a sword and then suddenly transforming into a Marine in a dress blue uniform. Woodall had enlisted right out of high school. He had great respect for MacIntosh, who was his team leader, and Thomas, who had served on occasion as squad leader. Woodall had heard stories about hazing

BATTLE, DAY 1: SOFIA DISTRICT

in the Marine Corps, but he saw none of that. When he showed up for duty with First Squad in January, Thomas shook his hand and said, "Hey, anything you need to know or anything you need to learn, me and Mac will teach you." Since arriving in Ramadi, Woodall had seen a lot. He was there when the Echo Company executive officer, Ben Kaler, was maimed in a roadside explosion. He witnessed another new recruit, Sean Carroll, being launched into the air by an IED explosion that took off that Marine's leg. Now, Woodall was side by side with Thomas in his first real gunfight.

Other stragglers showed up. There was Private First Class Kyle Katz, nineteen, who was left behind by the squad that was with Valdes; and two engineers, Corporal Shamel Edress and Lance Corporal Brett Dawson. Two other PFCs appeared, Russell Oguin and Fredi Navacastro.

After trying to follow Conner to the north side of Nova and losing him, Oguin and Navacastro had searched frantically for him and then made their way to Thomas and the others. Woodall asked them where they thought the squad leader might be and took off running to find him.

Thomas, meanwhile, led his men south across Nova to a large house that looked like a good defensible position. They knocked on the door, and when the family answered, they herded them into a back room while Thomas established gun positions on the roof and outside the building and had Carter notify headquarters they were under attack.

A quarter mile away at the far east end of the cordon, MacIntosh and Akey had been posted together on Nova. There was a palm grove and some houses just to the south. When the enemy attack started, a grenade exploded not far away, followed by enemy machine gun fire from the southeast. Both Marines headed toward where they thought Conner was located. But the sergeant was already on the move, and they never linked up.

The result was that MacIntosh and Akey were on their own. They cut through a house that was just off the roadway, and as they exited the south end, they saw to the left their first enemy fighter—a man running with an AK-47 in the direction both Marines had just left, clearly on his way to attack them. He saw them and fired. MacIntosh and Akey shot back, and the gunmen spun as if struck by a bullet and ran for cover. As it turned out, the area was crawling with enemy fighters. Akey and MacIntosh could see perhaps a half dozen or more heading toward them from the south. MacIntosh yelled for Akey to duck through an opening into a walled compound just off to their right while he stood and opened fire on the men before doing the same. They reached a house, and both headed into a carport where a white sedan was parked. A door and a set of double doors led into the house, but both were locked. What they had no way of knowing was that the residence was an enemy weapons and ammunition storage site. They could hear men speaking Arabic on the outside of the courtyard wall, as if planning how they would kill the Marines. Another man, possibly a resident of the house, came walking around a corner into the carport. He so surprised them that it was all Akey and MacIntosh could do not to open fire. Anxious and irritated at having to deal with this interloper, MacIntosh had him stand close by. The Marines were now effectively cornered. Those gunmen they had seen outside the courtyard were certainly coming in after them, and all they could do was wait. Akey took a knee near the front of the sedan. MacIntosh stood behind the front end of the car, against the wall. They waited with their rifles up. The first gunman suddenly appeared from around the corner, and both Marines opened fire. Then there was a second. Then a third. The bodies collected on the concrete floor. Finally, a fourth man stepped into the carport and, with a look of either shock or anger, tried to pull up as he saw his brethren lying in a growing pool of blood. Akey and MacIntosh shot him as well.

BATTLE, DAY 1: SOFIA DISTRICT

It was a hellish few seconds of gunfire and gore, and when it was over, MacIntosh stood for a moment almost in shock at their handiwork. He snapped out of his funk only when he heard Akey say, "They're still moving." MacIntosh wasn't going to risk a wounded enemy fighter pulling out a grenade or a hidden weapon. He fired kill shots into each of their heads. Meanwhile, amid all the shooting, the house resident they had grabbed had disappeared, fled somewhere.

"We got to move," MacIntosh told Akey. "We can't stay here."

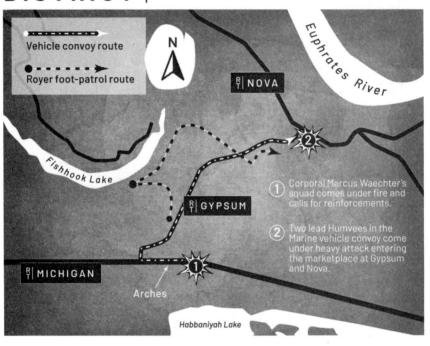

NORTH OF ARCHES,
3:20 P.M.

Far to the southeast of the sniper battle, Echo Company commander Kelly Royer finally realized he was marching his troops where nothing was happening. The gunfire that had attracted their attention was actually much farther away. And to complicate matters, he was just told over the radio that Valdes's First Squad—Sergeant Conner, Lance Corporal Thomas, and their Marines—was isolated up at the northern tip of the Sofia District and now also under attack.

Royer's only choice at that point was to get his men mounted up on trucks and Humvees and take the shortest route to the north end of the district. From the arches on Route Michigan, there was a road the Americans designated Gypsum that wound about a mile through a residential area of larger homes before connecting at a T intersection with Nova. There the convoy could make a left turn and follow Nova northwest about two and a half miles to where Conner and his men were fighting. Gypsum was part of the circular route that Echo Marines hiked nearly every day when they were conducting route clearance through the Sofia District. The insurgents had certainly seen them use it many times.

Royer radioed Second Lieutenant Wroblewski and told him to get his Marines and the vehicle convoy moving to meet him at the Gypsum-Nova intersection. Royer and his crew would double-time it there by foot. From there, the entire force could move en masse to relieve the troops fighting in the north.

There was a sense of urgency as Wroblewski and his Second Platoon men and Staff Sergeant Walker and the Marines of Third Platoon piled into the vehicles and headed up Gypsum. Leading the way in two open-backed Humvees was Walker with Marcus Waechter's squad that had first taken fire at the Arches two hours earlier.

Like many of the senior noncommissioned officers in the battalion, Walker, at twenty-eight, was a former drill instructor. His nickname at the San Diego Marine recruit depot was "the Beast," a label that spoke to his imposing six-foot-two frame. He had trained and influenced literally hundreds of new Marines, working through no fewer than nine thirteen-week cycles of recruits over the years. He was said to be fair but tough in his distinctive, flat-brimmed campaign hat worn by all DIs. After years of recruit training, Walker felt a duty to request a combat assignment. "How can I teach men to fight if I've never been to battle?" he asked his father, Kenneth Walker. And as a platoon sergeant with the Magnificent Bastards, he still employed the booming DI voice that demanded compliance. Walker was in the front passenger seat of the first Humvee, and the back of the vehicle was crammed with people—five Marines and a corpsman and a detainee who wore zip-tied handcuffs and was blindfolded.

Behind them in a second open-backed Humvee was Corporal Waechter, six other Marines, and two handcuffed detainees. Most of the troops in those first two trucks were—like so many others in the battalion—brand-new, right out of high school, boot camp, and the School of Infantry. Nearly all were eighteen or nineteen years old. Among them was the beanpole Matt Scott, a nineteen-year-old private first class from the state of Washington who was all of six foot four, 150 pounds. He was a Second Platoon Marine qualified to drive Humvees, so he was at the wheel of Waechter's truck. In Walker's Humvee was Private First Class Ryan Jerabek, eighteen, manning an M240 medium machine gun. A mortarman by training, he was excited to be assigned the automatic weapon. Jerabek had been an honor student at Pulaski High School outside Green Bay, Wisconsin, and planned to return there as a history teacher after serving in the Marine Corps and earning a college degree.[2] He was an idealist who had exhorted classmates in a 2002 speech to "thank those who fought and are fighting in the battles to keep this country at the pinnacle of freedom."[3] Fernando Mendez-Aceves, the corpsman on the first truck, had been accepted into the Navy's Basic Underwater Demolition School in 2002 to become an elite Navy SEAL but had been involuntarily

BATTLE, DAY 1: SOFIA DISTRICT 149

pulled from the program during its infamous "Hell Week" of brutal training because of hypothermia issues.[4]

Both lead Humvees were about as poorly armored as any of the vehicles the Magnificent Bastards had. Waechter's Humvee had steel half doors on the passenger and driver's side, and sheet metal bolted on both sides of the open-backed, troop-carrying portion of the vehicle. Walker's Humvee in front only had a steel half door on the front passenger side and an L-shaped steel door on the driver's side and no other armor protection. The Marines might as well have been riding in a hay truck. Wroblewski ordered that the Humvee with the M240 machine gun lead the way because it had the heavier weapon and a bullet shield.

The crossroads they were all heading for was a placid, trash-strewn plaza that lay about a quarter mile from where the Euphrates made a gradual bend to the east. The paved Gypsum rose up to meet the elevated roadway that was Route Nova, and along the intersection was a ramshackle business district made up of low-slung, cinder block buildings with thatched awnings and solid steel doorways, each housing an auto repair shop or other tool operation. Enemy gunmen had ordered the shopkeepers to leave that morning. "Today we are going to kill Americans," the insurgents said. They then began the business of preparing an elaborate ambush. Enemy fighters somehow hauled engine blocks and the husk of a white sedan onto rooftops to be used as firing positions. Across the intersection on the northeast side of Nova, there was a shallow fighting position dug out of the side of the road where a dishka heavy machine gun was set up to fire directly down Gypsum. According to one estimate, there were as many as ninety insurgents positioned in and around the killing zone. Many of them were disciplined cadres, likely veterans of Iraq military service and conflicts. They were disciplined fighters, leaving as little evidence of their efforts as possible to deny Americans any intel. As a result, they had resources for rapidly evacuating their wounded and dead. They even hung bags from their AK-47s to catch spent shell casings as rounds were fired. There were enemy fighters in reserve who could quickly step forward and replace wounded comrades so that fire superiority over the Americans could be achieved and maintained. Munitions were pre-positioned in fallback locations. And vehicles were close by—cars or even motorcycles—to provide rapid escape if US reinforcements got through. But there were also layered lines of defense to the south designed to stop or slow any quick-reaction force that arrived to rescue trapped Marines.

Of course, John Wroblewski and his men who were manning the convoy that was headed to this intersection knew nothing about any of this.

NORTH END OF SOFIA DISTRICT, 3:30 P.M.

Private First Class Justin Woodall left Lance Corporal Roy Thomas and the other Marines in his squad to plunge into a lush area of grasses and intermittent palm trees north of Route Nova and search for his squad leader, Christopher Conner. There were plowed fields and a few homes, and Woodall stumbled across some furrowed ground until he finally spotted the sergeant and ran to him. The two slipped into a storage hut as enemy fire started to zero in. They both knew the enemy would be eager to close in and kill two isolated Marines. Woodall tried to target one of them as he aimed out a window and, when he fired, was certain the man fell. That was one, at least. They were clearly cut off from the rest of the squad, and Woodall argued that they needed to push their way to the river to prevent becoming surrounded. He could see more insurgents arriving in cars and infiltrating a nearby tree line, maybe fifteen to twenty people.

"Fuck, we got to get out of here as fast as possible!" he yelled to Conner.

The sergeant, meanwhile, could hear over his inter-squad radio that MacIntosh and Akey were also trying to fight their way

BATTLE, DAY 1: SOFIA DISTRICT 151

out of encirclement and needed help. The short-range radio connected to a headset a Marine could wear under his helmet and had a microphone. Conner had no idea where MacIntosh was or, for that matter, where Thomas and the rest of his squad were.

He agreed with Woodall that heading to the river was the best idea. There was a house about thirty yards in that direction, and Conner instructed Woodall to make his way there. The PFC took off running. He got several yards toward the house before dropping to his knee in tall grass and returning fire. Woodall saw a gunman just as the man was pointing right back at him with an AK-47. They fired almost simultaneously, and the enemy fighter went down. But so did Woodall, shot through the left shoulder. It felt like someone hit him with a sledgehammer. The round passed clear through his body, and Woodall could feel warm liquid on his skin. He looked down to see his left arm drenched in blood. Still, he felt he could use the arm and yelled to Conner, "I'm hit. We need to move!"

When he turned back to look at the tree line where enemy gunmen had been gathering, he was astonished to see what looked like a skirmish line of fighters move out of the trees and down a slope in his direction. They weren't rushing or bounding but simply moving in unison. For a second, it reminded Woodall of those images of Revolutionary War soldiers advancing in lockstep. When he was lucky enough to shoot one of them, they'd simply drag the wounded man to the rear and the rest would keep moving. It was like they had no fear. They were now seventy-five to one hundred feet away and closing in with AK-47s and light machine guns, and Woodall could begin to see details of their faces and even their eyes. Some had checkered kaffiyehs. Most were wearing dishdashas. The Marine ran the last several yards to the house, and when he looked toward the enemy again, he could see more cars in the distance arriving to retrieve the wounded and drop off more fighters. He thought, *This shit is never going to fucking end.*

Conner watched Woodall reach the house. He chose to stay and fight where he was under ever-increasing enemy gunfire. One round ricocheted off an M16 magazine Conner carried in a pocket on his vest. The sergeant discarded it.

Dozens of yards away, Woodall was growing desperate. The enemy was taking him apart piece by piece. The PFC was lying on his stomach near a corner of the house, and when he tried to raise himself up into a firing position, a ricochet blew through a knuckle on his right hand. Now Woodall was struggling to reload his rifle, using his thumb and three bloody fingers to insert a magazine and slamming it home with his forearm. He reached the rear of the house and, from behind a pillar, could see a fence made of weaved palm fronds and an Iraqi man beckoning him in halting English. "Come here. Shelter."

Woodall stayed put, and as the man turned to yell something in Arabic to someone behind the fence, the Marine could see through his dishdasha the outline of an AK-47. Then the whole fence erupted with gunfire from one or more fighters behind it. Woodall pressed himself tight against the pillar and could feel flecks of concrete stinging his face from bullets impacting a wall near him. Two men finally came running toward him from around the fence, and he shot them down.

The Marine slumped to the ground, his back against the building. He felt trapped and overwhelmed with a sense of despair. His pathway to the river was obviously cut off. He was alone, wounded, and without a radio. The nineteen-year-old felt helpless and, though he knew it would do no good, started yelling for his Marine mentor: "Corporal Thomas! Corporal Thomas!"

But Thomas was far too distant to hear Woodall's plea. He was busy using his inter-squad radio to guide MacIntosh and Akey to safety.

The two Marines had slipped out of the carport where they had gunned down four enemy fighters and worked their way west around the residence. There was a driveway opening along the west side of the compound wall, but the gate was locked. For the moment, they held their position on the west side of the house.

MacIntosh was at the corner of the structure, and if he peered around it, the Marine could see the eastern opening in the compound wall through which he and Akey had entered minutes before fleeing the enemy. There was also, of all things, a cow standing in the courtyard. Cattle were allowed to roam all over the Sofia District, and troops were instructed not to harm them, or families would have to be compensated. From where he was tucked back around a corner, MacIntosh saw the bovine's big eyes and tufted ears suddenly twitch. The Marine leaned around the corner with his rifle up, and sure enough, there were enemy gunmen at the entrance of the wall opening. MacIntosh fired, certain he had hit one of them. And he pulled back. This gonzo interspecies collaboration went on for a few minutes. The cow would react, and MacIntosh would correctly discern that gunmen were trying to enter the courtyard, and he would open fire. During one episode, the Marine was flabbergasted to see that one of the four fighters they had shot down in the carport was still alive, trying to crawl out the same opening in the wall. MacIntosh raked him with gunfire.

Another insurgent boosted himself to peer over the courtyard wall at the Americans before dropping back down. MacIntosh called Thomas on his PRR. "Roy, we're fucking surrounded and fucked. We have to get out of here." From the description MacIntosh gave of his location, Thomas now had an idea in which compound the two Marines were located and urged them to make a dash for his location. "We're going to provide fire. You motherfuckers need to run," Thomas said over his inter-squad radio. As if on cue, an older man emerged from the residence, made his way over to the gated entrance, and unlocked it, either because he pitied the trapped pair, was weary of his property becoming a battlefield, or was worried an errant round might detonate munitions hidden inside the house.

Whatever the reason, Akey and MacIntosh exited that entrance and took off running across three hundred yards of field. They could see the house where the squad was located and even caught a glimpse of Marines there. From his end, Thomas and other squad members moved behind a wall to get closer to where MacIntosh and Akey would be approaching. Bullets ricocheted off the opposite side. Thomas could see the two running his way, but it felt like it was happening in slow motion. The two first tried to leap a ditch as enemy rounds struck the ground at their feet. They temporarily took cover behind the only two trees in the field. Then they made a final run to reach their comrades. Akey tumbled into a creek just short of safety and Thomas stepped from behind the wall to rescue him. An enemy round burrowed into one of Thomas's boots.

The house that he had chosen for their Alamo had walls on three sides, and the Marines defended different sectors. As the enemy began to close in, Thomas and MacIntosh tried repeatedly to reach Conner over their headset radios. But they never got through. Thomas, MacIntosh, Navacastro, radioman Carter, and one of the Marine engineers climbed a stairway to the roof and started targeting enemy gunmen to the east. Meanwhile, other insurgents had worked their way closer, a few of them reaching the opposite side of the wall that ran along the length of the house. They were easily within hand-grenade range, and suddenly one was lobbed onto the roof. MacIntosh, from a doorway leading downstairs, saw it first and yelled, "Frag! Frag! Frag!" The grenade came to rest a few feet from Thomas and Carter. Navacastro, an eighteen-year-old Chicago native, was steps away, trying to flee. Thomas yelled for Carter to run and gave him a shove before bracing for the explosion, using his rifle as a shield and lowering his head and helmet as if to weather a hailstorm. The bomb exploded. Navacastro was knocked down but otherwise unhurt. Carter caught shrapnel to the lower part of his left leg. Thomas took the worst of it. A shroud of metal bits laced across his left leg and left arm. A wrist was shattered. Worst of all, tiny pieces of shrapnel blew out his left eye with a few penetrating his brain.

The voice he heard screaming was his own. "Help me! Help me!"

7

BATTLE, DAY 1: THE AMBUSH

GYPSUM, NORTH OF ARCHES, 3:35 P.M.

ECHO COMPANY CAPTAIN Kelly Royer and his mix of about two dozen people had worked their way on foot along the eastern edge of a large marshy area and started heading east toward the intersection of Gypsum and Nova. They had a mile of ground to cover to the rendezvous point and were moving fast because of a growing urgency to reach embattled Marines. One of Royer's radio operators, Lance Corporal Victor Madrillejos, was struggling to keep pace, and the captain kept screaming at him. "Suck it up! Find it! Find it in your belly! You have Marines being shot at!"[1] The eighteen-year-old Northern California native—who, at five foot three, was known as "Shorty"—was hampered by combat gear, his weapon, and a bulky radio with a ten-foot antenna that kept catching on tree limbs and power lines. The radio had a cord connected to a handset, which Royer clung to, dragging his radio operator along. Madrillejos grew so exhausted that he started to throw up. For years afterward, he would remember bitterly how Royer shamed him to move faster because comrades "were being shot at."

Within a few minutes, Royer and his men got to a place where they could see the convoy moving up Gypsum. Royer reached Wroblewski by radio and told him to stop. The lieutenant ordered a halt, but not everyone got the word. The two lead Humvees just kept going. In the second one was Private First Class Zach Shores, a nineteen-year-old from North Carolina, who stood in the back of the truck with the bipod of his light machine gun resting on the roof of the cab. He saw the trucks behind them slow to a stop and tried to rouse Waechter, who was in the front passenger seat, by banging on the roof and yelling. Realizing what was happening, the squad leader tried to contact Staff Sergeant Walker in the first Humvee over the radio. But that vehicle, with Walker in the front passenger seat and eighteen-year-old Lance Corporal Kyle Crowley behind the wheel, was already disappearing around a corner up ahead. The Humvee was heading directly into an ambush.

Crowley was another boot who had arrived at the battalion in December. He had earned promotion to lance corporal, and his squad leader, Corporal Eric Smith, was so impressed that he chose Crowley to be a team leader.

The eighteen-year-old Marine now drove his Humvee through the middle of the market area approaching Nova. Shops were closed. Steel doors were locked tight. At the rear of the Humvee was Deshon Otey. A flex-cuffed detainee in slacks, shirt, and sandals was beside him and then the corpsman, Mendez-Aceves. Across from them were Private First Class Christopher Cobb, nineteen, from Bradenton, Florida; Lance Corporal Travis Layfield, nineteen, from Fremont, California; and Lance Corporal Anthony Roberts, eighteen, from Bear, Delaware. Jerabek, the seventh person in the jam-packed rear of the Humvee, was on the M240 machine gun that was mounted on a pedestal. The weapon had a broad gun shield attached to protect the gunner. All the Marines

BATTLE, DAY 1: THE AMBUSH

and the sailor had M16 rifles except for Cobb, who was carrying a light machine gun.

A few rounds hitting the Humvee were the first signs of trouble. Someone yelled that everyone should get down. Otey instinctively jumped out the back, thinking others would follow. There was suddenly a massive explosion of gunfire. Gunmen firing machine guns from rooftops east or southeast of the market area fired massive amounts of gunfire at the Humvee. Others blasted away with AK-47s. The most earsplitting sound was the steady hammering of a dishka heavy machine gun emplaced across Nova and firing from a distance of just seventy feet, its large rounds punching shattering holes through the Humvee windshield.

More than a hundred yards back down Gypsum, where there was a bend in the road, the second Humvee rounded that corner. Shores could see the enemy fighters several dozen yards away shooting down into Walker's truck. *Fuck that*, he thought, and he fired bursts from his squad automatic weapon into one enemy machine gunner after another. He could see them flinch from the impact of his rounds. Then he was shocked to see others move forward to take their places. In the back of the Humvee, two other rookie Marines also started firing at the insurgents: Private First Class Arnold Thao, who had just turned nineteen the month before; and Private First Class Ryan Downing, the new recruit who was gently scolded weeks before by Hospitalman Escalera about exchanging last letters with his best friend, Lance Corporal Travis Layfield.

Layfield, nineteen, was in the lead Humvee. He was one of five Americans who somehow managed to escape the vehicle that in a matter of seconds was becoming a deathtrap. Some didn't get far. Staff Sergeant Allan Walker died on the ground just a few feet from the front passenger side of the vehicle. One Marine died in the back of the truck still sitting on a side bench, killed by a hail of bullets before he could even get up to move. The handcuffed detainee died, too. Otey, already out of the Humvee, found what he initially thought was refuge near a wall on the west side of the street. At first, he didn't see anyone follow him. "There was a shit load of fire, like it was raining lead," he later wrote in his after-action report. Otey could hear the deafening staccato of the heavy-caliber machine gun and saw men all along the tops of buildings across the street firing into the Humvee. Suddenly, an insurgent emerged to his right from the buildings behind Otey, and the Marine shot him down. As bullets tore up the ground near his feet, Otey started dodging them as he sprinted down the street toward the second Humvee. Miraculously, he was untouched, though one round passed through his trousers and another snapped off the bayonet hook on his rifle.

Amid this hail of fire, eighteen-year-old Ryan Jerabek stood his ground at the M240 machine gun in the back of the lead truck. With barely any protection behind the weapon's gun shield from the hailstorm of bullets, the PFC somehow managed to pick his targets, pivoting the weapon to rake the heavy machine gun emplacement across Nova and, in the process, killed or wounded at least two of its crew. Several hundred yards to the southeast, where the greater part of Wroblewski's column of trucks had stopped along Gypsum, Private First Class Ryan Miller was high up in a machine gun turret on a seven-ton truck and first recognized the sound of the heavy machine gun followed by the more muted rhythm of Jerabek's M240. From the weapons' alternating bursts, it sounded as if they were locked in a deadly competition until all Miller could hear was the heavier enemy gun. Still, Jerabek's stubborn resistance had purchased precious seconds, allowing some of the others in his Humvee to at least get out of the vehicle. Downing, in the second truck a hundred yards away, watched this unfold. Enemy gunmen focused their attention on the young Marine firing from behind his bullet shield. Downing watched as the teenager was finally struck by gunfire and started to fall down. Downing could see him flinch when the rounds impacted. But Jerabek managed to catch himself from falling because he kept one hand on his weapon. He somehow muscled himself back up to resume firing

BATTLE, DAY 1: THE AMBUSH 159

before the volume of incoming rounds grew overwhelming and Jerabek went down for good.

Back at the second Humvee, the driver, Matt Scott, had gotten out and taken a knee. He heard the enemy heavy machine gun and was shocked that the Iraqi insurgents, who had seemed timid fighters when the battalion first arrived in Ramadi, could muster up such a devastating weapon. Scott caught sight of Otey running in his direction and provided cover fire. The squad leader, Corporal Marcus Waechter, had yelled for his men to get out of the Humvee before jumping from the front passenger seat into a nearby ditch. He could see the first Humvee being pulverized by massive gunfire and did his best to carefully aim and knock down enemy fighters with his M16. But as with Shores's experience, every time Waechter shot someone on a rooftop, the body would be dragged back, and another fighter would jump in to take his place.

Downing caught glimpses of a few Marines fleeing the lead truck and stumbling into alleys on the west side of the street. He suddenly remembered the detainees who had been sitting behind him and glanced back to see one of the men motionless on the floor of the truck bed. Waechter thought he saw bodies of his comrades draped over a side railing of Walker's Humvee.

Otey, still reeling from the decimation he had just fled, came running up, yelling, "Get the fuck out of the Humvee!"

Suddenly, a rocket-propelled grenade whooshed in from the east toward the second Humvee and exploded on the right passenger side of the cab roof, inches from where Shores was firing his machine gun. It felt like he was hit by a train. He was thrown onto his back in the rear of the truck and momentarily lost consciousness. A minute or two before, he had caught bullet fragments in his right leg. Now he had shrapnel across his shoulder from the RPG. The barrel of his light machine gun was shredded. Downing, who had been fighting next to him, was also flung back into the truck bed next to Shores and a detainee. He was momentarily deafened, and it felt like the skin on his face, arms, and neck was burning from where bits of metal tore his flesh. A taste of iron was in his mouth. Lance Corporal Justin Tate, a twenty-one-year-old native of southern Illinois and the tiny farm village of Eldorado, had one leg over the rear tailgate, in the process of stepping out of the truck, when the explosion pitched him clear of the vehicle and onto the ground. Waechter, who was in a ditch just a few feet from where the RPG impacted, was knocked down and stunned by the blast. He could hear Marines in the back of his truck screaming that they were hit.

Just several feet from the Humvee, on the west side of Gypsum, was a cinder block shed with a thatched-grass roof that was attached to a one-story building. A walled courtyard was on the south end, and a doorway into the shed faced the street. The Marines scrambled inside seeking cover, hoping to get into the rest of the structure and maybe onto its roof. Shores could hear the two detainees, who were left lying on the floor of the Humvee's troop-carrying area screaming. Inside the shed, a doorway into the other structure was locked, and the Americans were confined to the dirt-floor storage hut, a tight space of about eight by ten feet made smaller by the presence of an unarmed Iraqi man wearing a dishdasha. The Americans, spun up and agitated, pointed their rifles at the man, who pleaded, "No, no, mister, mister." Corporal Evan Null called for the rest of the Marines to get inside. They didn't need much encouragement. It seemed nearly all the enemy gunmen on various rooftops and on the ground were focusing their gunfire on the second Humvee. The Americans felt like they were taking incoming rounds from nearly every direction, and the rate of fire was growing. When Waechter ran across the street to reach his men, a bullet struck his rifle, and another was stopped by his body armor. Meanwhile, Tate and Null helped Downey and Shores out of the Humvee.

They all crowded into the hut—Null, the wounded Downey and Shores, Otey, Thao, Scott, Waechter, Tate, and the Iraqi man they had found inside.

BATTLE, DAY 1: THE AMBUSH

161

Some 350 yards back down Gypsum, where most of the convoy had come to a halt in response to Captain Royer's radioed command, troops found themselves in the center of an upscale area of Ramadi. Around them were homes two or three stories high with elaborate cornices and rooftop terraces.

After the vehicles had stopped, there was a second or two of silence as Lieutenant John Wroblewski got out of his Humvee and stood talking on a handset connected to the vehicle-mounted radio.

Others disembarked just as they heard the snapping sound of rounds passing over their heads, followed by a solid sheath of incoming fire. Almost simultaneously, there was a huge roar of weaponry and explosions from down the road at the intersection, including the unmistakable sound of a heavy machine gun. Marines in the column scattered for cover. Wroblewski took a knee with the handset to his ear. He read the crisis around him and knew he needed to inform headquarters that their situation was suddenly dire.

Corporal Eric Smith, a squad leader riding in the front passenger seat of the Humvee that was pulled behind Wroblewski, felt like the world around him had transformed in a heartbeat as he stepped out of the vehicle. The enemy was unleashing a wall of lead in their direction. He and four members of his squad leaped into a ditch alongside the road. From there, they took up positions behind a low wall that ran in front of a large house off the road to their right. Smith could see a gunman in a tree line not too far in front of them, took aim, and shot the man through the head.

Meanwhile, Marines manning vehicle-mounted medium machine guns began returning fire at any enemy they could see. Two of them were boots. Private First Class Ryan Miller, who had joined the battalion in January, was firing from the turret of one of the tall seven-ton trucks. Corporal Michael Stewart was blasting away on an M240 mounted on the back of the Humvee Eric Smith had been riding in.

In front of him, Private First Class Cody Calavan was the most exposed of the three, shooting his weapon from Wroblewski's Humvee, which was at the front of the halted column. The nineteen-year-old Marine had joined the battalion in November. He was from the scenic village of Lake Stevens, northeast of Seattle, and had tragically lost a younger brother to a drunken driver the previous summer. As sole surviving son of his family, Calavan could have avoided serving in a conflict zone. But he declined. Now as other troops took cover to return fire, he remained firing his M240.

Back at company headquarters in Combat Outpost, they were tracking radio communications in the far-flung battle, and Wroblewski could be heard over the radio trying to reach Royer. He got out the word "Six," which was shorthand for the company commander, before the transmission stopped. Back on Gypsum, a sniper had unleashed a round that penetrated the radio handset Wroblewski was holding up to his face, then blasted into his jaw. The lieutenant collapsed on the ground.

Shaun Lenz had seen it all. The twenty-two-year-old corporal, a native of Tulsa, Oklahoma, had been riding in a seven-ton truck behind Wroblewski's Humvee and heard his orders over a radio headset for the convoy to halt. Lenz was out of the vehicle and against a wall, where he could see Wroblewski down on one knee, talking into a radio handset he held with his left hand. He was behind the open door of the Humvee, but the shot came through a gap between the open door and the body of the vehicle. There was impact, and Lenz saw Wroblewski drop like a sack of potatoes.

From where he was directing fire for members of his squad, Smith heard someone yell, "Lieutenant Ski's hit!" The squad leader could see Wroblewski on the ground and without hesitation took off running across an open field swept by enemy fire, confident that his team leaders would cover him. It was a distance of more

BATTLE, DAY 1: THE AMBUSH

than fifty yards, and Smith moved in a straight line across it. When he turned to yell for the corpsman, Hospitalman Third Class Sergio Gutierrez, the twenty-four-year-old sailor was already up and running and about to pass Smith. Bullets were pinging off the dirt, the pavement of the road, the lieutenant's Humvee. Gutierrez's tunnel vision was such that he didn't even notice. An enemy round passed through one of Smith's cargo pockets, and when the corporal reached down there, it was wet, and he thought he might be bleeding. Later he found that the bullet had perforated a bottle of Purell.

Wroblewski was bleeding badly. The officer was on his right side with his face on the asphalt. He was rolled over onto his back, and the sight of his wound was shocking. The bullet had entered his upper-right jaw and exited his lower-left jaw. Smith was looking at a mass of blood, teeth, and bone. Remarkably, the lieutenant was conscious, and there was a distant and confused look in his eyes as if he were trying to comprehend what had just happened. Smith said to him, "Hey, we're going to get you out of here." Smith first tried to pull him by the drag collar on his upper back and then just took hold under both arms and started dragging, joined by Gutierrez. They pulled him some distance to another Humvee, where Smith and Gutierrez lifted him inside and the corpsman began to bandage Wroblewski's terrible wound and administer morphine. Smith retraced his steps back to where the officer had been shot because he needed to get on the radio and call for assistance, most importantly for a helicopter medevac. But he found the handset with a bullet hole through the push-to-talk button on the side. It was useless, and as a result, so was the radio.

So there was no communication. His platoon commander was direly wounded and in immediate need of surgical care. His platoon sergeant, by happenstance, was back at Combat Outpost. Royer and his people were somewhere in the area on foot. The first two Humvees in Smith's convoy had disappeared around a turn up ahead into a cauldron of intense gunfire—what had happened to them was anyone's guess. There were about twenty troops with Smith, and they didn't have a commander.

The twenty-one-year-old corporal was thinking, *What the hell am I going to do?* As the senior member of Second Platoon, he took charge. He decided to have three people drive the wounded Wroblewski nearly three miles back to Combat Outpost. One lone vehicle moving through the city was a risk, and there was no way to alert the base that they were coming. But Smith knew that the only way to save Wroblewski was to get him out of there and to a helicopter medevac as quickly as possible. The corporal was acting virtually as a platoon commander at this point and ordered Corpsman Gutierrez to accompany the wounded lieutenant, Lance Corporal Jonathan Brown to drive, and Calavan to man the M240 medium machine gun on the vehicle, telling him, "Listen, if anybody's on the street, fucking shoot them. I don't care. Nobody should be out right now." It took several minutes to maneuver the seven-ton trucks out of the way because Gypsum was so narrow. And then the Humvee took off with Smith thinking, *Fuck, I hope this works out.* During the race to get to Combat Outpost, Gutierrez did what he could for the wounded officer, asking him if he was wounded anywhere else. Wroblewski gave him a thumbs-down "no" in response. The corpsman feared that the one terrible wound the lieutenant had was fatal.

Back on Route Gypsum, Eric Smith returned to his squad members, and it wasn't long before he noticed that Wroblewski's helmet and his M16 were lying out in the open near where he was shot. Smith turned to one of his men, Corporal Misael Nieto. "Hey, man, I need you to do me a favor." But then he hesitated. "Never mind. I got it." And Smith left cover to again cross the fifty yards or more to reach the rifle and helmet and bring them back as enemy gunmen once again opened fire. He somehow returned to his Marines unscathed.

BATTLE, DAY 1: THE AMBUSH

ROUTE APPLE, SOFIA DISTRICT, ALSO AROUND 3:35 P.M.

The fighting grew chaotic as Weapons Company Captain Rob Weiler pressed an opportunity to destroy enemy forces arrayed along Apple as an ambush. Amid the cacophony of gunfire, enemy RPGs, and Marine MK19 rounds crisscrossing on the battlefield, overhead power lines were torn down, and the electrified wires hit the street, snapping and reeling. Out of a side street about a hundred yards or more away, an enemy fighter on a motorcycle came wheeling out and turned the bike toward the Marines, riding at them head-on. The man, whose head was wrapped in a scarf, was holding a shortened version of an AK-47 and firing it like a pistol. Sergeant Shane Nylin, twenty-five, of Phoenix, Arizona— who three days earlier had been eager to learn the condition of the mortally wounded Geoff Morris—now couldn't believe this suicide charge by the motorcycle insurgent. He and another Marine aimed and fired. One round penetrated the small fuel tank on the bike, and they could see flames that set fire to the man's shirt. He laid the bike down, and it exploded like some kind of Hollywood action movie stunt.

Weiler's men found their vehicle-mounted MK19 automatic grenade launchers—that spewed out 40mm grenades with their distinctive *chug-chug-chug* rhythm of fire—particularly effective, even against enemy fighters hiding behind walls. An exploding 40mm would rain lead down on the insurgent. At other times, the grenades simply tore the walls down. "Ten rounds into a concrete wall did what several .50-cal [armor penetrating] rounds could not," a battalion lessons-learned report later concluded. "MK-19 rules the battlefield." In one instance, a Marine manning one of the launchers reduced to a burning wreck a blue sedan that was dropping off more enemy gunmen. Similarly effective for another Marine was the M203 grenade launcher attached to his M16 rifle. All these various weapons, along with heavy machine guns, allowed Weapons Company to quickly overwhelm the insurgents while dismounted troops cleared houses along the street and beyond. By the time the enemy fire finally died out and the smoke cleared, Weiler counted eighteen dead enemy fighters.

In the middle of the gunfight, there suddenly appeared two Marine vehicles rolling up Apple from the west. The Weapons Company commander was shocked to see them moving through a battlefield with so little security. But the small convoy was an ad hoc relief force assembled from the remnants of Echo Company troops who had been left back at Combat Outpost. When word arrived that the snipers were under attack, and with all Echo Company vehicles in the field, these men had borrowed a Golf Company Humvee with a leaky transmission and taken a canvas-backed ambulance as Gunnery Sergeant Coleman was yelling for them to "go, go, go!"

One result was that Combat Outpost was now so stripped of personnel as the battle erupted and expanded that cooks and mechanics were serving as security personnel and had been sent to provide additional defense of the provincial Government Center.

Meanwhile, the last-minute relief force of thirteen Marines and a corpsman sought directions to the snipers from Weiler and his men, and so informed, went on their way.

TANK GRAVEYARD, ALSO AROUND 3:35 P.M.

As Lieutenant Valdes and a portion of his Marines, along with the only corpsman available, advanced across an open field toward a palm grove and the tank graveyard, Private First Class David Quetglas tried to treat some of the wounded left behind near Route Nova. He bandaged up Lance Corporal Brandon Lund, who had been struck by bullet fragments in his right hand and left shoulder. Nearby was Private First Class Miguel Martinez, whose left hand was wounded.

Quetglas used the platoon radio to call company headquarters and ask for a medevac for the wounded. Then he began firing at muzzle flashes in foliage off to their left flank. When he turned back, he could see, of all things, an unarmed Iraqi man riding up Nova on a bicycle as if it were a Sunday afternoon in the park. He pointed his weapon at the man. "Get the fuck outta here!" It took a beat or two, but the man grudgingly complied, planting both feet, lifting the bike, spinning it around, and pedaling away.

The three Marines sought better cover down the western embankment off Route Nova, but not before Quetglas and Martinez tried unsuccessfully to drag along with them the body of Lance Corporal Benjamin Carman still in the truck. The enemy gunfire and the heavy weight of the slain Marine was too much, and they left his body.

Martinez could still fight, despite his wounds, and Quetglas told him, "Kill anything that ain't fucking one of us!" He worried they were still too exposed and shifted Lund into some trees.

In the meantime, it looked like enemy fighters might have crossed Nova to their side and were creeping up on them from the north. Gunfire was increasing, and rocket-propelled grenades whooshed overhead. Added to that, incoming mortar rounds exploded nearby. "I was so scared," Quetglas would later write in an after-action report.

Valdes, from where he was located two hundred yards to the east, could see all the explosions and gunfire around the Humvee back on Nova. He cursed his failure to bring the squad radio with him from the truck and, on his inter-squad radio, began calling for Quetglas. Was he still alive? The PFC responded that he was okay, and Valdes told him to contact headquarters on the platoon radio and demand reinforcements. Quetglas said the radio was still in the truck. "Go get it," Valdes responded. Quetglas called out for Martinez to cover him and made a dash for the vehicle. He was under fire but managed to unlatch the door, grab the radio, and leap off Route Nova back into their position. He put in the radio call to Combat Outpost. But it wasn't necessary. In seconds, fresh troops flooded in.

The ad hoc relief force scrounged together at Combat Outpost came barreling down Nova from the northeast. Soon after, the Army brigade commander, Colonel Buck Connor, with his security team and a pair of Bradley Fighting Vehicles, came up Nova from the southwest. Connor had relocated from the battle in the center of Ramadi to help out Echo Company in the far eastern Sofia District.

With the arrival of reinforcements and particularly the Bradley Fighting Vehicles, enemy resistance dissolved, and the insurgents fled. Connor and his command sergeant major, Ron Riling, along with their two dozen security-detachment GIs joined the newly arrived Marine reinforcements from Combat Outpost in sweeping through the tank graveyard and palm forest to a cluster of houses six hundred yards east of Nova. A few homes were searched, and then the troops pulled back. Stayskal, Lund, and Martinez were evacuated to Charlie Med at Camp Ramadi. The body of Marcus Cherry was collected, as was Carman from the back of the Humvee where he had lain since being fatally wounded at the battle's outset. A newly arrived corpsman thought he detected a faint pulse. But Carman was either dead or on the edge of it. Meanwhile, Valdes pulled together the surviving members of the squad he had brought to the fight, and they headed by Humvee to support the lieutenant's other squad that had come under heavy attack. The Marines from Combat Outpost followed them, all linking up with Weapons Company troops who had finished their fight on Route Apple and were heading the same way.

NORTH END OF SOFIA DISTRICT, ALSO AROUND 3:35 P.M.

Roy Thomas was on his hands and knees after absorbing the grenade blast on the roof of the house he and the others were defending. He had blacked out for a second. But regaining consciousness, the twenty-one-year-old Marine born on the Fourth of July could see with his right eye blood pouring from the left side of his face like a fountain, and his first thought was, *Well, I'm dead.*

Maybe because of the adrenaline pumping through his veins, Thomas climbed to his feet and ran through the doorway leading downstairs. MacIntosh was there and helped him into the living room. The window in that room looked out on the wall behind which the enemy was throwing grenades, and Thomas wanted to move, so they shifted to the kitchen. The group had no corpsman, so MacIntosh, who had first aid training, applied bandages over Thomas's devastated left eye and held them in place by wrapping the top of his head with duct tape. Despite the severity of his wounds, Thomas had the presence of mind to ask for a favor even before MacIntosh finished bandaging him. Would he snap a picture of Thomas? MacIntosh told him to at least wait until he was done wrapping the wound, and then he took the disposable camera that Thomas had fished out of a cargo pocket and, with dishes and a stack of metal cooking pots as backdrop, took a photograph. With blood on his face and staining his flak jacket, Thomas became the portrait of a wounded Marine.

Hundreds of yards to the east, another casualty, Private First Class Justin Woodall, had been calling out Thomas's name in futile desperation. He finally realized that was pointless and he would have to reach Conner and his inter-squad radio to call for help. Woodall climbed to his feet and ran as fast as he could as insurgents opened fire. One round slammed into his back and threw the Marine onto the ground. The bullet was thankfully stopped by a SAPI (or small arms protective insert) plate, a square, ceramic piece of body armor, on the back of Woodall's vest. Still, the impact caused three compression fractures in Woodall's spine, though he knew nothing of this at the time.

He got up and kept running until he reached Conner. "Hey, man, we got to get the fuck out of here," he said to the sergeant. For the moment, they took up defensive positions, with the sergeant on one end and Woodall on the other and a wall separating them inside the structure. Eventually, Conner moved outside and began pulling away from their location, apparently assuming Woodall had done the same.

He began on his own a long, solitary effort to reach the river, all of it in stages. He would search out an area of concealment— either a small berm, a tree, or section of tall grass—wait for a lull in the gunfire, and race in a zigzag pattern to the hiding place. Then he'd scan for targets and repeat the process.

Woodall didn't realize Conner was gone. He had heard him shooting for a time. But then that stopped and he feared the squad leader was killed. Woodall moved carefully around the structure only to find the sergeant was gone. Falling back to his original position in the hut, Woodall could hear Arabic from enemy fighters in a tree line shouting at one another.

He was alone again but strangely felt no panic. His thoughts turned back to a chapel service from the previous day when he had taken communion from Navy chaplain Brian Weigelt. The Marines were always fascinated that the cleric never carried a weapon, and they would ask about it. "The God who protects me at home is the God who protects me here," Weigelt would say.

The nineteen-year-old Marine now took solace from those words even as he realized there were more enemy fighters hunting him than he had bullets left to shoot at them.

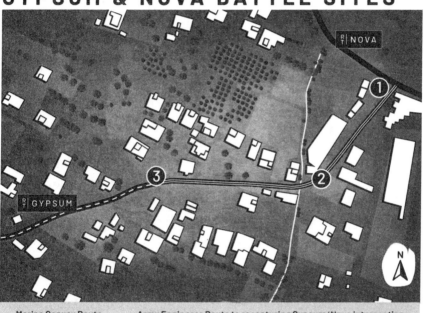

GYPSUM AND NOVA,
ALSO ABOUT 3:35 P.M.

AFTER WATCHING WROBLEWSKI'S convoy drive past and feverishly ordering him by radio to stop, Echo Company Captain Kelly Royer, Third Platoon Second Lieutenant Tom Cogan, and the two dozen or so troops with them started to head across Gypsum on foot. That's when they heard an explosion of gunfire and rocket-propelled grenades at the Gypsum-Nova intersection some six hundred yards away. Royer thought it was the loudest noise he had ever heard in his entire Marine Corps career. And then he and his troops began taking fire from several directions. "It was an enormous [enemy] kill zone," Royer told a Marine historian weeks later, "approximately 450 meters long by 200 to 250 meters wide. They had men all over the place." The captain and some of his men established a command control position on a nearby rooftop. Residential homes stretched out along Gypsum for several hundred yards. Royer was consumed with trying to reach everybody and anybody by radio, with the troops who had vanished into that crucible of gunfire up ahead, with battalion command, with company headquarters, with Wroblewski. He learned over the inter-squad radio that the lieutenant was hit, and he struggled to get more information but maddeningly lost touch with the troops who were with Wroblewski, for at least another forty minutes. The initial onslaught of enemy resistance made it increasingly clear that not only had the insurgents apparently created a slaughter pen at Gypsum and Nova but access to that area was sealed off by a stubborn phalanx of gunmen and machine guns nests on rooftops for hundreds of yards across the southern flank of that area.

The troops with Royer and Cogan had initially spread out as individual Marines sought cover. But little by little, they coalesced into small fighting groups that kept pushing east and north. Cogan led one of them. Weapons Platoon Sergeant Ronnie Ramos led another. One impediment was a broad field about two hundred yards east of Gypsum that stretched out along an area directly

BATTLE, DAY 1: THE AMBUSH

173

south of the Gypsum-Nova intersection. There seemed to be several enemy machine gun nests sweeping the field with interlocking fire as Marines began moving across it. Ramos was trapped for a time behind a palm tree as enemy rounds chewed up the opposite side of the tree where he was crouched. Lance Corporal Jeremy Bennet provided suppressive fire with a light machine gun, ultimately allowing Ramos to break away and retreat to better cover. Ramos and his men remained pinned down at a nearby house for another half hour. Cogan and his cluster of troops nearby were similarly stymied by heavy enemy fire. When they tried to close in on a building where there was a machine gun on the roof, they spotted booby-trapped grenades on the ground with trip wires covering alleyway approaches to the structure.

Cogan shifted west, linked up with Eric Smith's right flank, and arranged to use one of the MK19 automatic grenade launchers on a seven-ton truck to finally destroy the enemy position. The vehicle was moved forward and the weapon brought to bear. But the distance to the target building was too short. The grenade didn't have space to arm itself in flight, and the effect was little more than throwing big rocks. Holes were punched in the structure, but the machine gun kept firing.

The insurgents had succeeded in blocking Royer's relief force from reaching the two Humvees at the center of the ambush site for nearly an hour. Of the fifteen troops caught in that kill zone, seven Marines led by Corporal Marcus Waechter had barricaded themselves in a small cinder block hut off Gypsum. For them, it seemed as if time stood still.

When they first piled into the room, there was sweet relief from the onslaught of weaponry the enemy fired from behind engine blocks on nearby roofs and the countless AK-47 riflemen who drew a bead on the Americans when they were in the street. Waechter estimated there were dozens of armed insurgents out there. The Marines were shocked to find the man in the buttoned-up dishdasha standing inside when they entered. The first two Americans into the room literally had their rifle barrels pressed into his face as he pleaded in Arabic. The young Marines flooding the space were angry, frightened, desperate, and fighting for their lives. Who was this guy? All the shops had been shut down. If he wasn't a merchant, was he the enemy? Corporal Evan Null, the tough former high school wrestler who grew up in the Appalachians of southwest Virginia, threw the man on the dirt floor. The Iraqi could read the malevolence on their faces, and he was on his knees begging.

Attention quickly shifted to defending the hut. Null told Private First Class Matt Scott, who had been the driver of the Humvee, to cover the entrance facing Gypsum. "Sit right there and watch the door." The nineteen-year-old Scott was from Second Platoon while all the others were Third Platoon Marines he didn't know very well. Null and Lance Corporal Justin Tate took opposite corners of a large window facing west. Private First Class Arnold Thao, nineteen, tended to Private First Class Zach Shores's shrapnel wounds. Both had joined the battalion in January right out of the School of Infantry. Scott and Private First Class Ryan Downing were also brand-new Marines. Null gave Downing's shrapnel wounds a once-over and concluded they weren't too serious. Waechter and Otey, the survivor of the first Humvee, rounded out the group that was so tightly packed inside the hut that those not guarding the doorway or window were crammed up against a back wall nearly shoulder to shoulder.

There was still considerable gunfire and explosions outside. It wasn't completely clear whether enemy fighters knew where the Americans had sought refuge or were quickly figuring it out. At one point, machine gun fire raked the outside of the hut, and as rounds pulverized the cinder blocks, sending bits of cement, bullet fragments, or whatever else flying into the room, Scott scrambled to back away from the entryway. His boots kept slipping on the dirt. Downing reached over at the last second and grabbed Scott by the drag handle on the back of his flak jacket, pulling him farther inside the room. The Marines were expecting any second that an RPG round would come smashing through the walls and enemy insurgents would charge in. "I guess we're all going to die today," Null said in his Appalachian drawl. The air inside the cramped quarters was thick with dust.

Through the window, Null spotted an enemy fighter walking toward Gypsum from the north. It was a man wearing a dishdasha, and he had more than one rifle or other weapon hanging under his shirt rocking back and forth with each step, making him look thick and bulky. Clearly, the arms bearer had no idea he was walking past a window of a room full of Marines. He caught sight of them at the very last second, and there was a look of sheer terror on his face as Null, Waechter, and Otey opened fire from just a few feet away. Tate, who was on the north side of the window, actually pulled himself back as the shooting exploded in front of him. The man fell to the ground. Otey walked up, still seething from seeing his friends die minutes before, leaned out the window, pressed his rifle against the man's head, and fired half a magazine until the insurgent's skull came apart.

Good Lord, Tate thought.

Minutes later, two other men walked past carrying rifles and also oblivious that Americans were in the hut. The Marines could see the look of shock on their faces as they gunned them down and kept shooting into the bodies until they stopped moving. *They would have done it to us*, Downing was thinking. At one point, gunfire outside began to die down, replaced by the sound of intermittent, individual gunshots. Downing thought he knew what that was: *These fuckers are executing our guys. They're killing them.*

Meanwhile, Waechter and others with him who had intersquad radios kept trying frequencies to reach any commander, several of whom were only a few hundred yards away. But no one heard them or answered.

The space inside the hut crackled with nervous energy. What could they do? What should they do? Waechter, as leader, was carrying the weight of the world. He felt a strong pull to take action—do something—about comrades from the first truck who might still be alive. Beyond that, how much longer could they remain in this virtual prison cell? Any second, they expected the enemy to attack with overwhelming force and kill them all. "We can't sit here. We're going to die," Tate argued. But the other unknown was understanding where any enemy fire might come from if they stepped outside, in which direction they should shoot as they emerged. The insurgents had the high ground on rooftops, but in which direction? Had they shifted? Were the Marines surrounded?

Waechter remained plagued with a sense of duty to head back outside and lay down a base of fire in the direction of their lost friends. At one point, he and Scott ventured for a few seconds out into the courtyard, only to return as enemy fire pelted the walls. The argument over what to do continued. "Are you fucking crazy?" Downing exclaimed at one point. "We have no idea where anybody is." Otey was emphatic that they'd be as good as dead as soon as they stepped out that door and left the courtyard. Null agreed. They needed a better idea of what they were up against.

It was the most primal of existential debates, and a tortured dilemma for the twenty-one-year-old squad leader, whose Marines were out there somewhere. Finally, someone suggested a possible solution. Send the Iraqi out into the open and see if he survived. That would demonstrate the level of danger. Even to this, there were counterarguments. Someone remarked that it could make their circumstances worse. He would tell the insurgents where the Marines were located, how many there were, and so on. Others felt certain there was no way the enemy would shoot one of their own people. The Iraqi man had been curled up on the dirt floor during part of the fight. Now he was led to the entrance and told to run. Null thought the man wanted out. But to Shores, it seemed like he was terrified.

The man didn't make it more than several dozen yards before

CAVALRY

The soldiers of Second Platoon, Charlie Company, 1st Engineer Battalion, had been cooling their heels for hours until they were finally ordered into the field to support a squad of Marines under attack in the north end of the Sofia District—the men Second Lieutenant Valdes had left behind when he raced to assist the sniper team.

The Army engineers in the five armored personnel carriers raced across the southern edge of Ramadi and then up Route Michigan and turned left on Gypsum. They were heading for Route Nova, where they would make another left turn and drive two and a half miles to reach those Marines. But as they headed up Gypsum, they came upon a stalled convoy of Humvees and seven-ton trucks—Wroblewski's people.

By this time, the direly wounded officer had been transported back to Combat Outpost for helicopter evacuation to a hospital. The Echo commander, Kelly Royer, and Second Lieutenant Cogan had led troops across Gypsum from west to east and tried unsuccessfully to flank insurgents blocking their path to the Gypsum-Nova intersection where two of their Humvees had disappeared nearly two hours before.

The man left in charge of the Marine convoy that the Army engineers came across was Corporal Eric Smith, and he had no way to communicate with Royer or headquarters because the handset for his only radio had been destroyed when Wroblewski was wounded.

For Marines and the Army, the entire battlefield around this ambush site was hampered by an astonishing lack of situational awareness and communication. There was a true fog of war here.

178   **UNREMITTING**

Beyond hearing a horrendous amount of gunfire from the intersection of Gypsum and Nova, Smith, Cogan, and Royer had no idea what had happened to the two Humvees that disappeared in that direction. As a result, their company and battalion headquarters were equally unaware.

The only people who could have told them about the slaughter at that crossroads were Corporal Waechter and his seven men. But they were trapped in a tiny hut, under intense fire, and had no radio communication with anyone.

The engineer platoon was led by Second Lieutenant Wade Welsh, a twenty-four-year-old Iowan. It was a complete surprise to him when he and his men came upon a Marine convoy bunched up along Gypsum, and he certainly had no idea what had happened at Gypsum and Nova.

He only knew that a squad of Marines up to the north—Christopher Conner's men—were in dire shape. Welsh had learned by radio that they had casualties and that attacking enemy fighters had gotten within hand-grenade range. He needed to get up there as quickly as possible.

His APCs squeezed past the stalled convoy vehicles. They spotted a Marine prone on the ground manning a machine gun with spent brass shells all around. Another Marine near a seven-ton truck looked like he was waving them forward. Corporal Eric Smith saw them drive past and was befuddled. Why had these Army vehicles suddenly shown up? If they were there to assist, why hadn't they stopped?

Welsh thought that the Marine waving them forward was pointing them in the best direction to reach the squad miles to the north. He radioed to his men, "Keep going." The net result was that when the armored personnel carriers speeded up and quickly closed that last few hundred yards to the core center of the enemy ambush site, they had no idea what was waiting for them.

But neither did the insurgents know they were coming. The heavy-caliber dishka machine gun, which had been their primary

Battalion and company commanders for the Magnificent Bastards in Ramadi, 2004. Seated and standing from left to right: Headquarters and Service Company Captain Wilson Leech III and First Sergeant Joe Ellis; Echo Company Captain Kelly Royer and First Sergeant Curtis Winfree; Fox Company Captain Mark Carlton and First Sergeant Tim Weber; Battalion commander Lieutenant Colonel Paul Kennedy and Sergeant Major Jim Booker; Golf Company Captain Christopher Bronzi and First Sergeant Patrick DeHerrera; Weapons Company Captain Rob Weiler and First Sergeant Alfonso Mack Jr.

Left: Members of "the Bearded Guys" in disguise standing in front of their painted Opel sedan. From left: Corporal Amir Hekmati, Lance Corporal Amir Heydari, unknown Marine, Sergeant Major Jim Booker.

Below: Phony surveillance cameras developed by Army engineers to discourage the planting of IEDs. Attached to power poles in the city, they were so convincing that insurgents repeatedly tried to blow them up.

Second Lieutenant John Wroblewski photographed on patrol the day before he was killed.

The Philadelphia Inquirer / David Swanson

Above: Weapons Company Captain Rob Weiler in his hooch after a day of combat.

Left: Echo Company 1st Platoon commander Vincent Valdes, shown receiving promotion to first lieutenant.

Three detainees before the ambush at Gypsum and Nova on April 6. All rode in two Marine Humvees at the center of the attack, and it remained unclear what happened to them when the shooting started. Marines are, from left: Lance Corporal Deshon Otey and Lance Corporal Justin Tate, ambush survivors. Otey would later be killed in Marine sniper team assassinations.

Philadelphia Inquirer / David Swanson

Above: Minutes after being wounded by a grenade on April 6, Lance Corporal Roy Thomas asked his friend Lance Corporal Chris MacIntosh to take this picture.

Right: Tank graveyard in the Sofia District, scene of intense fighting on April 6.

Photo carried by several newspapers after fighting broke out across Iraq on April 6, 2004, shows the windshield of a Marine Humvee shattered by heavy-caliber rounds from an enemy machine gun. All but one of the Americans aboard were killed. Image was taken after the ambush when Private First Class Eric Ayon attempted to start the disabled vehicle. Ayon would die from a roadside bomb blast three days later.
Philadelphia Inquirer / David Swanson

Above: Bloodied glasses of Private First Class Ryan Jerabek found at the ambush where he was killed earning a Bronze Star for valor.
Philadelphia Inquirer / David Swanson

Left: Lance Corporal Nathan Appel carrying the remains of Lance Corporal Travis Layfield, killed at the ambush site of Nova and Gypsum on April 6.

Exhausted Golf Company Marines after fighting on April 7. Second row from left: Corporal Jonathan Embrey, Private First Class Daniel Tapia, and Lance Corporal Chris Grimes; front from left: Private First Class Thomas Kraesig and Private First Class Terrence Hayes.
Shutterstock / Maurizio Gambarini

Above: Marines fighting on April 10 from a sewage ditch along a wall where Echo Company Captain Kelly Royer had a bullet impact his helmet. Gun flash from an enemy machine gun is visible in the center of the photo.
Philadelphia Inquirer / David Swanson

Right: Battlefield Cross shrine at Easter Sunday memorial service for fifteen Marines and one sailor killed in combat during the previous eleven days. The battalion suffered seventy-two wounded in that time.
Philadelphia Inquirer / David Swanson

Left: Navy corpsmen Sergio Gutierrez (left) and Tyrynn Dennis, who treated some of the severest wounds during the Ramadi fighting.

Below: Army Captain Jodelle "Jody" Schroeder, critical care nurse who treated wounded Marines, shown with an Iraqi child during a school visit in Ramadi.

Marine Corporal Eric Smith, who would earn the Navy Cross for heroism on April 6, shown here after suffering shrapnel wounds and a concussion in an IED attack on May 27.

Charlie Med full to overflowing during Seabee mass casualty event on May 2.

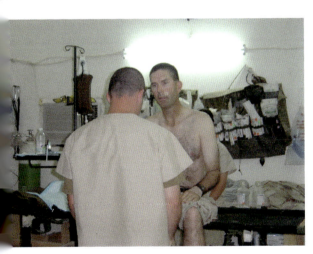

Above: Army Colonel Arthur "Buck" Connor Jr.—commander of 1st Infantry Brigade, 1st Infantry Division—being treated at Charlie Med after being concussed by a roadside bomb on May 26, the first of two severe head injuries for the officer.

Right: Aerial view of the destroyed house where a four-man Marine sniper team was assassinated on June 21. After the killings, the battalion had the building mined with explosives and blown up.

Left: A drawing of Marine Sergeant Kenneth Conde Jr. on display at his memorial inside a Marine Corps University building renamed in his honor at Quantico, Virginia.

Below: Lance Corporal Chris MacIntosh, nicknamed "Rabbit," goofing off.

Marines patrolling through a palm tree forest in the Sofia District of Ramadi.
Philadelphia Inquirer / David Swanson

BATTLE, DAY 1: THE AMBUSH

179

tool of destruction, was useless by then. It had jammed with about ten rounds left to fire. The enemy fighters had been busy gathering up all the weaponry of slain Americans, M16 rifles, Jerabek's M240 machine gun, Cobb's squad automatic weapon, night vision goggles, thermal sights, and bayonets.

The first personnel carrier coming down the road was armed with an American heavy machine gun, a Browning .50-caliber. The gunner was Private First Class Andre Soares, a native of New York City and the son of Brazilian diplomats who had grown up in Paris; he was fluent in French, Portuguese, and English. His buddies called him "Frenchie." As his tracked vehicle neared the final turn before Gypsum swung north to link with Route Nova, the first thing out of sorts that Soares spotted was a Marine helmet lying upside down in the road. *Oh shit, what's going on here?* he thought. Then he saw the RPG-wrecked Humvee that Waechter and his men had abandoned. None of this was what Soares and the other soldiers in the column expected, evidence that something was terribly wrong. And then, as the APC swung left on Gypsum toward the intersection more than one hundred yards away, Soares saw the first Humvee that had been carrying Staff Sergeant Walker and his men. Now there were maybe eight enemy fighters in and around it, looting and celebrating; some held rifles up in the air as if in triumph. In a fraction of a second, the twenty-four-year-old Army engineer opened fire with his .50-caliber, unleashing a burst of heavy rounds in their direction. He did that five or six times as the armored carrier drove into the market area. Enemy fighters fell or fled. The large rounds were pulverizing. One bearded, heavyset man wearing an American flak jacket had the entire upper half of his head ripped away. A gray-haired man in white shirt and trousers was struck in the meaty portion of his right thigh, and the impact nearly severed the limb. Other soldiers in the back of Soares's APC followed suit and raked the area with rifle and medium or light machine gun fire. Even the driver began firing his 9 mm pistol. In a matter of seconds, the soldiers had retaken the intersection. Lieutenant Welsh was in the second tracked vehicle, and everything happened so fast—Soares and the other soldiers firing from the first vehicle cleared the area of enemy fighters so quickly—that Welsh didn't fire the MK19 grenade launcher on his APC. The platoon medic, specialist Justin Springer, was riding in the back, along with the 1st Engineer Battalion's thirty-nine-year-old command sergeant major, Irving "Ray" Bush, who had chosen to join the mission that morning. As Welsh's tracked vehicle rounded the corner following the first APC, Springer caught a glimpse of Marines emerging from the hut where Waechter's men sought cover.

The Marines inside the shed felt a shot of elation when they heard the Army tracked vehicles approaching and Soares's .50-caliber open fire. "Fuck yeah!" one of them yelled. It felt as if they had been trapped in the dusty shed for hours. In fact, the ordeal had lasted about forty-five minutes to an hour. As the armored vehicles passed close by, thoughts turned to friendly fire. So a few cautiously stepped outside and started waving at the column of APCs so the Army could see they were American military.

The lead tracked vehicle with Soares was driven through the T intersection and into the field on the opposite side with insurgents fleeing ahead of it. The enemy stopped to launch a rocket-propelled grenade at the APC that fell short, and Soares responded with a burst from his heavy machine gun. Welsh's APC pulled to a stop directly left of Walker's devastated Humvee. The Marine vehicle was shot to pieces. The front windshield was a mass of gaping, shattered holes. The gun shield for Jerabek's M240 had been scored repeatedly by bullets. There was a large blast hole in the right-rear fender. All four Humvee tires were flattened. The bodies of two Marines lay in the back of the truck.

Behind Welsh, the Army medic, Springer, had been facing the rear of his tracked vehicle, and when it stopped, he looked right and immediately saw the body of an American face up on the ground. Springer was nineteen and from Ossian, Indiana. In high school, he had longed to be an Army infantryman, but that proved impossible after he enlisted and learned from testing that he was color-blind. Still, the Army needed medics, and Springer made that his second choice. The combat he found in Ramadi proved just as real for a medic as an infantryman. Just days before, Springer had lost his best friend in the Army when another medic, Michael Karr, was killed along with four other soldiers in the massive IED obliteration of an armored personnel carrier near Fallujah. Now, he was staring at fresh US casualties. He was in such a hurry to climb out the top of the APC and reach the man that Springer ripped off the holster with his 9 mm and hit the ground without any weapon. He ran over and quickly realized he'd found a corpsman. A medical kit was nearby, and the man was carrying surgical scissors in a front pocket. It was Hospitalman Mendez-Aceves, and he was dead. The APC driver, Army specialist Mike Elledge, twenty-four, of Warm Springs, Arkansas, was ordered to drop the rear hatch on the armored personnel carrier, and Bush and Springer dragged Mendez-Aceves's body inside the vehicle. Then the medic spotted more remains in an alleyway on the road's west side, not far from where he had found the corpsman, and headed out again. Greg Huebbe, a nineteen-year-old Army specialist from Naples, Florida, who had been riding next to Springer in the APC, disembarked to provide security for the medic as he worked.

Welsh, meanwhile, was in a tough spot. He notified Marine battalion command that they had dead troops at Gypsum and Nova. "You need to get these bodies out of here, because I can't escort them back," he told them. It was clear from radio traffic that the Marine squad to the north still needed help. Coming to their assistance was Welsh's original mission. Radios in the APCs had erupted with calls from the wounded radioman there, Lance Corporal Adam Carter, who was at the site where Lance Corporal Thomas had suffered grievous shrapnel wounds from a grenade, the worst of it the loss of his right eye. The Army lieutenant wanted to get going, but he couldn't just abandon this ambush site.

So he decided to split his force. His company commander, Captain Tyler Faulk, would take three APCs and continue up Route Nova to the north. Welsh would leave one vehicle at the intersection and have his APC head back down Gypsum a few hundred yards to fetch the Marines stalled there with their seven-ton trucks. By this time, many of the enemy gunmen who had been blocking the Marine advance had begun to withdraw when the column of Army armored personnel carriers first came up Gypsum. In short order, the lieutenant was back telling Eric Smith to move his men and vehicles up to the intersection. Welsh was frustrated and angry. He had led his platoon into an ambush site without any warning from anyone, and now he still had a mission to finish up to the north. "I'm an officer. You will obey my orders," he told Smith. Shaun Lenz, who was nearby, called out that they had no "comms" and needed a handset for the radio. Someone in the APC tossed one out, and Lenz caught it.

Soon, the Marine convoy was back in motion, following Faulk's APC back into the ambush site. Cogan, Royer, and their men would also be arriving on foot.

Back at the intersection, Springer ventured into the alleyway to reach the body he saw there. It was that of a young man lying face up with a huge, gaping head wound, and shockingly, there was still breath in his body. Springer recognized what was called *agonal respiration*, effectively a dying person's last breath. It quickly ended. Springer caught sight of a second Marine lying face down nearby. He began moving to get a closer look, only to back off when enemy rounds ricocheted off the wall above the medic's head. Insurgents had retreated to the west and were shooting from trees fifty to one hundred yards away. The medic, who had no weapon, pulled out of the alley and looked south on Gypsum, where he could see Waechter's men who had emerged from the cramped hut. Springer ran down to enlist their help, then headed back just as a seven-ton truck rolled into the market area.

Eric Smith found Waechter and asked what had happened.

The squad leader tried to explain the deadly results of the enemy ambush and what happened to the Marines in the first vehicle up near the intersection. "I don't know if they made it, man. I think they're all dead," he said.

Smith was stunned. "They're what?"

"The first vehicle is up there, and I don't think they made it," Waechter repeated.

The grim task of loading the bodies of dead friends for transport back to Combat Outpost commenced. Those who took part or who watched it being done while they held security positions around the intersection felt a confluence of emotions ranging from shock to disbelief, anger to a desire to see someone pay for it all.

As first on the scene, Springer started the process, finally dragging the body of the slain young Marine with the massive head wound out of the alleyway and lifting and pushing it up into the high bed of a seven-ton truck. It was a struggle, and as he labored to shove the body within the grasp of Corporal Frank Gutierrez, who was up in the truck trying to assist, a massive amount of body fluids poured down over the front of Springer's uniform clear down to his boots. The same thing happened to Gutierrez as he yanked the remains into the truck bed. The Humvee that Wroblewski had been riding in was now driven into the intersection. The back of the truck was lower to the ground, and bodies could more easily be loaded into it.

After pulling the second body out of the alleyway, Springer turned his attention to the blood-soaked bed of Walker's truck— the area in the back where most of the Marines had been riding. There were two dead bodies there. With the assistance of others who arrived with the convoy, both bodies were loaded into Wroblewski's Humvee. The medic pulled from his APC the body of Navy corpsman Mendez-Aceves that he had first found shortly after arriving, and the dead sailor was loaded with the others. Staff Sergeant Walker's body was found on the ground near the front-passenger side of his Humvee.

In addition to Walker and Mendez-Aceves, the other dead who were recovered were Lance Corporal Kyle Crowley, the Humvee driver; Lance Corporal Anthony Roberts; Private First Class Christopher Cobb; and Private First Class Ryan Jerabek, who had fought to the death behind his M240 machine gun. The decision was made to evacuate them, along with the wounded Ryan Downing and Zach Shores, back to Combat Outpost. Vehicles began turning around to head south on Gypsum. Springer climbed into Welsh's APC in preparation for resuming their mission to the north.

There were bodies of at least four insurgents scattered around the market area. From inside the armored carrier, Springer looked across the street and could see that one of them was still moving. The man was barefoot and lying on his back. As Springer watched, the large tires of one of the seven-ton trucks making a wide U-turn rolled over the man's midsection and kept going. Springer was certain the driver knew exactly what he was doing. The tire left a wide track across the man's belly and body contents from the pressure of a fourteen-ton vehicle gushed out of his mouth. Bush, the Army command sergeant major, saw it happen as well. Both men would never forget the sight of it.

Eventually, as Royer and his troops filtered into the Gypsum-Nova intersection and expanded their control of the area, and members of Wroblewski's platoon returned from delivering the dead and wounded to Combat Outpost, one other slain American was found. It was Walker's radioman, Lance Corporal Travis Layfield, who had somehow made his way—or been dragged or carried by the enemy—to the opposite side of buildings west of Gypsum. Layfield was found buried in scattered debris.

Meanwhile, an intel specialist with Echo Company, Corporal Charles Lauersdorf, surveyed the ambush site, taking pictures and notes of what he could find. "A prime area for an ambush," he wrote in his report. "This attack was well planned and coordinated." The Marines found two cars filled with weapons.

BATTLE, DAY 1: THE AMBUSH

Embedded photojournalists who were with Royer were also on the scene and began taking photographs. Some of the images would land on the front pages of newspapers covering the widespread violence unfolding across Iraq. There was a snapshot of a Marine carrying Layfield's body in a bag over his shoulder and another of Jerabek's crushed, bloodstained glasses lying in the dirt. One iconic image of Private First Class Eric Ayon, one of the seven-ton drivers. He had slipped into the driver's seat of Walker's Humvee to see if he could start the engine. The vehicle was disabled. But the photograph of Ayon's face behind the bullet-shattered windshield spoke volumes.

Some two hours earlier, back at Combat Outpost, Lieutenant Wroblewski had been brought in according to Eric Smith's improvised field evacuation plan and loaded onto a helicopter for a flight to a hospital. His platoon sergeant, Damien Coan, was there and called out to his commander, whom he respected and cared about deeply. Gunnery Sergeant Bernard Calvin Coleman did the same. Wroblewski gave them a thumbs-up. But the lieutenant was hemorrhaging from a severed artery near the site of his head wound, and during the flight, somewhere over Iraq, the twenty-five-year-old officer went into cardiac arrest and died.

The hatchback Humvee filled with the bodies of so many dead Americans was pulled into the cavernous hangar bay at Combat Outpost. Marines who hadn't been out on any patrols or missions that morning came rushing out of their quarters, some still in T-shirts and boxer shorts, completely unaware of what had happened until they saw blood dripping out of the back of the vehicle, and then stood transfixed as the hatchback was lifted to reveal a pile of bodies. Lance Corporal Derek Callaway was one of those watching. The nineteen-year-old thought he saw the body of Staff Sergeant Walker on top of the pile. Marines in the front of the truck were yelling something about "being under attack." Callaway couldn't really comprehend it all.

Navy corpsmen rushed to wave the Marines away—they didn't need to see any of that—and to lay the remains on the concrete floor, each covered with a white sheet. A small break room nearby where there was a TV and freezer for icing up water bottles would eventually be turned into a makeshift morgue. One of the sailors was Hospital Corpsman Third Class Kevin Barger. He was twenty-three and a native of tiny Big Creek in the Appalachian Mountains of eastern Kentucky who had been drawn to the medical field because a grandfather he idolized served as a Navy corpsman. Now, as he and the other sailors moved bodies of slain Americans, Barger was conscious of how well he knew so many of the dead, looked after them, nursed them, accompanied them on field operations, or helped one or more to bed after returning to the barracks falling-down drunk back in the States. He tried not to look at faces. He didn't want emotions interfering with the task at hand: conducting a final check for life signs, cleaning up each of the bodies, cataloging an official time of death. The plan worked until another corpsman stopped him. "Hey, HN3, be careful with this one. This is one of our own." Barger looked down to see the face of Fernando Mendez-Aceves, a fellow corpsman and close friend. It was a shock. He hadn't known that Mendez-Aceves was dead until he found himself lifting the sailor's body.

MISSING IN ACTION

After leaving Justin Woodall, Sergeant Chris Conner spent the next hour or more trying to make his way to the Euphrates, covering about five hundred yards. At one point, an enemy fighter with an AK-47 charged at him, only to dodge behind a tree when Conner raised his rifle to shoot. For a frightening few seconds, the sergeant's gun jammed, and he raced to clear it, working the mechanisms and inserting new magazines until he was finally able to discharge a round and shoot the man. As Conner continued

BATTLE, DAY 1: THE AMBUSH

to move toward the river, he could hear Arabic voices along the water's edge and feared insurgents were surrounding him.

Just then, two Humvee-mounted platoons of Weapons Company along with the company commander, Captain Rob Weiler, were approaching from the southwest after fighting their way up Nova.

The battered squad of Marines who had been fending off attacks from the house where Lance Corporal Thomas was wounded by a grenade fired a star-cluster flare to reveal their location, and the arriving quick-reaction forces linked up with them. Almost simultaneously, enemy forces along the riverbank to the northeast and in a house to the south of Nova opened fire with rifles and machine guns. Weiler directed one of his platoons, led by Lieutenant JD Stephens, to sweep the fields and the house with .50-caliber machine guns and MK19 automatic grenade launchers. Behind this carpet of fire, Weiler ordered his other platoon commanded by Lieutenant Dave Dobb to dismount and move troops across fields to the north side of Nova toward the river.

Weiler made his way into the besieged house, where he learned two men were missing—Conner and Woodall—and found two others wounded: Thomas and Carter, the squad radio operator. They also learned that Nova was blocked to the east by the IED the squad had found hours before during their foot patrol.

As Thomas was carried out on a stretcher, Stephens, his former platoon commander, called out to him, "Hey, Thomas, I bet I can beat you at PFT now," referencing physical fitness training.

Conner, meanwhile, had watched the Marines driving up Nova from an open field where he was hugging the ground as heavy machine gun fire raked the area around him. He could hear rounds impacting close by and passing overhead. Minutes later, Dobb's men approached on foot, and Conner was finally rescued. They also found two dead enemy fighters nearby, likely killed by the .50-caliber guns, and exchanged fire with a third one, who retreated down the riverbank, leaving a trail of blood.

188 UNREMITTING

Woodall was officially listed as missing in action at 5:05 p.m. The worst was feared. Marines were all too aware of what had happened in Fallujah the week before when the four security contractors had been intercepted and slaughtered in the streets.

Minutes earlier, however, Private First Class Woodall remained barricaded in the hut and was working carefully to make every shot count. This was basic boot camp firearms training, firing his weapon at the end of an exhaled breath when his aim was steadiest. But every time he came around the corner of the doorway to take aim, more of the enemy had closed in. At one point, he emerged with his rifle, and there was an insurgent with a gun, a man in his twenties, standing right at the end of Woodall's rifle muzzle. The Marine shot him down.

Seconds later, something detonated against the building. Woodall thought it might have been a rocket-propelled grenade. Surprisingly, the walls held, but debris billowed in and the air was thick with dust and grit. As he ran through the difficult paces of changing out a magazine with his wounded right hand, Woodall was terrified to suddenly see a man step in through the doorway. The enemy fighter was practically face-to-face with him, and the Marine moved almost reflexively for his military Ka-Bar knife attached to his vest by a cord. He grasped the knife and thrust the seven-inch blade into the man's throat, backing him out of the room, before pulling the knife out and watching the insurgent fall to the ground at the doorway entrance. Woodall was so jacked up on adrenaline that he finished loading his rifle and just started firing indiscriminately out the doorway. Then he cursed himself for having wasted so many bullets.

He was now down to his last magazine, and thought, *This is it. This is the way it ends.*

But to his astonishment, he could see the enemy falling back.

US reinforcements had arrived, including Bradley Fighting Vehicles from the west, along with Lieutenant Vincent Valdes and surviving members of the squad he had taken south to assist the snipers, and members of the relief force that had been assembled

BATTLE, DAY 1: THE AMBUSH 189

out of Combat Outpost. After Dave Dobb's successful effort to locate Conner, Weiler had Lieutenant Stephens and his platoon dismount and sweep along the north edge of Nova to find Woodall. He directed Valdes to do the same along the south side.

In addition, the Charlie Company engineers who had captured the Gypsum-Nova intersection where six Marines and a sailor were killed were approaching from the southeast up Nova.

Stephens and one of his people found Woodall. There were bodies of enemy fighters on the ground around where the Marine was holed up in his hut. Woodall could hear someone yelling over a radio, "We found him! We found him!" Lance Corporal Brian Telinda, who had fought with the snipers down at the tank graveyard, was nearby. He was the first person Woodall actually recognized, and when he caught sight of him, Woodall broke down in tears. The two men embraced. Woodall said he was craving a cigarette, and Telinda gave him his last one. The former MIA was led across two hundred yards of plowed ground to Army Lieutenant Welsh's APC, where medic Justin Springer—who had found so many dead troops back at the Gypsum-Nova intersection who were beyond his help—finally had the chance to treat someone who was alive—and he bandaged Woodall's wounds.

It turned out that the house on the south side of Nova from where enemy fire was directed at Weiler's forces when they first arrived was the same walled compound where Chris MacIntosh and Eric Akey had killed several enemy gunmen in the bloody carport skirmish.

With Marines and Army armored columns now approaching from east and west, the insurgents abandoned the house, and Stephens's troops cleared it. They found the carport and the car where MacIntosh and Akey had waited to make their last stand. And they found the pool of blood spilled by the enemy gunmen who were killed there. The bodies were gone. They also discovered an enemy storage area inside the house filled with weapons, IED-making material, and Iraqi cash. And there were signs that the sedan in the carport was being prepared to be used as a bomb, or as the US military would later designate by acronym, a VBIED, for *vehicle-borne IED*. An incendiary grenade was used to destroy it.

Sometime during the hours and days after April 6, battalion Sergeant Major Jim Booker arrived at Combat Outpost and sought out Marcus Waechter and his squad, who were told to assemble in their barracks, on their racks, and wait for the sergeant major.

Booker arrived and saw there was only a portion of the squad. Empty beds were everywhere. Booker exploded. "I told you, 'All Marines to be on your fucking racks!'" he yelled. "Where's everybody at?"

A moment of silence was finally broken by Otey, who, in a calm voice and without a hint of irony or defensiveness, simply began pointing at each empty rack around the room and saying, *He's dead. He's dead. He's dead. He's dead. He's in the hospital. He's in the hospital.*

Booker, who pulled up a chair, was speechless.

"Oh."

He hadn't realized how this one squad had been hit so hard and lost more than half its people to death or wounds. (Tate would soon be flown to a military hospital in Baghdad to have a tiny piece of shrapnel removed from his left cornea, damage a physician told him could have cost him vision in that eye. He fully recovered.)

Booker surveyed the room where empty racks now held new meaning.

"Holy shit," he said.

The sergeant major would spend the night of April 6 sleeping in the patient hold area of Charlie Med at Camp Ramadi, to be near his wounded men.

On April 6, the battalion suffered eleven Marines and one sailor killed, along with seventeen Marines and two corpsmen wounded, eight of them severely enough to be evacuated back to the US.

BATTLE, DAY 1: THE AMBUSH

Kenneth Conde, the twenty-two-year-old sergeant who took a bullet to the shoulder only to keep fighting, would receive a Bronze Star for valor because of his heroism on April 6. So would Roy Thomas, for leading Conner's squad and absorbing a grenade blast to save a comrade; Joe Hayes, for leading a defense of Marines after being wounded; medic Justin Springer, for braving enemy fire to reach slain troops at Gypsum and Nova; Lieutenant Wade Welsh for breaking the ambush at the same intersection; Marine Lieutenant Donovan Campbell for reaching an embattled squad in South Ramadi; and Ryan Jerabek, posthumously, for his fight to death at the Gypsum-Nova crossroads.

Eric Smith, the twenty-one-year-old corporal from Waxahachie, Texas, who took over from his mortally wounded platoon commander, sprinted across gunfire-swept fields more than once to retrieve his wounded lieutenant, organized that lieutenant's medical evacuation, and led Marines in fending off attacks before eventually moving to take control of the Gypsum-Nova intersection from Army engineers, would eventually be awarded the Navy Cross, second only to the Medal of Honor for heroism.

While the number of Americans who died in Ramadi that day sent shock waves through the community of battalion families back in the US, most American media coverage of the day's events—with the exception of David Swanson's account in the *Philadelphia Inquirer*—had little to say about the Ramadi fighting other than the number killed. Sucking up most of the news-cycle oxygen was the battle for Fallujah, where two Marine battalions on April 6 launched a pincer attack into the city to trap insurgents, and the continuing Moqtada Sadr Shiite uprisings in Baghdad and southern Iraq.

President Bush had delivered a speech on that Monday, April 5, vowing to "stay the course in Iraq."[2] But following the news of US losses in Ramadi, he kept a low profile at his ranch near Crawford, Texas, conducting a twenty-minute phone conference call with top cabinet officials over the Iraq events.[3] Defense Secretary Donald Rumsfeld told reporters that the number of Iraqi insurgents involved in the fighting was "relatively small."[4]

The unacknowledged reality was that on the same day the Marines seized the initiative to attack insurgents in Fallujah, twenty-five miles down the road, enemy factions seized the initiative to attack 2nd Battalion, 4th Marines. Joe Dunford, Mattis's chief of staff and a future chairman of the Joint Chiefs of Staff, would years later define initiative as deciding when and where to attack an enemy force.

"We're meeting them at a time and place of their choosing, which by definition means they have the initiative," Dunford said, adding that in Ramadi, "the enemy had the initiative."

That same evening, Buck Connor called Mattis to describe the battle and the surprising skill and coordination of the enemy. "This is a different breed of cat," he told Mattis. "They actually stand and fight."

Mattis thought it was proof the enemy had skilled junior-level commanders, something akin to sergeants in the Marine Corps, who showed discipline. "The sophistication that 2/4 ran up against was on the NCO level, and it was very, very good. Base of fire. Fire-and-maneuver elements. Skirmish lines. Snipers up in trees. Dragunov rifles. Marines killed with one shot to the head or neck," he told the author eight weeks later.

Battalion commander Paul Kennedy came away from the fight uncertain about the enemy strength he was facing. "It created a problem in our understanding of how big he was," Kennedy told the author weeks after the battle. The battalion commander was impressed with the insurgency's tactical military skills. It had organized two major areas of attack in separate sectors of the city and then within those two areas launched multiple assaults, including ambushes within ambushes designed to block reinforcements. "That's a military tactic. That's not Jethro and Jed getting out there with their shotguns." Enemy leaders had set up interlocking

BATTLE, DAY 1: THE AMBUSH

fields of machine gun fire, created preestablished fallback positions, and even made use of military sand tables—an age-old practice of planning attacks on a miniature battlefield, some of which the Marines found. Kennedy was certain that he had met with some of these enemy leaders during meet-and-greet sessions over lunches. "They're smart guys. You talk to these guys, the light is on. You know that he knows that you know—that kind of thing."

Echo Company commander Kelly Royer was equally impressed with the combatants his men fought in the Sofia District on April 6, particularly at the Gypsum-Nova ambush site. They were "professionals" in his view. "They didn't mutilate the [American] bodies. They didn't disrespect the bodies at all," he told a visiting Marine Corps historian weeks later.

As a precaution after the heavy attacks, the Marines began to erect silhouettes on some of their fighting positions—cardboard cutouts draped with a helmet and flak jacket to make it appear they had more troops defending a position than actually existed.

Reflecting on the fight, Booker was amazed that an entire city had managed to keep the attack a secret. "There seems to be a handshake they have that we'll never be able to penetrate," he told the author in June 2004.

Years later, Joe Dunford said that what the insurgents accomplished in Ramadi April 6 was unique. He said that while there were similarly sophisticated enemy tactics on display elsewhere in Iraq, "Ramadi was an example of the highest level of coordination that we saw in the insurgency."

Sergeant Kenneth Conde came away from April 6 with new-found respect for an adversary he now saw as formidable. "We were told again and again, 'These guys are cowards, and they're going to fire an RPG, maybe an IED, and they're going to take off,'" he told the author. "[But] these guys—it was really surprising to me—they would do the same thing we would do."

He recalled a man who fired a rocket-propelled grenade and then, rather than run, picked up his rifle to keep fighting. "He stayed there, knowing that we were going to kill him. . . . Knowing that death is imminent, and he chose to stay," Conde said. "I don't hate them. They're people just like me, fighting for something they believe in. And that's the worst kind of enemy."

The first night after the fighting, every time Sergeant Romeo Santiago closed his eyes, he would see the face of the sniper in black he had charged through the palm grove at the tank grave-yard to kill. He'd fall back to sleep, see the face, and wake up again. For the next several days, Santiago felt more comfortable leaving his body armor on all the time, even in the chow hall at Combat Outpost.

Ryan Miller's nightmare lasted years. The private first class who, at age nineteen, had fired hundreds if not a thousand rounds from his truck-mounted machine gun near the Gypsum-Nova intersection. He was transported back there in his dreams, clearing houses with other Marines. Always, no matter how many enemy fighters they killed, more kept coming, arising from the sand by the hundreds.

Deshon Otey's recurring nightmare was about dying. He was in Ramadi, somewhere trying to grab some sleep, the one commod-ity of which there was never enough. He had escaped the enemy on April 6 when he fled a bullet-riddled Humvee at the Gypsum/Nova intersection. But in the dream, that enemy finally finds him. They creep up on him in his slumber, and Otey struggles to rouse him-self to fight back. But they are too many and overwhelming.

8

BATTLE, DAY 2

EXTENDING THE HAND OF FRIENDSHIP

AFTER THE FIGHTING ended on April 6, Chris Bronzi met with his Golf Company Marines to tell them they would be going right back into combat the next day. Two of his men had been killed and four badly wounded. The mission for April 7 was simple: Find and kill those responsible. But he was careful with his rhetoric. This wasn't about revenge, it was about aggressive engagement if the enemy chose to fight. The thirty-year-old company commander was, after all, a student of Lieutenant Colonel Paul Kennedy's oft-repeated dictum about "battlefield character," the concept that however harsh the bloodletting, it was essential to retain one's honor and avoid anything that smacked of a war crime. Bronzi admonished his Marines accordingly that night. But he also wanted to instill in them the need to get the job done.

Come Wednesday, April 7, they would return to the battle-field, the same neighborhood where enemy gunmen had fought so hard to isolate and destroy two of Bronzi's squads the day before.

To err on the side of caution, the day would begin with an olive branch. A brigade psychological operations unit, or psyops team, would be escorted into the city. The two up-armored Humvees were equipped with loudspeakers and reams of leaflets, and the mission was to spread the word to Ramadi citizens in recorded and written Arabic that coalition forces were not the enemy. Weapons Company's Third Platoon would accompany the psyops mission with executive officer Lucas Wells, who had been a major player in the Valentine's Day brouhaha on the beach shortly before the battalion went to war.

Third Platoon was Kenneth Conde's unit, the sergeant who took a bullet to the shoulder and kept fighting the day before. He and his Marines had seen the worst of the enemy just twenty-four hours earlier. And now they were to hand out notes of friendship to anyone they could find. Wells could barely look them in the eye when he gave them the mission. They left Hurricane Point at 9:00 a.m. and within an hour were moving slowly down Route Michigan through the market area, where throngs filled the street. Marines dutifully delivered leaflets from the backs of their trucks, and Wells admired their discipline. Seeing comrades killed and wounded one day, extending the hand of friendship the next.

It was slapped away. An eerie quiet prevailed as a sea of angry faces peered back at the Marines. People began ripping up the papers, displaying the soles of their feet as a cultural fuck you, and finally, throwing rocks.

The convoy made its way to the Saddam Magnificent Mosque, where it was supposed to turn around and repeat the process on the return, but leadership thought better of it, and they headed east.

Meanwhile, the forty Marines and sailors of Bronzi's Second Platoon gathered at a soccer field rally point about four hundred yards north of Route Michigan, and three squads fanned out in a satellite patrol walking through the same market area and then on to the previous day's battlefield. The Marines approached on foot,

BATTLE, DAY 2

and the crowds that had swarmed the psyops mission dispersed. Merchants began closing up shops. All were unsettling clues of violence ahead.

The platoon was commanded by Second Lieutenant Erik Quist, twenty-six, the latest in a long line of Marines in his family. His father, Burton Quist, was a career officer who fought in Vietnam. The son had never intended to do likewise. But his tech job out of college, while gainful, did not satisfy. Erik always remembered the words his father brought home from work each night: "So what did you do for God and country today?"[1]

Satellite patrolling this time was not as spread out and disconnected as the day before. Squads kept about two hundred yards apart as they crossed Michigan and moved south across the cemetery where fighting had persisted the day before. At 11:15 a.m., as the troops moved southeast, a rocket-propelled grenade swooshed in and exploded. No one was hurt, but as Second Squad searched the house thought to be the source of the rocket, an explosion outside wounded Lance Corporal Richard V. Cantu Jr., and AK-47 fire rattled from the south and east. Cantu was pulled inside the house that the squad now used as a fort. Quist learned by radio that both of his other squads were also under fire. He called for assistance.

A familiar cycle of ambush, reinforcement, and counterattack began. The only difference this time was that additional troops were dispensed more quickly, and Bronzi made sure he had a firm idea of where his people were located.

First to respond was Lieutenant Dave Dobb's platoon, the same Marines who had located Sergeant Chris Conner near the Euphrates River the day before. The six-foot-four-inch Dobb, a native of Holland, Michigan, was commander of Weapons Company's sizable mortar unit. Prior to the deployment, when Kennedy turned Weapons Company into a mobile assault force, putting all its Marines on wheels, the mortarmen were broken into two platoons with the call signs Rainmaker and Sledgehammer. This left Rob Weiler, company commander, with the flexibility of five mobile assault teams. Since the deployment started, Dobb had been in direct command of Rainmaker and on April 7 led those thirty troops along a southern route into the city.

They drove into an ambush as soon as they turned north to link up with Quist's platoon. It bore a terrifying resemblance to the ambush that had decimated Staff Sergeant Walker's Humvee at Gypsum and Nova. There was a crew-served machine gun just off the roadway firing directly into the front of Dobb's vehicle, shattering the windshield. But the enemy attack was a rush job with a smaller number of fighters and no heavy machine gun like the one that killed so many Americans. In addition, Dobb's men quickly overwhelmed insurgents with return fire, thanks in large part to Lance Corporal Jeremiah Savage, who was manning an M240 medium machine gun directly behind Dobb in the lead vehicle. Savage, twenty-one, who had a daughter at home and an infant son born just four days before, destroyed the enemy machine gun nest with his weapon, killing two insurgents. Marines shot two more enemy gunmen as they advanced.

It was a short, vicious fight, and afterward, Marines policed up the bodies of slain insurgents and collected their weapons. Dobb was struck by the gritty reality of it all. The twenty-six-year-old had grown up amid the placid beauty of his hometown's Dutch heritage and iconic windmill, where the biggest deal all year was the annual Tulip Time festival. Now he was staring into the faces of freshly slain enemy fighters and gathering enemy weapons that were still hot to the touch. Dobb and his men had known there was a war waiting for them in Iraq, but this episode had somehow taken it to a new level.

With the Rainmaker platoon momentarily blocked, Weapons Company commander Rob Weiler immediately went out with First Lieutenant JD Stephens and his people, the same Marines who rescued Private First Class Justin Woodall on Tuesday afternoon.

Three of Weiler's platoons were now in the city and getting into gunfights.

BATTLE, DAY 2

After Dobb and his men cleared the ambush, they reached Quist and evacuated the wounded Cantu to Combat Outpost. Dobb then returned to support Golf Company as more reinforcements flowed into the city, including a squad of Fox Company Marines that had been posted to the Government Center, and Golf Company's Fourth Platoon with Bronzi along. Eventually, Second Lieutenant Jonathan Hesener and Golf Company's Second Platoon would join the fight, the same unit that was hit hard during Tuesday's combat. As insurgent forces tried to maneuver through alleyways to flank Golf Company, Dobb's Marines used their truck-mounted heavy guns to kill at least five.

After the psyops disaster in the marketplace, Duke Wells and Weapons Company's Third Platoon did a loop through the east end of Ramadi and then headed back west along Route Nova when, of all things, they spotted enemy gunmen firing from the tops of palm trees. They were suspended up there in tree-trimming harnesses, and Private First Class Nick Kelly, who was manning a truck-mounted MK19 automatic grenade launcher, angled his weapon upward and started pelting the frond canopies with explosives. Two fighters dropped down and were quickly captured. A third fell mortally wounded from some of the fist-size rounds hitting him in the stomach. When he tried to reach for his weapon, he was killed by Marine rifle fire.

Other insurgents who were in a house along Nova fired a covey of rocket-propelled grenades at the convoy. In response, Marines opened up with heavy weapons, .50-caliber machine guns and MK19s, hammering the structure. As troops dismounted to search the building, its riddled walls reminded Corporal Heath McKenzie of Swiss cheese. The enemy had managed to flee out the rear, although two were found slain nearby, their AK-47s still strapped to their chests. Shockingly, the Marines found a mother and her three children huddled in a bathroom of the riddled building. *Thank God they survived*, McKenzie thought.

As the Marines fell back from the enemy strongpoint they had captured, Lance Corporal Marshall Cummings III suffered a through-and-through gunshot wound in his back and went down. Other platoon members returned fire, and Sergeant Marcel Williams sprinted fifty yards across an open field to reach the wounded man. Williams was a thirty-one-year-old native of Cincinnati, Ohio, and built like a linebacker at six foot one, 217 pounds. He lifted Cummings up over his shoulder, picked up the Marine's light machine gun, and ran nearly seventy-five yards back to the trucks. Cummings was bleeding badly, and the convoy soon headed back to deliver him to Charlie Med at Camp Ramadi.

They left behind an area still crawling with enemy fighters, and as Wells and his men left, JD Stephens with Weapons Company's Second Platoon moved in. Captain Rob Weiler was with Stephens, and they had started the day looking for a fight. Here, they would find it, some of the stiffest resistance of April 7. They had intended to head up toward Route Nova. But the lead truck took a wrong turn down Route Apple, a road running parallel about 560 yards to the south. They stumbled into a full-on enemy assault. It was as if the entirety of Route Apple suddenly erupted in violence. The fight would go on for two hours. At one point, the enemy would unleash a storm of rocket-propelled grenades, with countless numbers of the projectiles fired down the axis of the roadway, many exploding or skipping off the pavement between Humvees. "The enemy possessed an endless supply," Weiler would write in his after-action report. Still, the Americans got lucky. One RPG that hit the front end of the lead truck turned out to be an inert training round. In another instance, Weiler was standing next to his Humvee speaking on the radio to Kennedy when a rocket-propelled grenade struck the open passenger door in front of him and slammed it shut. Mercifully, it also didn't explode but went spinning along the ground. As part of their response, the Marines used one of their heaviest weapons—a truck-mounted, anti-tank weapon, known as a TOW, for *tube-launched, optically tracked, wire-guided missile.* It has a fourteen-pound warhead. As the name indicates, the projectile when loosed would unspool thousands of yards of thin wire as it soared, allowing an operator to precisely guide the warhead to a target. The Marines used it twice, once to destroy the dome of a house from where enemy gunmen were congregated, immediately ending that threat; and the second time to atomize an enemy fighter who had been launching RPGs from behind a cinder block wall far down the street. When Sergeant Shane Nylin—who, the day before, had destroyed an enemy gunman on a motorcycle—suggested they use the TOW missile to kill the fighter, Stephens's knee-jerk reaction was "Are you serious? Do you know how much those things cost?" But then he read the looks on his men's faces and immediately gave the go-ahead. Nylin launched the TOW missile.

Weiler assumed the role of rifleman on the ground assault, throwing smoke grenades to help obscure his advancing Humvees from enemy fire. There were no parallel roads along this portion of Route Apple that might allow Marines to flank enemy positions. So they were left to fight from house to house, entering and clearing structures and then quickly setting up on rooftops to mark enemy positions down the road with smoke, allowing heavy weapons on Humvees to destroy them. In the end, it was a lopsided victory for the Marines. Weiler counted up twenty-one dead enemy fighters, more than were killed on any other Weapons Company mission. Six Marines and two corpsman suffered relatively minor shrapnel wounds, almost entirely from exploding rocket-propelled grenades. Among them was Stephens, the platoon commander, who caught RPG shrapnel in his left leg.

When any fight was over, Marines were always left with the grim task of collecting enemy—those bodies that weren't policed up by retreating insurgents. When this battle on Route Apple ended, slain insurgents were collected and searched for documents and identification. But rather than roll through the city with Humvees full of dead bodies, Weiler ordered that they all be dropped off at an intersection for Iraqi traffic cops to deal with. Stephens was later struck by the insanity of it all, imagining how horrified Americans would be if some armed group littered a neighborhood crossroads with dead people and then simply drove off.

Meanwhile, in the center of the city, it was déjà vu for Golf Company Captain Chris Bronzi. At the end of the first day of fighting on April 6, he had argued that his men remain in the streets for the night to prevent the enemy from reestablishing fighting positions for launching a new round of combat. Instead, he was told to decamp to Combat Outpost for the night.

Now, on this second day, and just as he had feared, Bronzi and his men were back buying the same real estate they had purchased in blood the day before.

The heaviest cost would be an hour or so into the fight. Three squads of Marines from Lieutenant Erik Quist's Second Platoon, along with another squad from Fox Company, were under enemy fire from nearly all directions as they fought to link up with each other through the same streets where Tuesday's combat had unfolded—an area from East Cemetery to the neighborhood where Staff Sergeant Rodriguez and his men had been trapped the day before, and finally to Easy Street. Bronzi and his Fourth Platoon, in a column of five Humvees and a seven-ton truck, had left Combat Outpost and worked their way west to near the Saddam Magnificent Mosque on Route Michigan before turning south to push toward Quist's First Squad of about ten troops. They were near the same place where Deryk Hallal and Moisés Langhorst had died twenty-four hours before. Enemy fire from the northwest and southwest was raking the area, and Marines from First Squad along with those from the newly arrived Fourth Platoon were basically shooting past each other in response, creating a deadly cross fire, where Private First Class Christopher Mabry from Second Squad fell with three rounds to the chest. They were fatal. The nineteen-year-old—another one of Kennedy's high school class of 2003 recruits—was an honor student from Chunky, Mississippi,

BATTLE, DAY 2

203

raised by his grandmother.[2] When Bronzi reached First Squad Marines who were holed up in a compound, Mabry was feverishly being worked over by a corpsman, and the captain quickly arranged a truck medevac back to Combat Outpost.

According to an after-action report, an examination of Mabry's wounds revealed that at least one was caused by a round from a Marine M16 rifle. At least one other was the result of a bullet fired from either an M240 machine gun or an enemy RPK machine gun. The report concluded that at least a portion of Mabry's fatal injuries were the result of friendly fire, though Bronzi would forever reject that his man's death was fratricide.

Within the hour, Golf Company's Third Platoon led by Second Lieutenant Jonathan Hesener would be sent out from Combat Outpost as additional reinforcements. That was the same platoon that suffered mightily the day before with two dead and four wounded. Now, as they headed into battle for the second straight day, they fired at any perceived threats they saw on the streets.

For the next four and a half hours, Bronzi and much of his company would fight their way south and east to clear enemy resistance. It would prove to be a steady slog.

A powerful irony in Ramadi was that the Marines, while shock troops of the world's most advanced military, were fighting without anything like the support that a top-tier force could bring. It was a stark contrast to their brethren advancing through the streets of Fallujah twenty-five miles to the east, who had close air support from Air Force F-16 jets and AC-130 gunships as well as Marine Cobra and Huey helicopters and who made use of the 120 mm cannon on M1 heavy tanks to demolish enemy resistance.[3]

While the Marines in Ramadi were begging for air support, the Marines in Fallujah watched with glee as helicopter gunships destroyed mosques and prayer towers where there were enemy fighters and ammunition depots. After one Cobra team put high-explosive rockets directly into a Fallujah mosque, the forward air controller congratulated them on their "good hits," and the pilots could hear the

Marines in the background shouting, "Fuck yeah! Oorah!" In some cases, the air crews even unloosed ordnance to kill individual insurgents who were trying to shoot them down with RPG launchers. The enemy had learned to modify fuses on the grenades so they would detonate at heights of two hundred to three hundred feet, the altitude where copters were flying. Several of the aircraft would return from these missions with bullet holes through canopies, rocket pods, and rotor blades, but there were no serious injuries.

By contrast, there were heavy restrictions on the use of artillery and air support in the provincial capital of Ramadi. Brigade commander Buck Connor had six self-propelled Paladin howitzers around the city, but they were largely forbidden from firing into urban areas for fear of killing innocent civilians and alienating the population. There were also attack helicopters overhead, but the pilots would decline to fire for the same reason. What the Magnificent Bastards were left with in Ramadi, so far as air support, was calling in F-16 or F/A-18 jets to do low lightning passes over the city, break the sound barrier in the process, and maybe frighten the enemy with the boom.

The reality was that with few exceptions, 2/4 Marines and the enemy they fought were at times evenly matched in firepower.

"WEAPONS COMPANY AND GOLF CRUSHED THEIR ATTACKERS WITH THE VENGEANCE OF THE RIGHTEOUS."

Still, the Marines steadily advanced. Bronzi was following behind Quist's Second Squad and was there when they were stopped at a cross street by a well-emplaced enemy machine gunner. He watched in awe as the squad leader, Sergeant Elijah Abbott, calmly slung his M16 rifle, lifted a bazooka-like launcher, and, on one knee and in one fluid motion, moved around a corner into the open, fired the rocket, destroyed the machine gunner, and then, grabbing his rifle, turned to his men, and said, "Let's go."

As Quist and his now-reunited platoon pushed east, they ran into another wall of resistance as they tried to cross Easy Street.

BATTLE, DAY 2

There were more enemy machine gun nests and fighters with RPG launchers positioned down a series of alleyways running east off Easy Street. The heavily defended section stretched about three hundred yards. While Quist and his men took up overwatch posts on rooftops along the avenue to return fire, the Fox Company squad commanded by Second Lieutenant Joseph Denman moved farther south and then east to outflank the insurgents. But the enemy saw them coming and raked the squad with machine gun fire. Five Marines were wounded, including Denman, who caught shrapnel in his right eye. The wounds were relatively minor and all of them eventually returned to duty. But in the short term, all had to be evacuated, and the advance was stalled until Weapons Company Marines arrived with truck-mounted heavy weapons to force insurgents to pull back.

More than five hundred yards to the south, Golf Company's Fourth Platoon, under the command of Second Lieutenant Craig Flowers, was fighting into the southern end of the city. Bronzi had moved with his radioman from Quist to Flowers and was working to link up with one of Flowers's squads that had pushed far out in front of the advance. Bronzi wanted to ensure they had radio communication. By the time he reached them, the squad of eight Marines was under intense fire. Four of them had shrapnel wounds and with Bronzi forced their way into a walled compound to take refuge in the house there. Suddenly, the Golf Company commander and those Marines were now isolated and effectively cut off. Bronzi attempted to lead them out of the compound to push east toward the large soccer stadium across Easy Street. But as soon as they stepped outside the walls, enemy machine gun fire erupted, and Lance Corporal Kevin Miller Jr., who already had shrapnel wounds to his left leg, went down when a bullet struck him in the back. Bronzi thought it was a serious wound, and they retreated back into the compound. But once inside, several of the troops broke out in laughter because Miller, in fact, was unharmed. The bullet had struck his armored plating. He just had the wind knocked out of him. Still, Bronzi thought they should stay put for the moment, and he and the others took up positions on the roof to return fire.

Lieutenant Jonathan Hesener and his Third Platoon coordinated with Bronzi by radio and moved to within about 350 yards of the captain's position, setting up a defensive line around the Al Farouk water tower southwest of the soccer stadium. They were prepped for anything, and when Corporal Jonathan Embrey—Chaps, who had fought at East Cemetery where Jeremiah Letterman was wounded the day before—saw a man with a rifle in a building window and opened fire, a dozen other Marines and an M240 medium machine gunner followed suit, unleashing a hailstorm of bullets that riddled the structure.

Bronzi had a flare sent up to show his position to Hesener. The wounded men with the captain could still walk, and the squad was now running low on ammunition. At their urging, Bronzi elected to make another break for freedom. This time, under enemy fire, they crossed the last few hundred yards to Easy Street and linked up with Hesener and his men.

Soon, Fourth Platoon joined them. Bronzi now had about sixty troops with him, and they were all under a steady stream of enemy fire from the east, west, and south. Despite whatever casualties they had suffered, the insurgent force was not going away. The captain was in radio communication with Cobra gunships overhead and made clear where he was located. Bronzi asked the pilots to open fire on any rooftop shooters they could see anywhere across the southern edge of the city.

It was all enemy territory, he told the pilots. But they refused. They wanted precise map-grid locations on each target and wanted to be talked in on each attack. Bronzi was getting angry but tried to comply. The pilots still declined. Fear of collateral deaths and damage in this provincial capital was just too strong.

The result was that Bronzi and his troops, along with a Weapons Company escort that eventually joined them, moved back to Combat Outpost under almost continuous fire.

BATTLE, DAY 2

The day's fighting was not entirely decisive for either side. While the Americans lost only one Marine killed in action, twenty-five troops were wounded, compared with nineteen on April 6. Fortunately, only two of the twenty-five required evacuation back to the States. The others eventually returned to duty.

The enemy, on the other hand, had paid a steep price. The Americans could see it from the miles of funeral processions that later weaved through the city, and there was a CIA report that about 180–200 bodies had been stacked up at the city morgue after two days of fighting. And those were bodies that weren't claimed by Ramadi residents, suggesting they were fighters from outside the city. Other reports put the total figure of enemy dead from the two days at 400 or more.

Perhaps the most profound evidence of a decimated insurgency was on the morning of the next day, Thursday, April 8, when Marines once again took to the streets and there were no attacks. That was despite earlier intelligence that the enemy planned a three-day offensive in Ramadi. And it wasn't as if the Marines didn't offer a target. In what was called Operation County Fair, Lieutenant Colonel Paul Kennedy had the battalion sweep through the entire residential area where Chris Bronzi and his men had fought for two straight days, a section of neighborhoods south of the Saddam Magnificent Mosque that covered about four tenths of a square mile. Beginning predawn, they went through every house. There was no resistance.

One of the most amazing discoveries in one location was more than $800,000 in American currency, more money than Bronzi had ever seen or ever would see, he was thinking.

Meanwhile, 1st Marine Division commander Jim Mattis felt certain the attack on Fallujah was just a few days from victory.[4] There were now four Marine battalions pushing into a city half the geographic size of Ramadi, where much of the population had fled. Winning quickly was vital. The general had stripped out battalions from areas outside Fallujah to feed the assault, and his overall forces across southwest Iraq were now stretched thin. "We are moving aggressively against the enemy across our zone," he wrote in an April 8 memorandum, "but there are enemy forces operating in areas where we have no forces and the Iraqi security forces are impotent."[5]

Indeed, hundreds of Iraqi soldiers and police trained by American troops and slated to fight alongside Marines had deserted. Many joined the insurgency. "Their treachery has certainly cost us killed and wounded," Mattis wrote.[6]

And the rebellion was metastasizing. Beyond Fallujah and Ramadi, and the Shia uprising in Baghdad, violence had spread to Iraqi provinces north and northeast of Baghdad.[7] More importantly in the short term, coalition supply lines were effectively severed during several days in April as enemy sappers destroyed a number of key bridges and highway overpasses along Route 1, the primary north–south artery for bringing supplies from Kuwait.[8] In addition, elaborate ambushes were set in place against supply convoys, killing American troops and civilian drivers, reducing dozens of US long-haul tractor trailers to burning hulks along desert highways. American forces began running short of fuel, ammunition, and food as a result. The most dramatic ambush was on Good Friday, April 9, against a convoy escorted by an Army reserve unit out of Bartonville, Illinois, that led to the capture of an American soldier, Private First Class Keith "Matt" Maupin, who would be listed for years by the US government as POW. The convoy was an assemblage of twenty-six vehicles that included seventeen Army tractors, each hauling five-thousand-gallon tankers, operated by American civilians working for defense contractor Kellogg Brown & Root. There were five escort gun trucks, and several of the soldiers, including twenty-year-old Maupin, rode shotgun in some of the tractor trailers. The convoy was traveling from a logistics center near Balad, north of Baghdad, to Baghdad International Airport and, as it neared its destination, entered an ambush zone extending four to five miles with 150–200 Mahdi Army gunmen. Fuel tankers exploded, and tractors were run off the road. One soldier and six drivers were

BATTLE, DAY 2

209

killed. Eight other soldiers and four drivers were wounded. A second soldier's body was found days later. Maupin and a driver were captured. The driver would eventually escape. Insurgents would initially release a video showing Maupin alive. A second video released in June would purportedly show his execution.

But it was of such poor quality that the US military would continue to search for the soldier and list him as a prisoner of war for four years until his body was located.[9]

The greatest setback for Mattis and his 1st Marine Division would also arrive on Good Friday with orders from Lieutenant General Ricardo Sanchez, commander of coalition forces, to halt the advance on Fallujah. Mattis was furious. He had never wanted the mission in the first place. But once ordered to do so, he thought it foolish not to finish the job, famously paraphrasing a Napolean quote to CENTCOM commander John Abizaid: "If you start to take fucking Vienna, take fucking Vienna!"

But if the Marines had been winning the ground war in Fallujah, they were losing the information war as international news outlets, including Al Jazeera, aired daily footage of the violence. Under growing pressure, members of Iraq's provisional governing council threatened to quit if the Marine assault wasn't stopped, and President Bush relented. A ceasefire commenced. Discussions between US military leaders and former Iraqi generals led to the formation of the Fallujah Brigade, made up of former members of the Iraqi military. Security for the city was eventually handed over to the new brigade, but the city ultimately became an insurgency haven and stronghold, as well as a major propaganda victory, as Marines withdrew.

Back in the United States, Marine Corps notification officers began fanning out into communities with their angel-of-death duties, notifying 2/4 families that their worst fears had come true. After two days of enemy assaults, thirteen Bastards had been killed and forty-four wounded. In the small Iowa village of Jefferson, hometown to Benjamin Carman, officers drove up from Omaha and stopped at a gas station, seeking directions to the family residence. So small is Jefferson, situated in vast fields of corn and soybean, that by the time the slain Marine's mother, Marie, was notified, word had already spread through town that something terrible had happened to one of their own. When Ben's father, Nelson, got a call at work to come home, his wife on the line was so distraught, he struggled to understand what she was saying.

Back in Ramadi, Paul Kennedy felt he had some explaining to do to those families back home.

Harkening back to Vietnam, Kennedy wrote in a letter to wives that "the last two days have been the hardest two days this battalion has faced in over 30 years. Within the blink of an eye the situation went from relatively calm to a raging storm."

His themes were an enemy that was tough, if treacherous, and a Marine fighting force—their husbands—that was unrelenting.

"The enemy did not run; they fought us like soldiers. And we destroyed the enemy like only Marines can. By the end of the evening [of April 6] the local hospital was so full of their dead and wounded that they ran out of space to put them. Your husbands were awesome."

So far as the fight on the seventh, Kennedy wrote, "Weapons Company and Golf crushed their attackers with the vengeance of the righteous."

"The news looks grim from back in the States," he wrote. "We did take losses that, in our hearts, we will always live with. The men we lost were taken within the very opening minutes of the violence. They could not have foreseen the treachery of the enemy and they did not suffer. . . . It will be a cold day in Hell before we are taken for granted again."

When Kennedy wrote this letter, ninety-one members of the battalion had been wounded and sixteen killed in combat since the deployment began. Neither he, nor anyone else, could know that the Magnificent Bastards were not even halfway through their toll of casualties from Ramadi.

9

BATTLE, DAY 3

I'm a rolling thunder, pouring rain,
I'm comin' on like a hurricane.

—"Hells Bells," AC/DC, played at
the outset of combat, April 10

THE DAY AFTER Paul Kennedy wrote his letter of condolence and bravado to the families back home, the battalion suffered another death.

It was Echo Company, and the circumstances were almost mockingly familiar—another roadside bomb, another tragedy at the dreaded Gypsum-Nova intersection, and another story about a Marine named Eric Ayon.

Ayon was a native of Southern California, who married his high school girlfriend, Angie Vasquez. He set aside a childhood dream of joining the Marine Corps when his son, Joshua, was born. But when the boy was old enough that Ayon believed Joshua would remember his father if anything happened, Eric Ayon enlisted.[1]

BATTLE, DAY 3

He was twenty-six and a military truck driver who had fought on April 6 at the Gypsum-Nova intersection where six Marines and a sailor were killed. By sheer chance, he had his photograph taken that day sitting in the front seat of a bullet-shattered Humvee by an embedded journalist, David Swanson of the *Philadelphia Inquirer.* The next day, when Swanson showed Ayon how the photograph had been published by several newspapers, the Marine smiled shyly as buddies patted him on the back.

On Good Friday, April 9, he was at the wheel of a seven-ton truck accompanying troops conducting a route clearance mission along Nova, and an IED exploded near the rear of his large truck as the convoy reached the Route Gypsum crossroads. Ayon was unharmed. But as he stepped out of the driver's seat after that blast, a second buried explosive detonated, and a piece of shrapnel blown skyward from the ground struck him in the middle of the face, killing him instantly. It was two days before his son, Joshua, would turn seven.

At least three others were wounded, including corpsman Tyrynn Dennis, who had treated casualties April 6 during fighting at the tank graveyard. Dennis had been thrown up against a building by one of the blasts and was banged up enough to be flown to a military hospital for closer examination. He ultimately returned.

Ayon wasn't the only Marine killed on Good Friday. The 1st Marine assistant division commander, Brigadier General John Kelly, and his security team were ambushed just outside Ramadi when an IED went off, disabling a Humvee, and enemy gunmen nearby opened fire. Private First Class Chance Phelps, a nineteen-year-old from Colorado, was wounded by the blast but continued manning a machine gun in a Humvee turret until other casualties were pulled to safety. He was then suddenly killed when a bullet struck him in the eye. A Marine lieutenant colonel, Michael Strobl, later wrote an essay about escorting the slain service member's remains back to the US. Headlined TAKING CHANCE, it was the basis for an HBO movie with the same title.[2]

That night, Colonel Buck Connor revisited his diary after a combat hiatus and recorded the heavy casualties from the previous days and growing violence. "All of Iraq is aflame," he wrote. "I am counter-attacking tomorrow in the Sofia area of Ar-Ramadi."

Saturday, April 10, would be different. Unlike the grueling combat of April 6 and April 7, US forces would take the initiative. Backed up by Army Bradley Fighting Vehicles and armored personnel carriers filled with combat engineers, hundreds of Marines from Echo, Golf, Fox, and Weapons Companies would flow in and around the Sofia District in the city's northeast sector, where they believed the enemy was hiding.

The mission was designed much like Operation County Fair on April 8 but on a larger scale, with the Sofia District divided into sectors, each assigned to a different company of 2nd Battalion, 4th Marines for conducting predawn raids. Working off what intel they could gather, the troops would target in the darkness specific homes of purported bad guys—a rogue officer from the Iraqi Civil Defense Corps believed to be an insurgent commander, a dissident sheik, IED manufacturers. Then the mission would turn to searching every house in the area. Paul Kennedy wanted to provoke a response. His goal was simple, to kill or capture enemy fighters whom leadership believed had pulled back to the Sofia area from central Ramadi after April 6 and 7. Kennedy didn't want to give them a chance, as he would say, to lick their wounds and regroup. He didn't want them to get away. The mission for April 10 was code-named Bug Hunt, a named Kennedy chose from the 1959 science fiction novel *Starship Troopers* by Robert A. Heinlein, where alien arachnids were hunted. An interpretation of the novel was later the basis for a 1997 film of the same name.

There would be almost an operatic quality to its inception, at least in the vein of a rock musical. As convoys filled with Marines

BATTLE, DAY 3

and Navy corpsmen headed out three hours before sunrise to set up at staging areas, the visuals accompanying their movements were spectacular. The Army's heavy artillery at Camp Ramadi began filling the skies over the Sofia District with illumination rounds that would burn magnesium under descending canopies for ninety seconds. The Paladins kept firing for twenty to thirty minutes, turning night into day. Marine mortars fired high-explosive rounds aimed at detonating into the waters of what the Americans called Fishhook Lake located at the center of Sofia.

As denouement, giant speakers on psyops trucks began blasting AC/DC's "Hells Bells," with its twenty-second funereal overture of a tolling bronze clapper, all of this dripping in grim reaper symbolism. (Echo Company Captain Kelly Royer would feel a chill run up his spine at the sound of the deep chime.) "Hells Bells" was the lead song of the Australian hard-rock group's best-selling *Back in Black* album of July 1980, a tribute to the death of lead singer Bon Scott, who had suffocated on vomit after a heavy night of drinking.

There were even recorded Arabic taunts played by the psyops crew over the same loudspeakers that challenged the enemy to come out and fight. Weapons Company Captain Rob Weiler got so caught up in it that he commandeered one of the speakers and with the microphone to his mouth yelled, "We're right here! Come and get us, motherfuckers!"

Whether all this had the intended effect of scaring the bejesus out of an enemy roused from slumber remained to be seen, but it definitely jacked up the Marines. They were already stoked with knowledge that the people they were targeting had launched the attacks on April 6. Now they were a force of nature carried aloft by their own movie soundtrack with AC/DC lyrics admonishing to take no prisoners and spare no lives. Some Marines gripped their rifles and felt for that moment like kings of the world.

The adrenaline lasted only so long. As platoons fanned out across the district in the darkness and Americans surrounded target homes and began to enter and search premises, many of the raids turned out to be a bust. Enemy leaders were not found or were never there. In one instance, there wasn't even a structure at the coordinates the troops had been given. So they would move on to another house and start the process over. Given the morning's cinematic start, it was a letdown.

But the enemy was there. In the eastern section of the Sofia District, an area assigned to Echo Company, not only were there scores of insurgents ready to do battle but a good many were fanatically committed to fighting the Americans to the death.

Kelly Royer's Echo Company was arrayed in three tiers for three separate raids from north to south along Sofia's east side: First Platoon just off Route Apple, Second Platoon eight hundred yards southeast, and Third Platoon another three hundred yards south beyond that.

Royer and a small headquarters contingent started out the morning with Second Lieutenant Tom Cogan and Third Platoon. Second Lieutenant Vincent Valdes led First Platoon. And with the death of John Wroblewski on April 6 and pending arrival of a replacement officer, Second Platoon was still under the command of Sergeant Damien Coan, with the position of platoon sergeant going to Corporal Eric Smith (who would receive a battlefield promotion to sergeant for his heroics on April 6).

All three platoons had completed initial searches beginning precisely at 5:00 a.m. None of them found the suspects they were seeking, and they moved to other homes. In Cogan's case, there was no house at the coordinates he and his men were provided, so they started with the nearest building.

Sergeant Romeo Santiago's sniper team was assigned to support First Platoon and were dropped off at a power plant just east of the unit's location. With the wounded Corporal Richard Stayskal medically evacuated back to the US, Santiago had

BATTLE, DAY 3

two remaining team members, Corporal Ted Stanton—still doing missions despite recovering from a through-and-through gunshot wound to his left shoulder four days before—and Corporal Cameron Ferguson. To fill out the team, they were joined by another member of the sniper platoon, Tommy Parker Jr., twenty-one, a corporal from Arkansas who was married and the father of a two-year-old girl, and one of the most amiable members of Echo.

The battlefield for the day was a green region of palm groves and cultivated fields broken up by scattered farmhouses and clusters of the usual walled residential compounds skirting dirt roadways that ran west from Route Nova. The area was crisscrossed with cinder block walls and earthen berms, and since there was no sewer system to speak of, flowing streams of human waste. Every home had an outhouse. Families typically owned two or three cattle that lolled about their property with their calves until the shooting started and too many of them became bloated corpses. The enemy, meanwhile, had by force or cooperation pre-staged weapons and ammo at various residences—grenades, AK-47s, RPG launchers, medium and light machine guns most commonly known by their Russian initials, PKM or RPK. This allowed them to quickly establish strongpoints on rooftops or from windows to provide flanking fire against advancing US forces. As a result, the battle that followed was anything but linear with squads of Marines pushing forward here or there, or in some instances, pulling back. Always, there was the constant struggle to gain fire superiority during these furious small-unit clashes—fire more bullets more accurately and more destructively at them than they were firing at you—until the adversary was fleeing or dead.

The Iraqi insurgents in their dishdashas or black pants and shirts, wearing red-and-white kaffiyehs, always fought better in daylight. The first report of Echo troops pinned down came just a few minutes after sunrise.

"THANKS A LOT, ASSHOLE."
FIRST PLATOON

When Valdes was alerted that the other two Echo Company platoons were under fire, he quickly began moving his men in their direction. First Squad, under the formerly missing-in-action Sergeant Christopher Conner, was left to safeguard the platoon vehicles on Route Apple while the other squads headed out on foot. Valdes accompanied Second Squad, and his platoon sergeant, Staff Sergeant Jeffrey Craig, took Third Squad. The blue-eyed, blond, über-fit Craig, a thirty-year-old native of Oil City, Pennsylvania, had engendered a love-hate response from his Marines. They respected his warrior skills but were growing weary and even angry with how he treated them, behavior they believed bordered on hazing.[3] Like many other platoon sergeants, Craig was a former drill instructor. But when he transitioned to a combat unit, he never eased back on the yelling and incessant training that for his men took on a mindlessness in the venue of a combat zone. His nickname, even outside of Echo, was "Staff Sergeant Psychopath." He had men doing the kind of remedial exercises at Combat Outpost—textbook sandbag preparation and repeatedly mounting and dismounting trucks in full gear—they thought they'd left behind in boot camp. It was bad enough they were in a combat zone getting shot at, mortared, and killed.

But Craig, who joined the platoon in January, felt compelled to drive them relentlessly so they could survive Ramadi. He could see the deployment was rushed without the necessary months to prepare, and he thought they lacked unit proficiency, cohesion, and tactical skills. The mounting deaths through the summer only validated Craig's fears. So he pushed them still harder, knowing full well they hated him for it.

On this day, Second and Third Squads moved in tandem off Apple southeast toward the sound of gunfire with Santiago and his sniper team on their right flank moving from house to house, occupying the high ground on rooftops to provide "guardian angel"

BATTLE, DAY 3

overwatch. It was right about at this point when Lance Corporal Theophilus Tor earned the nickname "Cow Killer." Born in Monrovia, Liberia, the only son of an only son, Tor grew up in Sacramento, California, where his father worked as a computer engineer. Tor enlisted in the Marine Corps before he was a US citizen. His first night with the battalion, he was so wound up and demonstrably angry about possible hazing that he turned to his team leader, who happened to be Chris MacIntosh, and declared, "Yo, I might have to beat up a lot of these guys." MacIntosh defused the tension with a dry response. He told Tor he was going to bed. "Please don't kill me while I sleep." Tor instantly liked him.

As First Platoon Marines headed off Route Apple, the twenty-year-old Tor took his assigned position in support of the sniper team when suddenly Ferguson came running out of a walled compound with a cow right on his heels. Soon both men were fleeing this animal when it suddenly occurred to Tor: *I have a gun.* He unloaded on the bovine with his squad automatic weapon. Ferguson followed suit. It wouldn't be the only cow killed in combat, with the battalion compensating in cash any family that lost one.

Nor was that the only instance of absurdity. Just ahead was an enemy gunman with a light machine gun at the base of a palm tree firing at the Marines from 150 yards away. Santiago and Stanton, who had fought long enough together to anticipate each other's rhythms, were on his flank. Tactics called for one of them to lay cover fire while the other advanced, but who moved out first?

"Well, I'm not going to do it," Stanton said.

"I'm a sergeant. You do it," Santiago responded.

"Come on, we don't have rank in this thing."

"All right, fine."

Rock-paper-scissors.

Stanton lost, and as Yago opened up with his M16, the corporal began moving past him. But the gun jammed. "Thanks a lot, asshole," Stanton complained as he advanced while Santiago worked to clear his weapon.

"Hey, I'm sorry. I'm sorry."

Ultimately, Marines enveloped and killed the gunman, only to move on to a tougher strongpoint that stopped the entire platoon—a two-story house with multiple enemy machine gunners on the roof.

Army troops that morning had blocked all entry and egress points to Sofia District. There would be no enemy reinforcements. Many of those fighters who woke up in the district that morning didn't seem to care. They were concentrated in Echo's target area, a mix of trained cadres and residents willing to take up a gun and start shooting. Rob Weiler called the latter *minutemen*. With daylight, insurgents armed with light machine guns took up fighting positions on rooftops, behind berms, or in tall grass, waiting for Americans to come within range. Others wandered about looking for targets of opportunity. Only a few stumbled into clusters of Marines and simply surrendered. First Platoon took some of these people into custody.

Most resisted. A few hundred yards east of where the snipers had been fighting, Staff Sergeant Craig and eight men from Third Squad were picking their way south through rows of palm trees. Lance Corporal Brian Telinda and Lance Corporal Jarad Cole were on point about thirty feet ahead of everyone else. Both had fought at the tank graveyard on April 6. Cole, who was nineteen, was a big, sensitive fellow who struggled, like all his comrades, to cope with the grinding loss of friends to death and injury, and the inability to sleep because of the emotional trauma. But his method of managing was unique in a warrior culture. When they were back in their barracks at Combat Outpost, Cole would start to weep. He caught hell for it from the others. But it worked for him. It eased the tension.

On this day, Cole had prepared for combat. After running out of ammunition for his light machine gun on April 6, he wasn't taking any chances. He was weighed down with five drums, each with two hundred belted rounds. Cole adored his M249 squad

BATTLE, DAY 3

automatic weapon, which could fire hundreds of rounds per minute. He loved being able to run with it, blasting away on fully automatic, shooting from the hip.

On this morning, he was the first to see eight armed Iraqis walking away through the palm forest and alerted Telinda, who called out in Arabic and English for the men to stop. Telinda was following the coalition's rules of engagement, which dictated first a verbal command, even when someone was carrying a weapon. He couldn't just shoot them because they had guns. Their answer was to swing about in unison and open fire. The two on each end cut loose with light machine guns; the other six fired AK-47s. Telinda and Cole, who were about fifteen feet apart, barely had time to take cover, each stepping behind the trunk of a palm tree that offered little protection. The enemy gunmen blasted away, their rounds chiseling hunks of stem from the palm tree trunks. Exposed sleeves and cargo pockets on Marine uniforms were frayed by bullets. From where he was frozen in place, unable to even reach for his radio without exposing a limb, Telinda could see Cole's tree trunk getting chewed up by the flying lead and yelled at him not to move until there was a pause in the hailstorm of bullets. "Then jump out and we'll both open up!" At one point, Telinda tried to peek around to see the enemy only to have pieces of stem explode in his face from AK-47 rounds. The shock of this caused the Marine to fall back on the ground.

Cole saw it happen and thought Telinda was killed and he was now alone. "Fuck it," Cole said and stepped out from behind the tree to cut loose with his SAW, advancing toward the enemy. Telinda heard the epithet and saw Cole's actions. He climbed to his feet and joined him, shooting his M16. The enemy was fleeing. Telinda thought he knocked at least one of them down, and the man crawled or fell through a window into a house about sixty feet away on the Marines' left flank, where other fighters took cover. The insurgents would eventually escape out the back of the house, dragging any bodies of comrades with them.

There was still incoming fire from two directions as other Marines in the squad arrived. Much of it was from an enemy machine gunner on the roof of a house to the southwest. Cole, who was on an adrenaline tear after stepping out from behind the palm tree, jumped over a three-foot wall to fire at more insurgents—he thought he shot three—only to get dragged back for his own safety by Telinda. Meanwhile, a man armed with an AK-47 tried to climb over a wall on the squad's left flank right in front of the unit leader, Corporal Ramon Barron. The Marine raised his rifle, the muzzle all but touching the insurgent's face, and pulled the trigger. The entire back of the man's head exploded, and the gruesome sight for young Americans on their first days of heavy combat was an eye-opener. The Marines continued to exchange fire, particularly with the rooftop machine gunner, but their position was growing tenuous. Craig was certain the gunner was trying to pin them down while enemy riflemen maneuvered to their left. "If we don't fucking move out of this area, we are going to get flanked!" he yelled, ordering his men back toward Route Apple at a run with enemy gunfire at their backs. There the shooting continued as insurgent fighters chasing the Americans neared and, in some instances, crossed the roadway. Barron left the squad to race northwest more than one hundred yards across an open field swept by enemy fire so he could reach the platoon trucks on Route Apple and retrieve fresh ammo. But as he made the same dangerous journey back, weighed down by several ammunition containers, he was shot in the lower leg. Craig sprinted to reach Barron, at one point draping himself across the wounded squad leader to protect him. As the platoon trucks moved closer along Apple, both men managed to gather up the ammo cans and covered the distance back to the squad. Additional troops from Echo Company's headquarters platoon and from Weapons Company—Lieutenant Dave Dobb's Rainmaker people—would soon arrive on trucks to help clear Apple of enemy resistance.

Meanwhile, Lieutenant Valdes and Second Squad, which

BATTLE, DAY 3   223

had originally been on Craig's right, were preparing to attack a stubborn strongpoint where three insurgents were firing machine guns from a rooftop. The enemy gunmen seemed impervious to efforts by the sniper team and other Marines to kill them from a distance. The only alternative appeared to be a direct assault on the building. As Valdes and his men drew closer, they threw grenades onto the roof and maneuvered to an east entrance into the house. It was Valdes, Tor, Private First Class Jose Texidor Jr., and Lance Corporal Nathan Appel, who had been photographed by journalist David Swanson on April 6 as he carried the bagged remains of Lance Corporal Travis Layfield over his shoulder. Tor threw a grenade into the building, and they entered to find a shrapnel-wounded man on the floor dressed in black and begging for his life. "Mistah, fisherman. Mistah fisherman!" The Marines found a light machine gun nearby and cuffed the man.

Valdes entered. "Anybody clear the upstairs?" He started up steps to the roof, and his men followed—Texidor, Tor, Appel, radio operator Samuel Rutledge, and Corpsman Kevin Barger, the sailor who had helped unload the bodies of dead Americans at Combat Outpost, only to discover among them his friend Fernando Mendez-Aceves.

The stairway led to a landing and then another short series of steps to a covered rooftop entrance. The Marines could see the body of a dead insurgent in the doorway and stacked themselves one behind the other in preparation for charging onto the roof, with Valdes in front. Texidor was second and could feel the adrenaline pumping through his veins. He suddenly remembered that he had no grenades with him, but there was no turning back, and he bumped Valdes to let him know he was ready. It was a tight space. The lieutenant said he would go right and Texidor should go left, but the PFC didn't hear the instructions. Valdes took a step out to the right and, for a fraction of a second, he could see two enemy gunmen alive on the roof, one of them just outside the roof entrance to the left. All the grenades thrown up there hadn't finished them off. The man, dressed in black and armed with an RPK light machine gun, stepped across the entrance of the doorway just over an arm's length away and opened fire at close range with a five- to seven-round burst before disappearing from view. A bullet or fragments of bullets struck Valdes. He could feel an impact into his body armor near his ribs and another into his heel. Texidor got it far worse. The twenty-year-old Marine had been in mid-step with his left leg when a round entered the inside portion of the limb, smashing through the bone, muscle, and flesh behind his left kneecap. It felt like he had been hit by a car, and Texidor fell back hard onto the floor. Valdes was still on his feet up against the wall of the roof entrance. Texidor sat straight up and for an instant thought, *If I can wiggle my left foot, I'm good to go.* But he wasn't. Blood was fountaining from the wound, and Texidor could tell his femur was shattered. He lay back down, staring back at Tor, who was behind him. He quietly said, "Yo, son. Yo, I'm hit. They shot me." Tor could see the leg was wrecked. Texidor's left foot was pointed the wrong way. Suddenly, the pain kicked in, and Texidor started to scream. Barger, the corpsman, and Tor pulled him downstairs to the main room. Lance Corporal Appel, who had been right behind Tor, stepped forward to the entrance onto the roof. He could see his squad leader, Corporal Robert Hernandez, down in the yard trying to signal where the enemy on the roof was located, and when Appel came around the corner of the entrance with his rifle up, he was met by a fusillade of automatic weapon fire from that direction. Appel immediately pulled back, but not before an enemy round managed to shear off the pinkie finger on his left hand.

Downstairs, Barger began working on Texidor's damaged leg. There was part of a knee joint, but virtually everything else behind his kneecap was destroyed. Barger administered morphine, began placing a tourniquet, and started stuffing the wound with Kerlix bandage rolls and wrapping it. Navy corpsman Manaia Alaimalo

BATTLE, DAY 3

arrived and started intravenous fluids. As the sailors labored, Barger kept talking to Texidor to calm him. "Hey, so why do they call you Tex?" he asked. "Because my name is Texidor and it's just short, and Marines are lazy," he said. "I'm not even from Texas. I don't like anything from Texas. I'm from Jersey."

Minutes earlier, when Texidor was being dragged down the stairs, battalion Sergeant Major Jim Booker showed up. Seeing senior officers in the midst of a battle was a tonic for Marines, and that was particularly true with Booker.

The sergeant major had first arrived on the battlefield that morning with Kennedy, Rob Weiler, and Dave Dobb's mounted Rainmaker platoon, rendezvousing with Echo Company's First Squad on Route Apple about ninety minutes after the fighting started. Kennedy and Booker almost always stayed together during combat. But in this instance, fighting grew to such a fever pitch that the sergeant major left Kennedy and chased after an insurgent who had been blasting away at the Marines.

He took Lance Corporal Pedro Contreras with him, and they pursued the enemy gunmen, who, like so many others, was dressed all in black. He led them to a two-story house that became the stubborn enemy stronghold with machine gunners on the roof that Valdes and his men would assault. Booker showed up after the lieutenant's unsuccessful attempt to charge the rooftop. The sergeant major and Contreras threw grenades onto the roof and then went inside the building, where they found the wounded Texidor on the floor. Booker had never seen so much blood, and he felt certain the Marine was dying. He had seen too many of his men killed in the last few days and was determined to end this threat on the roof once and for all. Booker organized another attack up the stairs, with him in the lead, followed by Valdes and Contreras. When they reached the same roof entrance, Booker threw a grenade and then went left. Valdes went forward, and Contreras went right. The grenade killed one of the two insurgents who had still been fighting on the roof. Booker found the other. It was the same man he had been chasing from Route Apple, now mortally wounded and struggling to breathe.

"You motherfucker," Booker said to him, pointing his big M14 rifle at the man's face. "You mujahideen motherfucker. You see my white, Christian face? It's the last thing you're ever going to fucking see."

"OH FUCK! I GOT SHOT IN THE HEAD!"
SECOND PLATOON

The fight by Second Platoon Marines in the middle of the Echo target area largely mirrored the experience of First Platoon, with one exception. Shortly after company commander Kelly Royer joined them, he was nearly killed, managing to escape only by crawling with other troops through a sewage ditch flowing with human waste.

The captain started the morning with Third Platoon on the south end of his mission site, and after a few homes were searched there, he took his small headquarters unit and moved northwest to link up with Second Platoon, just a few hundred yards away. Marines there had surrounded and searched a house where there were supposed to be dissident members of the Iraqi Civil Defense Corps who were working with the insurgency. But no suspects or incriminating evidence was found. Nine men were detained and later released. The squads fanned out to search other houses, often finding only terrified women and children and men begging on their knees not to be harmed. Once, after a fruitless effort, Corporal Joseph Magee Jr., the leader of Third Squad, took pains to apologize to the homeowner for any inconvenience. As sunrise broke, enemy fighters began to attack.

Royer was crossing a field with his men and photographer David Swanson and had been joined by members of Second Platoon when they came under fire and took a knee, first in the open and then along a cinder block wall. As enemy machine gun positions in buildings to the west and east raked the area, Royer yelled for his men to take cover in the sewage ditch that ran adjacent to the wall. It was filled with three to four inches of liquid muck and had a foot-high berm on one side. Adam Clayton, the company senior corpsman, got some of the blackish water into his mouth when he dived in and could actually taste what he thought must have been human feces. He fought the urge to retch.

Clayton, twenty-one, grew up in the Salt Lake City area of Utah, the oldest of three boys. In his youth, he aspired to be a Marine, but in high school, he also discovered an interest in medicine. He learned he could embrace both by joining the Navy and serving as a corpsman.

Initially on April 10, it was unclear from which direction enemy gunmen were firing. Sergeant Kenneth Hassell left the ditch to find a higher vantage point at a nearby building. He would eventually come back and climb over the wall, jumping into the ditch and screaming out in pain as his lower left leg shattered on impact. Royer, meanwhile, still had his head up trying to spot the source of gunfire, when a round struck the front center of his helmet, snapping his head back and knocking him down. Sergeant Damien Coan saw it happen and immediately thought, *Shit, they just killed the company commander.*

Then the Marines heard Royer call out, "Oh fuck! I got shot! I got shot in the head!"

Clayton instinctively raised himself out of the ditch and ran in the open to reach the officer. Crouching over Royer, he groped with his sewage-stained fingers the captain's face and head, frantically searching for a bullet entry wound. Royer had quickly realized that the round failed to penetrate his helmet, and while he admired Clayton's heroic response, he yelled at him to stop feeling around, get the hell off, and take cover. Enemy fire increased, and the troops laying in the slime could see rounds hitting the ground close by and chipping at the block wall. Corporal Charles Lauersdorf, the intel specialist who had assessed the ambush site on April 6, was struck in the legs by bullet fragments from the rounds that ricocheted off the cinder blocks. David Swanson was hurt. Shortly before everyone had sought cover in the ditch, the photographer was shocked to find that he had been grazed on the inner part of his right bicep by an enemy round. Among the thirty-nine-year-old's first thoughts: *My wife is going to freak.* For Lance Corporal Omar Morel Cruz, twenty-two, the unfolding mayhem reminded him of battle scenes from the movie *Saving Private Ryan.* Royer notified battalion headquarters by radio of his predicament and was asked if he needed reinforcements. Royer said no. "We can handle the fight."

After about forty-five minutes, he and the nine men with him managed to crawl along the sewage trench for several yards to where they could more safely emerge from the filth, their uniforms blackened. Hassell had to drag himself along and was screaming in pain. At one point, Royer was yelling into the radio and accidentally sat back onto Hassell's broken limb. Clayton had to push the officer off. The corpsman had lost much of his medical gear in the sewage trench and wound up fashioning a splint for Hassel's leg out of a few stiff palm fronds.

The near-death reality of the chaos had a quelling effect on Royer. On any other day, he had a domineering way of carrying himself as company commander that many of his men felt bordered on arrogance. "You get the fuck over there. You hurry the fuck up. You start fucking shooting." He seemed to bark his orders. Many of his Marines found it irritating. An Echo Company nickname for him was "Captain America." But in the minutes after he was nearly killed, the tough-guy persona momentarily drained away. Eric Smith was targeting insurgents from behind a palm tree when he turned around and was shocked to see several filth-covered Marines emerge from a ditch, Royer among them. The captain made his way over to Smith. "You see this shit?"

Royer said, gleefully showing Smith the divot in his helmet. "They almost got me!"

As troops assaulted houses where enemy gunfire originated, they kept finding weapons and ammunition that had clearly been pre-positioned. The insurgents had planned ahead. They were familiar with coalition rules of engagement prohibiting troops from firing on unarmed people and were taking advantage of that rule to move fighters around the battlefield or bound from one location to the next during a retreat.

The most exhilarating moment for Second Platoon that morning was when Lance Corporal Benjamin Musser unleashed a round from one of the bazooka-like AT4 anti-tank weapons with extraordinary accuracy. The Marine had been with the battalion just five months and had never fired the weapon. When the advance was momentarily held up by a second-story gunman, Musser volunteered to use an AT4 to kill the man. Sergeant Coan ordered a couple of Marine SAW gunners to provide cover fire so the twenty-one-year-old could step out into the open and avoid hurting comrades with the backblast of his anti-tank weapon. To the cheers of those brethren, he fired a round precisely on target. The shooting ceased, and two squads charged across the field to clear the building.

Corporal Magee was out front, and he saw two wounded enemy fighters on the ground reaching for their rifles. He shot each of them twice in the chest. Surprised to see one of them still moving and pulling out a grenade, the corporal shot him three more times in the chest. But the man's fingers were still working to grasp the pin until Magee finished him off with two final rounds to the head.

Such fight-to-the-death resistance continued as Marines entered the building. They found a man coming down a stairway from the roof, an AK-47 on the steps below. "Don't go for it! Don't go for it!" a Marine yelled out. But he did and Magee killed him with three shots to the chest.

Coan, the acting platoon commander, was impressed time and again with the courage and selflessness of his men. In one instance, after they had secured a building, Coan felt a tap on the shoulder and turned around to see one of his corpsmen, Hospitalman Alfred Moore. "What do you need, Doc?"

Moore, a quiet man who never seemed to have much to say, asked if they would be holding that position for a bit longer. "We'll be here for a few minutes. Why?"

"I just got to patch something up." The corpsman had been all over the battlefield that morning tending wounds or fighting the enemy. Coan thought he was talking about yet another wounded Marine who needed help.

"Who's hurt?"

Moore pulled down his trousers to reveal a leg wound he'd received and had been too busy to address. A bullet had gone clear through his thigh.

Coan stared in amazement. "Do you need to get medevacked?"

"I'll be all right," the sailor quietly responded and began to finally treat his own wound.

COMBAT'S CAPRICIOUSNESS
THIRD PLATOON

Of all Echo Company, Tom Cogan's men conducted the most coordinated attacks against enemy positions.

The second lieutenant, who had organized assaults on April 6, led his men on this day first west and then east and then north across or along the edges of a broad field south of where Second Platoon was fighting.

When the morning started, Cogan was working off the same flawed intelligence that the other platoon commanders had received. His mission was to apprehend a dissident sheik, and it was sensitive enough that Royer wanted to accompany Third Platoon initially.

BATTLE, DAY 3

But not only did Third Platoon not find the sheik, there wasn't even a house at the coordinates they were provided. So Cogan had his squads begin to search nearby residences. As a precaution, he sent a two-man sniper team to provide overwatch from a rooftop on the northeast corner of the field where Cogan and his men were operating. To provide security for the snipers, the lieutenant sent along three riflemen, all veterans of the successful March 25 night assault on the enemy mortarmen who had been firing on Combat Outpost—Lance Corporal John Sims Jr., Lance Corporal John Huerkamp, and Private First Class Jeremy Ramirez, a boot who'd joined the battalion in November.

Third Platoon first began to take enemy fire from gunmen to the west across a stream. Cogan directed his men to a house where they opened fire with grenade launchers, light machine guns, and M16s, pummeling four to five enemy combatants who had taken up positions in a structure on the stream's opposite side. Then Cogan got word that the snipers and his three Marines with them were coming under intense fire from the east. Cogan left two of his squads to maintain fire superiority to the west, and he led an attack in the opposite direction with seven of his men, clearing three homes along the southern edge of the field until he and his team were on a rooftop 150 yards south of the Marine snipers. With the alternating enemy attacks, Cogan suspected the enemy was coordinating movements by cell phone. He directed the men with him to start targeting any enemy fighters they could see to the east. "We just started killing guys right and left. They were all over the place," Cogan told a field historian weeks later.

But for the five Marines in the sniper building, enemy fire only grew more intense. The two Marine snipers and Sims were on the uppermost section of the rooftop with the least amount of cover, and it was about that time that Sims was shot in the back under his left shoulder. He was pulled out of the line of fire, and Huerkamp tried talking to him. But the wounded man didn't respond, and his face was turning a shade of blue.

A wall and heavy enemy gunfire separated Cogan and his men from the sniper house and reaching the wounded Sims. He radioed Second Platoon and spoke with Corporal Eric Smith, who had set up a casualty collection point in a large house to the northwest. Cogan asked if a team could be sent to retrieve Sims, and Smith did exactly that, deploying Lance Corporal Jason Birmelin with some men and a stretcher to reach Sims. Navy corpsman Sergio Gutierrez went along.

Combat's capriciousness had been tough on Gutierrez, the oldest of three children from Orange County, California, raised by a mother who cleaned college dormitories for work. Sergio had joined the Navy to escape the gangs of Santa Ana and Anaheim. The cost for his service in Ramadi would be years of severe post-traumatic stress disorder.

Much of that stemmed from the first several weeks of the deployment, when Gutierrez was again and again thrust, by the vagaries of war, into some of the worst carnage Echo Company endured. Again and again, he was left to cope with horribly wounded Marines who had little or no chance of surviving. There was the terrible roadside bomb explosion March 30 that blinded Lance Corporal Jason Murray and literally blew in half combat engineer William "Whiskey" Wiscowiche. Gutierrez helped pick up body parts. On April 6, he had tried mightily to keep alive Second Lieutenant John Wroblewski after the officer was mortally wounded with a gunshot to the face. He had Wroblewski sit up to better manage breathing, but the horrible choking and gurgling sounds would later haunt the sailor in his sleep.

And now he was faced with an interminable struggle to save Sims. He and Smith and other Marines took turns breathing for the wounded man or performing chest compressions, though Sims never showed more than a weak pulse and almost no breath. Gutierrez led the effort, cycling in other Marines to take over mouth-to-mouth resuscitation when the corpsman grew exhausted. It would seem like an eternity before Sims would be medevacked from

BATTLE, DAY 3

the battlefield to a medical facility. A helicopter was summoned, and Smith sent troops out to secure a section of field for a landing area. "Listen, I've got enough guys here," he was telling someone over the radio. "I'll pop smoke in that field. . . . Land the bird!"

But no helicopter would touch down. Smith was furious.

Cogan, meanwhile, intent on killing the insurgents who had been firing at the sniper house and had wounded Sims, consolidated his platoon and then led four men on a flanking maneuver, occupying a house to the east. But there were gunshots coming from the direction of Second Platoon—friendly fire. He twice radioed for them to cut it out, but Cogan and his men remained pinned down.

He finally managed to link up with Army engineers who arrived in armored personnel carriers. Once again, it was Charlie Company of the 1st Engineer Battalion. Just as they had broken enemy resistance on April 6 after the deadly ambush and massacre of Americans at Gypsum and Nova, so the engineers showed up this time to help quell enemy fighting and deliver Sims to a doctor's care. Company commander Tyler Faulk was in charge, this time with a different platoon. Cogan told him the direction he needed to go to reach Sims, and a decision was made to simply smash through the wall to reach the casualty.

Faulk did just that, directing his own vehicle to plow through, the driver flooring it just before they hit the wall. Other APCs in the column followed. At least one of them wound up with broken bits of wall on the front end like a wreath of stone.

The tracked vehicles arrived outside Smith's casualty collection site, and Sims was loaded into an APC. Engineers departed. But too much time had passed since the Marine was wounded—two hours—and he was beyond saving.

"WHEN I SIGNED UP FOR IT, I SIGNED UP FOR IT ALL."
RAINMAKER PLATOON

Weapons Company commander Rob Weiler had three of his mobile assault platoons in the field on April 10. One was conducting house searches west of the Fishhook Lake. A second had set up a vehicle checkpoint near Gypsum and Nova. And Weiler rode with the third unit, which was Lieutenant Dave Dobb's Rainmaker assault platoon, conducting searches along Route Apple.

When violence exploded in Echo's area, Weiler thought the battalion had a perfect opportunity to crush the enemy. If Echo Marines could drive insurgents east toward the open fields and palm groves stretching toward the Euphrates, the Weapons Platoon at Gypsum and Nova could attack into the enemy's left flank and Rainmaker would hit the right. "It appeared to be a perfect situation," Weiler would later write in his after-action report, "the enemy was surrounded."

But it soon became clear that Echo had its hands full and wasn't going to be pushing the enemy in any major way. Lieutenant Colonel Paul Kennedy and Sergeant Major Jim Booker met up with Weiler, and Kennedy urged him to take the pressure off Echo.

Dobb and his Rainmaker troops attacked northeast along Route Apple. Weiler was with them, as were two women soldiers—members of the Lioness teams—in what at least one historian would later say would be the first instance of female US military members involved in direct ground combat.

Both women had quietly been breaking gender barriers in the military for years. Staff Sergeant Ranie Ruthig, thirty-one, had grown up amid the soybean and cornfields of South Dakota, the daughter of a long-haul truck driver and Vietnam veteran. Her mother chose the name "Ranie" from a female character in an episode of *Bonanza*. Ranie's first flight in an aircraft was traveling to Army in-processing. Specialist Shannon Morgan, ten years younger, had been adopted and raised by her paternal grandparents in the tiny village of Mena in southwest Arkansas. Hers was a childhood of sports and hunting. She grew skilled with a rifle but also at playing classical music on the piano at her mother's insistence. Ruthig joined the military for the college benefits. Morgan signed up out of patriotic fervor after the 9/11 attacks.

Since 2013, women have been allowed to serve in any position in the military for which they can qualify. But for Morgan, and particularly for Ruthig, who joined in 1992, there was a Byzantine slate of restrictions all predicated on somehow keeping them out of combat. To qualify for limited GI Bill benefits in 1992, Ruthig was restricted to a small set of the least popular noncombat jobs, and she chose tracked vehicle mechanic. Even there, she couldn't work on tanks or armored fighting vehicles, because they were part of combat units. An exception was armored personnel carriers. In South Korea, she was the only woman among eleven mechanics, and she joined the Army engineers when that branch finally accepted women in 1995. Her growing maintenance knowledge allowed her to advance through the enlisted ranks, but not without naysayers in her unit claiming she slept her way to higher rank.

Morgan also became a tracked vehicle mechanic, and after she and Ruthig deployed to Iraq in September 2003 as part of the 1st Engineer Battalion, both jumped at the chance to conduct missions outside the base with the Lioness program. They were qualified on a wide range of weapons, and because of her shooting expertise, Morgan became the only woman in the battalion assigned to carry a light machine gun, or SAW. After the Magnificent Bastards arrived in February 2003, battalion leaders quickly grasped the value of the Lioness program in conducting house searches or vehicle checkpoints, and soon began employing them. They'd asked for certain teams over and over, and the pair of Ruthig and Morgan was one of them.

On April 10, the women were with the Rainmaker platoon when they began searching homes in the predawn hours, and they were with them when fighting broke out at daybreak. For the two female soldiers, it would become among the most profound episodes of their lives.

They saw stark differences between how Marines and soldiers fought. Marines seemed more aggressive, eager to draw the enemy into battle. A clear example were the loudspeakers challenging insurgents to come out and fight on the morning of April 10. The Marines were also different in how they attacked. There was a constant tension to keep moving forward. When the Rainmaker platoon dismounted and began pushing from house to house along Route Apple, the women were the tail end of a squad that always kept pressing ahead. It was doctrinal for the Marines.

"Squad leaders and platoon commanders need to be single-mindedly aggressive," a lessons-learned battalion paper emphasized. "Once contact is made there must be Marines racing to trap the rat. Cautiously evaluating the situation and slowly bounding only serves for the insurgent to move to another house or get in a vehicle to his next pre-staged RPG."

There were moments during the fighting that Saturday when Ruthig would bring her M16 up to fire only to see a Marine suddenly charge out in front of her. At one point, as the squad began to move with each tapping the person behind to signal they were advancing, Morgan was at the end of the line and didn't get tapped. She was looking in the other direction, and when she turned back, she found herself alone. She was scared and furious.

The Marines and Ruthig had reached a house and climbed to the roof, where the staff sergeant saw her battle buddy below. "Shannon, what the fuck are you doing? Get up here!" Ruthig yelled. Morgan made her way to the house, up to the roof, and confronted the lance corporal she was convinced had left her behind. "You fucker!" she yelled, proceeding to kick him in the balls. Fortunately for him, the Marine was wearing a groin protector for shrapnel and reacted only with an "Oof." His comrades broke into laughter. The combat would go on for hours. At various times,

BATTLE, DAY 3

the women fired on enemy positions, carried enemy corpses, and dodged enemy fire. *I am truly in war,* Ruthig thought.

Weiler wrote of the women in his after-action report: "They performed courageously throughout the engagement."

For Morgan, it was a clarifying moment in the struggle for gender equality. In joining the Army, she had wanted only to be treated equally but sometimes felt she had to work twice as hard as men to make that happen. On the battlefield, however, discrimination drained away fast.

"You really wanted there to be no separation," Morgan thought after that day. "Well, the bullets really don't care when they're flying downrange what gender you are. They just wanted us dead. Period. So you need to be able to deal with everything just like your male counterparts. When I signed up for it, I signed up for it all."

As the Rainmaker platoon pushed forward along Route Apple, the scattered number of enemy gunmen opposing them were running out of room with the Euphrates River at their backs, and they seemed doubly determined to fight to the death. At one point during the movement down Apple, Weapons Company troops saw a young girl, probably six or seven, standing alongside the road. An IED detonated. None of the Americans were struck by shrapnel. But the girl was completely obliterated. They couldn't see a trace of her.

One fighter more than two hundred yards away stepped out into the open to launch a rocket-propelled grenade that exploded near the advancing Marines. Then he took cover. The platoon sergeant, Felix Garcia, knew the man would try again and carefully aimed his M16 where he saw him disappear behind a wall. "I got him. I got him," he said. Sure enough, the man popped back out, and Gacia shot him through the chest.

A blood trail led the Marines into a nearby house where the wounded fighter lay face down on the floor. When they pulled back a blanket, there was blood pouring out of an exit wound in his back. He was rolled over, and Lieutenant Dave Dobb stood over him with his rifle when the insurgent suddenly reached up and grabbed the barrel of the M16 with both hands and pulled it down as if he wanted the officer to kill him. A struggle ensued. Dobb, who was six foot four and 220 pounds, actually had to stomp the man's chest with his foot and jerk his rifle back to wrest it away, shocked at the strength of the dying man. The insurgent was cuffed and loaded into an open-backed Humvee, where he died before they could get him back to a medical facility. Elsewhere, at least two other wounded enemy fighters who were begging to be killed after being captured, even as a corpsman tried to treat them, succumbed to their wounds.

The platoon pushed on and flushed three more gunmen into a field and pinned them down from a rooftop position. One of them was wounded and captured, and two squads of Marines swept a field to find the others.

As the Marines worked their way through tall grass, an enemy fighter armed with a light machine gun was waiting for them, hidden in a small depression. The Americans were spread out before him—among them, Rob Weiler and Dave Dobb—and the insurgent opened fire. Everyone hit the ground. The lone exception was Lance Corporal Reagan Hodges—the tough Marine who had tried to intimidate the captured Adnan Hassan Farhan into giving answers the night of April 5. He stayed on his feet and kept moving toward the gunman, firing his rifle.

The enemy fighter, lying prone on the ground and dressed in a dishdasha, was shooting wildly. Hodges was a dozen feet away and advancing step by step, steadily firing one shot after another. The insurgent, for all his unleashed firepower, hit nothing. Hodges shot him at least six times. The Marine was unscathed, the enemy fighter was dead.

Weiler, for one, was certain Hodges saved his life. Lance Corporal Joe Herscher, who witnessed it all, walked up to Hodges seconds later and said, "I'm really glad you're on our side."

The battle drew to a close. Cobra and Huey helicopter gunships

BATTLE, DAY 3

conducted strafing runs near where Echo Company's First Platoon was fighting, ending resistance there. The Army armored personnel carriers that arrived where Echo's Second and Third Platoons were engaged sent insurgents fleeing. And the Rainmaker platoon had pushed its way to the river. The last thing those Marines came across was a building filled with medical supplies, many of them carrying UNICEF labels from the United Nations Children's Fund. Rob Weiler was convinced it was an enemy field hospital. Through an interpreter, the captain had questions he wanted to ask. What could they reveal about the insurgents? Were they happy to see these violent people killed by the Americans? Did they understand that some Marines gave their lives to do this? He got nothing in response. The hospital workers said they hadn't even seen any insurgents. Weiler was livid. He had them all brought out to a courtyard in front of the building and ordered them through the interpreter to applaud his Marines for the work they had done. They meekly complied.

The interpreter, unhappy with Weiler's actions, complained about it later to Kennedy, who, in turn, expressed displeasure with the Weapons Company commander.

But for the young captain, the entire incident held meaning. He saw that the goal the Marine command had set for itself was built on sand. Major General James Mattis had spelled out in his "Letter to All Hands" that coalition forces would destroy the enemy and thereby make good with the Iraqi people. But Weiler realized there was no daylight between the insurgency and the population. Marines would never kill their way to victory.

10

LUNACY

"WE FIGHT THE SAME GUYS AGAIN AND AGAIN."

BY THE END of the fighting on Saturday, April 10, one Marine was killed, John Sims. Twelve Marines and a sailor were wounded or injured, including three who had to be medically evacuated back to the United States. The battalion leadership believed, on balance, the day was a victory because they had regained the initiative and in the process, killed another forty enemy fighters, maybe more. The fewer bad guys, leaders argued, the better. And in fact, for the next twenty days, through the end of April, just nine Marines were wounded during various mortar, grenade, or IED attacks, most of them lightly enough to return to duty. Three had to be sent home. To the extent this was a reprieve from the drumbeat of violence, it was brief.

The infamous Abu Ghraib prisoner abuse scandal would be made public during a *60 Minutes* broadcast on April 28, further stoking Iraqi hatred of coalition forces. Less than a month later, 454 prisoners would be released as a result, a move US military intel officials were certain refreshed the ranks of the insurgency.

"The prisoner release system is spiraling out of control," intel officer Kyle Teamey would note in his journal. "We fight the same guys again and again."

In the wake of heavy fighting in early April, Silver Stars would be awarded to Captain Chris Bronzi, commander of Golf Company; Captain Rob Weiler, who led Weapons Company; Second Lieutenant Tom Cogan, who commanded Echo Company's Third Platoon; and Sergeant Major Jim Booker. Army Brigade Command Sergeant Major Ron Riling would also receive a Silver Star for valorous actions on April 6.

During five days of the Ramadi battle, 2nd Battalion, 4th Marines lost 15 troops in combat. By contrast, during twenty-one days of the Fallujah battle, four Marine battalions lost a combined total of 27 troops.[1] April would prove to be one of the two bloodiest months of the Iraq War, with 135 US troops killed. (November 2004, when the second battle of Fallujah was fought, was the deadliest month, with 137 killed.)[2]

A memorial service was held on Easter Sunday, April 11, for the fifteen Marines and one sailor who died during the previous eight days. Troops assembled in formation inside the hangar bay at Combat Outpost. In front of them was arranged a Battlefield Cross, the traditional shrine for honoring troops killed in combat. There was a weathered pair of combat boots, a rifle with the barrel pointed down, and a helmet perched on the stock. Sixteen dog tags strung from the rifle grip hung down in a cluster like a silent wind chime. One by one, service members stepped out of formation and walked forward to kneel and pray, stand and salute, or simply reach out and touch a portion of the memorial.

Tom Cogan watched it all, holding his chin in his hand, his eyes moist with emotion, his face a portrait of sorrow. Six of the dog tags belonged to his men. Cogan's platoon had suffered higher losses than any other, all but one of them on April 6.

"It was the worst day of my life," the twenty-three-year-old told a *Philadelphia Inquirer* journalist during a satellite phone interview immediately after the ceremony. "It's my job to take care of these guys and get them home as safe as possible. It's my duty to them and their families. It makes me feel like I failed. Like I could've done something better or different."[3]

Battalion chaplain Brian Weigelt chose his words carefully that morning. He knew it was essential to acknowledge the swell of emotions among surviving Marines. "We have experienced the great joy of brotherhood and the sinking emptiness of grief," he told the troops.[4] But Weigelt understood that part of his role was to also keep the troops in the fight, to urge them in the wake of such loss and heartache to recommit themselves to the task ahead. They still had a job to do in Ramadi.

He was echoing the concerns of battalion leaders when it came to dealing with death. "Excessive mourning is an indulgence and distraction," a lessons-learned paper concluded. "The mission is to keep the rest alive."

"SERGEANT MAJOR SAID I CAN'T SHAVE OR CUT MY HAIR ANYMORE."

Sometime in early April, Sergeant Major Jim Booker came up with an idea. It was unorthodox, risky, and viewed by more than a few as crazy. Yet his commanders approved. Booker had two inspirations for it. One was the night of March 31, when the senior enlisted officer dressed up like an Arab and was driven behind enemy lines to record specific target locations for future raids. The other was a movie (that was followed by a book based off the screenplay) about a cadre of rogue undercover Los Angeles police. *Extreme Justice: The Secret Squad of the LAPD That Fights Violence with Violence*, the book title screamed.

Booker loved the movie and even got a chance to meet some of the actual police officers after its 1993 release. In Ramadi, he thought similar undercover tactics could work to catch enemy

LUNACY

243

fighters in the act of burying an IED, setting up mortars, or preparing an ambush. What he needed was a handful of Marines who looked like Arabs and who would accompany him to roam the city day or night. Booker himself could grow a pretty thick beard. He began recruiting people he thought physically fit the role. He chose a sergeant from Weapons Company. A second Marine joined but later got cold feet and dropped out. Then there was twenty-year-old Corporal Amir Hekmati from headquarters, whose parents were Iranian immigrants and who spoke fluent Arabic.

A fourth member was Lance Corporal Amir Heydari, twenty-two, from Fox Company, who was born in Iran and whose family immigrated to the United States when he was a toddler, settling in the Washington, DC, area. His father started a building contracting business in the US after serving as an enlisted military member in Iran before the shah was overthrown. Heydari's mother was a seamstress. Amir grew up fluent in Farsi and chose to join the Marine Corps after 9/11 out of a desire to fight for his adopted homeland after the terror attacks, and to fight for his family. He had relatives in Iran who died during the country's brutal eight-year war with Iraq in the 1980s. With a US invasion of Iraq looming after 9/11, Heydari wanted to be a part of it. When the invitation from Booker came through, Heydari volunteered with "hell yeah" enthusiasm.

An immediate perk for the few men Booker recruited was the requirement that they stop shaving. This was a big deal. It was the very first thing Heydari told Fox Company First Sergeant Tim Weber after joining the group.

"What did the sergeant major want?" Weber asked.

"Sergeant Major said I can't shave or cut my hair anymore," Heydari announced.

"What the fuck for?"

"We're going to be doing some things, First Sergeant."

The division, particularly under Major General Mattis, was obsessive about personal hygiene among troops and emphatic that they shave *with a razor* every day. It was seen as good order and discipline with the added benefit of requiring regular use of soap and water. ("Electric razors are merely a cosmetic exercise.") Mustaches were allowed, but limitations were such that most looked terrible. Being granted dispensation from shaving made a Marine feel part of something exclusive, and it gave rise to the battalion nickname for Booker's team: the Bearded Guys.

In a garage out at Combat Outpost, they found a red Opel station wagon with which to prowl the city. They wanted to change the color and could only find a bucket of white house paint. It worked. But it was sticky and started flaking off. They kept an arsenal under a tarp in the back—Claymore mines, M249 light machine guns, grenades. They were trained to use and carry AK-47s. Their basic protocol, in the event they were discovered, was to take control of a house and set up a defense until help arrived. But still, there were enormous risks. There were areas of the city where the enemy operated freely when Marines weren't around, setting up roadblocks, inspecting vehicles, or barricading streets. Precautions were taken. A drone was reserved to watch over Booker and his men. Marine units ran parallel missions blocks away. And Weapons Company was required to have a platoon up and ready with engines running throughout the duration of the reconnaissance. That would be a future point of friction.

In the meantime, the Bearded Guys headed out in their Opel with their kaffiyehs and floor-length dishdashas (with combat boots poking out below) on their first mission, slowly driving through the market area and observing. It quickly turned dangerous. As the daily traffic congestion closed in and slowed down, another driver rear-ended the Opel. It was a fender bender at most, but the driver got out and started studying the damage. The Marines weren't sure how to respond. Should they get out and express annoyance? There certainly wouldn't be any exchange of car insurance. The Bearded Guys finally elected to just drive away, albeit at a crawl because of the congestion, hoping the uniformed Iraqi soldier who walked up wouldn't spot their weapons and raise a fuss.

They reached Hurricane Point, and Lieutenant Colonel Kennedy was waiting. Headquarters had been monitoring the whole event. "There was a pucker factor on that one," he said.

The next mission was less alarming than it was embarrassing. Again, they were in the Opel, this time parked near the large soccer stadium on the city's southeast side, simply watching. An improvised piece of tradecraft was to chain-smoke cigarettes in the car with the windows rolled up to generate a haze that might obscure them from lookie-loos. All the inhaled smoke, however, made them a little sick to their stomachs. Surveillance went fine until a boy approached showing a growing interest in these men in their smoky car. The Bearded Guys kept trying to shoo him away. But the boy ignored the furtive gestures and kept inching closer and closer.

Finally, Hekmati rolled down a window and in Arabic directed the child to leave. The boy listened and then smiled.

"You're Americans."

Busted.

The boy backpedaled and walked away, grinning ear to ear.

The Bearded Guys stayed in operation for about a half dozen missions before it was decided to retire the idea. But not before a clash erupted between Booker and Weapons Company commander Rob Weiler. At the center of the dispute was the one thing troops could never get enough of in Ramadi—sleep. There was such a drumbeat of missions and so much to do when Marines weren't outside the gate that a good snooze was always at a premium. This was particularly true of Weapons Company, which, in addition to being the battalion go-to force for any emergency, was constantly tasked with other missions whether it be raids to capture enemy leaders or escorting supply convoys or coalition support vehicles. Now they had the added duty of remaining in their vehicles for hours with the engines running in the event the Bearded Guys needed rescuing. When it was First Lieutenant Dave Dobb's Rainmaker platoon with the duty one night, he asked Weiler if his exhausted crew could remain in the barracks with their gear on to get some rest. Weiler consented, believing they could rouse those in their bunks and get them saddled up in the few minutes it usually took to launch a mission. But when Jim Booker found out, he was livid. He raised the issue with Paul Kennedy, who summoned Weiler into his office and ordered an investigation. Weiler knew it was entirely possible he could be fired over it. At some level, particularly given his growing fatalism over surviving this perilous deployment, Weiler didn't care. And eventually, it all went away, although not without creating temporary friction between certain senior officers.

Meanwhile, Weapons Company had come up with its own label for Booker's team: the Bearded Ladies.

Dispensing nicknames was the crudest and most rudimentary art form in the military, and it was practically in the DNA of this battalion because all the members were, after all, Magnificent Bastards. The highest levels embraced the practice. Paul Kennedy chose Porcupine as a call sign for Echo and Joker for Chris Bronzi's Golf. His pet name for the hulking leader of Weapons Company, Rob Weiler, was "Wookie," something none of Weiler's men dared call him to his face.

Many nicknames generated within the ranks required zero imagination. "Tex" for Jose Texidor. "Yago" for Romeo Santiago. "Shorty" for five-foot-three radio operator Victor Madrillejos. Weapons Company platoon leader JD Stephens handed them out to his men like hors d'oeuvres: "Knife," "Deuce," "Big Boy," "Swede," "Tweeter," and "Neck" (for a Marine with, well, a large neck), to name just a few.

On occasion, a little free association caused a label to stick. For Chris MacIntosh, it happened the year before Ramadi during training in Okinawa. A handful of his buddies, Deshon Otey among them, were watching a violent gangbanger film called *Belly* in which there were clips from another movie—the avant-garde *Gummo*, depicting two poor white trash boys blasting away with cap guns at a third adolescent wearing rabbit ears. "This shitty-ass rabbit stinks!" one yells. Always afterward and throughout the fighting in Ramadi, MacIntosh was known as "Rabbit."

He grew to like it.

If it all sounded bat-shit crazy, that's because it was. The Marines, after all, were living in a dangerous city among people who wanted them dead. They were preoccupied with not being maimed by a mortar round or obliterated by an IED or shot by a sniper or thrust into a kill-or-be-killed gunfight. They were adapting to this madness, even becoming seasoned at it. But there was still life in the margins where basic human needs and desires existed. A good night's sleep. A decent meal. Staying hydrated in triple-digit heat. The simple enjoyment of getting momentarily lost in a video on their laptop (circulated selections ranged from, surprisingly, the romantic drama *The Notebook* to the bloody *Sopranos* series) or catching a few precious moments on the internet or satellite phone with family. Talking smack with a bunkmate, rave dancing in the barracks, or delving into life's meaning with another Marine during long hours of guard duty. Just plain missing wives or girlfriends or parents or children. Or sex. Trying to reconcile those longings with the reality and demands of Ramadi was preposterous, and it was folly even to try. All a sane person could do once in a while was laugh at it.

There was never a timeout from any of this for Marines, of course. The Army, since it required soldiers to deploy for a year, allowed a two-week leave to go home. But the Marine combat tour was seven months, and so there was no break. On rare occasions, if a Marine had a major emergency, such as a death in the family, they were allowed to go back to the States for at least a few days, and when they asked their buddies if there was anything they should bring back, the response was always the same and often announced in unison: "Porn."

They were, after all, young men brimming with testosterone, and when such images were available, one thing would lead to another. On a base like Combat Outpost, the one location where a Marine could be relatively assured of privacy was one of the heavy plastic portable toilets.

On a very hot day in late July, an Echo Company lance corporal in shorts and a T-shirt headed out to one. He was a team leader and veteran of some of the toughest combat Echo had endured. Since there was the threat of a chemical attack that day, he was required to wear a gas mask outside. He carried his M16 in one hand, mandatory for any trip across the base, and in his other hand, a device of assistance graphically labeled with the illuminating nickname of "pocket pussy." For some reason, it was lime green. He liked to call it his girlfriend.

The problem was that just about the time he was attending to business inside the toilet, the base came under a mortar attack. Rounds whistled in and exploded. Following one of the blasts, the Marine heard what sounded like gravel hitting the outside of the john and instinctively hit the floor. The filthy, disgusting, God-knows-what-is-on-it floor. It's amazing the incentive an enemy attack will engender.

He cracked open the door and could see the tires on nearby Humvees flattened by the shrapnel. Then he burst out of the portable toilet and beat a path to his barracks several yards away, a sight to behold. Rifle in one hand, girlfriend in the other, skivvies down around the knees, and wearing a gas mask. Corporal Frank Gutierrez, with Echo's Weapons Platoon, was on guard directly above the toilet and saw the whole thing. He couldn't resist yelling out, "Did you finish?"

The "gravel" that hit the toilet was actually shrapnel, bits of it slicing into the flesh on the back of the lance corporal's right arm. He didn't even notice right away and was one of four wounded in the attack that day. They would all, of course, be awarded Purple Hearts. There was a ceremony and a few knowing smiles when the team leader received his medal "for wounds received in action."

These were the kinds of images the Marines loved to recollect

LUNACY

(as opposed to the ones they longed to forget), memories stacked up neatly at the intersection of hilarious and harrowing.

Like the time a 107 mm enemy rocket smashed into Golf Company's operations center and punched through the roof into the quick-reaction force assembly room. The thirty-three-inch projectile, which had a blast radius of forty feet, blessedly failed to detonate and instead went spinning like a top on the floor. Marines watched in wonder.

When the shower water at Combat Outpost produced an odd smell, men clambered on top of the water tank for a look-see. An Iraqi contractor maintained the facilities, pulling water right out of the Euphrates and pumping it unfiltered into a tank. The Marines could see catfish swimming around in the same liquid they'd be using to clean themselves and their clothing. Real slapstick stuff.

While there wasn't any photo memorializing the fish or spinning rocket or lance corporal fleeing the portable toilet, there was a snapshot of Golf Company Marines lounging poolside. Sort of. Someone had gotten their hands on a large, plastic children's wading pool, set it up in the courtyard of the company barracks, and filled it to the brim with water. Marines stripped down to their shorts and happily lolled away, "brown faces and pale bodies pointed at the sun," Lieutenant Donovan Campbell later wrote in a memoir.[5]

Another popular image among members of Echo Company Marines was of Chris MacIntosh dancing naked at the Graveyard Observation Post just out of sight of his platoon commander. The post was one of several eventually set up along main thoroughfares in Ramadi. Marines could watch the roads to see if IEDs were being planted, a far superior approach than patrolling the same street to spot bombs already buried and risk annihilation in the process. Manning the outposts meant long hours of sitting and staring, and idle minds. An errant idea like "let's do something stupid" might bubble up. For MacIntosh, whose difficult combat experiences hadn't yet eclipsed his impetuousness, it led him to strip down to only a ballistic vest, shoulder an AT4 bazooka-like weapon, and grin into the camera. Somehow, amid the madness that was Ramadi, the image struck the perfect note.

Nor were these sublime or ridiculous moments confined to the rank-and-file. Weapons Company Captain Rob Weiler and his executive officer, Lieutenant Lucas Wells, were out with some of their troops in the industrial area of central Ramadi along a curving road the battalion called the Racetrack. An IED had been found and an explosive ordnance disposal (EOD) team summoned to blow it up. These kinds of events—waiting for EOD to arrive and then, finally, to get the job done—could take hours. Weiler and Wells wandered through an empty apartment building nearby and found cold bottles of Sprite. They settled on the ground with their backs against a garage behind an expensively appointed home of a sheik, sipping soda and waiting for word from EOD. Word arrived that detonation was ten seconds away. The power of the explosion, which occurred in the street opposite the sheik's home, was far greater than expected. The shock wave rippled through the building and bucked both men onto a back street from where they watched as a major appliance came soaring through the air. It was a large, modern refrigerator that was blasted through sliding glass doors in the sheik's home and landed about seventy feet in front of the two stunned officers. They looked at each other in pure disbelief and then broke into smiles. They had barely avoided becoming the most unusual killed-in-action cases of the war—death by refrigerator.

Then there was the time Tom Cogan caught endless ridicule from his men because the California legislature managed to get him married while he was in Ramadi. True story. The Philadelphia native, who fought his way to earning a Silver Star for actions April 6 and 10, had learned after arriving in Kuwait that his girlfriend, Theresa Arnold, was pregnant. He wanted her medical expenses covered during the birth of their daughter and death

LUNACY   251

benefits paid in the event he was killed. Cogan, who commanded Echo Company's Third Platoon, couldn't go home to get this done, and marriage by proxy was not legal in California. It was the lieutenant's boss, Captain Kelly Royer, who suggested petitioning the state to change the law. The twenty-three-year-old platoon commander had family in Philadelphia who had legal contacts in California working the issue, and after a period of months, Governor Arnold Schwarzenegger signed a bill allowing service members serving overseas to marry through a legal stand-in. At 11:00 a.m. on September 11, at the county clerk's office in San Diego, with family present and a close friend as proxy for Cogan, the couple exchanged vows by cell phone, a first in California history. (It was 10:00 p.m. in Ramadi.) Theresa's wedding gown was peach. It was a good-news story in the middle of so much violence, and newspapers ate it up. WTH THS RNG I THEE WD—IRAQ MARINE MARRIES CALIF. GAL BY CELLPHONE, heralded the *New York Post*.[6] Cogan caught heaps of derision and felt awful when it came time to travel across Ramadi to sign legal papers. Any trip through the streets of the city was dangerous. "Hey, guys, I apologize for this," he told his men.

In years to come, other service members would take advantage of the new law to do the same thing.

Comedy relief extended to the Army as well, like the time the senior physician for the entire area of operation injected himself with fifteen milligrams of morphine by mistake.

Army Captain Randy Radmer, forty-five, was the brigade surgeon, a family medicine specialist from St. Joseph, Missouri. On August 23, Radmer was riding in a security detail with Connor near a mosque in Ramadi when the convoy came under attack and a rocket-propelled grenade exploded, wounding an Army specialist in both legs. Radmer was preparing to ease his pain with some morphine. Connor and other soldiers were clustered around when some commotion caused Radmer to fumble with the syringe and grab it upside down so that when he pushed it into the soldier's thigh, he stuck himself in the hand instead. Quickly realizing his mistake, Radmer looked up at Connor.

"Sir, I fucked up," he said.

"What?"

"I gave me the morphine and not him."

Connor could see Radmer's eyes start to glisten. "Well, that's no fucking good. You probably ought to head in."

"Yes, I probably should."

Radmer was getting high. But for the next ten minutes, he was still able to administer two morphine shots to the wounded soldier and apply a dressing. Then he and the wounded GI were both carted off by armored ambulance to Camp Ramadi, where the attending physician at Charlie Med noticed Radmer had three empty injectors even though he said he had only given the soldier two.

"I may have accidentally gotten one of those," Radmer explained.

The physician laughed. "I don't even want to know."

11

PERSEVERANCE

"RHONDA, WE NEED TO PRAY. WE NEED TO PRAY RIGHT NOW. IT'S JEREMIAH. I JUST KNOW IT'S JEREMIAH."

VIOLENCE DROPPED TO relatively low levels through the remainder of April in Ramadi. The Battle of Fallujah that began on April 6 drew to a close by the end of the month as security for the city was turned over to the Fallujah Brigade of the former Iraqi military. The general consensus among military leaders was that the negotiated result would only create a haven for the insurgency that would have to be defeated at some point. It certainly allowed a base of operations from which insurgents could launch future attacks against the US troops in Ramadi. "Today we surrendered to the insurgency," Buck Connor lamented in his diary.

Meanwhile, fighting raged along the Syrian border in the Al-Qaim District with the heaviest combat during a two-day period beginning April 17 in the village of Husaybah, where five Marines were killed, including a company commander.

Three days earlier, in a small village nearby, a squad of Marines was searching vehicles for weapons when an insurgent leaped out of one of them and grappled with the unit leader, Corporal Jason Dunham. The Marine wrestled the man down and saw on the ground a live grenade he'd released. Dunham shouted a warning to his men and covered the explosive with his helmet and body, absorbing the blast. He died of his wounds eight days later and was posthumously awarded the Medal of Honor, the first Marine to receive this highest valor award since Vietnam.

In Ramadi, a brief hiatus from dying was almost over. While the heavy ground combat had subsided, the enemy relentlessly pursued other ways to kill or maim Americans. They would manage to succeed at times to flood centers with more dead and wounded than could be handled.

The greatest carnage was Sunday, May 2, as Navy Seabees assembled out in the open on Camp Ramadi. The famed Naval Construction Battalions (*Seabee* is a heterograph of the initials *CB* for *Construction Battalions*) have origins dating back to World War II, when these sailor-builders constructed military facilities and airfields around the world. The men sent to Ramadi were part of a reserve Seabee unit based in Jacksonville, Florida. They were citizen-soldiers with jobs such as mechanics or construction workers when they weren't called up to active duty. Many of them were older sailors in their thirties who simply volunteered to serve their country. The four hundred Seabees of the battalion who were deployed to Iraq in April 2004 were scattered across US installations stretching from the outskirts of Baghdad to the borders of Syria and Jordan, building and expanding facilities. Among the dozens assigned to Camp Ramadi were the escort teams that provided security for Seabee convoys moving between the bases. During one of their earliest missions on April 30, they were returning from delivering building supplies to Al-Qaim when their convoy was attacked. Two sailors were killed and six wounded. Like the Army and Marines before them, the Seabees began welding armor to their Humvees.

PERSEVERANCE

Buck Connor had seen these sailors gathering outside at Camp Ramadi for convoy briefings. They didn't report to him, but he directed his command sergeant major, Ron Riling, to warn that assembling outside for any length of time was dangerous. Insurgents watched from across the Euphrates and would launch mortar rounds or rockets into the sprawling base.

On the Sunday afternoon of May 2, a Seabee convoy made the short trip from Camp Ramadi to Blue Diamond to pick up a newly arrived high-level commander, Rear Admiral Charles Kubic. They escorted him back to Junction City, where the plan was for Kubic to visit with Seabees a few hours and then be transported back to Blue Diamond—all of it utterly routine.

But disaster struck shortly after Kubic arrived at Camp Ramadi. At 2:30 p.m., dozens of Seabees were standing in a south-facing half circle in their motor pool area, receiving further instructions. They were expecting to meet with Kubic, who was several yards away inspecting a damaged vehicle from the April 30 attack. Just then, powerful enemy 120 mm mortars opened fire. Investigators later surmised each round was fired from the back of three trucks positioned in an apartment complex to the southwest, allowing the enemy to flee quickly and avoid capture. There were theories afterward that one of the installation's hired workers, acting as a spy, helped enemy gunners take aim.

But it was a very windy day, and it would have been challenging, if not impossible, for any mortar team to successfully strike a specific location, particularly insurgents firing out of the backs of pickup trucks. More than likely on May 2, the Seabees were victims of monstrously bad luck amid the reality that in Ramadi, a simple human urge to linger outside carried with it the risk of sudden death.

The first shell landed near a battalion headquarters and a hunk of shrapnel came through a window and struck Army Captain John Tipton in the head. The thirty-two-year-old officer and married father of two young children was killed. Seven other soldiers were wounded.

Twenty to thirty seconds later, the second round landed not far from the west end of where the sailors were standing in a semicircle. The ground in the motor pool was so hard that it absorbed little of the shrapnel. The flying shards instead ripped the sailors grouped nearby. It was a bloodbath. Seabees were torn apart. Wounded were screaming in pain. Other cried out for help. Some left blood trails as they crawled for cover underneath a nearby Humvee.[1] One Seabee had a piece of shrapnel sticking out of his stomach, and both legs were shredded below the knees. He would be airlifted out only to die from his wounds. There were dozens of casualties. Ground ambulances and other vehicles began to ferry them to the nearby Charlie Med, where casualties on litters supported by sawhorses filled every available space and spilled out into a reception area under an outside awning.

Army medical personnel working with critical care nurse Jody Schroeder, whose empathy had touched so many wounded Marines in the previous weeks, heard the explosions and scrambled to prepare. The first to arrive was the mortally wounded Tipton. Schroeder had had dinner with him just the night before in the mess hall, where he spoke of his excitement to soon be going home to his family.

Word of the Seabee disaster arrived, and Schroeder called out to the staff. "There are going to be a bunch of Seabees showing up in a few minutes," she said. "We need to prep for a mascal," using the term for a mass casualty event, every medical facility's worst nightmare. Surgeons and medics from a special operations base nearby rushed to assist. Schroeder triaged every wounded patient, quickly deciding who required urgent care, who could wait, and who was beyond saving. Major Clint Murray, a thirty-year-old infectious disease physician, was Charlie Med's senior doctor. He circulated through a tableau of bedlam—countless scrums of medical workers, each hunched over a bleeding service member in

PERSEVERANCE

agony. Murray could see a level of control and patient-processing that was achieving results. Airways were cleared. Bleeding staunched. Body fluids restored. One by one, wounded sailors and soldiers were made ready to be carried out and loaded onto large Marine helicopter transports for flights to higher-level hospital facilities. The first copter left with casualties one hour after the blast. Four medevacs would be required to fly all the wounded out.

The mortar attack created forty-five casualties, including at least thirty-six sailors. One Seabee brought into Charlie Med was already dead. A second one died during treatment. Twenty-seven people required an air medevac for more complex care, twenty-two of them sailors. Three Seabees and Tipton would not survive. A June 4 after-action report listed lessons learned, starting with never gathering in groups out in the open.

The event would be the deadliest day for Navy Seabees since Vietnam.

The Magnificent Bastards suffered almost identical numbers of casualties in May; they simply occurred throughout the month. Forty-seven Marines and Navy corpsmen were wounded. Six Marines died. If the enemy's willingness to stand and fight in large numbers had abated after the battles of early April, their thirst for killing Americans wherever and whenever possible was never slaked. There was in May an average of one casualty-producing attack nearly every other day, mostly from IEDs. (Events involving roadside bombs, where they were found or exploded without causing injury, were far more numerous.)

The very first one was shortly before 9:00 p.m. on May 1, when a Weapons Company convoy passing through a western area of the city not far off the banks of the Euphrates Channel was hit by a roadside bomb. It was believed the trigger man, working with a remote-controlled device, was on the other side of the channel, about 140 yards away. It targeted the Rainmaker platoon that had seen so much action already. The bomb struck the third vehicle in the convoy, and the driver took the worst of it with shrapnel raking his left leg and ankle. His left thumb hung on by a shred of tissue. Lance Corporal Reagan Hodges—who had selflessly charged a machine gunner during combat on April 10—was in the front passenger seat and caught shrapnel in his face. He got out and ran over to the driver, who was twenty years old, in shock and pain and screaming, "Mama! Mama!" The sight of a young man in agony was heartbreaking. But Hodges also was furious that the enemy might relish seeing a Marine crying out that way. Hodges grabbed him. "You have got to shut up screaming for your mother!"

Five other Marines were wounded. Two of them, including the driver, would require medical evacuation out of the country.

Less than two weeks later, the hard-luck platoon would be hit again, and this time, it would be much worse. For three hours on the Wednesday morning of May 12, Rainmaker, with Lieutenant Dave Dobb in command, had been engaged in a civil affairs mission, a bland title for what were gestures of goodwill. Weapons Company commander Rob Weiler was with them, as was his executive officer, Lucas Wells. The task was to visit schools in the Sofia District and hand out soccer balls, Frisbees, candy, and gum to children. At one stop, the Marines dropped off a generator to provide power for a school. Many of the men, particularly those with their own kids, loved the job. There was no hatred or suspicion in the young faces, and for at least a few minutes, war's oppressiveness lifted. Then it was back into the Humvees with their jerry-rigged armor and off into streets where no good deed went unpunished.

Rainmaker was headed to its third and final school, traveling on Route Nova near the infamous Gypsum intersection, where so many Americans had died in April, when explosives buried in the roadway were remotely detonated by the enemy. The blast was directly adjacent to an open-backed Humvee loaded with troops, forcing the vehicle off the road and into a gully. Such Humvees had hillbilly armor bolted on, but the plates of steel on the sides only extended up so far, leaving the necks and heads of Marines

PERSEVERANCE

riding in the back unprotected. And it was worse for the machine gunner who rode standing up behind the vehicle cab. The gunner was basically exposed from the waist up. The blast hit the left side of the Humvee. The driver, Lance Corporal David Reigelsperger Jr., was covered in shrapnel, unconscious but alive. His jaw would have to be wired back together. Dave Dobb was in the front passenger seat and momentarily blacked out.

Most of those riding in the back escaped serious injury, though the pressure wave was so powerful it blew out eardrums for most of them. For four of the Marines in the truck, including Reigelsperger, it was the second time each had been wounded during the deployment. When Dobb regained his senses, one of the first things he heard was Lance Corporal Jeremiah Savage cry out. He had been manning the machine gun.

"I'm dying," the twenty-one-year-old said.

A corpsman rushed to treat him, and outwardly, it looked at first like an uncomplicated wound. A piece of shrapnel had struck him in his lower-left back and exited out the right side of his neck. He was conscious. When they rushed him back to Combat Outpost, Dobb and the others felt certain he would survive. He was put on a helicopter for transport to a hospital.

Just the day before, Savage's wife, Cassandra, had told him by phone that photographs of his newborn son were in the mail. Back in his hometown of Livingston, Tennessee, where it was morning when the bomb went off, Savage's mother, Eva, was starting her day at work at a Pamida department store. Jeremiah had called her on Mother's Day, the Sunday before. On this Wednesday morning, she was preparing to move dresses out to the sales floor when she was suddenly overwhelmed with a feeling of dread. She turned to her manager. "Rhonda, we need to pray. We need to pray right now. It's Jeremiah. I just know it's Jeremiah."

The shrapnel that had struck her son tore through his body, slicing across the largest artery of the human body, the aorta. Whether Jeremiah Savage could sense that his insides were terribly damaged when he said he was dying, no one will know. But he did not survive for long.

Eva Savage attended Wednesday-night church service and after returning home was in the kitchen looking out the window when a vehicle pulled up and three Marines in dress uniforms disembarked. She knew exactly why they were there.

Back in Ramadi, brigade commander Buck Connor recorded the events in his diary. "It was a bright sunny day. Nothing happening. And then suddenly, we had a man killed and more wounded by an IED." This was life in Ramadi, he wrote: "Mind-numbing repetition punctuated by quick, violent, horrible events."

Many weeks later, during an interview with a historian at Combat Outpost, Lance Corporal Reagan Hodges reflected on the terrible calamities that never seemed to stop. "You can train all day long how to medevac and get a casualty out of a situation. But what you can't train for is the mental part," he said. "When you hear one of your friends screaming in pain and you look at him and he's a bloody mess, how can you react to that? . . . Those are things you cannot train for. Those are things that you have to be squared away within yourself. Nothing in this world can help you."

As May drew to a close, the pace of attacks quickened. On the morning of Wednesday, May 26, Connor and his five-vehicle security entourage were traveling east on Route Michigan when an IED detonated next to his vehicle—the third in line—about three hundred yards east of the arches. The colonel was in the front passenger seat of a Humvee that only had metal plates bolted on the lower half of the passenger doors. The blast went off close by, sending a cloud of debris two hundred feet into the air that seemed to swallow the truck. For whatever reason, perhaps the angle of the blast, shrapnel struck only the Humvee roof. Connor had tiny pieces in his skin that left him covered in small, bleeding wounds. Still, the explosion was powerful enough to blow out the windshield and leave the colonel unconscious from the pressure wave. He tried to scream for his driver to stop, but produced only a squawk. His lungs and nostrils were filled with a metallic taste and after climbing out of the truck, Conner took two woozy steps, and collapsed. Soldiers drove him back to Camp Ramadi, where the colonel fell down again and was transported by ambulance to Charlie Med.

In addition to soreness, Connor had classic symptoms of a brain injury—nausea, dizziness, and headache. Later, there would be vomiting and near convulsions. Senior physician Clint Murray wanted the colonel flown to another facility to undergo a CT scan to see if there was bleeding in the brain, but Connor adamantly refused. Randy Radmer, the brigade surgeon who often acted as Connor's personal physician, reluctantly acquiesced.

The day after the brigade commander incident, Eric Smith, who would be awarded a Navy Cross for valor on April 6, was wounded along with two other Marines and a corpsman in a roadside bomb attack in eastern Ramadi. They had been riding in one of the tall seven-ton trucks when the bomb went off. Injuries were relatively minor, and everyone eventually returned to duty. But in the immediate aftermath, as an unarmored Marine ambulance raced through the streets of Ramadi carrying Smith—who was strapped into a litter and had been stripped down to his underwear—another IED went off outside. It caused no injuries, and the ambulance kept moving. But it jarred Smith, who angrily demanded that the corpsman who was with him, Adam Clayton, hand over his 9 mm so the corporal would have something to fight with if they got into more trouble.

"Dude, no, I'm not giving it to you!"

They arrived safely.

By then, doctors at Charlie Med had already been working frantically to keep another Marine alive whose wounds were far more grievous. Earlier that morning, Golf Company's First Platoon had come under attack in south-central Ramadi. They had headed out in a convoy to an elementary school so that new building improvements the battalion had financed could be inspected. The trucks were parked along an adjacent street for several minutes. Lingering anywhere for any length of time was always dangerous, allowing enemy fighters time to be alerted and assembled for an attack, and that's what happened. There was an eruption of enemy rifle fire, and rocket-propelled grenades were launched. None of the troops were hit as they immediately returned fire, including with heavy, truck-mounted machine guns. But one of the RPGs exploded amid a gaggle of young children standing outside the school. It was a nightmarish spectacle as small limbs and bodies were thrown in every direction. Two boys and a girl were killed outright. Marines pursued the enemy fighters who had fled while others with a corpsmen tended to the mangled children still alive. As fearful as he was of more attacks, the platoon commander, Lieutenant Donovan Campbell, ordered his men to remain at the school and care for the children until civilian ambulances arrived. Campbell—who had earned a Bronze Star on April 6 for playing a key role in the rescue of trapped Marines—established a defensive perimeter. "We were United States Marines and a bunch of dying children needed our help," Campbell would later explain in a memoir.[2]

His worst fears soon followed. An insurgent cautiously approached and launched an RPG from down a nearby street, and the projectile exploded near one of the parked Humvees. The driver of the vehicle, twenty-three-year-old Lance Corporal Todd Bolding, a native of Texas, was kneeling nearby. The rocket exploded against a light post, and shrapnel sheared off his left leg a few inches below the hip and his right leg just below the knee. As corpsmen reached him to start wrapping tourniquets, silence enveloped the schoolyard, broken only by Bolding's screams.

Critical care nurse Jody Schroeder was the first to meet the Humvee that arrived with Bolding. He was conscious but going into shock. The amputated portion of his right leg lay beside him on the litter. Medical personnel were stunned by the extent of the

PERSEVERANCE

destruction even beyond his mangled legs. The senior physician, Clint Murray, saw that the Marine's pelvic area had severe damage, perhaps reaching into the abdomen. Wounds were dressed as much as possible, and the team began the delicate process of reaching the right balance in restoring some of the vast amounts of lost blood—an area of severe trauma care that was still a learning process.

The fluids had to be restored, but only to a degree. Administering too much could raise blood pressure to a level that might break loose clots and cause more hemorrhaging. Normal blood pressure is about 110 over 70. In treating Bolding, they were shooting for a systolic number—the higher one—of no more than 90. At some point, it went too high. Bolding's brain became infused with blood, and he sat bolt upright in the litter, alarming Schroeder, Murray, and others. They finally achieved an equilibrium, stabilizing the Marine to the point where he could be flown out to higher-level care. He was carefully transported from one facility to another until arriving at a major Army hospital in Germany. Ten days after he was wounded, Bolding passed away there with his family at his bedside.

The death of Savage and the fatal wounding of Bolding were not even the worst of what happened in May. That horror was reserved for what occurred two days after the elementary school slaughter.

It was a Saturday, May 29, three weeks before the start of summer, with the temperature already rising to 110 degrees by 9:00 a.m. A Weapons Company platoon was conducting another of the dreaded route clearance missions on the far east end of Ramadi. Two combat engineers were on foot, using a mine detector to find buried bombs. It was the same dangerous gamble Marines had faced too often before—locating a concealed explosive before an enemy insurgent, watching from a hidden location at some distance, detonated it. The bet this time was lost. An artillery shell shrouded in sand exploded, throwing both engineers—Lance

Corporal Ryan Elkins, twenty-three, and Private First Class Dustin Howell, twenty—into the air. Elkins suffered shrapnel wounds to his face and lost an eye. Howell was also blinded in one eye and had damaged vision in the other. He had a broken leg and shrapnel damage to his midsection. Both were headed home.

That was only prelude to the most catastrophic event of the day, which happened just down the road five hours later. An Echo Company convoy led by a new commander of Second Platoon—Second Lieutenant Michael Martley, who replaced the slain John Wroblewski—was heading west on Route Michigan back to Combat Outpost. Martley was twenty-four and a graduate of the Citadel military college of South Carolina. He was a quiet, reserved young man who had been given the unenviable task of replacing a beloved officer to lead men who had long since become seasoned and battle hardened. His platoon sergeant, the irascible Damien Coan, would eventually warm up to Martley. But in these early weeks as the new lieutenant found his footing, Coan had little patience and a short fuse. His men joked that Coan would kill Martley before the deployment was done.

On this day, the lieutenant and his Second Platoon troops were on a retrieval mission, fetching members of Weapons Platoon for transport back to Combat Outpost. Utterly routine. It was about 2:00 p.m. Earlier in the day, battalion commander Paul Kennedy and his security detail were traveling through that portion of the city and spotted an abandoned station wagon parked on the north side of Route Michigan about a mile east of Combat Outpost. The fact that it hadn't been stripped was suspicious, and headquarters was notified about a possible VBIED, or car bomb.

What happened to that message remains unclear. But when Martley headed out with his people, he was unaware. After picking up the Weapons Platoon Marines, the troops headed back in a four-vehicle convoy along Michigan and approached the parked car.

PERSEVERANCE

Like so many things in this dangerous city, fate sometimes rested on the most inconsequential circumstances. Two team leaders for Second Platoon, Corporal Misael Nieto and Lance Corporal Jason Birmelin, were discussing where each would ride in the convoy. This was no small matter, because both men knew then when it came to IEDs, the enemy trigger men typically keyed off the first vehicle in a convoy when detonating a bomb so that the explosion, when it occurred, hit the third or fourth truck. The two Marines played a quick game of rock-paper-scissors. Birmelin won. He rode in the front of the first vehicle. Nieto climbed into the passenger seat of the last truck. It was an open-backed Humvee, similar to the one in which Savage was fatally wounded a few weeks earlier. There was steel plating along the flanks, steel L-shaped doors on the passenger and driver's sides, a ballistic glass windshield, and panels in the back filled with ceramic armored plates like the ones troops wore as body protection. It was all jerry-rigged. As with Savage's truck, the troops riding on benches in the back facing inward had protection only up to their shoulders.

Even more exposed was the machine gunner, who in this case was nineteen-year-old Private First Class Cody Calavan. He was the gunner on the improvised mission on April 6 that delivered the mortally wounded Lieutenant John Wroblewski back to base.

The other bit of chance was where people chose to sit in the back of the truck. In this instance, those who happened to sit on the right caught the worst of what was about to happen. Those on the left escaped relatively unscathed.

Birmelin, in the lead vehicle, spotted the station wagon with its hood up, as if disabled, and immediately became suspicious, telling his driver to "go on the other side of the road." But when the last vehicle passed, it was only six feet from the parked car. The station wagon was weighted down with four or five artillery shells, plastic explosives, and ball bearings for shrapnel. The car disintegrated on detonation.

The blast shredded the right side of the Humvee and the tires. The steel plates held. But where they didn't extend high enough, ball bearings slammed into the heads and faces of Marines sitting on the right side of the truck.

Calavan was killed outright. Another one of Kennedy's high school graduates of 2003, he left behind a Washington State father who had lost his wife to cancer and his only other son to a drunken driver.

Also dead or dying was Corporal Rafael Reynosa Suarez, twenty-eight, of Santa Ana, California. The day before, in the Combat Outpost chow hall, Suarez had proudly showed another Marine, Theophilus Tor, ultrasound pictures from his wife's pregnancy. Rafael and Dinora had been high school sweethearts. "I'm having twins," he proudly told Tor.

"Bro, I know you're going to be a great dad."

Two other Marines sitting on that right side of the truck were barely alive. Five more and a corpsman were also wounded.

Marines and sailors in the convoy moved rapidly to reach and begin tending to the casualties and set up a perimeter around the blast site. In a crowd of people nearby, several Iraqi men dressed in police uniforms could be seen laughing at what had happened. They were taken into custody.

The scene was a chaotic horror show. A Marine with a gruesome, gaping hole to the back of his head was conscious and fighting those trying to hold him down to be bandaged, all the while yelling incoherently. Elsewhere, a corpsman was bellowing, "Stay with me!" to a grievously wounded Lance Corporal Benjamin Gonzalez Jr. He was a twenty-three-year-old Texas native and combat replacement just two months from going home, where he had plans to marry.[3]

Navy hospitalman Manaia Alaimalo, twenty-one, of Long Beach, California, who had helped Corpsman Kevin Barger on April 10 treat Jose Texidor, was riding on the left side of the Humvee. He had shrapnel wounds on his right arm, and his eardrums were blown out. Blood trickled from his ears. But he was conscious, flipped himself over the left side of the truck, and began treating Sergeant James King, who was riding in the back of the truck. The sergeant's left leg was nearly severed at the knee, and he had lacerations to his skull. Alaimalo worked to apply a tourniquet.

Corporal Frank Gutierrez, who had helped load up slain Americans at the intersection of Gypsum and Nova on April 6, was in the first truck of the convoy. He raced to assist and found a close friend, Lance Corporal Anthony Alegre, lying still and covered in blood. Gutierrez felt certain the twenty-year-old Marine was dead or nearly so and moved on to help with another casualty.

The driver of the blasted truck was Private First Class Gregg Arneson, who had wounds to his face and a broken left foot. Corporal Nieto—who had lost at rock-paper-scissors—was in the passenger seat, closer to the explosion. He had severe internal damage to his midsection and would lose his spleen. His hands were badly mauled, and he had a broken right foot.

Trucks started to ferry the wounded and dead to Combat Outpost, the nearest location for treatment and helicopter evacuation. It was a small battalion aid station with one doctor, Navy Lieutenant Colin Crickard, and the event quickly became overwhelming.

The battalion had two Navy doctors, Crickard and Lieutenant Kenneth Son. The two men alternated between an aid station at Hurricane Point and another at Combat Outpost. In conjunction with Navy corpsmen, the doctors handled routine health care and battlefield wounds. More serious cases were transported to Charlie Med at Camp Ramadi in the far west end of the city. But where Marines suffered severe wounds during fighting in the city's east end and required immediate airlift, they could be taken to the Combat Outpost aid station to be stabilized and flown out by helicopter to a larger treatment facility.

Son, a graduate of the University of Southern California, was also versed in acupuncture and treated hundreds of troops for a variety of maladies from sleep disorder to back pain to combat stress. Even Paul Kennedy partook.

Crickard was a six-foot-six former high school wrestler who won the 215-pound weight class state championship in New York State in 1994. A Naval Academy graduate, he earned his medical degree at the Uniformed Services University in Bethesda, Maryland.

The clinic at Combat Outpost was tiny. There were only four stations available for treating major wound cases, essentially litters set up on sawhorses. The whole point of the aid station when it came to the severest casualties was to make certain airways were clear and patients could breathe, intubating them if necessary, checking dressings, and then sending them off by helicopter. The wounded from the car bomb explosion arrived in two waves as trucks pulled in. There were six very severe cases. Three of those had been sitting on the blast side of the open-backed Humvee: Gonzalez, Alegre, and Corporal Bumrock "Bum" Lee. (The fourth Marine on that side, Suarez, was already dead.) Lee, a twenty-one-year-old Californian whose family had brought him from South Korea at age four, was one of the most beloved, popular members in the battalion and had been working to acquire his US citizenship.[4] The other three urgent cases were King, whose left leg was mangled, and the two men sitting in the front of the vehicle, Arneson and Nieto.

Crickard had to make a difficult choice. As the four litter stations quickly filled, a corpsman with each patient shouted out vital signs and what care needed to be delivered. Crickard moved from one patient to the next, quickly realizing he had more gravely wounded people than he had places and people to prepare them for air medevac. He resorted to triaging, deciding who could be saved and who was beyond saving. Arneson, the driver of the Humvee, looked to be in a better condition than any of the others and was set aside for the moment. Gonzalez, on the other hand, was so disfigured by the blast—he had one arm missing—that no

PERSEVERANCE

one knew who he was. His dog tags were gone. Someone finally recognized his tattoos. Gonzalez had been intubated and undergone a chest decompression to assist with respiration. But he didn't appear to be breathing or bleeding from wounds any longer. Crickard decided there was nothing else to be done. They had no blood products to provide. They needed his treatment station for another casualty.

"Okay, he's expectant," Crickard told his corpsmen. "Move him out because he's not really alive at this point in time."

The four casualties in the treatment stations were Lee, Alegre, King, and Nieto. Gonzalez was carried outside the building, where Hospitalman Adam Clayton with the help of some other Marines continued CPR and administered ten milligrams of epinephrine or adrenaline to stimulate the heart. It seemed to work. Clayton thought he had a pulse and told others to pass word along. Crickard was stunned and directed that Gonzalez be air medevacked with the others. It was also the beginning of what would be years of second-guessing for the physician as he served out his time in the Navy and later went into private practice, haunted by whether he made a terrible mistake on that day in Ramadi.

But Clayton himself was not certain Gonzalez was alive. And indeed, he was pronounced dead not long after he was flown away.

Bum Lee had suffered a massive open head wound and would live only two more days.

Of the five men who took the full force of the blast—the four riding on the right side of the truck and the machine gunner— only Alegre survived. The explosion and shrapnel had cracked his skull like an eggshell. This would actually help him to survive, as it allowed space for his injured brain to swell until it could begin to recover. Doctors retained the portion of his cranium that had cracked loose and later surgically reassembled Alegre's skull. He would remain hospitalized for sixteen months.

The killing of four Marines in the car bomb attack May 29 was the worst loss to the battalion since the April 6 battle.

It was becoming increasingly clear for the troops of 2nd Battalion, 4th Marines that the enemy hadn't gone away after the April heavy fighting. If the insurgents couldn't defeat the Americans on the battlefield, they were clearly committed to running up the number of US dead and wounded by almost daily attacks with bombs or hit-and-run ambushes.

The Magnificent Bastards kept aggressively counterattacking when the opportunity presented. They sifted intel and used it to launch raids across the city—twenty in May—to capture or kill enemy operatives and uncover weapons-storage areas. (A good number turned up nothing.) Simultaneously, they kept working to forge alliances with the nonviolent sectors of Ramadi, continuing to finance school and mosque renovations, street improvements, soccer stadium upgrades, and even paying for trash and debris removal—ultimately $2.9 million of investment.[5] And they kept handing out candy and soccer balls to children.

Beginning in late spring, the Marines began shifting from the dangerous route clearance missions to static observation posts from which to conduct twenty-four-hour surveillance of Route Michigan to guard against enemy fighters planting IEDs—the same tactic Army Captain Nicholas Ayers had used to great success with his tanks and Bradley Fighting Vehicles along Highway 1 north of Ramadi. Chris Bronzi ended the route clearances for his Golf Company on May 24.

As the Magnificent Bastards reached the halfway point in their deployment to Ramadi, the insurgency's stubborn, unrelenting violence bred an unalloyed contempt for the enemy among the Americans that would seep through in unexpected ways.

Echo Company commander Kelly Royer had accompanied the delivery of a wounded insurgent to Charlie Med at Camp Ramadi. Captured enemy fighters were to be provided medical care just as robust as any delivered to wounded US service members, and Royer watched with fascination as doctors tended to the man. Royer noticed a pretty, blond nurse on the team.

It was Jody Schroeder, who had her own feelings about the enemy. She had treated scores of them. Did so willingly. And despised them just the same. "The badly wounded bad guys are assing up all the resources," she complained to her diary back in April. On one previous occasion, Schroeder was working on a wounded Iraqi police officer who had to be restrained on a stretcher because he was belligerent and fighting with medics. When they started to release him, the man grabbed the stethoscope wrapped around the nurse's neck and tried to yank her down. She fought him off, and he was once again restrained, this time as an Army battalion commander stood nearby with his 9 mm.

On the day Royer showed up, the Echo Company captain was so impressed with their generous treatment that he approached Schroeder and said, "You really do care for the enemy the way you do our own troops."

"You want to know the solution to that?" she responded.

"What?"

"You guys need to aim better."

12

MISTAKES

"GODDAMN IT, THEY FELL ASLEEP."

PAUL KENNEDY ALWAYS dreaded the sound of flip-flops on the stone floor outside his quarters at Hurricane Point. The battalion commander would be asleep in his rack. It might be 2:00 a.m. But the patter of those shower shoes getting closer and closer would rouse him, and he'd sit up in his cot, waiting.

It struck him how he had become like the blind cobbler and central character of Depression-era writer Wilbur Daniel Steele's short story "Footfalls," able to memorize the sound of a killer's footsteps.

For Kennedy, it was the footfalls of his operations officer, JD Harrill, who, more often than not, brought bad news about killers. Somewhere in the city, there was an enemy attack that left a young Marine dead or forever changed. The first few times Harrill padded in, there'd be a windup as he started to explain circumstances.

But Kennedy grew weary with that. He didn't need the preamble. "Just tell me the punch line," he'd say. "Who's hurt and who's killed? What are we doing about it?"

MISTAKES

Tactical decisions in the wake of a tragedy always came first. Calculating resources. What to ask of the brigade. Shifting manpower to compensate for casualties. Gauging what response would make the enemy pay a price. Divining what the insurgency would do next and how to meet that threat. After all of that, there remained questions Kennedy reserved for himself. How had he not anticipated? Where had he failed to ensure orders were carried out? What, if any, mistake did he make?

The enemy certainly gets a vote. But commanders had been dismissed for giving that vote too much weight. Whatever happened to the Magnificent Bastards, Kennedy knew he bore ultimate responsibility. Buck Connor could discharge him. James Mattis had built a mystique around firing people. He sacked a colonel, a regimental commander, during the Iraq invasion for not being aggressive enough. Kennedy witnessed it.

Whatever higher-ups made of his performance, Kennedy knew it was out of his hands, and no purpose was served by dwelling on it. Still, just the reality of working in a fishbowl where he was being watched and judged couldn't help but play with his head.

Mattis sketched out the contours of that fishbowl when he arrived at Combat Outpost in June and delivered a pep speech to Marines in the chow hall. "Ramadi must hold," he said in no uncertain terms. "If we don't hold the government center, if we don't hold the provincial capital, the rest of the province goes to hell in a handbasket."

Kennedy was confident in his own decisiveness.

But it was the internal dialogue of self-doubt that was always a distant bell for any commander when the enemy proved surprisingly resourceful and the result was dead Marines. *Was I ready for that? Am I the right person to do this? Am I really an imposter?*

Ramadi had a way of getting under the skin that way with its thicket of unforeseen consequences. Its people, its geography, its weather, even the flow of its river always left the Marines zero margin for error.

274 UNREMITTING

It was a hard lesson learned by Fox Company in early May. Based out of the Snake Pit combat post on the city's far west end, Fox was led by Captain Mark Carlton, a thirty-three-year-old graduate of history and political science out of Eastern New Mexico University.[1]

Carlton and his men operated in a part of the city where there was less violence than what Golf and Echo Companies were encountering. Apart from suffering the battalion's first killed-in-action casualty with the death of Lance Corporal Andrew Dang on March 22, Fox had through April lost no other people. With some exceptions, it had also sat out much of the major fighting that month.

In late April, commanders hit upon a daring mission for Fox. Intelligence officers had gotten tips that the enemy was using a large island in the river as a weapons storage depot. It was also believed that mortars were being fired from there. Fox Company troops in an observation post atop the city's largest hospital, 750 yards southwest of the island, had seen boat traffic to and from the island. It was an area of land in the Euphrates covered in grass and trees that was about 680 yards long and 170 yards across at its widest. It lay just 150 feet from the river's south shore.

It just so happened that Fox Company had special training in waterborne assaults, and several of its Marines had taken a scout-swimmer course. The battalion had also been drilled in conducting river crossings.[2] The plan would be to send three, two-man teams of swimmers over to the island to secure the shoreline and then pull over by rope inflatable Zodiac boats with landing teams aboard—everything done in total silence. Once in place, Marines would search for a weapons cache using mine detectors.

Some of the rank-and-file in the company were skeptical from the start. They could see the island almost every day as they patrolled along Route Nova. They'd not observed any activity there.

Kennedy thought the assault plan was sound while Harrill was

MISTAKES

concerned that intel on enemy activity wasn't strong enough to warrant the mission. Sergeant Major Jim Booker, who had more experience than anyone as a scout sniper and had conducted boat missions in the past, wasn't consulted on the planning. He didn't oppose the mission. But he warned the team to be careful about the current; it might look placid on the surface but, depending on the depth, could be roiling just below.

Operation Treasure Island was delayed a few days, and then Carlton gave it the green light for Saturday, May 1, and shortly before 11:00 p.m., six members of Fox Company entered the water. There were three corporals, Albert Pretrick, twenty-six, and Dustin Schrage and Jeffrey Green, both twenty; two lance corporals, Craig Atkins, twenty-one, and Brandon Winneshiek, twenty-two; and the company gunnery sergeant, Dirk Lens. It was Lens who had struggled back in March, with company First Sergeant Tim Weber, to find a dignified way of disposing of some final remains of slain combat engineer Andrew Dang after he was beheaded by a rocket-propelled grenade.

All six were considered expert swimmers, although they hadn't been in the water for months. The team, including the men who were to assault from Zodiacs, had practiced landing with the inflatable boats over at Hurricane Point.

Each pair pushed off from the shore in slightly different locations. Schrage and Atkins were farthest upstream, then Lens and Pretrick, then Green and Winneshiek. They wore trousers, swimming booties, and inflatable life vests. Each was weighed down by an M16 and ammunition. One thing missing from the crate of swimming assault gear that arrived in Iraq were fins, but they were thought unnecessary for such a short distance.

Lens, who would drag the rope that would be used to pull Zodiacs across once the swimmers reached the island, had a waterproof pack that provided buoyancy. The others elected not to use one, though Winneshiek had decided before he shoved off from the shoreline to partially inflate his life vest.[3]

The swim was deceptive. While only 150 feet of distance—not even two lengths of a recreational pool—the bottom of the river was a V-shaped trench that dropped to a depth of 35 feet. The current pushing through that narrowing section was far swifter than the deceptively calm flow on the surface.

The result was that as they sidestroked through the water, each began fighting an undertow, and as they neared the island, some grew exhausted. "I'm not sure I can make this one," Schrage called out.[4] Atkins, who was his partner, couldn't respond, because he was struggling to catch his breath. He could hear Schrage calling out his name. Just downstream, Pretrick had made it ashore, and Lens was behind him. Farther downstream, Winneshiek was nearing the shore and kept checking on Green. "Okay," the corporal kept responding. Winneshiek grabbed reeds along the shore and finally pulled himself in. He looked around, and Green was gone.

As Atkins was thrashing about, he slipped under the water. He had tried to inflate his life vest, but it failed. As he sank, the Marine suddenly grasped something. It was the rope held by Lens. Atkins yanked on it and then grabbed hold of the gunnery sergeant in a panic. "Motherfucker!" Lens called out. "Take the fuckin' pack, goddamn it." He shoved the floating device to Atkins. The two made it to shore. Schrage had vanished.

The covert mission was now completely overt and no longer a mission as Marines yelled out the names of missing comrades. Carlton, from the shore, realized something had gone terribly wrong and ordered his men to launch the Zodiac and begin rescue efforts. Eventually, helicopters and fixed-wing aircraft joined the search. Marines walked the bank of the river for three miles. Army and Navy divers pitched in. But three days passed with no results. Finally, on the Wednesday evening of May 5, shortly before recovery efforts were to end for the day, Navy divers found Green's body submerged just short of the island. He still had his boonie cap on and his M16 strapped to his back. Weber, Lens, and

MISTAKES

277

Booker motored over to the island in a Zodiac and, in knee-deep mud, pulled the remains into a body bag. Back at shore, they carried Green to a waiting truck as troops who had crowded around watched in silence, their helmets removed.

Divers found Schrage's body twenty-four hours later at the very bottom of the deep trench within the channel. Again, the Zodiac went out for retrieval. Schrage's body was bloated, heavy, and difficult to move. An M16 was still strapped to his back. Unforgettable for those who were there was the expression of horror on the dead Marine's face.

At the memorial service held the next week, Navy chaplain Brian Weigelt, searching for a way to make sense of what had happened and offering solace to the Marines of Fox Company, focused on their exhaustive effort to locate their friends.

"You searched tirelessly. All were committed to finding your missing brothers and you did not stop until you found them."[5]

Carlton took the deaths hard. Weber tried to console him. But the captain seemed overcome with grief, blaming himself for sending his men on a treacherous crossing.

In June, Echo Company would suffer its own tragedy, losing four men in a single nightmarish event. Captain Kelly Royer would deal with the situation far differently than Carlton.

Since taking over command of Echo days before the deployment, Royer, with his overbearing style, had managed to alienate a growing number of his troops. It was clear as early as the fighting in early April. When word arrived at company headquarters that John Wroblewski had died of his wounds, his men needed to be informed. Royer informed Damien Coan, the platoon sergeant, "I'm going to tell your platoon."

Coan's famously short fuse began sputtering. "No, you're not." Coan thought Royer was pulling rank in the midst of tragedy.

"Who's the company commander?" Royer said.

Coan's fuse burned down. "The only captain in the room, that's you! But I'm telling my platoon this."

Royer relented and walked with Coan to the assembled platoon to stand by as the sergeant delivered the heartbreaking news. For Coan, there was no way he would allow Royer to be the only one to break the news, and for one reason—he believed the men hated Royer. In the years to come, Royer would say he had no recollection of Coan's account.

First Lieutenant Sean Schickel arrived later in April to assume the post of Echo Company executive officer. He was an Illinois native from a family with a long, fulsome lineage of serving in the Marine Corps. He was the youngest of five boys, four of whom joined the Marines. Sean enlisted. Loved it. And after leaving enlisted life and graduating college, he earned a commission as an officer. When he showed up at Echo Company as the new number two, Schickel was a thirty-one-year-old first lieutenant.

As Schickel surveyed company operations, he found a number of problems such as a lack of accountability for weapons and gear, and graffiti on portable toilets, trucks, barracks, and sandbags. A lot of it was the usual Marine humor, but some of the defacement was aimed at Royer, including a reference to him as Captain Casualty. After the fighting and killing they'd seen, Echo troops were grasping for a way to make sense of it all. As the month of June began, two-thirds of the troops killed in combat were from Echo or working with the company. The unit was one of five companies in the battalion, and yet Echo accounted for a whopping 70 percent of the severest casualties that required medical evacuation back to the US.

Suddenly, there were wild conspiracy theories that Royer was somehow responsible, that he had intentionally placed his men in dangerous situations to win glory for himself as a leader in tough combat. There was no evidence any of this was true. But the mere existence of these unfounded theories added to a souring state of mind within the company.

At the battalion level, Paul Kennedy was unaware of Echo's morale issue. But there were things about Royer that annoyed him.

He had, after all, given Royer the Porcupine call sign for being prickly. In addition, Kennedy had been overheard on the radio during combat complaining to Royer that "you got to fight your company, quit fighting your platoon," meaning he needed to focus on managing his entire command, not just a portion of it.

But beyond such concerns, Kennedy gave Royer solid marks in a combat fitness report at the end of May, describing the captain as highly intelligent, articulate, strong-willed, and an aggressive officer who had "single-handedly reshaped a company in sore need of a leader." The only caveat was a recommendation that for future assignments, he would "best be employed as an independent operator."

In the months ahead, Kennedy's views would change radically.

In the meantime, one of several challenges that Royer would face would be management of snipers assigned to his company.

The role of these sharpshooters became more crucial as the battalion, in May and June, moved away from the hated and dangerous route clearance missions and started using observation posts to guard against IEDs being planted.

Less essential roads such as Route Nova would no longer be the focus as resources were concentrated on watching the main thoroughfare of Route Michigan twenty-four hours a day.

Echo oversaw about four and a half miles of the road at the east end of the city. Squads conducted observations from concrete bunkers. One section of roadway was watched by a four-man sniper team covertly posted in a building. Royer's snipers—Sergeant Romeo Santiago and three other men, operating under the call sign Headhunter—had famously come under attack by a column of insurgents on April 6 and fought their way through it, suffering two wounded, including one evacuated home.

Now they were assigned to a mission—the Route Michigan overwatch—for which they clearly didn't have enough people. Other snipers in the battalion faced the same predicament. So the decision was made to have regular Marines assist sharpshooters, doubling their manpower. It wasn't an ideal solution since those troops didn't have the same intense training as snipers, but it provided some help.

For Headhunter, the snipers were Santiago and his three corporals, Tommy Parker Jr., Cameron Ferguson, and Ted Stanton, who had been wounded on April 6. They were now joined by four Marines pulled from Echo ranks: Corporal Christopher Gonzales and three lance corporals, Juan Lopez, Pedro Contreras, and Deshon Otey, the lone survivor of Staff Sergeant Allan Walker's ambushed Humvee from April 6.

With eight people, Headhunter could alternate two four-man teams every twenty-four hours to watch Route Michigan.

But it was still an exhausting pace. Sometimes Santiago was handed an entirely separate mission and so had to beg or borrow sniper resources from Golf Company to keep up surveillance of Route Michigan. Even then, it was challenging because a twenty-four-hour mission always took longer than twenty-four hours. A group would leave Combat Outpost after dark and on foot to quietly work its way along tree lines and ditches to avoid detection to reach an abandoned house, and then do the same on the way back. This added hours to the job, leaving less time to eat, rest, and recover before going out again. Another hitch was that there were few abandoned houses for snipers to hide in along Echo Company's assigned area. Really only two. Which left open the possibility the enemy might figure out where the snipers were hidden.

A favorite location, with a sweeping view of Route Michigan, was a new, unfinished structure three stories high with a vaulted front entrance accented with towering columns. It was located about eight hundred yards east of Combat Outpost. The house was designed to be a lavish residence with tall Arab windows, expansive rooms with high ceilings, and a stone stairway in the back that led to a second level and then to a roof encompassed by a parapet. A panoramic view of Habbaniyah Lake with its glistening

MISTAKES

waters lay to the southeast. Sniper teams had been using the house since March without protest by the owner.

One problem, however, was that workers were showing up on occasion to continue construction, and there was very little doubt that people knew Marine snipers were hiding there.

Santiago didn't like it one bit. First Lieutenant Nate Scott, who commanded the battalion sniper force, shared Santiago's concerns. The lieutenant was a soft-spoken, twenty-six-year-old former Chicago business consultant who had quit his job after 9/11 and earned an officer's commission in the Marine Corps. His platoon of snipers was broken into teams assigned to each of the rifle companies.

Snipers were trained to be clandestine, operating with stealth and never going the same route twice. But now they were locked into conducting surveillance from virtually the same location twenty-four hours a day where their cover had essentially been blown. In addition, the hours were long and repetitive, with the kind of grueling tedium that breeds complacency.

In the latter half of June, Santiago was handed yet another mission for his snipers. Combat Outpost had been getting mortared from somewhere up in the Sofia District. The sergeant needed to take a team up there, then locate and kill the mortarmen. In the meantime, he also had to maintain the daily overwatch of Route Michigan. The dilemma was how to staff both missions. A Golf Company sniper team would help alternate on the Route Michigan overwatch. But Santiago had to divide up his own men in the best way possible. The Sofia assignment was more dangerous, requiring three to four days operating covertly some distance from Combat Outpost in an area sparsely patrolled. Santiago elected to use the most experienced men for the mortar mission—himself, Stanton, and Ferguson, and the corporal, Gonzales. He'd leave Parker to run the overwatch with Lopez, Contreras, and Otey. Scott approved.

Both teams headed out on foot from Combat Outpost in the wee hours of Monday, June 21, Santiago leading his men northward and Parker and his Marines heading to the overwatch house to the east. It happened to be Santiago's twenty-sixth birthday.

Some time prior to this, intelligence operatives at the 1st Marine Division headquarters at Blue Diamond intercepted an enemy cellular phone call. There are varying accounts of what information was collected. According to a report completed a year later by the Naval Criminal Investigative Service, what was overheard was an authorization to assassinate Parker's team. Someone was going to "do these Marines." Jim Booker said he learned months later that a phone call to the owner of the house had been recorded. In that conversation, someone alerts the owner that "we're going to kill these fuckers when they come back again."

Whatever was in the intercepted call, it never reached the battalion before June 21.

Parker and his men checked in by radio on the half hour as required all night. But the calls stopped by midmorning. The nearest Americans were Second Platoon troops who were in a bunkered position east on Route Michigan near a cemetery. Damien Coan was there and took a squad of ten Marines in a pair of Humvees to see what was going on at the sniper team's location. Lance Corporal John DeGoede IV led a fire team into the building and up the back stairs, calling out to Parker and his men as they climbed the steps. "Hey, are you sleeping in or what? They're trying to get ahold of you on the radio." Seconds later, DeGoede called out, "Corpsman!"

He and the team had reached the rooftop to find all four Marines dead and blood everywhere. Coan headed up to see for himself, and word spread fast. Sean Schickel was asleep after working a late shift during which he spoke with Parker and his men before they headed out from Combat Outpost. Now he was being awakened to learn they'd been killed. He swung around and

MISTAKES

sat up in his bunk. "Goddamn it, they fell asleep. Lieutenant Scott was right."

Paul Kennedy and Jim Booker had been in a meeting at the brigade headquarters at Camp Ramadi and were leaving when Royer called by radio from the kill site with a clipped summary that caught Kennedy off guard.

"Headhunter 2B is dead," he said, using the team's call sign.

"What does that mean?" Kennedy responded.

"They're all dead. They've been assassinated."

"Stay there."

Kennedy headed for the house. Colonel Buck Connor was also on his way.

Mike Wylie, the battalion executive officer, was astonished to see images of the dead Marines broadcast on television within minutes after he learned about the killings. Insurgents filmed the carnage and quickly delivered a tape to the Associated Press.

The scene on the rooftop was heartbreaking. There were very few signs of any struggle, just 9 mm shell casings all over the roof. It was speculated there were four assassins.

Two of the Marines appeared to have been killed while they were asleep. One of them, Tommy Parker, was wrapped in mosquito netting. Pedro Contreras was the other. Both suffered several gunshot wounds. Juan Lopez was sitting in a corner of the rooftop, with his back against a parapet wall, a radio by his side. Someone who saw him thought he might have been asleep as well. He had been killed by a single gunshot fired down through the top of his head.

Deshon Otey was the only one who may have been alert when the killing started, although how much warning he had was unclear. A blood trail suggested he was wounded near the stairway entrance and stepped across the roof before collapsing. He had defensive wounds on his left hand as if he had tried to block gunshots, and several wounds to his upper body. He had also been beaten or kicked.

It was a death that bore an eerie resemblance to the nightmares Otey had been suffering since April 6, men coming to kill him.

The assassins made off with two sniper rifles, a radio, a thermal sight, four M16s, and ammunition.

There were endless questions. Protocol allowed for two men on the team to be resting or sleeping while two were on duty. So how did the enemy gunmen make their way undetected up two flights of stairs? Those stairs should have been booby-trapped with a Claymore mine, and a doorway usually blocked by a steel barrel that would have made plenty of noise if someone was pushing their way through.

One Marine would have been watching the stairs while a second was watching the street.

In the daytime, snipers typically moved to the second level of the house where they were out of the sun and less obvious. But Parker and the others were still up on the roof by midmorning.

There were also signs of the kind of complacency Nate Scott had worried about. At least some of the team were in their T-shirts. One was not wearing boots, and there was a pair of shower shoes present. There was also a MiniDisc player and a car magazine.

One theory was that the Marines had grown accustomed to seeing workmen on the lower level. The killers may have infiltrated the construction crew and befriended the Americans over time. There were carpentry tools found on the roof, leading to speculation the workers had been allowed access.

As the senior Marine on the mission, Tommy Parker received much of the blame for what appeared to be a failure to stay alert, a conclusion that later angered the corporal's wife and family.

Royer drafted a statement the day after the killings that appeared to fault Santiago for how he divided up his snipers ("I did not authorize this") and described in detail all the security lapses evident when the bodies were found.

Santiago and the others who were on a multiday sniper mission were immediately brought back to Combat Outpost. Santiago

MISTAKES

wept when he heard the news and was overwhelmed with guilt, second-guessing every decision he made about the mission.

Rank-and-file Marines were devastated by the crushing loss of four friends. Contreras was funny, popular, and a risk-taker admired by his comrades. Parker was widely viewed as a genuinely nice guy. And Otey was in a special class as the sole survivor of an ambush.

The irrepressible Chris MacIntosh, for the first time in the deployment, broke down in tears at the news of his friends' deaths and then slipped into a spiral of despair that caused others to urge him to see the chaplain. "I don't want to fucking talk to you," he said to Brian Weigelt, then went back to his squad.

Thanks, in part, to the insurgents' video, the story of the four slain Marines was widely reported.

Lopez's burial created a minor international stir. He was a Mexican national, and his family wanted him interred in his home village of San Luis de la Paz north of Mexico City. Six pallbearers from 2nd Battalion, 4th Marines were flown in from Camp Pendleton in California. The embassy provided a color guard that included two Marines carrying ceremonial M14 rifles without ammunition. Armed Mexican soldiers appeared during the graveside ceremony to enforce a national ban on foreign troops carrying weapons and demanded the M14s. There was a tense standoff for forty minutes until the Mexicans finally withdrew.[6]

Back in Ramadi, Royer summoned Santiago and Stanton, his two most senior snipers, into a meeting and after showing them graphic photographs of their dead friends—pictures they hadn't seen—reprimanded them for allowing complacency within sniper ranks.

Santiago was struck by the cruelty of it.

13

WICKEDNESS

"I'M GOING TO DIE WITH MY HEAD UP."

IN THE DAYS and weeks after the four Marines were assassinated, the battalion tried to hunt down those responsible. The owner of the house was located and brought to division headquarters at Blue Diamond. JD Harrill personally interrogated him alone in a room with just the two of them, clearly frightening the man, who would soon flee to Syria. Operations launched in early July to round up the killers had resulted in a few suspects being detained and sent to Abu Ghraib prison.

Meanwhile, the enemy used the killings to taunt the Americans, spreading word of a future attack when they would get more of the same.

The one tangible response the battalion seized upon was to simply blow up the house where the men were murdered. Paul Kennedy gave the order. Marine combat engineers planted 460 pounds of C-4 explosive throughout the structure, with long, narrow blocks of the plastic explosive duct-taped around columns and laid in bundles every eighteen inches or so along the floor and wall

WICKEDNESS

joints. It was detonated in the early hours of June 29, the house thoroughly reduced to rubble. While a spectacular show, it got mixed reviews. Romeo Santiago, the sniper team leader who was deeply affected by the loss of his four men, was not impressed. *It was dumb,* he thought. *Why make the statement of blowing it up? It made you feel better?* Commanders knew for weeks that the sniper teams were not being employed correctly. *Maybe some of the resources used to blow up the building should have been applied earlier to support the sniper teams and those men would be alive,* Santiago thought.

Hours before the detonation, in a late-night ceremony in the heavily fortified Green Zone of Baghdad, Iraq regained the sovereignty it had lost in the wake of the US-led invasion the year before. The transfer of power occurred two days earlier than scheduled to frustrate disruptive efforts by the insurgency. The Coalition Provisional Authority led by Paul Bremer was dissolved. The first elections were set for January 2005. The interim prime minister was a politician and disaffected Ba'athist named Ayad Allawi.

In Ramadi, the Marines purchased 1,500 small Iraqi flags for a dollar apiece and handed them out to citizens to promote national sovereignty.

More importantly, Kennedy and his troops responded to the transition by dramatically reducing their footprint in the city. Where before they ventured into any neighborhood daily, they now restricted movements. Apart from continuing to conduct raids based on new intelligence, the Marines largely confined troops to the Government Center and stationary observation posts along the main thoroughfare of Route Michigan to guard against IEDs on that crucial artery.

But fear persisted of a "Fallujah model" taking root, leaving security for vast areas of the city to Ramadi police or national guard troops intimidated by the insurgency or, worse, collaborating with an enemy seeking to control areas of the city.

"We've done everything we agreed to—We've stayed out of the neighborhoods 99 percent of the time," Kennedy told a gathering of top Iraqi security officials in July. "Now we're asking that the [police] generals take the next step and ensure this stretch of road [Route Michigan] is safe—and they can walk their babies down the road."[1]

The challenge of handing over governance was finding trustworthy leadership. The governor of Al Anbar Province, Abdul Kareem Burgess (also sometimes spelled *Bergis*, *Berjes*, or *Burjis*), a politician and former police investigator, had originally been chosen as mayor of Ramadi by the sheiks of the province and elevated to governor by US commanders. He had a history of cooperation with the coalition. But while he had considerable influence with the sheiks, he had no direct control over government ministries that reported to Baghdad, most crucially the police. When he met with US Iraqi administrator Bremer shortly before he left the country at the end of June, Burgess described his governing circumstance as tenuous. "I can no longer trust anyone," he said to Bremer. "I don't know if people are working for me or for the resistance."[2]

The head of law enforcement when the Marines arrived was a burly fellow with a gray handlebar mustache, named Ja'ardon Mohammed Habeisi, also known as Ja'ardon Mohammed Al Alwani. Habeisi had shown leadership skills in revamping what had been an incompetent agency when he took charge. He had also been the target of at least three assassination attempts by the insurgency, including one in which his oldest son lost a leg. Nonetheless, Kennedy was growing impatient with what he saw as mounting evidence that Habeisi was playing both sides of the fence, placating the Marines while abetting the enemy.

Meanwhile, the war didn't wait while leadership sorted itself out. In a little more than forty-eight hours after the transfer of power in Baghdad, the Magnificent Bastards suffered another body blow.

WICKEDNESS

The tragedy came just as they began to acquire in June the first of dozens of new factory up-armored Humvees the Pentagon had ordered months before. These were essentially metal-encased vehicles that could withstand at least the first generation of enemy IEDs being used. (The bombs would grow larger and more penetrative against steel in years to come, requiring the US to respond with even more heavily armored military transport.) One tactical issue with the new up-armored Humvees was that they were only capable of carrying five people—a driver, three passengers, and someone in the gun turret—and there remained a need for larger, cargo-bearing Humvees for transporting more troops. Convoys venturing into the city rode in the up-armored vehicles, but some troops still had to travel in the kind of open-backed Humvees in which Marines had died at the Gypsum-Nova intersection ambush on April 6 and the vehicle-bomb attack along Michigan on May 29. There were efforts to make these high-back trucks more bombproof with steel shielding along the sides, armored doors in the back, sandbags on the floor, and L-shaped steel doors on the passenger and driver sides of the cab. But it was far from foolproof.

Through the night of June 30, Weapons Company's Third Platoon conducted an overwatch of Route Michigan at the city's far east end to guard against the planting of any IEDs. They wanted to make certain nothing would mar festivities on July 1 when an Iraqi police academy graduation would be held nearby. After the all-night mission, the platoon was heading back west along Michigan from the arches—the Marines thinking of the breakfast they were going to enjoy at one of the lavisher Army chow halls at Camp Ramadi.

A roadside bomb exploded at 6:45 a.m. directly to the right of one high-backed Humvee. Several men in the rear of the truck were wounded. The worst case was Lance Corporal William Nackers, who was turning twenty that very day. He suffered shrapnel wounds to his left leg. But Nackers and the others in back still scrambled to get out of the truck, knowing full well that their squad leader riding in the front would be the first one on the ground yelling for them to assemble.

As they clambered out, however, there was silence from the front seat. It was Kenneth Conde, who had earned a Bronze Star while fighting with a bullet hole in his shoulder on April 6 and who was one of the most well-respected Marines in the battalion.

Weiler was in the Humvee directly behind the truck and ran forward to see what had happened. The buried artillery shell that was detonated threw shards of steel shattering the ballistic windshield and penetrating the engine frame. Other pieces had been deflected by the steel passenger-side door. But one hunk of metal shot through the L-shaped opening of the door and struck Conde in the head.

He was alive but struggling to breathe and clearly suffering a massive brain injury. The sergeant was pulled out, and Weiler, who had been riding in the vehicle directly behind, tried to bandage him. Meanwhile, houses near the attack site were surrounded and searched. One suspect was detained. During these efforts, Americans spotted a group of men standing not far away who looked amused by it all and were laughing. Weiler caught sight of them and was beside himself with fury. Covered in Conde's blood, he began moving in their direction, literally contemplating gunning them down one by one until he got answers about the IED trigger man. It was an explosive moment broken only when one of Weiler's sergeants, Marcel Williams—who on April 7 had carried a wounded Marine on his back seventy-five yards to safety—stepped in front of the officer. "We got this, sir," Williams told him, reading Weiler's intentions. The sergeant had harbored similarly dark thoughts himself. But he chose discretion over bloodlust and defused his company commander's rage, sparing the battalion a potential atrocity.

Conde was transported to Combat Outpost, where he was helicoptered to a higher level of care. Weiler, who considered the squad leader not only one of his best Marines but a good friend, was relieved to hear he was in stable condition and took that to mean he might survive. Weiler shared the information with the other troops.

But by the time the platoon made its way back to Hurricane Point, Paul Kennedy was waiting to tell them Conde had died. It was crushing news. The young leader had turned twenty-three just a week earlier.

Shortly before that birthday, the sergeant had spoken with the author about his own mortality and the risks they faced in Ramadi.

"The nature of the beast is that people are going to get hurt and killed," Conde said. "The thing about it is, how are you going to die? When people remember you, when you go back, are you going to know, 'I made it back, but I was ducking down the whole time, and not watching my buddy's [back]'? Or are you going to go back in a body bag, but at least you died with honor?

"It may sound kind of funny to say that. But it makes sense to me," he said. "If I'm going to die, that's how I'm going to die. I'm going to die with my head up. They can do things to me. But they can't take away the honor that I feel."

Conde was the only member of the battalion killed in July. The steady flow of deaths that plagued the Magnificent Bastards from their first weeks in Ramadi was finally slowing down thanks to several factors, including a reduction in patrols, a greater reliance on static observation posts, and the acquisition of up-armored Humvees.

In response, the enemy simply adjusted tactics, relying on hit-and-run ambushes, mortar attacks, and in some instances, snipers and organized assaults. Even though battalion deaths declined, there were a continuing number of Marines and corpsmen wounded through June and July. Among the first was Lance Corporal Nickalous Aldrich, a twenty-year-old native of Austin, Texas, and a former Future Farmers of America member, who suffered RPG shrapnel wounds to both legs and his backside during a

June 8 attack. The round had been fired at a Golf Company observation post atop an Islamic library and study hall the Americans called, for some reason, the Agricultural Center, located about a half mile east of the Saddam Magnificent Mosque. It would prove to be a popular target for the insurgency. About a week after Aldrich was wounded, Lance Corporal Jason Rosman was shot in the back as he and others hiked back to Combat Outpost from the Islamic library observation post. The eighteen-year-old, who would later write about his experiences in a self-published book titled I Should Have Gone to College, was struck near his shoulder blade by the bullet that narrowly missed his armored plate. The damage from the round caused the teenager's lung to temporarily collapse. He would be evacuated to the United States. The day after Conde was killed, two Echo Company lance corporals standing guard at Combat Outpost were wounded in a mortar attack. For each of them—Kevin Gaeden, nineteen, and Brandon Lund, twenty-one—it was a second Purple Heart. Lund's left elbow was shattered, and he headed home.

The steady erosion of the battalion ranks was not confined to people killed or wounded in battle. Marines were sent home for any number of ailments that couldn't be treated in the war zone, such as abscesses, complex dental problems, a torn ACL, or serious auto accident injury. In a few cases, they accidentally shot themselves with their own weapons.

As the summer advanced, a new category of injury began to occur—heatstroke. Ramadi is a desert city, and it baked in the hottest months with temperatures reaching 120 degrees and higher.

Meteorologists in the States often cite the "heat index" in hot weather, which considers air temperature and humidity to provide a sense of what the heat feels like against the skin. But for decades, the military has used a far more precise measurement that gauges the danger of hot weather. It's called the *wet-bulb globe temperature*, or WBGT, and it tracks air temperature, humidity, wind speed, and sunlight to provide a reading that dictates when outside

WICKEDNESS

activity should be limited. The standard says that any reading of ninety degrees WBGT or above requires mandatory breaks in outside activity after only fifteen minutes. And those breaks needed to last at least forty-five minutes before venturing back outside. A standard used for college athletics dictates no outside exercise with any reading of ninety-two degrees WBGT or higher.

But when combat broke out in Ramadi during the summer, mandatory breaks in outside activity were impossible. In addition, troops were never spared from wearing their blouses and trousers beneath heavy flak jackets with body armor, and under a load of weaponry, ammunition, and helmets. During several hours of combat on July 21, the WBGT reading hovered between ninety-two and ninety-four degrees, and sixteen Marines fell out because of heat exhaustion. They were all from Lieutenant Donovan Campbell's platoon in Golf Company.

"Did you realize that you had sixteen fucking heat casualties?" Golf commander Chris Bronzi said to Campbell in a harsh dressing-down. "Sixteen? You know that I consider every heat casualty a leadership failure!"[3]

The theory among Marines was that the enemy used the hot weather to advantage, forcing the heavily clad Americans to struggle through the heat while insurgents fought in sandals and loose-fitting garb.

Temperatures were brutal, inescapable, and sucked every bit of moisture from the face. Lips were left bone-dry. Skin cracked.

By midsummer, the air-conditioning units in the barracks were working consistently, and that was a means of relief by day's end. But during hours of sunlight, the troops perspired through every layer of clothing and outerwear, including flak jackets. Sweat squirted out of boots. Hydration was a religious ritual, with the downing and refilling of canteens in formation. Squad leaders were required to conduct urine checks to ensure the piss was clear in color, verifying hydration. Platoon Sergeant Damien Coan's famously remembered admonishment of these days was "Drink water, asshole!" (He had said it after discovering a Marine heading out on a mission with a load of soda pop.)

Hydration was even written into operational orders: "Each man will drink 1 quart of water 1 hour prior to the mission, and 1 quart within 1 hour following the mission. Unit leaders must ensure that men remain hydrated and have a rest plan throughout the mission. Random urine checks will be conducted before and after the mission by no less than a squad leader."[4]

Trying to get cold or cool water to the troops locked in a gunfight was a logistical hurdle until someone hit on the idea of transporting into the field fifty-five-gallon plastic drums partially filled with water bottles overlaid with ice. Even as the ice melted away, the water stayed cool all day. A fallback was liquid intravenously administered. At the end of a day, Marines would strip down to their skivvies and lie back in a lower bunk with an IV bag hanging from an upper bunk draining into a vein. In worst cases where corpsmen could spot the beginnings of heat exhaustion on the battlefield, a saline solution was hooked up to a war fighter with the bag tucked into a flak jacket so he could keep fighting.

By far, the most serious heat casualty in the battalion was Sean Gustavison. His core body temperature rose to an astonishing level when he suffered a heatstroke in early June and the twenty-two-year-old had to be medically evacuated out of the country.

Private Gustavison was a Michigan native with a weight problem who struggled in the Marine Corps almost from the time he was in boot camp. He was originally assigned to 3rd Battalion, 5th Marines but missed that unit's deployment during the Iraq invasion because of a knee injury. There was hazing and allegations of malingering, and in general, Gustavison had a miserable experience with the battalion. By his fourth year in the Marine Corps, he was still a private and volunteered to join a combat casualty replacement unit made up of Marines nearing the end of their enlistments. He was assigned to the Magnificent Bastards and became a member of Echo Company's Second Platoon. He

WICKEDNESS

found the experience different with 2/4 and the troops there more inclusive.

On the first day of June, the battalion conducted a repeat of the Bug Hunt operation that ended in heavy fighting in early April. But it was a mixed result. There was no enemy resistance, and while some weapons caches were found, all the suspects detained were eventually released for lack of evidence. In the course of it, some Army tracked vehicles ran over power cables at Combat Outpost, temporarily cutting electricity to barracks, and troops sweltered all night in the heat.

By the next day, the temperature of the air felt like that first blast of heat when someone opens an oven door. When Second Platoon headed out on foot for an overwatch mission, Gustavison, with his heavy body weight and his gear, was already laboring. By the time he collapsed on the way back, they were still a half mile from Combat Outpost. Gustavison was with Eric Smith's squad, and they pulled out a poleless litter—essentially a tarp with handles—and took turns with four Marines carrying him while others provided security. They'd switch out as the bearers grew weary.

A corpsman had already started intravenous hydration by the time Gustavison was carried into Combat Outpost. Corpsman Adam Clayton was with the team treating Gustavison and thought the Marine was so hot it was like he was cooking. Records show his core body temperature was an astonishing 107 degrees. The National Institutes of Health say anything more than 104 degrees is associated with either long-term or permanent neurological damage. Working with Dr. Colin Crickard, the medical crew stripped off Gustavison's clothes, packed plastic bags of ice near crucial areas of his body, kept his skin damp and fans blowing on him—anything they could think of to reduce his temperature. Within an hour, a helicopter arrived to carry him away. He was headed home.

Amid all the losses suffered by the battalion, Golf Company got good news in July. Joe Hayes was back. The Marine who had earned a Bronze Star during vicious April combat, who fought after being wounded by a grenade, and who had led his men in prayer under enemy fire had determinedly made his way back to the war, one of the few combat casualties evacuated to the US to do so. (Another was Vincent Moudy, of Echo Company, wounded in the fight with the enemy mortar team on March 25.)

He didn't have to. The system wasn't really set up for such return trips. When Hayes returned to Camp Pendleton and convalescence, he found his life being pulled in two directions: love and war. His near-death experience had revealed how much he was in love with Candace Neighbors, his girlfriend of more than a year. Within two weeks of being wounded, Hayes had purchased a ring and proposed marriage, and she started making wedding arrangements. But as the weeks and months of physical therapy passed, Hayes kept hearing how his friends back in Ramadi were fighting and dying—Todd Bolding, Pedro Contreras, Deshon Otey. *I can't go on the rest of my life knowing that I could have gone back*, the twenty-one-year-old thought. *I wouldn't be able to live with myself.* There were also traces of something else. Combat had been terrifying. But there was an undeniable element of thrill more powerful than any similar feeling Hayes ever had. He would learn later in life about dopamine and adrenaline and how they become very much like addictive drugs. But this thrill-seeking pursuit would become a driving force in his future decision to take on dangerous assignments as a police officer. For now, he just knew he wanted more of it. As Candace was making her plans, Joe told her he was going back to Ramadi. She struggled with what he said but didn't try to dissuade him. Hayes would remember all of it as the toughest decision of his life.

Golf Company Gunnery Sergeant Winston Jaugan led the convoy that picked up Hayes after he arrived by helicopter at Hurricane Point. Jaugan had not told anyone in Hayes's platoon. When they arrived at Combat Outpost, he led the platoon sergeant, Damien Rodriguez, out to the Humvee and told him, "I got a present for you." The two bear-hugged, and Hayes was led over to see everybody else. The Marines went nuts.

Hayes arrived in time for some of the toughest combat since April.

"A BOY OF 13 CRYING, WHIMPERING."
FIRST OF THE WICKED WEDNESDAYS, JULY 14

The day began with a rude welcoming for visiting troops from 2nd Battalion, 5th Marines, the battalion that would take over for Paul Kennedy's people in September. Captain Patrick Rapicault was part of 2/5's operations staff. His nickname was Frenchy. Rapicault was born on the French Caribbean island of Martinique and grew up in the French Riviera before coming to the southern US as a teenager, earning his citizenship and becoming an officer in the Marine Corps. He was a standout, particularly with his distinctive blended accent reflecting France and Mississippi. Rapicault was on an orientation mission the morning of July 14, traveling with Weapons Company along Route Michigan when an IED that was a mixture of fuel and plastic explosive detonated, engulfing in a fireball a Humvee carrying the thirty-four-year-old officer. The vehicle had armored plating bolted on the sides that provided protection, but Rapicault still suffered blackened burns on the right side of his face.

(Rapicault later was the subject of a *60 Minutes* broadcast that documented his death on November 15. A CBS crew was riding in a convoy led by the captain when a suicide car bomber detonated explosives adjacent to Rapicault's Humvee, killing him and two other Marines. He was a popular leader, and it was a terrible blow for 2/5 battalion.

(One of the others who died November 15 was Corporal Marc Ryan, twenty-five, of Gloucester, New Jersey. Ryan had served in Afghanistan from 2001 to 2002 and volunteered in May 2004 to be a combat casualty replacement for the Magnificent Bastards in

Ramadi. When the Bastards went home in September, Ryan stayed on in Ramadi as part of 2/5 and as the gunner in Rapicault's Humvee. Jim Booker would always consider Ryan an honorary member of the Magnificent Bastards and yet another of the battalion's many KIAs in Ramadi.)

Six hours after the fireball IED, the enemy launched a coordinated assault, attacking the battalion observation post atop the Islamic library and ambushing Colonel Buck Connor and his security team along Route Michigan. It all unfolded along a six-hundred-yard stretch of the roadway just east of the Saddam Magnificent Mosque. Connor and his team were traveling west, having returned from lunch with Army officers at a base in Habbaniyah. The attack began, as usual, with a roadside bomb detonating next to his truck. It was a fully armored Humvee, and apart from an injured left shoulder, he was unhurt except for effects of the blast shock wave. The jolt broke the stock of his Mossberg shotgun. Connor took two steps after climbing out and collapsed. He had suffered another blast concussion. Connor's driver came over to assist. As others poured out of their Humvees, enemy gunmen opened fire from nearly every direction. The soldiers were in the parking lot of a car repair complex, and they worked their way east along Michigan trying to return fire as rocket-propelled grenades whistled overhead. Connor spotted a man with an AK-47 on the upper floor of a building across the street firing his weapon on a fully automatic setting, just spraying bullets. The colonel was down on one knee, took careful aim, held his breath, and fired a slug from his shotgun that struck the insurgent right below his throat as he was turning to flee. The body was later recovered.

Marines were rushing reinforcements. A Golf Company platoon left Combat Outpost. Paul Kennedy and his security detail and Weapons Company troops reached Connor and his people within minutes.

Connor, a historian by education, recorded the sights, sounds,

WICKEDNESS

and emotions in his diary days later: "The explosion again, then the RPGs, the machine guns, the high-pitched crack of AKs, hugging walls, crouching, suddenly seeing enemy on the roof, dropping to a knee and firing. . . . Completely covered in sweat, in my eyes, dehydrated, reloading my shotgun. Where are the Bradleys? The [Marine] gun trucks opening up with caliber 50, moving up and back on the street keeping the attackers away. Iraqis huddled inside the buildings. A boy of 13 crying, whimpering. . . . The sound a bullet makes when it is close, so close to you. Covered in dirt and oil and filth."

Cobra attack helicopters were soon flying overhead, and the Bradley Fighting Vehicles finally arrived. Marines were getting even quicker and deadlier at responding to attacks with the overwhelming force of their truck-mounted heavy guns and automatic grenade launchers. When Golf Company ground troops pushed north to occupy a building from which they had been receiving enemy fire, it had been so pummeled by Marine weaponry that resistance was gone. There were only wounded insurgents and others who had thrown down their weapons. The structure turned out to be the headquarters for a local chapter of the coalition for Iraqi Unity, a political organization. It contained a huge arsenal of firearms and ammunition. Kennedy brought to the site retired Marine Corps officer and Fox News celebrity Oliver North, who hosted a Fox program called *War Stories with Oliver North*. He and his film crew had embedded with the battalion, and Kennedy wanted to show North the perfidy of Iraqi politicians.

"I've [previously] met the director of this political party," Kennedy told Oliver North on camera in front of the building. "He's going to jail."

The fight lasted four hours and was a lopsided victory. Apart from a few minor wound cases, the Americans emerged unscathed. By contrast, twenty-one enemy fighters were killed, and twenty-five were taken into custody.

"I MARVELED AS I WATCHED THEM WORK."
JULY 21

The enemy tried again exactly one week later. The Magnificent Bastards came to call these successive attacks in July "Wicked Wednesdays."

It began the same way in nearly the same place. This time, the ambushed commander was Major Mike Wylie, battalion executive officer. He had headed out from Hurricane Point that morning in a four-vehicle convoy equipped with the new factory up-armored Humvees. They arrived at Combat Outpost, where Wylie surveyed the compound, checking on troop welfare and conditions. It was a four-mile trip back to Hurricane Point, and eventually, he and his security detachment would have to risk it.

Insurgents were waiting. Intelligence reports would later reveal that there were several groups operating in the city, and each was bringing in more fighters and improving coordination with one another. They preferred operating in the same densely populated central area of Ramadi where they had battled Golf Company on April 6 and 7. There was a web of streets through which to maneuver and flee if necessary. Residents in this area were submissive, and police didn't interfere.

Former Iraqi military officers directed operations, and fighters were drawn from three locations: Ramadi, the nearby Khalidiyah area that had bedeviled 1st Brigade soldiers for nearly a year, and the insurgency haven of Fallujah.

In the afternoon, the enemy shot rockets that fell short of hitting Hurricane Point, fired a rocket-propelled grenade at the Marine observation post atop the Islamic library and research center—a stubborn target of the insurgency nearly every day—and lobbed mortar rounds at Combat Outpost.

Wylie decided to head back to Hurricane Point at about 3:00 p.m. Even in the stifling 120-degree heat, it was eerily calm. "Hey, it's really quiet," Wylie said over the radio to battalion headquarters.

"Of course it's quiet. It's hot. It's the middle of the day" was the response.

"No, I get that. It's not that. It's something else."

The *something else* was the usual opening salvo, an IED that blew up just as the convoy passed beneath a green footbridge directly in front of the car repair garage where Buck Connor and his team were pinned down the week before. It was another fireball explosion like the one that had singed Rapicault. There were no injuries, but fighters dressed in black emerged from buildings or from around corners and opened fire on the trucks, their bullets pounding the outside of the heavy armor like hail. Rocket-propelled grenades were next, one after the other, firing and exploding, reminding Wylie of bongo drums. The .50-caliber in the turret of his Humvee jammed, and the gunner couldn't return fire. The other weapon on the convoy was an M240 medium machine gun on a high-backed Humvee at the rear of the line manned by a corpsman, and he was hammering as many targets as he could find. Wylie had the convoy keep pushing through. The massive Saddam Magnificent Mosque was five hundred yards down the road, and as they raced by, Wylie could see gunmen on the walls.

The gauntlet didn't end until the trucks were west of the mosque. Paul Kennedy told them to come in and he would begin organizing a response. He and Jim Booker were waiting outside headquarters, leaning up against a wall of sandbags, as Wylie pulled up.

"Hey, Mike, good to see you alive," Kennedy said.

Inside the operations center, with sweat pouring down his face, Wylie laid out what happened and where on a tactical map. "They started the ambush with an IED. As we pushed through—I mean there was really nothing we could do. They were right along here on the high ground."

Kennedy flooded the area along Route Michigan with nearly the entire battalion.

In the east, there was fighting around the Islamic library and research center involving Golf Company. A portion of Lieutenant Donovan Campbell's First Platoon defended the roof of the structure, keeping up a stream of counterfire. "I marveled as I watched them work," he would later write.[5] An Iraqi policeman who chose to fight alongside the insurgents was killed. Two Golf Company Humvees were disabled in the attacks.

In the west, a Weapons Company convoy came across an abandoned vehicle parked in front of a children's hospital only a mile out of Hurricane Point. They destroyed it with a TOW missile, and subsequent explosions revealed they were correct in suspecting it was a vehicle-borne IED.

In the center of the city, Kennedy and his command element along with Weapons Company Marines took fire from two directions, from the east and northwest. Insurgents attacked the column with IEDs along with rifle, RPG, and machine gun fire. A cameraman with Oliver North's team was along for the ride and captured footage of Marines leaping out of their vehicle to exchange fire with enemy gunmen who were 100–150 yards away.

Fox Company Marines waded into what would prove to be some of the unit's fiercest fighting of the deployment. The nearly ninety troops were led by Captain Mark Carlton, who two months before had been riddled with guilt after sending his men on a river mission that left two of them drowned. On this day, he was at the front of the fighting when an insurgent stepped out from around a corner and let loose a rocket-propelled grenade. The explosion sent shrapnel into Carlton and his radioman, twenty-year-old Lance Corporal Brandon Barclay. It was Barclay's second wound in Ramadi and severe enough this time that he would be heading home.

Oliver North's film crew interviewed Carlton not long after. "I saw the signature blast when it was actually fired, and just like in the movies, slow motion, hit the ground once in front of us,

WICKEDNESS

skipped, and then detonated right in the middle of us," he said. Carlton suffered more than a dozen shrapnel wounds to his face, neck, one arm, and both legs.

When he hobbled up to Kennedy after the attack with dressings on his leg and neck, determined to stay in the fight, he reminded Kennedy of the bandaged, limping fifer in the famous *Spirit of '76* painting that depicts three marching patriots under an American banner.

(Carlton would try to stay with Fox Company, telling North, "If for nothing else, I'm out there because those boys are out there. So there's no other place for me." But his wounds and the resulting pain were too much, and he was eventually evacuated back to the States.)

The fighting would last through the heat of the afternoon and into the evening, resuming the next morning with sporadic gunfights as Kennedy directed his troops to sweep through neighborhoods. Apart from the many heat casualties, all of whom recovered, the number wounded in action included nine from Fox Company, four from Golf, and one from Weapons. All but two of them managed to return to duty. An estimated twenty-five enemy fighters were killed, including two imams caught up in the fighting who had been preaching against the Americans.

In a final intel analysis, battalion officers concluded that enemy tactics had grown more sophisticated with the coordination of mortar and rocket attacks with the detonation of IEDs along with rifle, machine gun, and RPG fire from insurgents in the streets. But somehow the fierce resistance that had proven so deadly in the April combat was no longer at play. Enemy foot soldiers, perhaps mindful of cutting losses, were too willing to give up ground or put down their weapons rather than stand and fight.

Still, the militants displayed a stubborn resolve to keep on the attack. "The enemy is trying to take Ramadi. That cannot be allowed," brigade intel officer Kyle Teamey wrote in his journal.

"I AM SINGLE ENGINE AND I THINK SINGLE PILOT."
JULY 28

Enemy leaders altered tactics exactly one week later, and it proved successful. Through the late morning and early afternoon, reports started surfacing that insurgents were going to launch attacks against various Marine outposts and combat bases. Shops in the city began to close, always a telltale sign of violence to come.

Shortly after 1:00 p.m., virtually every military base in or near Ramadi came under mortar fire. There were four casualties at Combat Outpost, including the lance corporal who was hit by shrapnel while he was in the portable toilet with his lime-green girlfriend. At the Blue Diamond base across the river, a gunnery sergeant who was part of the 1st Marine Division headquarters, thirty-three-year-old Shawn Lane, was killed by a mortar round. He was married and the father of a four-year-old boy.

Under cover of this bombardment, about eighty insurgents closed in on the home of the provincial governor, Abdul Kareem Burgess. The compound was located five hundred yards southeast of the Islamic research center, where there was a Marine outpost just then under fire. The enemy fighters were dressed in Western-style clothing and wore masks. They calmly approached Iraqi police guarding the governor's residence and coerced them to submissively abandon their post.

Burgess wasn't there. But his wife and four sons were home. His wife was working in the garden. At least two rocket-propelled grenades were launched at the house, and a grenade exploded. The family surrendered. The house was looted and set on fire, and Burgess's three adult sons were taken away by the enemy gunmen. Two hours later, three gagged men were seen being pulled from the trunk of a car in Fallujah. That city had become an insurgent stronghold since the Marine offensive led by Major General James Mattis had been halted in April. Islamic militants in Fallujah were led by Abu Musab al-Zarqawi, a Jordanian-born terrorist and al-Qaeda's leader in Iraq.

WICKEDNESS

Meanwhile, just a few hundred yards southeast of the governor's residence, two Marine Cobra helicopters supporting ground troops were in-bound, flying one hundred feet off the ground. They were led by Lieutenant Colonel Bruce Orner, who commanded an attack squadron of Cobras and Hueys located at Al Taqaddum Air Base just across Habbaniyah Lake. The forty-seven-year-old officer had twenty years of flying experience and, on June 24 over Fallujah, was able to expertly land a Cobra after both engines were disabled by a shoulder-mounted surface-to-air missile. Orner and his copilot managed to walk away from the crash site.

On this July 28 mission, the second Cobra was flown by Lieutenant Colonel David Greene, thirty-nine, a reservist who had been called back into active duty in January.

The two helicopters had already flown a few missions that Wednesday, including escorting medevac helicopters carrying the remains of slain Gunnery Sergeant Lane and other wounded troops in the mortar bombardment of Blue Diamond. Now they were being summoned to provide air cover for a Weapons Company convoy taking fire as it drove through southeast Ramadi. Because of radio issues, Orner had Greene take the lead, and they flew a course that cut across the southeast corner of the city. Greene's copilot was another reservist who worked as an airline pilot in his civilian life, Lieutenant Joe Crane, thirty-seven. From his front seat in the aircraft, Crane was having difficulty trying to spot enemy fighters through a telescopic sight. "I don't see anything."

"Roger that, coming left," Greene responded, turning the aircraft south to avoid overflying too much of the city. Passing over built-up areas of Ramadi was a good way to attract dangerous ground fire. It was during that left turn when the aircraft's profile was parallel to the ground that there was suddenly a sound like someone had swung a baseball bat against the side of the helicopter.

Several things started happening at once. The aircraft halted its left turn, causing Crane to call out, "Come left! Come left!

What did we get hit by?" The helicopter began a gentle descent, which was frightening because they were only a hundred feet off the ground and there were buildings and power lines below. A master caution alarm sounded a steady *beep, beep, beep* with a panel light flashing, signaling that the left engine was shutting down. Crane turned off the alarm and said, "We have lost our number one engine." He took the controls to stop the descent, noticing immediately that there was no resistance. Greene wasn't flying the aircraft.

Crane peered over his left shoulder. There was a bullet hole through the left side of the canopy, and the interior was splattered with blood. His pilot was slumped forward. Crane turned back in shock and tried to absorb it all as he flew the aircraft south and then east toward Al Taqaddum. His initial urge was to radio about what had just happened. But he thought the enemy might be monitoring, and he didn't want to give them satisfaction.

On an inter-flight frequency, he finally notified Orner. "I am single engine and I think single pilot."

From where Orner had been flying off to the left, puffs of white smoke could be seen adjacent to Greene's Cobra, and Orner first thought it might be flares that had been launched to draw off missiles. Now with Crane's transmission, he drifted up alongside and could see the hunched-over figure of Greene in the rear seat.

"Yes, it looks like you are single pilot."

Crane responded that he was heading back to base. Then his radio communications went out. He signaled as much to Orner by tapping his helmet and giving a thumbs-down. Crane carefully flew the damaged Cobra on its remaining engine the seven or eight minutes to Al Taqaddum, his thoughts racing about Greene and his wife and two children back in Vermont, one boy and one girl. *Maybe he's still alive*, Crane wondered.

Orner touched down at the airfield first, and his copilot

climbed out and ran over to where Crane landed. He inspected the bloody cockpit and began disarming the weapons system. A corpsman approached, saw the bloody carnage in the cockpit, and shook his head at Crane. A bullet had struck Green in the lower left side of the neck and passed clear through. He was dead.

In all, five rounds had struck the helicopter, including one that disabled the left engine. All were likely fired by a gunman on the ground who was simply taking aim with an AK-47. Orner later thought the man either knew exactly what he was doing, leading the aircraft just enough to deliver precise shots, or he was incredibly lucky.

Greene would be among the highest-ranking officers killed in Iraq at that point in time.

"SPIRITUALLY, IT APPEARED THAT HE DID EVERYTHING RIGHT."

Back in Ramadi, there was a growing concern within Paul Kennedy's staff that the city was starting to turn into another Fallujah-like terrorist haven, despite the presence of hundreds of US troops.

The decision to pull back from routine patrolling and concentrate largely on watching over Route Michigan from fortified outposts was effectively leaving large swaths of the city to the enemy. With the transition of governing authority in late June, the Marines had hoped to rely on Iraqi police and national guard to provide security, or at least assist with tamping down the insurgency. But that wasn't happening. Exhibit A was how easily law officers abandoned Governor Burgess's family to insurgents, who proceeded to kidnap three of his children.

In July, when Paul Kennedy had demanded that police officials clamp down on the growing violence, one top official, Brigadier General Jassim Mohammed Badaa, explained his predicament: "We will give orders, but maybe the police and soldiers will not obey them."[6]

By early August, the battalion was receiving reports of insurgents taking physical control of the streets with roadblocks and checkpoints, particularly through the notorious Malaab area of Ramadi. This was a densely populated area stretching south from Route Michigan where Golf company had waged intense fighting on April 6 and 7.

"While we know these groups [establishing roadblocks] were small and disorganized," a battalion intelligence summary noted, "we also knew that over time, without a professional and secure presence of ISF [Iraqi Security Forces] in the Malaab district, the cancer of Fallujah would spill over and more insurgents would flock to Ramadi and cause fence sitters to fight."

The battalion intelligence chief, Captain Wyeth Towle, met with Badaa on August 1. The police official warned that corruption was spreading among his officers. Police were not manning checkpoints to block the infiltration of insurgents into the city.

Badaa was a pious Muslim and a quiet man with three wives, who hated the radical Islamists and their twisted religious views. He offered a kind of unvarnished truth about what the Marines were doing right or wrong. For his collaboration with Americans, he lived under the constant threat of assassination.

"Jassim is what we consider the last honest man in Ramadi," Towle wrote in a report after the meeting.

Meanwhile, enemy coercion of the governor paid off. Burgess was told by insurgents to resign and surrender to Zarqawi or see his three sons killed. He relented, advocating for US forces to leave Ramadi. Days later, insurgents released a video showing Burgess standing in front of the flag of Zarqawi's militant group and abdicating: "I announce my repentance before God and you for any deeds I have committed against the holy warriors or in aid of the infidel Americans. I announce my resignation at this moment. All governors and employees who work with infidel Americans should quit because these jobs are against Islam and Iraqis."[7]

WICKEDNESS 309

American forces in Ramadi responded with a show of force. Operation Traveler was launched at 3:30 a.m. on Tuesday, August 3. As four of Colonel Buck Connor's Army battalions sealed off the city, hundreds of Paul Kennedy's Marines conducted a house-by-house search of the entire Malaab neighborhood. During the next seven hours, thirty suspects were rounded up and several caches of weapons and IED material were uncovered. There was no resistance. Six days later, an identical mission was launched through the city's industrial area northeast of the Saddam Magnificent Mosque, and more munitions were found. This time, the enemy fought back on a limited basis, firing mortar rounds into a staging area the Marines were using at a soccer stadium. Eleven troops suffered minor wounds. Among them were Adam Clayton, the corpsman who had rushed to assist Kelly Royer during fighting on April 10, and Eric Akey, who had fought with Chris MacIntosh in the carport on April 6. Throughout the month of August, the Magnificent Bastards tried to keep the pressure on the insurgency by launching nine more operations.

The best news for rank-and-file Marines was that they were getting tantalizingly close to mid-September and a trip home.

The enemy, meanwhile, kept trying new ways to kill or injure them. Unable to defeat the Marines in a straight up fight and with IEDs proving less effective because of more heavily armored US vehicles (all of which would change with time as roadside bombs got bigger and more penetrative), insurgents became more resourceful.

The assassination of the four-man sniper team on June 21 was one example. Another was a gas attack on Hurricane Point on June 8. Forty-five troops wound up in the infirmary for what was later determined to be tear gas from exploding mortar shells.[8]

The enemy worked its levers of corruption within the police force to gain advantages.

The Marines undertook a $500,000 contract to transform a Saddam-era intelligence facility on Route Michigan into a new police station. It was located just over a mile outside Hurricane Point, and construction began on June 16. Renovation would include construction of perimeter walls, guard towers, and an armory. Furnishings would include printers, scanners, copiers, and internet access—a shiny example of the new Iraq. But somehow during the construction, explosives were planted and detonated on July 3 in a bid to level the structure. Damage was extensive, though the building remained standing.

The police chief, Ja'ardon Habeisi, promised additional security, and following repairs, construction resumed. But hidden explosives were once again planted, and a second blast in late July caused even more damage. The project was halted.

Perhaps the most audacious enemy scheme was to destroy an entire Fox Company outpost located on the roof of a Ramadi high-rise by blowing up the top stories of the building.

The high-rise outpost was atop one of the tallest buildings in the city, one that housed various government offices. The structure was on the north side of Route Michigan more than a mile east of Hurricane Point in Fox Company jurisdiction. Fifteen troops were on the roof keeping watch over the city on the Wednesday afternoon of August 18 when explosions ripped through the building's top floors.

Some men were actually thrown into the air. Lance Corporal Jonathan Hancock was sitting on a parapet when he went airborne and for a second thought he was going to free-fall down seven stories to the ground. Then he landed on the roof next to another Marine.

"Holy shit, we're not off the building. We're okay," the twenty-one-year-old Hancock said in amazement.

The plan was obviously to collapse the roof. Marines later theorized that if charges had been planted on a lower floor and fully detonated (some appeared to have failed to explode), the resulting damage combined with the weight of the upper stories might have brought the building down. As it was, the explosions blew out large sections in different areas of the top floors and cracked the concrete roof. But it held. Two men who were nearest to one of the blasts below suffered concussions, with one of them bleeding from his ears.

But all of them wound up trapped for a time. A steel door leading to the only stairwell was damaged and wedged shut. It was ninety minutes before a rescue crew arrived to cut through it. In the meantime, the men on the roof congregated at the center, believing that it was somehow the safest place to be if something started to collapse.

The mistake by commanders had been leaving security for the building entrance and lower floors to the police. They proved useless, allowing enemy sappers to plant explosives.

Three days later, a meeting was arranged at Camp Ramadi with Police Chief Ja'ardon Habeisi. It was a ruse. He was taken into custody and sent to Abu Ghraib. The decision to arrest him had been made weeks earlier. According to a July intel document, the reasons were myriad: corruption in the Ramadi police department, tacitly aiding the enemy with guns and cash, and suspicion of assisting fighters in Fallujah with the same. A press release issued the same day Habeisi was detained said he was suspected of "corruption and involvement in criminal activities to include accepting bribes, extortion, embezzling funds, as well as possible connections with kidnapping and murder."[9] Brigadier General Jassim Mohammed Badaa was put in charge of the police.

But where the bomb blasts in the high-rise outpost failed to kill Americans, a sniper succeeded in August.

Jonathan Collins was the last one of Kennedy's class of 2003 high schoolers to die in Ramadi. He graduated the year before from Crystal Lake Central High School, about forty-five miles northwest of Chicago, where he competed in swimming and soccer, dabbled in theater, and worked for years at a popular local pizza parlor. He joined the Marines right after graduation and the Magnificent

Bastards in November at age eighteen. He was a devout Catholic and wore on a necklace the medal of Saint Michael, patron saint of the military. In his right breast pocket, he carried a prayer card of Saint Joseph, the husband of Mary, mother of Jesus. "Oh, Saint Joseph, whose protection is so great, so strong, so prompt before the throne of God, I place in you all my interest and desires," it begins.

"Spiritually, it appeared that he did everything right," Fox Company First Sergeant Tim Weber, who had the task of inventorying the young man's possessions, later wrote in his diary.

Lance Corporal Collins was part of a squad manning an observation post atop a run-down apartment building about three hundred yards east of Fox Company's Snake Pit encampment called OP Ghetto. A five-and-a-half-foot wall of sandbags had been erected on the roof for protection, with openings allowing troops to keep watch on Route Michigan. At 6:50 p.m., Collins was standing with his back to one of those openings, chatting with his squad leader, when he was struck in the back of his head by a single round that penetrated his helmet. He died instantly.

A quick-reaction force that arrived soon after from Snake Pit found the men of Collins's squad, their rifles ready and tears in their eyes, scanning futilely for a glimpse of the enemy gunman who killed their friend. Weber arrived and told the squad leader to get his men back in their post positions and have them wipe the tears away. This was no place to grieve, Weber said.

Collins's remains were transported to Charlie Med at Camp Ramadi, where nurse Jody Shroeder took up the task of cleaning blood off Collins helmet and out of the truck that carried his body, all under the mournful eyes of comrades who brought him there. "This shit sucks," she wrote in her diary that night.

For the Marines, the sniper threat added a new and terrifying element to the overwatch missions, particularly in the city where there were endless places for an enemy marksman to hide. With

WICKEDNESS

each shift, a Marine had to worry whether he was in someone's crosshairs. "Is this my moment?"

Eventually, bulletproof shields cannibalized from wrecked Humvees would be erected behind which service members could stand. But not before tragedy struck again nine days after Collins was killed.

This time, it was Caleb Powers. The twenty-one-year-old Marine had lived a life of perseverance long before he enlisted and was sent to Ramadi. Stricken with emotional disorders as a young child and given up by his mother, Powers was placed with the renowned Childhelp USA organization, becoming one of the first residents of the group's Northern Virginia village for children. Powers flourished there, mentored by a former vice chairman of the Joint Chiefs of Staff who volunteered his services. As a young teenager, Caleb was placed with extended family in rural, upstate Michigan, where he dreamed of becoming a Marine. As he grew older, he became an outspoken advocate of Childhelp USA and assisted with fundraising and talks with children.

A sniper in Ramadi zeroed in on Powers when he was in the High-Rise OP overlooking the city at 5:15 p.m. on August 17. (It would be the next day when militants would attempt to blow apart the upper stories of that building.) One shot killed Powers instantly. There were hundreds of buildings below where the sniper might have been hidden. Marines carried Powers's body down seven stories. Once again, Jody Schroeder was at Charlie Med when the slain Marine was brought in. She felt helpless and angry to see a terrible thing repeated. Weber was there to collect the body and accompany it to Al Taqaddum Air Base for the flight home. Schroeder found him and sat with him, listening intently as he poured out his feelings and frustrations. It was a bit of a sanctuary for the first sergeant who otherwise had to appear strong for his Marines. She listened intently as he unburdened himself. Weber would never forget her kindness.

The death of Caleb Powers would be half of a double tragedy for his sister, Rosanna. She had preceded her brother into the Marine Corps by a year. The day after Caleb was killed, the man she was planning to marry and who was the father of her son—Marine Sergeant Richard "Ricky" Lord, twenty-four—died of wounds suffered in Iraq. "It's probably the hardest thing ever," she later told CNN about losing a brother and a fiancé in two days. "Nobody should ever have to go through it."

Fox Company would abandon the High-Rise OP after the bombing attack of August 18, much like Golf Company had chosen earlier in the month to abandon its outpost atop the Islamic library and research center out of concerns their presence there was taken by Ramadi residents as a desecration of a religious site. Both companies set up new outposts.

The final weeks of the deployment were rapidly approaching, and yet the bloodletting wouldn't stop. In the twenty-six days between the killing of Caleb Powers and the last day of the deployment on September 12, the battalion suffered twenty-six casualties from roadside bomb explosions, mortar attacks, and small arms fire. Two were severe enough to warrant evacuation back to the States. Four were hurt when a civilian dump truck rammed a Humvee.

The worst event was during the predawn hours of Friday, August 27. A Golf Company foot patrol was working its way east along the four-lane Route Michigan. They walked in a staggered formation along either side of a concrete median. Among them was Lance Corporal Nickalous Aldrich, who had just turned twenty-one. Two and a half months earlier, he had suffered shrapnel wounds from an RPG and earned a Purple Heart. He and the others were about nine hundred yards west of Combat Outpost.

Meanwhile, a Golf Company convoy had left the base heading west on Michigan toward the Government Center. In the lead vehicle was Lieutenant Donovan Campbell, the Princeton graduate who had earned a Bronze Star for valor on April 6. According to his memoir, *Joker One*, he had his convoy travel west on the eastbound lanes at an accelerated speed to avoid IEDs. As a safety precaution, the vehicles were traveling without headlights on. Approaching from the west were civilian trucks with headlights blazing. They were coming head-on. Campbell wanted to stay where he was, with his Humvees hugging the median, to force oncoming traffic to swerve out of the way. The four-lane highway at that point was about twenty yards wide. Campbell had been briefed that there was a Marine foot patrol out there somewhere.

Aldrich would have seen the Iraqi trucks coming from the west, if not the blacked-out Humvees traveling from the east at fifty miles per hour.

As the civilian trucks passed with their blinding headlights, Campbell and his driver could feel a sickening *thump-thump*. The driver slammed on the breaks, screaming, "I think we just hit a fucking Marine!"[10] Aldrich was found lying on the north side of Michigan with a massive head injury. He was dead in a few hours, sixteen days short of going home.

Aldrich would be the Bastard to die during the deployment.

The growing number of wounded in these final weeks was such that many were earning their second Purple Hearts.

That was the case with Chris MacIntosh. His first one was March 24, when he suffered a concussion from a roadside bomb explosion that maimed two other Marines. He was given a satellite phone to call his mother and tell her he was okay. He was handed the phone again after the bitter fighting on April 6 to let Lauren MacIntosh know that he once again survived. The men were encouraged to make these calls as a way of easing anxieties back home. But Lauren MacIntosh, who had a uniquely close bond with her youngest child, was becoming an emotional wreck each time the phone rang and she could hear Chris's voice come over the staticky line. She knew it meant another terrible thing had happened in this distant place where she had zero control over his fate.

She was always his guardian angel. When Chris had first been assigned to 2nd Battalion, 4th Marines, Lauren had accompanied him to his new billet, like a mother taking her son to his freshman dorm—much to Chris's consternation. When he had returned to Camp Pendleton late after a leave to go home, she had called the Echo Company first sergeant to explain his tardiness and keep him out of trouble.

MacIntosh tolerated the mothering with bemusement. She was his best friend, after all. But now in Ramadi, he worried these repetitive calls might be doing more harm than good.

On the morning of August 20, MacIntosh was in his bunk when mortar rounds hit. The shells were fairly accurate, and havoc ensued. Windows in the chow hall got blown out. Portable toilets were destroyed. A backup generator for a command center was disabled.

Three Marines suffered minor wounds: MacIntosh, Corporal Robert Hernandez, and Echo Company Gunnery Sergeant Bernard C. Coleman. All would be patched up and return to work, and as usual, MacIntosh was told to call home. He was fearful about his mother's reaction, and his instincts proved correct. When Lauren MacIntosh answered and heard her son's voice, she went to pieces. "What happened *now*?" she asked through her sobs.

14

EXIT

"BACK HOME YOU GO TO JAIL FOR DOING SOMETHING LIKE THIS."
KILLING

A YEAR AFTER the Magnificent Bastards fought in Ramadi, Colonel Paul Kennedy testified before the House Armed Services Committee that "we fought full-scale combat on the city streets of our assigned area accounting for nearly 1,000 enemy dead."

It was an extraordinarily high number of enemy KIA attributed to the actions of one Marine battalion. It rivals the estimated number of militants killed in the second Fallujah battle—between 1,000 and 1,500—that lasted six and a half weeks and was believed to be the biggest clash of the Iraq War, involving six Army and Marine battalions.

The reality was that actual combat experience for the vast majority of troops sent to Iraq or Afghanistan was the exception rather than the rule with so many of them confined to fortified bases or relegated to less hazardous duty. The Marine Corps recognizes those who truly engage in fighting with something called the Combat Action Ribbon, awarded for being "under enemy fire [IEDs included] while actively participating in . . . combat." During the heaviest years of fighting in Iraq and Afghanistan, only about one in five Marines earned Combat Action Ribbons.

But among the Magnificent Bastards, Combat Action Ribbons were handed out wholesale, at a rate of more than 90 percent in some rifle companies. The troops were under fire at least every week, if not every day or two.

For one battalion to kill a thousand enemy fighters in seven months where there was no US air and artillery bombardment to magnify enemy losses required individual Marines and sailors to shoot and kill over and over.

The result was that taking life, if not routine, was certainly not unusual for many of Paul Kennedy's people. Golf Company's Jonathan Embrey was one example. The twenty-two-year-old Marine, who was nicknamed "Chaplain" or "Chaps," kept a diary of his combat experience in Ramadi. In his daily narrative of events, Embrey briefly touches on the killings, not as a means of keeping a tally but simply because they were a part of the fabric of his Ramadi experience.

So he writes about putting a bullet through the head of an enemy fighter on a rooftop who was shooting as Embrey fought his way through a cemetery on April 6, and how he "wasted a few more people" at the end of a road from where gunfire had wounded another Marine. The next day, he and two other Americans shot down four enemy insurgents running for their car. Twenty days later, Embrey fired into an enemy vehicle from which troops had been taking fire. He raked the car with an M240 medium machine gun and saw it explode, killing all the passengers. Then he cut down three combatants trying to flee with one machine gun burst. After his team was ambushed on July 21 and took refuge in a house, Embrey and his men made it to the roof, from where he shot a gunman through the face from a distance of forty meters. And on August 11, Embrey and his team were conducting an overwatch mission when militants started firing into a Marine vehicle. "I shot the guy with the RPG and he kept running. I think I hit him at least five times."

Jason Rosman wrote in his memoir about the first time he killed someone, on April 7. The eighteen-year-old member of Golf Company felt a sense of elation:

"'Fuck yeah,' I thought, thinking about my friends from high school probably partying in college at the same time I just shot a dude in the neck. Holy shit what a rush! Back home you go to jail for doing something like this. I had never felt so free in my life."[1]

Years later, Chris MacIntosh would remember how the use of deadly force became second nature in Ramadi. "Especially if you start losing all your fucking friends and everything around you is falling apart, it's very easy to pull the trigger," he said.

The cost was at times the accidental killing of innocents, which could carry its own scarring emotional baggage. Jonathan Hancock, the Fox Company Marine who was trapped for a time on the roof of a high-rise after an insurgent bomb attack, was haunted for years by an incident on September 12, the last day of the deployment. It would contribute to the post-traumatic stress disorder he would later suffer. Hancock was in an observation post on the roof of a bank on Route Michigan, lobbing grenades from an M203 launcher on his rifle into a courtyard where there were enemy gunmen. As he let loose a final round, he watched the projectile arc toward the target.

"It just hung in the air for fucking ever and as it was hanging in the air, I see this—this kid running across this field," Hancock recounted in a documentary about his psychological ordeal years later. "And it just—it just impacted right at his feet as he was running and just . . . gone."

Sometimes, Marines would seek out the chaplain—their only ready source of counseling—when they wrestled with the rightness of taking life, particularly after the battles of April, when hundreds of enemy fighters were killed. Brian Weigelt heard similar questions from each of them. *How will I face eternity for what I have done? Am I going to be condemned for killing people? What are the eternal consequences?*

Weigelt would patiently listen. He would acknowledge that war was inherently evil and that it was vital for these men, when they carried out their duty as Marines, not to allow this darkness to define them.

There were a handful who felt overwhelmed by the killing, as if their humanity were slipping away. They were based out of Combat Outpost and primarily fought as gunners on truck-mounted heavy weapons that were far deadlier and more indiscriminate. To help them cope, Weigelt and Sergeant Major James Booker brought each back to Hurricane Point for a few days. The battalion headquarters was relatively safer, with better food, showers, and lodging. There they could rest, exercise, and collect their thoughts. Booker would talk with each one for hours on the back terrace of the palace that contained the battalion headquarters. It overlooked the Habbaniyah channel that flowed southwest from the Euphrates River. Weigelt had them write about their feelings, and then he'd discuss the essays with them. He felt it was a pathway for separating them from their experiences and reconnecting with who they were as people, separate and apart from the killing. It seemed to work.

Paul Kennedy was always proud of the fact that despite the challenges his men faced in Ramadi, they were never accused of overly aggressive conduct of the type that other units fighting in Iraq engaged in. The only potential exception that occurred in Ramadi while Kennedy and his people were there involved Marines who worked, of all things, as security for James Mattis.

The major general had twenty-nine troops acting as his personal security guard, riding in up-armored Humvees and eight-wheeled Light Armored Vehicles, or LAVs that look like tanks on rubber tires. On the night of June 7, the security team minus Mattis was driving along a dangerous, curved section of

EXIT

roadway known as the Racetrack, about a mile west of Combat Outpost, when they were ambushed with an IED. The blast killed Lance Corporal Jeremy Bohman, twenty-one, of Sioux Falls, South Dakota, and wounded three other troops. Mattis's men opened fire. Quick-reaction forces from Golf and Weapons Companies arrived at the scene. There were reports of unarmed people killed. An investigation later ensued, although the outcome remained unclear.

The one military tool immediately available to gauge the emotional impact of combat was the Post-Deployment Health Assessment survey. Troops were required to fill out the four-page questionnaire as they prepared to go home.

It queried them about physical wounds and injuries received and any sicknesses suffered, anything from a runny nose to diarrhea to skin diseases. It also asked about combat. "Did you see anyone wounded, killed or dead during this deployment?" "Did you ever feel that you were in great danger of being killed?" "[Have] you discharged your weapon [in combat]?"

There were questions aimed at uncovering evidence of depression, nightmares, hypervigilance, isolation, and even suicidal ideation.

A landmark study, published in the *New England Journal of Medicine* just a few months before the Magnificent Bastards ended their tour in Ramadi, found that about one in six soldiers or Marines who served in Iraq combat appeared to be suffering from major depression, generalized anxiety, or post-traumatic stress disorder (PTSD).

The rate of such illnesses among 2nd Battalion, 4th Marines may very well have been far higher. The 1st Marine Division had one psychiatrist, Navy Captain Bill Nash, a twenty-six-year veteran of the service. He regularly visited all the far-flung battalions and instructed chaplains and medical and senior enlisted personnel on how to spot mental health problems among troops and what to do about them. He was also provided some overall results on what the

Post-Deployment Health Assessment surveys showed regarding mental health issues and conducted psychiatric evaluations.

Nash was told by the 2/4 medical personnel who administered the surveys that over half of the battalion's troops showed signs of PTSD and that one in five were suffering "significant and persistent symptoms." Nash traveled out to Combat Outpost to do full psychiatric evaluations of troops who showed the severest signs of emotional issues in their survey responses. Over the course of two full days in early September, the psychiatrist met with these men. There were dozens of them clearly afflicted with PTSD, more than he had found for any other battalion.

"The first day, I started at about 9 a.m. and finished a little before midnight. The next day was almost as long," he wrote in a letter to friends and family shortly afterward. "Many of these guys will heal up over time and be OK, but some will not. For many, I just listened (as much as I could with so many of them and so little time), let them tell their stories, and tried to help them make sense of what had happened. Reassurance and education go a long way. But for many, medications and other treatments are needed. One of the tragedies out there was the belief by many of the [M]arines in Echo Company, which has had the most casualties of any in the 1st MARDIV, that some of their losses could have been prevented by better leadership and decision-making over the past seven months. That's a bitter pill to swallow, if true."

"GO ASK THE COMPANY."
KELLY ROYER

Shortly after noon on Monday, August 23, Marines of First Platoon, Echo Company, came under fire from the Al Haq Mosque, a hotbed of anti-American sentiment off Route Michigan about seven hundred yards west of Combat Outpost. Brian Telinda was among those there. He looked up and saw muzzle flashes from one of the windows. The platoon commander, Lieutenant Vincent

EXIT 323

Valdes, notified headquarters and requested permission to enter the mosque.

Raiding a Muslim house of worship could be touchy, but not impossible, especially if US troops were plainly under attack from enemy fighters inside. Eventually, during the deployment, a few dozen members of the Iraqi armed forces were attached to Golf and Echo Companies and could more readily conduct such searches.

On this occasion, battalion headquarters approved the search. If they were being shot at, they could go for it. At the same time, however, Echo Company Captain Kelly Royer pressed Valdes hard about doing so. Was he certain the enemy was inside? If you entered, you had better find a weapon, Royer told him. Valdes gave the order, and his men smashed through the front doors with a Humvee and went inside. Telinda reached the second floor, where he and other Marines found a few unarmed people, including a man in a wheelchair, some shell casings by a window, and evidence of gun residue. But no weapon. Back downstairs, Valdes informed them that an AK-47 had been located.

It wasn't until a day later that it was discovered Valdes had planted the gun. Someone saw him do it. Royer was livid and wanted him relieved of command.

"Why did you do what you did?" he asked him at one point.

"Well, sir, because you told me I'd better find a weapon in there."

Royer consulted with Kennedy, and the decision was made to delay any punishment.

The reality was that by the final months of the deployment, Royer had alienated much of his staff. His inflexible and overbearing command temperament had left some platoon commanders either rattled, like Valdes, or just plain fed up. Tom Cogan, who would wind up among the most highly decorated officers in the battalion, was particularly weary of it all. He couldn't tolerate how Royer intruded on Cogan's management of Third Platoon and openly complained to Echo Company executive officer Sean Schickel, even ruminating about shifting over to battalion logistics to get away from Royer. It wasn't a formal request, but Schickel, who had also grown concerned by Royer's leadership style, alerted the company commander. Royer saw Cogan as one of his best people and pulled him aside for a talk. "Well, sir, as a matter of fact," Cogan began, "I fucking don't like working for you. You yell at everybody about everything. Everybody winds up walking on eggshells around you." Somehow, the chat worked. In Cogan's estimation, Royer seemed to back off.

Major JD Harrill, who ran battalion operations, wanted Royer relieved of command, most importantly because he believed Royer should have more rapidly shifted his men from the dangerous route clearance missions to static observation posts along Route Michigan. To this day, Royer denies that there was any delay.

The battalion executive officer, Major Mike Wylie, had even stronger feelings. He had grown to dislike Royer and thought he was a bad company commander. Wylie believed that an errant commander could create a toxic atmosphere where things just went wrong, and he suspected that Echo's high casualty rate was not just bad luck.

But Paul Kennedy resisted making a change. He felt some deference was important when judging an officer who had led men through some of the toughest combat the Marine Corps had seen since Vietnam.

Amid all of this, one person who remained committed to Kelly Royer and was always willing to explain and provide context for his command style was his company first sergeant, Curtis Winfree. The thirty-six-year-old Houston native who had served eighteen years in the Marine Corps believed he had the closest relationship with Royer and thought many of his actions were grossly misunderstood. He believed the company commander cared deeply about his troops and agonized over decisions he made before

EXIT

325

placing them in harm's way. But he also saw Royer as a fireball type who wanted things done his way, and Winfree could see how that rubbed people raw.

Winfree was one of two senior staff noncommissioned officers for Echo Company. The other was Gunnery Sergeant Bernard C. Coleman, thirty-seven. He was born in Lynchburg, Virginia, the son of an Air Force aircraft refueler who shifted his family to locations around the world every four years, including South Dakota, Germany, Delaware, and Japan. The younger Coleman graduated from a high school outside Tokyo, and his father sent him back to the States, believing his son was a disciplinary problem.

The teenager enlisted in the Marines and wound up making it a career, impressed as a Black man that the Marine Corps was color-blind when it came to promotions. He grew into a tough, disciplined enlisted officer with consistently high regard from superiors and lower enlisted alike—that is, until Kelly Royer took command of Echo Company.

If Winfree, as first sergeant, was the senior enlisted adviser to the company commander on matters related to troop morale, the gunnery sergeant—Marines called them *Gunny*, for short— was the infantry expert who kept troops stocked with everything they needed—or at least everything Coleman could get his hands on in a service branch that too often lacked necessary gear like vehicle armor. In Corps parlance, he was the beans, bullets, and Band-Aids guy.

But in Echo Company, Coleman was far more than that. He was a sounding board for platoon commanders angry about Royer and struggling to deal with the man.

Coleman would hear the snickering from squad leaders in the barracks after word got around about Royer's background as an Air Force chauffeur. The joke was that he aspired to go from bus operation to becoming the next Erwin Rommel, the brilliant German field general of World War II.

Coleman took after the task of eradicating negative graffiti about Royer that sprang up around Echo Company's area of Combat Outpost. The caricatures in some instances were obscene. He would spray-paint over them himself or direct platoon sergeants to get it done. It meant checking the portable toilets and vehicles regularly.

In Coleman's estimation, Royer wasn't a malicious man or incompetent. In fact, the gunnery sergeant thought Royer was a strong tactician. His failing, in Coleman's view, was a lack of people skills. To some, Royer had an abrasiveness and bravado that left him incapable of leading without offending or creating disharmony.

Coleman said he experienced this himself during a loud exchange with the Echo commander in front of several Marines during a night mission in late March. Frustrated with what he thought were pointed and pointless questions, Coleman suddenly blurted out, "I'm tired of your shit!" Royer later reprimanded him for it, even counting up the number of troops who witnessed the exchange: seven.

The two men had strong personalities, and a clash was inevitable. Royer would make a move to prevail, and it triggered a series of events that would end his command of Echo and his chance for advancement in the Marine Corps.

On July 14, Royer signed a fitness report for Coleman, portions of which appeared contradictory. A brief narrative section was mildly complimentary, lauding Coleman's hard work, successes, growth, and combat bravery. But the rating marks were below average in nearly every category.

Coleman viewed it as a career ender after eighteen years in the Marine Corps, and he showed it to the battalion sergeant major, Jim Booker. It evolved into a conversation about the morale of Echo Company that was missing from anything communicated by the company first sergeant, Winfree. (Years later, Winfree would say he was unaware morale was so low but should have known and alerted Royer. "That's on me," he said in 2024.) The battalion high command concluded it had a problem that needed to be addressed. At Kennedy's direction, Major Mike Wylie put together a climate survey, a questionnaire the military sometimes uses to gauge troop sentiment. Coleman had urged Booker to do exactly that. "Go ask the company," he told him.

On Sunday, August 29, Kennedy contradicted Royer's fitness report on Coleman. "I strongly non-concur with the low distribution of marks for this outstanding Marine gunnery sergeant," he wrote in a section devoted to reviewing-officer remarks. He lauded Coleman for being the "ballast" in a company "that has seen the most friction and turbulence of any in this battalion" and said he was among the top 10 percent of gunnery sergeants with whom Kennedy had worked. "I would trust the lives of my own children with this man."

Two days later, Major Harrill rode in a convoy across the city from Hurricane Point, and copies of the climate survey were passed out to the members of Echo Company gathered in the chow hall. More than 90 percent of the unit participated, or upward of 175 people. The responses were gathered up and brought back to battalion headquarters, where Kennedy pored through them.

A Marine 1st Division officer's written summary of the survey results said:

> The battalion's staff officers, senior enlisted leaders, and the leadership within Company E, describe Captain Royer as overbearing, dictatorial, and out of touch with his Marines. More importantly, the results of the command climate survey reveal a broken bond of trust between the leaders and the Marines in the company. Morale is consistently described as poor. Captain Royer himself is personally cited in the vast majority of the statements collected and there is not one positive comment; he is characterized as stifling initiative, being overbearing, arrogant, selfish,

abusive, and unprofessional. A significant number of the statements call for his relief.

Kennedy decided Royer had to go. He and his command staff headed to Combat Outpost the next day. Royer was summoned to the Golf Company briefing room, where he found Kennedy by himself with a stack of survey results on the map table. Kennedy told him he was relieved and to pack up his things so he could immediately head back to Hurricane Point with Kennedy and his people.

Royer felt numb and utterly deflated, thinking, *What a dishonor. I have to live with this for the rest of my fucking life.*

The same day, Kennedy wrote up his thoughts on Royer in a fitness report explaining that he had totally lost confidence in the man's ability to "inspire, mentor or appeal to the better nature of his Marines and sailors. . . . His authoritarian style and 'zero defects' mentality have placed the morale and esprit de corps of his Marines in jeopardy." Kennedy described how Royer used intimidation and public humiliation to achieve results, chastising officers in front of junior Marines. Kennedy said the high marks he gave Royer in a May fitness report "were obviously flawed and should be viewed with circumspection as information was not forthcoming by his men concerning this leadership environment within the company."

In the ratings area, Royer received less-than-average marks in every category, including the worst, an adverse finding, in four categories: leading subordinates, developing subordinates, setting the example, and ensuring well-being of subordinates.

In the days that followed, Royer filed a response ten times the length of Kennedy's remarks. He wrote a history of command of Echo, citing challenges faced and detailed rebuttals of each of Kennedy's criticisms. He brought up the Valdes incident involving a planted weapon to argue that he used it as an opportunity to mentor officers about ethics. He denied publicly humiliating any of his men.

If morale was flagging, Royer argued, it was because of tough combat, high casualties, and difficult living conditions. He also cited efforts by him and his wife to successfully solicit donations of soft drinks, juices, soups, clothing, and video movies for his men.

"The bottom line is that though I am extremely demanding of my men . . . I do love and care for them," he wrote.

The issue of Royer's firing went up to Colonel Joe Dunford for review. He was by that time the assistant division commander of the 1st Marine Division headquartered at Blue Diamond and was soon to be promoted to brigadier general. Dunford knew Royer from when the officer served on the division staff during the Iraq invasion the year before. He now conducted an inquiry, reading every questionnaire response, reviewing documents submitted by Royer, and speaking with Kennedy and officers and senior enlisted members of Echo Company. Sean Schickel, who had been executive officer and was elevated to acting company commander after Royer left, was summoned to Blue Diamond to see Dunford. Schickel told him that for seven months, the men of Echo Company had been fighting two wars, one with the enemy and the other with Royer.

Dunford endorsed Kennedy's decision. While he found a host of qualities in the officer—extraordinarily conscientious, bright, very aggressive, hardworking, and committed—he was particularly struck by the results of the climate survey. He found the survey results much harsher than those conducted within other division battalions, including those in similarly tough combat and living conditions.

At the root of Royer's failure was a style of leadership that created a disconnect between what he wanted to achieve and how that was interpreted. What he said and how it was heard.

330 UNREMITTING

"He was clearly ineffective in communicating with his subordinates in such a way as he engendered their trust," Dunford wrote. "Seniors, peers and subordinates continually question[ed] Captain Royer's motivation for his actions; they generally assumed the worst of him."

After Dunford's decision, Royer filed one last rebuttal. A new wrinkle was that he had been allowed to read thirteen redacted climate survey results. "I was terribly shocked," he wrote. "Sadly, this misunderstanding [of my intent] contributed to their discontent and to a dampening of their morale; for that, I am sincerely remorseful."

The new division commander who had switched out with Jim Mattis in August, Major General Richard Natonski, endorsed the Kennedy and Dunford findings. Royer would keep fighting his dismissal in the months ahead from back in the States, but his future in the Marine Corps was finished.

"I'M TIRED OF KILLING PEOPLE."

There was an almost palpable relief within Echo Company after Royer was gone. Schickel was a far more relaxed commander, and tension that had gripped Echo for months melted away.

Even more importantly, the entire battalion was in the final stages of going home. For all the thrilled anticipation, it was a strange adjustment for those men who had learned to cope with combat by forcing themselves to accept the likelihood of their own deaths, which gave them the freedom to fight unfettered by fear. But now, in these last days, there was suddenly a very real possibility they were going to survive. This brought back caution and a dampened willingness to take risks. Why die now at the very end?

Nor was the enemy easing up. There were mortar attacks, Route Michigan ambushes, and small arms fire at observation posts every single day.

What made matters worse was how these final missions had to be carried out alongside the new incoming troops from 2nd Battalion, 5th Marines—whose slogan was "Retreat, Hell"—under the command of Lieutenant Colonel Randy Newman. Before leaving, the outgoing Marines had to accompany and orient the incoming Marines about this dangerous city. Kennedy's people were keenly aware the newcomers had not yet learned how to fight in Ramadi, and how to read the urban terrain to quickly outmaneuver and defeat enemy ambushes. The last thing they wanted was to get killed by a rookie mistake. Some were hesitant to even go out on these final missions.

The newly arrived "Retreat, Hell" troops had heard about the heavy casualties 2/4 suffered and fierce combat endured. They had a taste of it early when one of their operations officers, Captain Patrick Rapicault, was in an IED explosion during a reconnaissance visit to Ramadi in July. It was scary stuff, so much so that a captain in command of 2/5's Weapons Company, too unsettled by the dangers of the city, was sent home. Rapicault took his place.

At the same time in September, Buck Connor's 1st Infantry Brigade of the Big Red One division finished its tour and was replaced by the Army's 2nd Brigade, 2nd Infantry Division. Connor himself left Camp Ramadi the morning of Sunday, September 12. He had lost more than sixty troops under his command in a year's time, well over half of them from 2nd Battalion, 4th Marines.

There were mercifully few casualties for 2/4 in these final weeks, all minor injuries or wounds. By the weekend of September 11 and 12, most of Paul Kennedy's people had been shifted to the Camp Ramadi base on the far west end of the city in preparation for going home. They were relatively safe there, whiling away hours playing softball.

City security was now in the hands of Randy Newman's 2/5 battalion, and the enemy took advantage of these untested troops by launching widespread attacks across the city. For the few dozen

Kennedy people still acting as advisers or providing base security, it was a final round of violence before going home, almost as if this dangerous city wasn't about to loosen its grip until the very last minute.

During fighting near the Government Center on September 12, a flustered tank commander with the 2nd Brigade threw his seventy-ton M1 into reverse and started to back up, crushing at least one Humvee in the process. A handful of Rob Weiler's men who had stayed behind to assist 2/5 Marines barely managed to jump out before their vehicle was flattened like a beer can.

Enemy mortar rounds began hitting with accuracy inside the Government Center perimeter, wounding two Weapons Company Marines on their very last day of combat. Shrapnel from one of the blasts broke Sergeant Brad Diaz's left leg.

Across town at Combat Outpost, two of Chris Bronzi's men—Sergeant James Heredia, twenty-four, and Corporal Glenn Hamby, twenty-six—were acting as advisers to help the incoming battalion's Golf Company adapt to this violent city. The learning curve grew steep as fighting broke out across the city over the weekend. Two of 2/5's Golf Company platoons came under attack along Route Michigan. A third platoon, with Heredia and Hamby along, left Combat Outpost on foot from a northwest gate with the idea of flanking the enemy. Things quickly began to go wrong. The new troops were unfamiliar with the area, and the platoon lieutenant led his men in the wrong direction. By the time Hamby was able to convince him of his mistake, the platoon came under attack. Heredia and Hamby, by now hardcore veterans of urban warfare, directed troops to get out of the narrow streets and onto rooftops, where they could more effectively kill the enemy. Even then, the new arrivals seemed hesitant to rise from behind cover and fire their weapons—or maybe they just didn't like being told by another Marine how to fight. Still, the two advisers tried to set the example by keeping up a steady stream of return fire. At one point, after several minutes of Marines frantically trying to

EXIT

333

locate the source of the sniper fire, Hamby spotted muzzle flashes from inside a building through a hole in a wall created by a missing brick. He used a grenade launcher to blast a large opening through the wall to expose the sniper position and then riddled the interior with his M16 to kill the man.

The fighting lasted six hours. The platoon commander was finally convinced to move his troops through the streets—with Heredia and Hamby on point—and link up with the rest of 2/5's Golf Company. As the fighting continued, Heredia and Hamby ran across open areas of enemy gunfire to resupply troops with water and ammunition. Both Bastards would earn Bronze Stars for valor for their actions.

The incoming battalion lost its first man that Sunday, all while 2/4 Marine Jonathan Hancock looked on helplessly. Lance Corporal Hancock had been among those members of Fox Company who, one month earlier, were nearly blown off the roof of a high-rise building along Route Michigan. On September 12, Hancock was acting as a squad adviser for 2/5 Marines. They were set up in an observation post on the roof of a bank just across Michigan from the old high-rise structure. A 2/5 sniper team was with them. The day before, Hancock had spotted a suspicious vehicle parked along the eastbound lanes of Route Michigan about four hundred yards to the west. He suspected it was a car bomb, and in fact, enemy fighters had planted IEDs across the city in preparation for ambushing American troops that weekend.

From the bank outpost where Hancock was located, radio communication was down because of dead batteries. So he used a telephone to call the battalion tip line and warn about the potential VBIED. He felt certain the American who answered would alert battalion headquarters.

But on Sunday, the car was still there, and Hancock could see a 2/5 convoy headed directly toward it from the west. Frantic, he ran down to the four-lane highway and stood in the middle,

334   UNREMITTING

hoping they would see his silhouette. He tried waving his arms, motioning for the convoy to cross over to the westbound lanes and avoid the car. It was to no avail. As Hancock watched, the car detonated just as the convoy passed. The explosion wounded three Americans and killed Lance Corporal Jason Poindexter, twenty, of San Angelo, Texas.

Minutes later, Hancock could hear a crescendo of gunfire from the west in the direction of Snake Pit combat outpost. A force of more than a hundred insurgent fighters had massed there in a desperate bid to overrun that fort.

Snake Pit was a walled enclave off Route Michigan just east of Hurricane Point wedged between Route Michigan and the two-hundred-yard-wide Euphrates Channel. It had been home to 2/4's Fox Company. But by the weekend, most of Fox Company had been moved to Camp Ramadi along with most of Kennedy's battalion. Only Fox Company's Weapons Platoon, under the command of First Lieutenant Abel Guillen, was still there providing base security through Sunday.

As 2/5 Marines and Army resources were drawn into street combat across the city, Guillen and the twenty troops with him were all that were left to defend Snake Pit. They were set up in machine gun nests around the base perimeter and had some fire support from observation posts at nearby Hurricane Point and the south end of a bridge-dam crossing over the Euphrates. The Sunday had started out fairly routine, with individual enemy gunmen taking potshots at the base in the morning. But as the afternoon wore on, that gunfire grew heavier, peppering Marine Corps positions from buildings to the north across Route Michigan and from a run-down, war-scarred apartment complex 250 yards to the east known as the Ghetto. It was in an observation post atop those apartments, since abandoned, where Lance Corporal Caleb Powers had been killed by an enemy sniper on August 17.

Guillen, twenty-nine, was the child of migrant farmworkers who emigrated from Mexico to pick fruit in the orchards of

EXIT

Washington State. He enlisted at seventeen and was eventually urged to enter officer training and earn a commission. He had received a Purple Heart during the same fight on July 21 that left Fox Company commander Mark Carlton grievously wounded. On September 12 at Snake Pit, the only other senior leader with him was the 2/4 battalion's weapons specialist, thirty-seven-year-old Chief Warrant Officer Rick Dunham, simply known as the battalion gunner. Among Dunham's duties during the deployment were keeping troops trained and up to speed on their various weapons and sighting systems.

From their barricaded outposts or tower positions around the base, the Marines were armed with their rifles, a few M240 medium machine guns, and a collection of squad automatic weapons, or light machine guns. There was also an MK19 automatic grenade launcher set up near the base entrance on the side facing the channel. (An entrance onto Route Michigan had been barricaded with a berm on the inside.) The weapon could be angled in the direction of the Ghetto, but Guillen forbade firing it because he knew there were families still living in some of the apartments.

As incoming fire grew heavier and enemy gunmen began maneuvering down narrow roads perpendicular to Michigan, Guillen tried to decipher what the insurgents were planning. At first, he thought they were simply trying to keep the base Marines pinned down to prevent reinforcements from reaching troops fighting deeper in the city—perhaps not realizing how lightly Snake Pit was garrisoned. Then Guillen began to worry that the enemy was planning to overrun them. Either way, his men were rapidly burning through what ammunition they had on hand and in the base armory.

To the west, between Snake Pit and Hurricane Point, was a two-story Iraqi National Guard barracks where five Marines manned a sandbagged position on the roof. Among them was Lance Corporal Amir Heydari, who had been recruited months earlier by Sergeant Major Booker to serve as one of the Bearded

Guys. Things were largely quiet in their sector, although they could see several men moving through an abandoned building 250 yards to the north. No one was ever in that structure. Suddenly, there were shots fired from there, and the Americans could see muzzle flashes. One of the men got permission to fire a bazooka-like weapon called a Shoulder-Launched Multipurpose Assault Weapon, or SMAW. It was a difficult shot at 250 yards, but he put the rocket right through a window, and the men whooped and hollered as the warhead exploded inside. Enemy fighters came pouring out of the structure, and Marines manning a bunkered position on the south end of the bridge-dam crossing the Euphrates opened fire on them. That threat was over.

But elsewhere, from the north and the east at the Ghetto apartments, growing numbers of enemy fighters kept a steady stream of rifle and automatic weapons fire directed at Snake Pit. Water towers for the base showers were riddled with bullets. Corporal Brandon Honeycutt, fighting from a position atop company headquarters, took a ricochet in his left arm. At one point, Heydari began to yell out, "Alamo!" the call sign for when Marines would prepare to make their last stand in the event of an enemy attack to overwhelm the base.

At the far opposite end of the base, atop barracks in the southeast corner of Snake Pit, three Marines were set up in a bunker on the roof, drawing withering enemy fire. Manning the M240 medium machine gun was Private First Class Dan McNaghten, the twenty-year-old son of a police officer from Kirkland, Washington, who was inspired by 9/11 to enlist in the Marine Corps' Delayed Entry Program. Now, with enemy gunmen shooting at his position from the Ghetto apartments, he was under the most intense fire of the deployment, and on his last day. McNaghten was certain he was killing some of the enemy fighters on top of those apartments.

Individual enemy gunmen moved through nearby streets or down Route Michigan in a reckless bid to close in on the base.

The Marines, from their sandbagged positions, would cut them down with rifle and machine gun fire. But with so much ammunition carted off that morning by the 2/5 platoons heading into the city, the Snake Pit defenders were quickly running low on bullets. There wasn't any belted ammunition for the squad automatic weapons. So magazines were used instead. They had to be changed out frequently and tended to cause the weapons to jam. Dunham was rushing from one position to the next, helping Marines clear their guns and resume fire. He encouraged men to alternate their bursts of fire to conserve ammo.

Many of the enemy combatants seemed heedless of the concentrated gunfire from Snake Pit observation posts. Marines would see them crumple as bullets struck, their bodies collecting in the street or being dragged to cover by comrades who would themselves be exposed to Marine Corps fire. The behavior was so foolhardy that some of the Americans suspected the insurgents were under the influence of narcotics. Manning the gun post over the headquarters building with the wounded Honeycutt was Lance Corporal Phil Nohren, a lanky, six-foot-four native of rural Missouri.

Ammo was running desperately low. Guillen tried to contact battalion headquarters by radio to plea for a resupply, but communications were consumed with frantic chatter from across the city. He finally used a text messaging system to warn that ammo needed to arrive soon. He was told the battalion was fighting across the city and the request would be passed to Army brigade headquarters. As a fallback, he and Dunham decided to distribute captured AK-47s from the armory to the troop fighting positions. Dunham had base cooks load up magazines and carry them out to troops.

The Marines were within minutes of switching to captured enemy weaponry to continue holding back the enemy onslaught when Army Bradley Fighting Vehicles arrived with resupply. The tracked vehicles approached the Snake Pit entrance on a road running along the Euphrates Channel. They swung into a field to the east of Snake Pit and began firing rounds from their 25 mm cannon into the Ghetto apartments.

As had happened so many times when Army heavy weapons arrived, enemy resistance faded away. Guillen would later tell Paul Kennedy that his men had killed perhaps fifty enemy insurgents during the fight, and that was a conservative estimate.

Minutes before the Bradleys showed up, when it seemed the enemy fighters would never stop sacrificing themselves to Marine gunfire, battalion gunner Rick Dunham was on the rooftop of the headquarters building, moving from one position to the next.

Suddenly, he heard one of the young Americans call out something that would stay with him, something he would repeat to Paul Kennedy as coda to the day's bloodletting.

"I'm tired of killing people," a Marine said before handing off his light machine gun to a comrade. "You kill some."

EPILOGUE

"I DON'T THINK THE BATTLE OF RAMADI CAN EVER BE WON."

RAMADI HAD PROVEN to be such a violent city that after Paul Kennedy and his Marines left, the number of US troops patrolling the streets was doubled. Army Colonel Gary Patton, who commanded 2nd Brigade, 2nd Infantry Division and who had taken over security for the Al Anbar Province, decided in October more troops were needed in the city. Now, in addition to Lieutenant Colonel Randy Newman and his "Retreat, Hell" Marines, there would be a battalion of Army infantry handling the city's east end.

Never again would a single battalion be responsible for such a large swath of Ramadi as were the Magnificent Bastards in the summer of 2004. During 184 days in Ramadi after taking over combat operations March 13, the Magnificent Bastards suffered 238 Marines and sailors wounded (17 of them twice; Kenneth Conde was wounded and then later killed in combat) and 34 lives were lost. For a roughly 1,100-man unit, that's a combat casualty rate of 25 percent, among the highest of any battalion that fought in Iraq or Afghanistan. (Casualty rates among some individual 2/4 companies that were in the thickest fighting were even higher.)

Eight weeks after 2/4 went home, the second battle of Fallujah began. It was a sweeping house-by-house, room-by-room slugfest where more than ten thousand US troops, most of them Marines, were plunged into the city to finally eradicate that insurgent haven. The result was widely believed to be the bloodiest fight of the Iraq War and the toughest since Vietnam. Two thousand Iraqi soldiers fought alongside the Americans, and the interim government was in full support. In the weeks leading up to the battle, residents were urged to flee, and neighborhoods were nearly empty when the attack began. A massive disinformation campaign by US forces preceded the fight. It included the construction of a fake military base that successively convinced enemy commanders the upcoming assault would originate from south and southeast when in fact it came primarily from the north.[1] The invasion of the city took about ten days, followed by several weeks of dangerous mopping up.[2]

American casualties included a hundred or more troops dead. At least a few thousand insurgents were killed, many of them fighting to the death inside houses that US troops had to enter and clear one by one. Marine Corps veteran and author Bing West, who embedded with the US military during the battle, wrote that there were more than two hundred close-quarters fights inside Fallujah buildings.[3]

The heroism on display in these frenzied, kill-or-be-killed episodes yielded America's highest valor awards, including a Medal of Honor for an Army staff sergeant, a Distinguished Service Cross for an officer, and nine Navy Crosses for enlisted Marines, some of whom didn't survive the battle. Four of those Devil Dogs were members of 3rd Battalion, 5th Marines—the Darkhorse battalion—whose officers brawled with Kennedy's men during the infamous Valentine's Day soirée on the beach just before 2/4 left for Ramadi.

While the destruction of the insurgent sanctuary in Fallujah dampened enemy resistance in Al Anbar Province for a short time, the familiar pattern of deadly roadside bomb attacks and ambushes

EPILOGUE

fueled by hatred of American forces and the Shiite-dominated national government in Baghdad persisted, much of it in Ramadi, burnishing that city's reputation as a very dangerous place. During the first free parliamentary elections held in January 2005, only about seventeen thousand voted in Al Anbar Province, or just 2 percent of eligible voters.[4]

As time passed, the demands of continually cycling troops into Iraq and Afghanistan war zones was taking its toll on the Marine Corps. By summer 2005, three Marine battalions were on their third rotation into combat in as many years. (The same multiple-deployment strain would befall the Army in years to come as soldiers began to accumulate two-, three-, or four-year-long combat tours.)

One of the Marine units was 1st Battalion, 5th Marines, which had replaced Randy Newman's 2/5 troops in April. About 150 members of 1/5 had been on all three combat tours. First, the invasion. Then fighting in the first battle of Fallujah in 2004. And now, Ramadi, where they were losing more people—thirteen in the first few months—than in any of the other engagements. "I just want to live an easy life," Corporal Mike Kelly, twenty-three, of Boston, told the author that summer, after declining a $20,000 bonus to reenlist. "A normal job. Nothing fancy. A working stiff. That's my dream."

The battalion's Alpha Company was the hardest hit. The commander, thirty-six-year-old Kelsey "Kelly" Thompson, reflected on the city's persistent violence. "I don't think the Battle of Ramadi can ever be won," he said. "I just think the Battle of Ramadi has to be fought every day."

The Darkhorse battalion that took part in the second battle of Fallujah headed to Iraq for the third time in January 2006 and was posted just east of Ramadi in Habbaniyah. In June, one of the battalion's sniper teams spotted an enemy marksman in a parked vehicle and killed him with a single shot as he prepared to fire a rifle. Another insurgent trying to drive the vehicle away was also gunned down. The weapon the marksman was using turned out to be a Marine Corps sniper rifle that had been seized by the enemy during the assassinations of Tommy Parker, Deshon Otey, Pedro Contreras, and Juan Lopez two years before.[5]

In November of that year, 2nd Battalion, 4th Marines returned to Iraq, this time under a different commander but with dozens of the same Marines who had fought in 2004. Two companies, Echo and Fox, were once again posted in Ramadi, although Echo would later be shifted out of the city. For two men who had survived the unremitting violence two years earlier, luck would finally run out.

One of them was the man who replaced Sergeant Major Jim Booker as the battalion's senior enlisted officer. Joe Ellis had served as first sergeant for headquarters company in 2004. He arrived back in Iraq as sergeant major of the Magnificent Bastards. Three months into the deployment, he was killed by a suicide bomber at a checkpoint in Barwana, Iraq, northwest of Ramadi.

The other veteran lost was Clinton Ahlquist, who was one of Paul Kennedy's class of 2003 high school graduates when he joined the battalion in January 2004. In high school, he had been editor of the yearbook, class vice president, and prom king. He fulfilled a dream of military service when he rolled into Ramadi as a private first class with Fox Company. When Fox Company returned to Ramadi in 2006, Ahlquist was a sergeant and squad leader. He was killed by a roadside bomb on February 20, 2007, as he led the evacuation of a wounded Marine and he was posthumously awarded a Bronze Star.

In the 2006–2007 time frame, it was beginning to seem as if the violence that had first exploded against the Magnificent Bastards in 2004 would never go away. Rules of engagement had relaxed since Kennedy and his men were there. Troops made wider use of air attacks, artillery, and tank fire in the city. Destruction was more widespread, and Ramadi, one officer said, was beginning to look like Stalingrad. Still, the insurgency fought on. "We

EPILOGUE

343

have killed a very substantial number of these guys, and yet the level of attacks has continued to go up," said a deputy commander of Marine forces in Iraq, Brigadier General Robert Neller, in January 2007.[6]

Ramadi stubbornly remained untamed with resistance led chiefly by al-Qaeda–connected terrorists. In August 2006, the operations intel officer for the Marine Corps in Iraq, Colonel Pete Devlin, drafted a grim state-of-affairs secret report about the insurgency in Ramadi and across western Iraq. A summary of the contents was leaked to the media. One unnamed Army officer who read the report told Thomas Ricks of the *Washington Post* that "we haven't been defeated militarily but we have been defeated politically—and that's where wars are won and lost."[7] Years later, another intel officer said that all the US had succeeded in doing in Al Anbar Province since 2003 was tread water.

The irony was that amid the pessimism, the worm had actually begun to turn for certain Iraqi leaders. By late 2005, tribal chiefs had grown weary of the ruthless, score-settling tactics of al-Qaeda. In the far western area of Al Qaim—where Corporal Jason Dunham had earned a Medal of Honor in 2004, open warfare broke out between tribal members and the terrorist group. The coalition ultimately stepped in to help support and organize a government militia of tribal members to battle al-Qaeda, and it was the first stirrings of what would be called the Awakening.

Ramadi was where it began. Early signs of the so-called Awakening in late 2005 were brutally quashed by al-Qaeda. But the American military tracked al-Qaeda leader Zarqawi to a safe house north of Baghdad in June 2006 and killed him with an airstrike. Three months after that, Sheik Abdul Sattar Abu Risha, who lived with his family in an estate west of Ramadi, announced the formation of the Al Anbar Awakening tribal movement. Marine Major Alfred "Ben" Connable, a senior intelligence analyst who spent years in Iraq, described Abu Risha "as the right guy at the time."

344   **UNREMITTING**

"He had insurgent credentials, he had smuggling credentials, and he was enough of a kind of criminal vagabond, these kind of suave criminals that became so popular in Western Iraq," Connable told researchers in 2009.[8]

Among the greatest successes was convincing young tribal members to join Iraq security forces and work with the US military to defeat al-Qaeda.[9] Security within the city and other areas that embraced the Awakening movement vastly improved, with daily attacks dropping precipitously in 2007. Abu Risha, however, would not live to see peace return to his city. Ten days after he shook hands with President Bush at an air base in Iraq in September 2007, he was killed in an IED explosion outside his Ramadi home.

Still, the insurgency that had spread across Iraq in the spring of 2004 was finally receding. Despite years of bloody warfare, its high-water mark for coordinated attacks against US forces remained the early April offensive against 2nd Battalion, 4th Marines in Ramadi that had failed. The US would withdraw its forces from Iraq four years later, in 2011. But the end of that conflict didn't end the misery of that blighted city. From the remnants of al-Qaeda in Iraq sprang a Sunni terrorist group called the Islamic State of Iraq and Syria, otherwise known as ISIS or ISIL. A crucial battleground became the provincial capital of Al Anbar Province. From 2014 to January 2016, Ramadi was transformed into a wasteland as ISIS took control and then was driven out by Iraqi government forces. The majority of structures were destroyed, bridges were blown, power was all but severed, and vast numbers of citizens fled into the desert.

Not until after that nightmare ended did Ramadi finally begin to flourish. The city population gradually returned to pre-invasion levels. Billions of investment dollars flowed in, and new construction spread. It included a shopping mall, hospitals, universities, and new government offices.[10] A luxury hotel and restaurants occupied the southern banks of the Euphrates just upstream

EPILOGUE

from where two Marines from 2/4's Fox Company drowned in a failed river assault. Signs of war remain in the pockmarked exteriors of residential housing in city neighborhoods and out in the Sofia District where Marines had been locked in desperate combat. But so much other evidence of war has been swept away. A sparse grove of stately palms marks the field once known as the tank graveyard. The wrecked armor is long gone, and new buildings ring the area. An asphalt soccer court stands astride the field where Chris MacIntosh and Eric Akey ran for their lives to escape enemy machine gun fire on April 6. And at the intersection where seven members of Echo Company were gunned down in an ambush, many of the old machine shops where insurgents set up machine gun positions on rooftops have been replaced with new businesses. The outline of the fateful intersection the Americans called Gypsum and Nova is still there. And a few bullet-scarred huts remain. But now, just steps from where Corporal Marcus Waechter and seven Marines took refuge from a hail of gunfire, there's a pizza parlor with the cartoonish image of a smiling, winking chef beckoning customers to come in off the street and enjoy refreshment.

"I WANT TO START LIVING THE SECOND HALF OF MY LIFE."

It took a generation to finally rebuild the brick-and-mortar destruction of war in Ramadi, and at least as long for the medical reconstruction of some young Americans ripped apart by blasts and bullets in that city. Sometimes that meant years of trial and error as surgeons used metal plates and screws and bits of borrowed bone or flesh to fashion a new jaw or length of leg. Bouts of infection might arise to ruin the work done and cause doctors to start all over again as their patients grew into middle age, holding out hope for some return to normalcy.

From the moment Jose Texidor suffered a gunshot wound to his left leg on April 10, 2004, doctors would spend the better part of twenty years trying to salvage that limb. Almost everything behind the kneecap had been destroyed. At Bethesda Naval Hospital in Maryland, a steel plate and skin grafts were used to hold it together, and after eighteen months of rehabilitation, Texidor was taking tentative new steps. But new infections set in. He would finally fly to Los Angeles and seek help from a highly regarded program at UCLA called Operation Mend. The cooperative effort between UCLA and the US military that began in 2007 was designed to provide advanced surgical and medical care for the most direly wounded of the Iraq and Afghanistan wars. For Texidor, it first meant months of treatment with antibiotics to clear out the infections of bone and flesh, then a total knee replacement. That was in 2017. Setbacks and further recovery would follow. There would be a broken left ankle and an unrelated bout with testicular cancer. While he eventually became ambulatory, the mechanics of taking a step are far from perfect. "It's been a long, long road," Texidor said in 2023, now married with three children. "I want to get back to school. I want to start working again. I want to start living the second half of my life. I want to enjoy it. I want to be stress-free."

The medical saga of Brian "Mack" McPherson was even more complicated. Rebuilding a face where the lower jaw was gone—destroyed in the explosion of a roadside bomb—was a challenge for doctors in the American military. Civilian physicians would have to step in, and even then, it was a struggle.

McPherson, who was twenty-five when he was among the first casualties for 2/4 in Ramadi, always ranked himself as the first Bastard killed in combat. That was because he later learned his heart stopped twice after he was evacuated from the battlefield. In the first effort to rebuild his face, military doctors removed muscle from McPherson's latissimus dorsi muscles on his right side to use as connective tissue for a new jaw. The foundation was built from pelvic bone grafted onto a steel framework that McPherson

EPILOGUE 347

likened to an Erector set. It was a monthslong endeavor because every time bone or flesh was extracted from one part of his body, McPherson had to heal before that harvested material could be used to fashion a new jaw. But ultimately the effort failed because of stress, surgical fatigue, and McPherson's generally diminished physical and emotional state.

Years passed. McPherson eventually learned about Operation Mend. In 2016, doctors there attempted a second reconstruction, this time pulling bone and soft tissue from McPherson's left leg below the knee and used what portion of the original jaw reconstruction remained viable. Once the lower jaw was assembled, dental implants could eventually be emplaced. McPherson would be finally able to chew food.

But as always, there was the risk of failure. One challenge for McPherson, who met and married his wife, Heather, in 2018, was the same difficulty other recovering veterans face who live in remoter areas of the country. The best health care was often too far away if something went wrong. After finally undergoing dental implant surgery in his newest reconstructed jaw in 2018, McPherson developed another serious infection. He and his wife drove seventy-five minutes to a Department of Veterans Affairs hospital in Oklahoma City and were there for twelve hours without learning anything definitive, then were ultimately sent home and mailed antibiotics.

As McPherson's condition grew worse over the Christmas holiday season, Heather drove him to a large public hospital in Norman, Oklahoma, where a maxillofacial surgeon considered surgically removing part of McPherson's newly reconstructed jaw—a terrifying prospect for the veteran who was thinking, *I don't have bone to spare.* The physician insisted that otherwise the Marine veteran would not survive long enough for UCLA physicians to treat him after the holidays. Within twenty-four hours, McPherson was flown to Los Angeles, where an Operation Mend resident or doctor in training pulled out the infected implant and administered more antibiotics. The jaw was saved. In 2019, more than fifteen years after the explosion in Ramadi, McPherson finally began enjoying the simple luxury of chewing food.

While some of the men harmed in Ramadi took years to recover, others carrying hidden wounds only got worse. One was Buck Connor. Long after the Army colonel had retired and started work in the private sector, he was diagnosed with Parkinson's disease, an illness of tremors that stems from nerve cell damage to the brain. Doctors told Connor that the disease was very likely the result of his repeated exposure to blasts when he was in Ramadi.

Brain damage from blasts was little understood in the early years of the Iraq and Afghanistan wars as IEDs grew prevalent. By 2006, military medical experts were warning that the Pentagon lacked a system-wide plan to identify and treat soldiers with traumatic brain injury, or TBI.[11]

A RAND Corporation study released two years later estimated that three hundred thousand US troops suffered at least mild brain injuries.[12] Scientists who conducted imaging studies of soldiers impacted by the shock wave of a blast found a different pattern of brain damage from a traditional blow to the head by a blunt object. In cases of blast exposure, there was a more dispersed pattern of cell damage in the brain. In moderate or severe cases, blood vessels could inexplicably spasm and cut off oxygen flow, causing permanent brain damage. The Pentagon began more aggressively dealing with the issue. By 2010, it initiated a battlefield policy requiring that anyone caught within fifty meters of an explosion had to remain out of combat for at least twenty-four hours or longer if symptoms such as vertigo or headaches persisted.[13]

Connor believed he was exposed to at least eight blast events during his year in Ramadi. In the two severest cases—May 26 and

EPILOGUE

349

July 14, 2004—he momentarily lost consciousness and for days suffered from dizziness and vomiting, sometimes retching while he was down on his hands and knees. All the while, he insisted on not being taken out of Ramadi to undergo imaging studies or in any way leave his command.

In recent years, his tremors from Parkinson's have grown severer. His regimen in 2024 was a dosage of three different pills four times a day and a powder to be inhaled as needed. The combination provides some relief from involuntary movements.

Beyond concussions from blasts, another frequent war injury in Ramadi's intense summer was heatstroke, and the Marine who suffered from this worst of all was Sean Gustavison. When he collapsed during a combat patrol in June 2004, his core temperature reached 107 degrees.

His body's ability to adjust to heat or cold was shattered. In the years to come, whenever ambient temperature rose above eighty-five degrees, it would feel like his body was screaming to escape. Gustavison would retreat to the basement of his Saginaw, Michigan, home, where it was usually fifteen degrees cooler. "I move down there and become nocturnal," Gustavison said in 2023.

An extraordinarily high core temperature, if the victim survives, can profoundly impact the brain. In fact, family members say Gustavison was changed by the experience. "They say that I am damaged."

Paul Hizo came home from Ramadi with a wound that eventually killed him. He enlisted in the Marines out of high school in central Illinois in 2003, joining 2/4 that November. On the morning of April 28, 2004, the private first class with Fox Company was walking at the front of his squad down Route Michigan. Fox Company had by then stopped doing the dangerous route clearance missions and started using observation posts to guard against IEDs. Still, troops had to patrol the dangerous streets to and from these static positions.

UNREMITTING

On this occasion, the squad was heading back to base when an IED detonated immediately to Hizo's right. He was thrown to the ground and was bleeding badly from shrapnel wounds to his head, right side, and right thigh. He couldn't see. Ultimately, Hizo was flown back to the States and discharged from the Corps the next year. Surgery to remove shrapnel from his left eye eventually restored sight there. But he remained blind in his right eye. And there was still a piece of shrapnel too deep in his brain for surgical removal. He died from a stroke in 2018. An autopsy later revealed an abscess in his brain likely from the shrapnel that may have caused his death, said his mother, Donna Tomich.

Hizo was buried in Arlington National Cemetery, the last of those from the 2004 deployment to die from enemy wounds.

"IT FEELS LIKE HOME."

Hizo is among four from that combat tour buried at the cemetery on the south slopes of the Potomac River, hallowed grounds visited by more than four million people each year. The graves for Jeremiah Savage, Caleb Powers, and John Wroblewski are located in the vaunted Section 60 portion of the cemetery, made famous because it is the final resting place for so many American troops killed in Iraq and Afghanistan.

The father of Wroblewski, John Wroblewski Sr., fulfilled a irresistible impulse to travel into the Iraq war zone and visit the precise location where his son was fatally wounded during heavy fighting on April 6, 2004.

This was made possible with the help of then Major General John Kelly, who had been James Mattis's assistant division commander in 2004. By 2008, Kelly was in command of all coalition forces in western Iraq. The elder Wroblewski was an athletic director for a New Jersey high school. He was an outspoken proponent of the war who had expressed views on CNN's *Larry King Live* and even managed to meet with President Bush. He and his wife,

EPILOGUE

351

Shawn, had four boys, of which Lieutenant John Wroblewski was the oldest.

With the support of the US military, the father made a trip to Iraq in 2007 but was unable to reach Ramadi. In 2008, he was back, and in the company of Kelly, he finally traveled to that stretch of roadway the Marines called Route Gypsum where his son was fatally shot in the face.

It was just one of countless ways that people marked the sacrifices of 2/4 troops after the 2004 deployment. Roadways were renamed for Wroblewski, Benjamin Carman, Dustin Schrage, and Jeremiah Savage. A California high school built a small monument honoring Kyle Crowley, who had died months after graduating. Moisés Langhorst was honored with a memorial in his hometown of Moose Lake, Minnesota. A Florida American Legion post was renamed in honor of Christopher Cobb.

Filmmakers memorialized the life and death of Lance Corporal Juan Lopez, one of four Marines in a sniper team assassinated on a rooftop on June 21. The twenty-two-year-old Mexican immigrant had attended high school in northwest Georgia and then enlisted in hopes of earning US citizenship.

Filmmakers had read of Lopez's dream of citizenship through service in the Marine Corps, all to improve the life of his family. That concept was used as the basis for a short film titled *Una Causa Noble*, or *A Noble Cause*. Shown at film festivals in the US in 2006, it was a fictional story about a young Mexican man who leaves his wife (as Lopez did) to go to war as a Marine and loses his life in the process. Lopez had posthumously earned US citizenship.[14]

Rob Weiler, the former commander of Weapons Company, had long dreamed of a way to honor Sergeant Kenneth Conde, the beloved squad leader in his company who had earned a Bronze Star in combat after fighting with a shoulder wound on April 6, only to die in an IED blast three months later. After a lobbying effort that included assistance from Paul Kennedy, Weiler's wish came true. A new school building on the campus of the Marine Corps University in Quantico, Virginia, was dedicated to the sergeant and named Conde Hall. Hundreds attended the ceremony in 2011 for what was the Staff Noncommissioned Officer Academy. Conde's father was there wearing his son's combat boots. A memorial to the sergeant was set up in the academy entryway. Among other things, it contained a portrait, medals, and the Bronze Star citation. There is also a plaque that reads: "His leadership before, during and after the battle symbolizes all we have come to expect from a noncommissioned officer."

Perhaps the most affecting memorial to the lost Bastards was not something made of stone or bronze but rather annual ad hoc assemblages of aging Bastards over beer, tears, and muscled embraces. The rituals began as the veterans chose to mark Memorial Day by gathering at the grave site of a fallen comrade. Parents would be invited to witness how much their child was loved, respected, and missed. The veterans themselves would draw solace from one another, rejuvenate their time-honored bonds, and, for a brief period, spend time with each other: people who understood exactly what they had been through, how they had suffered, and the emotional scars that persisted.[15]

"You never find this kind of brotherhood anywhere else," Derrick Kepler told the *Tennessean* newspaper after a graveside gathering in 2019. "When we come back to have all of us together, it feels like home."

Kepler had been a Golf Company lance corporal who was wounded in a mortar attack at Combat Outpost during heavy shelling on July 28, 2004, and later returned to duty. He and others of Golf had gathered at the burial site of Richard Quill III near Nashville, Tennessee, who came to 2/4 as a replacement and returned to Iraq with the battalion two years later, only to die of a sudden illness on February 1, 2007, at the age of twenty-two.

The veterans feted Quill and knew they'd be at another grave site in another year. Whenever they finally ran out of places to visit, the plan was to start all over again.

"Every single one of us will be here until there is two of us left meeting up at someone's grave when we're ninety-five years old," Kepler said.

"A GOOD AND DECENT MAN."

In the first forty-eight hours after the Magnificent Bastards got home, Chris MacIntosh wound up in jail. The highway patrolman who pulled up to where MacIntosh's car had broken down found the Marine with a blood-alcohol content of just over the legal limit and was unsympathetic despite being a Marine veteran himself.

MacIntosh asked if he knew about the Magnificent Bastards.

"Yes, I did hear about them," the officer responded. "And I'm glad to hear more about them in jail."

MacIntosh was locked up for twelve hours as his mother, Lauren, who had arrived in California to welcome him home, searched frantically.

While a good many veterans of the Ramadi fight scattered to their new lives after the deployment, young members still on four-year enlistments remained and, in fact, returned to Iraq and even Ramadi.

A few key players in the 2004 events went on to nearly reach the status of household names.

Mattis was elevated to three-star general in late 2004 and earned a fourth star in 2007. Three years later, he was placed in charge of Central Command, or CENTCOM, overseeing all US military forces from the Horn of Africa to Central Asia to include Iraq and Afghanistan. He clashed with the Obama White House during a period over Iran policy and was cycled out of that post five months early. He retired from the Marine Corps in 2013.

In 2016, he was chosen by President-Elect Trump to be defense secretary, an appointment that required a congressional waiver. The law requires at least a seven-year gap from the time someone leaves the military before taking such a cabinet position as a gesture toward ensuring a separation between the uniformed service and civilian oversight of the military. Congress, for only the second time in history, granted the waiver. In the Senate, the vote was 98–1. Mattis served until he resigned in protest in 2018 when Trump, over the secretary's objections, wanted to pull US troops out of Syria where they were conducting anti-terrorism operations. Mattis later coauthored a book on leadership, *Call Sign Chaos*, which became a *New York Times* bestseller.

John Kelly, who had been Mattis's assistant division commander during the Ramadi fight, reached the rank of general in 2012 before retiring four years later. He was tapped in 2016 to head the Department of Homeland Security in the Trump administration and was named White House chief of staff in July 2017. Kelly served eighteen months, longer than anyone else in that post during the administration.

Joe Dunford, who took over for Kelly as Mattis's assistant division commander and approved the firing of Kelly Royer, rose higher in the ranks than any of them. He received his first star in 2004, his second and third stars in 2008, and was elevated to four-star general in 2010. Chosen to lead US and NATO forces in Afghanistan from 2013 to 2014, Dunford picked Jim Booker to be his sergeant major. The next year, Dunford was named commandant of the Marine Corps and, months after that, was nominated by President Obama to be chairman of the Joint Chiefs of Staff— the military's highest position.

After leaving Ramadi and command of 2/4, Paul Kennedy served as the Marine Corps liaison with the House of Representatives. After promotion to colonel, he led a regiment into combat in Helmand Province, Afghanistan, in 2010, during what would be the bloodiest year for US forces in that war. It was the first full

EPILOGUE

355

year of President Obama's surge of troops into Afghanistan. One of Kennedy's battalions was led by Mark Carlton, who had commanded Fox Company in Ramadi. During a meeting with tribal leaders in January 2011, Kennedy was struck in the head with a rock by an Afghan trying to kill him. Kennedy's security Marines quickly shot and killed the assailant. Kennedy suffered a concussion and a broken nose and would receive a Purple Heart.

Elsewhere in Helmand Province, JD Harrill, the former operations officer in Ramadi, was by this time a lieutenant colonel commanding a battalion of Marines. In March 2011, Harrill was with his troops as they entered a walled compound in a village in Helmand Province. A twenty-five-year-old staff sergeant standing five feet away stepped on an IED that blew him in half. Harrill was riddled with shrapnel to his face, back, and left leg and thrown against a wall. A section of vertebrae was broken, and Harrill was in considerable pain. But he refused helicopter evacuation because he didn't want the Taliban to see him flown off the battlefield. Instead, he walked with his troops an excruciating three miles back to base and then declined medical evacuation out of the country, remaining until the deployment ended in September. Back surgeries would follow. Nerve damage in his left leg led to some muscle atrophy. Harrill retired from the Marine Corps in 2012.

After Afghanistan, Kennedy served as head of Marine Corps public affairs, commanded a Marine Expeditionary brigade in the Pacific, and led recruitment efforts before retiring as a two-star general in 2019.

Jim Booker, who had inspired many of the Marines in 2/4, returned home in 2014 after his final combat tour as senior enlisted adviser for Dunford and for his successor in Afghanistan. When Dunford became commandant, Booker was considered for the job of sergeant major of the Marine Corps. But another person was selected. "He [Booker] was beyond qualified," Dunford said in 2023. Booker retired in 2015. Six months later, he suffered a massive stroke that left him with considerable paralysis that included difficulty walking and talking. But over the next eighteen months, he saw significant improvement. With his wife, Carla, he took to entertaining 2/4 veterans at their hilltop home in central Texas.

The two captains Kennedy saw as his best and brightest in Ramadi were Rob Weiler and Chris Bronzi, and both seemed destined for great things. Weiler led Weapons Company and was named battalion operations officer in 2005. As a company commander with 2nd Battalion, 24th Marines, he deployed to Afghanistan in 2006 and then twice more as an operational planner. In 2012 as a lieutenant colonel, Weiler took command of the Magnificent Bastards and then in 2019 led 5th Marine Regiment as a colonel.

He was to receive his first star as a brigadier general in 2023 but, along with hundreds of other officers, saw promotions delayed. This was due to a highly publicized legislative tactic by Republican Senator Tommy Tuberville of Alabama, who was protesting a Defense Department policy allowing travel reimbursement for troops seeking abortions. Tuberville finally lifted that hold in December, but not before the Senate had to approve individual promotions in a time-consuming process.

Republican Senator Dan Sullivan of Alaska placed Weiler's nomination up for a floor vote in November, arguing with impatience that the officer's advancement should never have been held up. He made his point by reading from Weiler's Silver Star citation regarding combat in Ramadi.

"'He continued to fearlessly [lead] Marines as they destroyed this tenacious enemy,'" Sullivan said before looking up from the text. "He's no woke guy. He's no desk jockey."

As brigadier general, Weiler was made assistant commander of 1st Marine Division.

Bronzi, who had led Golf Company, seemed on an even steeper trajectory after Ramadi. Kennedy nominated him for the coveted

EPILOGUE

Leftwich Trophy, awarded to Marine Corps captains who show outstanding leadership in combat, and Bronzi won it. In the years that followed as he rose in the ranks, Bronzi earned two advanced degrees, including a master of arts in defense studies from King's College London. He became a staff officer with 1st Marine Regiment, served in Afghanistan, commanded a battalion, and then was appointed to the Joint Staff in the Pentagon before eventually assuming command in 2019 of the 15th Marine Expeditionary Unit, a rapid-response task force of more than two thousand troops.

But it all changed on a breezy summer day off San Clemente Island, seventy miles northwest of San Diego. Bronzi was leading the task force in a training exercise, and Marines were being delivered from the island to a nearby ship by amphibious assault vehicles, or amtracs. One of the squat, rectangular tracked vehicles with sixteen personnel aboard began taking on water shortly after 6:00 p.m.

As the Associated Press would later report, based on the investigation that followed, nearly everything went wrong.[16] The Marines were inadequately trained in the event of such an emergency. The fourteen amphibious vehicles in the exercise were in poor condition, and prior repairs had been rushed. The foundering vehicle sprang leaks. The transmission was without oil. The generator went out. A pump was failing. Emergency lights didn't work. And an escape hatch was unmarked. (Marines would end up searching for it in the darkness with their cell phone lights.) Still, the vehicle remained afloat for forty-five minutes, more than enough time for the troops to have evacuated. But no order was given to jettison their heavy gear and get out. Another assault vehicle arriving to assist collided with the flooding amtrac, causing it to turn in to a wave and take on even more water through an open hatch. The vehicle quickly sank in nearly four hundred feet of ocean.

Eight Marines and a sailor were killed in "one of the deadliest Marine training accidents in decades," the AP reported. A host of officers, up to and including the 1st Marine Division commander, were relieved or otherwise punished. Bronzi was one of them. He left the Marine Corps in 2024.

Kelly Royer would spend months trying to expunge the damning fitness report that led to him being relieved of command in Ramadi and years fighting for a promotion to major. In a bid to find some kind of error or unfairness, Royer retained a former Marine Corps judge advocate who pushed relentlessly, and ultimately unsuccessfully, to get a copy of the survey of Echo Company troops showing rock-bottom morale. The material assembled included supportive statements about Royer from more than a dozen people who were in Ramadi in 2004. They were a mix that included Echo platoon riflemen, Marines temporarily attached to the company, members of Royer's headquarters staff, the company radio operator, a combat replacement, and an Iraqi translator. Their statements were laudatory.

"I could go on for days giving example after example of how Capt. Royer is an exceptional leader and extraordinary Marine," company intel specialist Charles Lauersdorf wrote in 2006. "But I believe his record can speak for itself, with the exception of one, disputable, discriminate blemish that I believe was given for very unjust reasons. Echo Company's many successes are attributed not just to the hard-working Marines, but also just as much to Captain Royer's steadfast devotion to duty. For that reason, I would gladly serve under Capt. Royer's command in any clime or place."

One of the last letters of support Royer received in 2007 was, ironically, from his former gunnery sergeant, Bernard C. Coleman, by then a first sergeant. Coleman attributed most of the problems in the company to communications issues between Royer and his men that never resolved after he was made their commander on the eve of deployment. "I feel that he was placed in a no-win situation," he wrote. Coleman said he had mixed emotions when he heard Royer was removed from command.

EPILOGUE

In May 2005, Royer was featured prominently in a *New York Times* front-page story with his photograph. The article shed important light on the critical issue of Marines traveling in Humvees that had minimal or no armor and noted that most of Echo Company's deaths involved troops riding in these vulnerable trucks. But the article also seemed to imply that Royer's critical views about how the Marine Corps's handling of the armor issue was somehow related to his being relieved of command. In fact, he had been relieved as commander of Echo Company on September 1, 2004, and his whistleblower-like comments ran in the *Times* eight months later.[17]

That didn't stop members of Congress from seeing a connection when they cited the article during a House Armed Services Committee hearing a week after the story was published.

"I am absolutely overwhelmingly offended when I read reports that a Marine captain, Kelly Royer, commander of E Company, a company that suffered the largest casualties of any company in the theater in the six months they were there, is perhaps being railroaded out of the Corps because he simply spoke up about the troops that he was leading," said Curt Weldon, then a Republican congressman from Pennsylvania.

Both Mattis and Kennedy testified and gave assurances that Royer's firing had nothing to do with any critical comments.

"I will tell you that Kelly Royer is a good and decent man and initially a strong combat leader," Kennedy told the committee. "In over 90 days of intense combat my confidence in his ability to lead eroded to the point of necessitating his relief. . . . It was strictly a matter of leadership shortfalls brought about by long-term exposure to combat."

None of Royer's efforts to win a promotion beyond captain worked. He retired shortly after reaching twenty years in the military in 2009.

"I HAVE BEEN DELUDING MYSELF."

A few other veterans of the Ramadi fight generated headlines. Among them was the curious case of Amir Hekmati, who had been one of Jim Booker's undercover Bearded Guys. He would be portrayed at various times as a hero, then a victim of Iranian oppression, and finally, something quite different.

Hekmati, who was twenty-one when the combat tour in Ramadi ended, was honorably discharged from the Marine Corps in 2005 and for a time worked as a Defense Department intelligence analyst in Afghanistan. As the American-born son of Iranian immigrants, he held dual citizenships and, after leaving the job in Afghanistan, traveled to Iran to visit family. While there in 2011, he was detained by Iranian authorities, accused of being a spy, and sentenced to death, although that was later commuted to a prison term. Hekmati's lawyers would assert that he was tortured, and the Associated Press also reported that he was whipped and beaten. During Hekmati's four and a half years in prison, Secretary of State John Kerry demanded he be set free, and Vice President Joe Biden visited his family. The Obama administration negotiated his release in 2016, along with four other Americans, including *Washington Post* reporter Jason Rezaian.

Within months, Hekmati had obtained a $63 million default judgment against Iran for his treatment and used the court decision to apply for compensation from a Justice Department–operated fund for terror victims obtained from seized assets. He was awarded $20 million. But on the eve of collecting the first $839,000, Hekmati's eligibility for the money was revoked based on an FBI investigation that raised suspicions that the Marine veteran went to Iran to sell US secrets he obtained working as a defense contractor. He vehemently denied the accusation, and no criminal charge was filed.[18]

But the controversy continued. In December 2023, Hekmati filed suit in federal court alleging that the Justice Department had wrongfully revoked his eligibility for the $20 million.

EPILOGUE

Publicity was generated around former Echo Company sniper Richard Stayskal over his success, years after Ramadi, in single-handedly changing military medical malpractice law because of his own personal misfortune. Stayskal had been wounded during fighting in the tank graveyard on April 6. An enemy sniper shot him through the left lung during that combat, and Stayskal was evacuated back to the States. He was honorably discharged from the Marine Corps the next year. And while Stayskal felt he never fully recovered from his war wound, he chose to reenter the military, successfully applying to become a member of the Army's elite Green Berets. He passed their grueling physical tryout and worked his way up the ranks of noncommissioned officers.

After being chosen to attend a combat dive school in early 2017, Stayskal underwent a physical that included a chest x-ray and, later, a CT scan at the Womack Army Medical Center at what was then Fort Bragg, North Carolina.

The scan showed evidence of something suspicious in Stayskal's right lung. But he was never alerted to it and was cleared for dive school. Over the weeks and months that followed, Stayskal started having trouble with respiration and coughing up blood. By June, he was diagnosed with advanced lung cancer, and a doctor said there was clearly evidence of something wrong back in the January CT scan.

Stayskal, by that time married with two daughters, was devastated. He and his wife, Megan, wanted to sue the Army for medical malpractice. But a 1950 Supreme Court decision barred such lawsuits against the military. Stayskal lobbied Congress, and in 2019, over the Pentagon's objection, federal legislators passed the Sergeant First Class Richard Stayskal Military Medical Accountability Act, allowing for malpractice redress through an administrative law process.

Hundreds of service members have since taken advantage of the law, as did Richard and Megan Stayskal, who filed claims seeking $40 million in March 2023. But their demands were rejected by the US Army Claims Service after a finding that there was no evidence Stayskal would have had a better health outcome if the cancer had been treated five months earlier. He and his wife were stunned by the decision and planned to appeal to the overarching Defense Health Agency.

"I definitely felt like this should have been an easy decision, a slam-dunk," he told the *Washington Post*.[19]

The most highly publicized story about one of the Magnificent Bastards after Ramadi was about Damien Rodriguez. The career Marine had left Ramadi with both a heroism award and psychological trauma. He particularly struggled with his PTSD when he was drinking alcohol and during the anniversary of the April fighting. In 2017, he became violent in an Iraqi restaurant in Portland, Oregon, attacking one of the employees while shouting hateful and racist remarks. Prosecutors were uncertain how to proceed because the evidence showed Rodriguez was a bad actor and a victim at the same time; he had done harm in the DarSalam Restaurant on Northeast Alberta Street, but he had also been harmed in Ramadi in the service of his country.

A headline in a *New York Times* analysis of the case raised the question: WAS IT A HATE CRIME OR PTSD?[20]

In addition, there had already been a certain level of swift punishment. After his arrest, the decorated Marine was forced to retire from his rank as a sergeant major in the Marine Corps.

At the emotional heart of Rodriguez's war experiences—that included four combat deployments—were memories and the trauma of April 6, 2004, when his squad was ambushed along narrow residential streets in south-central Ramadi. Images of that experience had never left Rodriguez: Jimmy Gentile shot through the face; enemy insurgents trying to break into the house where Rodriguez and his men had found refuge; the fly-covered remains of one of his men, nineteen-year-old Moisés Langhorst.

Within the marbled walls of a Portland courthouse on March

EPILOGUE

2, 2018, Rodriguez stood before a sentencing judge in a dark blue suit and tie, fourteen years older since Ramadi, his hair graying at the temples, and proceeded to read prepared remarks he held in his hands.

He began with an apology to the owners of the Iraqi restaurant. "I reacted violently and irrationally seemingly out of nowhere and frightened you and your patrons."

Then he tried to explain.

"I participated in one of the war's bloodiest battles in Ramadi. We experienced intense combat almost every single day for seven months," Rodriguez said. "The incident that took place in your restaurant breaks my heart. That is not the man and Marine I am. But what took place only underscores that I have been deluding myself."

Based on Rodriguez's emotional trauma, prosecutors backed off on seeking a hate crime conviction that could have resulted in prison. Instead, after pleading guilty to second-degree intimidation and attempted second-degree assault, Rodriguez was placed on five years of probation and fined $21,000.

He offered a fervent wish at sentencing. He said he stopped drinking, was committed to outpatient therapy, and had volunteered to assist elderly war veterans as an act of contrition. "I would like to live as . . . [a] peaceful, an honorable man, father, and citizen," he told the judge.

"I'LL FIGURE IT OUT ONE DAY. IT'S NOT TODAY, THOUGH."

The military—and Marine Corps specifically—was unprepared for the surge of combat veterans flooding back from Iraq with mental health needs. Rodriguez and several other members of 2nd Battalion, 4th Marines were at the forefront of that group.

The Navy provides health care for the Marines, and in the early years of the wars in Iraq and Afghanistan, it simply didn't have enough therapists to meet the demand.

The Department of Veterans Affairs would also struggle to care for the traumatized men and women flowing out of the active-duty military. By 2014, a thousand Iraq and Afghanistan veterans were being diagnosed each week with post-traumatic stress disorder.[21]

Shannon Morgan, the Army engineer who was part of the Lioness program and fought beside Marines in Ramadi, left the service and arrived home in Arkansas with emotional issues. Family members urged her to seek help at a VA facility in Little Rock. After working up the courage to finally discuss the haunting memories of violence that plagued her, Morgan told a VA psychologist she thought she might be suffering from PTSD.

"Over what?" the therapist asked.

"The frontline combat I've seen," Morgan responded.

His response was brusque and dismissive. "There are no females in frontline combat, so try again."

She was stunned. He was essentially calling her a liar. The combat experiences of the Lionesses had been written up in the *Army Times*, and Morgan couldn't believe the psychologist was unaware. She felt adrift with nowhere to turn for help. A suicide attempt followed. Her parents found her, and she was admitted to a VA inpatient facility, where they began taking her problems seriously.

Post-traumatic stress disorder, with its litany of symptoms such as flashbacks, nightmares, emotional numbness, and hypervigilance, often leads veterans to self-medicate with alcohol or drugs. In the severest cases where a person feels hopelessly overwhelmed, self-destruction becomes a risk.

Attempted suicides in the Marine Corps reached record levels in the five years after the Magnificent Bastards rotated home.[22] The Army's rate of suicide doubled during that period and remained disproportionately high for years after US involvement in Iraq and Afghanistan wound down.[23] By 2018, the VA reported that an average of nearly nineteen veterans were killing themselves every day. That pace later eased. But suicides remained a crucial problem among active-duty troops. In 2022, the Marine Corps had the highest suicide rate of any of the service branches—nearly thirty-five deaths per one hundred thousand.

Suicides also plagued the Marines who had fought in Ramadi and were agonizing for their brethren when word of each one quickly spread.

They had started coalescing as a veterans group, connecting on Facebook, keeping one another on speed dial, and attending reunions. To see one of their own suddenly die by their own hand brought powerful feelings of guilt and frustration.

"Gentlemen, reach out to your Brothers and TALK TO THEM DAILY, WEEKLY, ALL THE TIME," stated a frustrated post after the 2021 suicide by Golf Company Marine Jeremy Reynolds. "Don't assume that you see them on social media and 'all is fine.'"[24]

Bereaved families would blame a Department of Veterans Affairs bureaucracy they said was failing to keep pace with a growing river of troubled veterans.

When Fox Company Marine Jonathan Schulze came home to Minnesota, he suffered from nightmares, flashbacks, and hyper-vigilance. He drank to excess and, in his sleep, screamed the names of dead comrades.[25]

Schulze had written to his father and stepmother during the deployment about the terror of IEDs. He was among those who defended Snake Pit from being overrun on the last day of battalion combat.

In January 2007, Schulze sought residential treatment at a VA facility in St. Cloud, Minnesota. "I feel suicidal," he told an intake worker, according to his mother. He was asked to come back the next day because there was no one to screen him. Then he was told the residential treatment center was full and he was twenty-sixth on the waiting list. Days later, he hanged himself in a basement with an electrical cord. "This young Marine died of wounds to the soul and not the flesh," stated a memorial website. (A VA inspector general investigation could not verify that Schulze said he was suicidal during his visit to the St. Cloud facility. But if he did, the hospital should have done a better job of screening him, the report concluded. It said that while there were no beds available for the residential program, there were beds available for someone suicidal.)[26]

William Draughon's family held the VA accountable for his suicide in 2010, obtaining a $480,000 judgment.[27] Draughon had served as a corporal with Golf Company and left the Marine Corps in 2006. He suffered from drug and alcohol abuse and had been diagnosed with PTSD. His family told an NPR affiliate in Kansas City he was a changed man after Ramadi. According to court papers, Draughon was "separated and divorced, fathered two children from different mothers, abused alcohol and drugs, accumulated a significant amount of debt and consistently struggled to control his depression."[28]

He fatally shot himself at his home in Kansas City, Missouri, in March 2010. The VA was accused, among other things, of removing from his electronic file a red flag notice that Draughon was a high risk for suicide.

Nearly five years later, an Echo Company veteran ended his life. Simon Litke had been one of the class of 2003 high schoolers joining the Marines right after graduation, showing up at the battalion just weeks before heading to Iraq. He arrived in Ramadi as a private first class and fought as part of Second Platoon, including the April 10 battle in the Sofia District.

Litke returned to Ramadi in 2006 a combat-hardened corporal. "He was a handsome kid with brown hair and striking blue eyes," his 2006 company commander, Scott Huesing, later wrote in his book *Echo in Ramadi*.

"Litke had a malicious squint most of the time—not for

EPILOGUE

367

acuity of vision, but as part of his demeanor, the kind of way he let everyone know he was the real deal. And he was. He was a legitimate badass who never took shit from anyone," Huesing wrote.[29]

Litke left the Marines in 2007 and suffered emotionally from, according to Huesing, "all that his mind could never un-see." No one knew how severe it was. On that November night in 2015, Litke met friends for a few drinks, texted old comrades from 2/4, and then, alone in his car, fatally shot himself.[30]

> With congressional passage of the National Suicide Hotline Designation Act in 2020, the federal government established a simple three-digit number for veterans and service members in crisis to call: 988, then press 1. The law was fully implemented by 2022, supplementing the existing Veterans Crisis Line, 1-800-273-8255 and press 1; text to 838255; or chat at VeteransCrisisLine.net/Chat.

The toxic mix of alcohol and PTSD would sometimes lead in other deadly directions. Golf Company veteran Bradley Erickson had a blood-alcohol content nearly twice the legal limit in Wisconsin when he smashed his vehicle into a car stopped on the median of a highway in 2010. Three college students were killed. A fourth narrowly managed to survive by jumping out of the way. They had been changing a flat tire. Erickson was convicted on three counts of drunken vehicular homicide and sentenced to thirteen years in prison. The sentence was half of what prosecutors sought because the judge saw Erickson's severe PTSD from combat in Ramadi as a mitigating circumstance.[31]

His fate would be a cautionary tale for Ramadi veterans.

In his best-selling 2014 book on PTSD, *The Body Keeps the Score: Brain, Mind, and Body in the Healing of Trauma*," Dutch psychiatrist Bessel van der Kolk explained that the cure for the disorder lies in addressing the symptoms:

Nobody can "treat" a war, or abuse, rape, molestation, or any other horrendous event . . . what has happened cannot be undone. But what *can* be dealt with are the imprints of the trauma on body, mind, and soul: the crushing sensations in your chest that you may label as anxiety or depression; the fear of losing control; always being on alert for danger or rejection; the self-loathing; the nightmares and flashbacks; the fog that keeps you from staying on task and from engaging fully in what you are doing; being unable to fully open your heart to another human being.[32]

Relationships were a common casualty. Marriages disintegrated when Marines came home. One of them was Paul Kennedy's, who wrestled with his own demons from Ramadi.

"I'm not a victim. I don't claim victim status. But my unwillingness to confront all that stuff had [nearly] led to two divorces directly attributable to 2004," he said in 2023. With continued therapy, Kennedy has worked to save the second marriage.

In the summer of 2024, he took the unusual step as a retired Marine major general of publicly urging the FDA to approve the drug MDMA, a key ingredient in the street drug ecstasy, for assisting the treatment of post-traumatic stress disorder. The Department of Justice classifies it as a stimulant and psychedelic.[33] Kennedy cited promising research results showing the drug quells the disorder and argued that new treatments are desperately needed at a time when PTSD is a national crisis that particularly impacts veterans.

"I heard stories of lives affected by post-traumatic stress disorder that commonly included troubled marriages, substance abuse and turbulent post-service lives," Kennedy wrote, citing what he witnessed at the twentieth anniversary reunion in April marking the Ramadi battle.[34]

Van der Kolk described the risk of trauma becoming addictive,

EPILOGUE

what he called *the pain of pleasure and pleasure of pain.* "Many traumatized people seem to seek out experiences that would repel others," he wrote. "Patients complain about a vague sense of emptiness and boredom when not angry, under duress or involved in some dangerous activity," in what might be an unconscious effort to gain control over or resolve a painful situation.[35]

An example of this was the experience of Joe Hayes. Like many veterans of Ramadi, he would later segue from the Marine Corps into police work. (Others who did the same included Jonathan Embrey, also from Golf Company; and from Echo Company, Jason Birmelin, Cameron Ferguson, Ryan Downing, Justin Tate, and Marcus Waechter.) Hayes—who received a Bronze Star for actions on April 6 and after being sent home as a casualty recovered enough to return to Ramadi—later worked for a small police department in Shafter, California, an agricultural town plagued by drugs and gang activity, about eighteen miles northwest of Bakersfield. Hayes volunteered for the night shift, drawn irresistibly to the street dangers the job offered. "I would seek out bad guys that I knew were wreaking havoc in a community," Hayes explained in 2023. "I knew who they were and where they lived and what they were doing. I would go after them." He made arrests that led to a high felony-conviction rate. It was obsessive. Every time he went out, Hayes felt the same rush he experienced heading into combat in the streets of Ramadi.

"That is a drug that is so addictive," he said.

But it also came with a cost. There were near-death experiences. Within a span of five weeks in early 2012, he was involved in two shootings. The first was a man armed with a gun, who was resisting arrest by Hayes and another officer. When the suspect tried to pull out his firearm, the Marine veteran shot him to death. In the second case, Hayes was alone trying to investigate a crime when a man came up and tried to grab his firearm. Hayes broke loose, but the man continued to come at him until

Hayes shot and wounded him. Both shootings were found to be justified.

The constant amped-up sensations were exhausting. His heart rate would get so high, his adrenaline so rampant, that Hayes would almost get dizzy and have trouble talking on the radio. Sleep was difficult. The PTSD he had brought home from Ramadi was getting worse. For that and orthopedic injuries suffered on duty, Hayes received a medical retirement after eleven years as a policeman. He and his wife and three children moved to Oklahoma, where he builds homes and occasionally hosts Christian podcasts drawn from his life experiences.

Van der Kolk also wrote about the sense of becoming emotionally numb and losing a sense of one's self. He cited the case of a Vietnam veteran who despite a successful legal career "always felt as though he were floating in space, lacking any sense of purpose or direction."[36]

Some of this was reflected in the life of Chris MacIntosh. Living modestly on full medical disability from the VA for his wounds and emotional issues, the once irrepressible "Rabbit," who touched everyone he met in 2/4 with his humor, began drifting.

His mother and best friend died in 2015 and his estranged father passed away several months later. The deaths sent him into an intense emotional funk.

"I'm just lost, that's all," MacIntosh said in 2022. "I'll figure it out one day. It's not today, though."

What's worked for him in the interim was purchasing a home in Michigan within minutes of his combat buddy, Roy Thomas. Thomas had lost an eye and received a Bronze Star for heroism on April 6. MacIntosh had dressed Thomas's wounds that day in a farmhouse kitchen, and their kinship outlasted the war.

"Having him here helps me more, probably more than he ever knows," said Thomas in 2023, who shares a home with his wife, Melissa, and their two children—daughter, Gracie, and son, Brock.

MacIntosh is Gracie's godfather. He and Roy frequently play

EPILOGUE

golf. They dissect the torments of the past. And they talk in a language of experience only other Bastards can understand.

Many have discovered their own coping mechanisms. When 2/4 veteran Jonathan Hancock finally vanquished his Ramadi demons, his success had the serendipitous twist of becoming an award-winning documentary.

Hancock, who survived an enemy effort to blow off the top of a Ramadi high-rise building, was in a psychiatric ward of a Maryland VA hospital in 2014 recovering from an overdose of pills when he was inspired by a feature story on television. It was about a former Army Ranger who was walking across the country carrying a series of American flags on which he had written the name of every American service member killed in the wars of Iraq and Afghanistan.

Hancock decided he would do the same to honor his comrades who died in Ramadi. Along the way, he planned to visit his surviving brethren or the family of those killed. Hancock sold what possessions he owned and set off on September 11, 2015, with his seventy-pound backpack, walking stick, and a red Marine Corps flag draped around his shoulders. He was scared and second-guessing himself and within two weeks called his mother, Maura Hancock, to say, "I don't know what I'm doing. I don't know why I'm doing it, whom I doing it for. I just feel I should quit."

But he didn't, winding his way across the United States, covering 5,800 miles in fifteen months until he finished at Camp Pendleton, California. More than a thousand miles into the walk, in Slidell, Louisiana, he was contacted through a close friend by cinematographer Brian Morrison. Hancock and Morrison had actually both attended Arundel High School in Maryland, although they did not know each other. Morrison had seen a story on Hancock's adventure and approached him about filming a documentary. The Marine veteran agreed. For the next several months and at the end of the walk, Morrison would catch up with Hancock to collect footage of his hike or his visits with Gold Star families and

Ramadi veterans. (One was Chris MacIntosh.) The resulting film, *Bastards' Road*, received eight documentary awards in 2020.

Through it all, Hancock felt he was healing. He took the opportunity of his solitude to concentrate on his memories of Ramadi and his tormenting images of war, such as the sight of that young boy obliterated by Hancock's launched grenade on the final day of combat. He found he could control memories, stepping into them when he chose, rather than seeing them reemerge involuntarily as flashbacks. Hancock compared his success to evidence-based PTSD treatments such as cognitive behavioral therapy, a talking therapy that helps people manage memories by repeatedly revisiting them.

The discovery led Hancock and his wife, Tiffany, to form in 2021 the Bastards' Road Project, a nonprofit organization aimed at assisting veterans with their mental-health issues through hiking therapy.

A second documentary to arise from Ramadi combat focused on the exploits of the Lioness unit of women soldiers led by Captain Kate Pendry (who married shortly after the deployment and became Kate Guttormsen). The documentary *Lioness*, with interviews of several of the team members, premiered in 2008 and would receive three documentary awards. (A streaming series that debuted in 2023 and was called *Special Ops: Lioness* had a fictional storyline with a group of combat operatives whose origins dated back to the actual Lioness program run out of Ramadi in 2003/2004.)

"KNUCKLE-DRAGGING, BRAINWASHED."

Nine weeks after the Magnificent Bastards left Ramadi, the Marine Corps celebrated its 229th birthday with an annual ball. Two honored guests at the celebration were two Army officers who had treated the wounded of 2/4—Major Clint Murray, who had been the Charlie Med senior physician, and Captain Jody

EPILOGUE

Schroeder, the facility's critical care nurse who had so endeared herself to the Marines.

Murray would remain in the Army, rise to the level of one-star general, and take command of the US Army Medical Center of Excellence at Fort Sam Houston, Texas, in November 2023. He would remember his time in Ramadi as the pinnacle of his military career because of the relationships he formed and the experience of treating the severest wounds combat can generate, events for which Murray said in 2022 he remains extremely proud.

Schroeder found the Ramadi experience life-altering. She learned the crucial skill of high-level functioning even amid horrendous sights and sounds of a combat emergency ward. She grew confident in her instincts and learned better how to assert herself in a male-dominated world when she knew she was right. "In Ramadi, I got to a point where I was like, 'You know what? Life is short. If I don't want to do something, I need to speak up. Or if I think that's the wrong answer, I need to speak up,'" she said in 2022. "That was such an epiphany."

Schroeder stayed in the Army, rising through the ranks. As a colonel in 2024, she was named interim chief of the US Army Nurse Corps. In April 2024, she was invited to attend a reunion of 2/4 veterans marking the twentieth anniversary of the April 6 combat.

"For some of you, she literally saved your life, her and her team," Kennedy told the assemblage as he introduced Schroeder. There was a long-standing ovation. She blew kisses to the veterans and said, "I will love you all for always."

One of the most remarkable ways Ramadi changed someone's life was with Justin Weaver, the Pennsylvania native who as a junior in high school witnessed hijacked Flight 93 in the sky seconds before it crashed. Weaver fought with Weapons Company in Ramadi, serving in the Rainmaker platoon under Lieutenant Dave Dobb. Jeremiah Savage, who died in an IED attack on May 12,

2004, was one of Weaver's best friends. After the service, Weaver returned to Pennsylvania and took a job at the North American Höganäs steel plant in Hollsopple, Pennsylvania. He was standing in line at a BP gas station one day wearing a hoodie with the word RAMADI emblazoned on it. The woman waiting behind him suddenly spoke up and said, "That's where I'm from."

Samar Majid was an electrical engineer the same age as Weaver. She was from an Arab Christian family that immigrated to the US from Iraq. The two hit it off and began dating. He was wary at first about revealing his combat experience. "I thought she was going to say, 'You ruined my life,'" Weaver said in 2023.

But the two eventually fell in love and planned to marry. "She's my world. She's been one of the best things that's happened to me," Weaver said. Her family embraced him as well, even though an uncle had been killed during fighting in the city on April 7, 2004. Weaver learned Arabic, and in the summer of 2022, he traveled with Majid's family back to Ramadi. He buried a small bottle filled with memorabilia at the location where Savage was fatally wounded and did the same at a second place where Geoff Morris was killed by an RPG.

As the vast majority of Magnificent Bastards left military service, Ramadi remained a lifelong milestone, if not a traumatic experience.

Some took occupations or lifestyles far removed from the savage violence they knew in Iraq.

Evan Null, who became trapped with other Marines in a small hut while comrades were slaughtered at the intersection of Gypsum and Nova, would wind up facilitating a drug rehab program at a federal prison in West Virginia.

Damien Coan, the ball-busting platoon sergeant with a hair-trigger temper, retired from the Marine Corps after reaching the rank of sergeant major. He took a human resources position at a 911 dispatch center in the state of Washington and began working on a master's degree in organizational leadership.

EPILOGUE

Kevin Barger, the former corpsman who unloaded dead bodies at Combat Outpost on April 6 and patched up Jose Texidor on April 10, established a self-sufficient and self-sustaining homestead on ten hillside acres northeast of San Diego. He and his wife, Jacquelyn, raised chickens and goats and taught their three youngest children still living at home (their oldest child, a daughter, is a police officer married to a Marine) a peaceful style of life that focused on faith and family.

Miguel Escalera, who received a Bronze Star for braving gunfire to treat wounded Marines during night combat with an enemy mortar team, returned to the state of Washington, where he transferred to the naval reserve and ultimately took a reservist position with the Coast Guard, serving as a lieutenant medical officer. Escalera retired from the Coast Guard in 2023 to work full-time as an orthopedic specialist at an urgent care facility in Washington State. He has never gotten comfortable with talking with family and friends about Ramadi.

It took fifteen years for the Marine Corps, notoriously stingy about high-level valor awards, to finally recognize Eric Smith's heroism on April 6 with a Navy Cross. He had left the service after making staff sergeant and returned to his beloved hometown of Waxahachie, Texas, with his wife, Shelly, and their son, Hayden. Smith joined the Irving Fire Department and was eventually promoted to captain. It was as a firefighter that he began meeting with a therapist who treated PTSD and started to talk about lingering anger issues that had plagued him since Ramadi, the ones that Shelly blamed for making him a changed man since the war. Eric was pushed through therapy to recall his combat experiences and could feel the fear and adrenaline rush, and even sensations of heat, the sound of gunfire, and the smell of blood. Gradually, Smith came to terms with his PTSD.

Through it all, he remained steadfastly proud of fighting alongside fellow Marines. "I feel honored that I got to walk among giants," he said.

For years, Romeo Santiago remained plagued by regret over the assassination of his four-man team on a rooftop in June 2004. He had led a separate mission that night thought to be riskier. But the soul-searching has never stopped. Should he have kept his eight-member team together rather than splitting them up? Did he choose the right man to lead the rooftop mission in Tommy Parker?

"I still struggle with guilt," said Santiago, who left the Marines to become an investigator for a prosecutor's office.

Many of the Bastards say Ramadi brought perspective to their lives—nothing will ever be harder than surviving that city.

"Everything else is gravy since I made it through that," said Jonathan Embrey in 2022. The Marine veteran from Golf Company whose nickname was Chaps later worked for the US Border Patrol and then took a position with the Illinois State Police.

"I got a second chance, so I try to make the most of everything," said Dave Dobb, the ex–Rainmaker commander. He left the military to work his way through the ranks of the United States Secret Service. "When it gets bad, or times are tough . . . you look back on that, and it gives you an angle on things that a lot of people don't have."

"I saw combat in Afghanistan, a lot of it," said JD Harrill, the former operations officer. "But nothing of that magnitude of death and horror."

Tom Cogan, the Philly native who led an Echo Company platoon and received the Silver Star, later joined the Marine Forces Special Operations Command, its elite commando force. He retired from special operations in 2023 at the rank of lieutenant colonel with the opportunity of returning to his beloved ice hockey. Cogan took the position of player development coach for USA Hockey's National Team Development Program, which trains and mentors top high school player prospects.

Cogan did countless missions when he was with special forces. But he said the most intense fighting of his life was in Ramadi.

EPILOGUE

377

In special forces, there was more opportunity to plan and considerably more resources available. In Ramadi, it was all guts and tenacity by the very young Marines he led.

"They were resilient," Cogan said. "We had ended up losing eight guys in the platoon over that deployment, and a ton more were wounded. But they'd still have rave parties in the hooch at night. They found the best part of it and just kept moving."

In simplest terms, Cogan said, "They were goofballs."

Others echoed the sentiment.

"I'll tell you this, the Marines were fearless," said Ron Riling, the fullback-size former command sergeant major of 1st Brigade of the Army's Big Red One. "Those young corporals and lance corporals, they weren't afraid to die at all. I almost felt you had to put a leash on those kids once in a while to slow them down."

Navy corpsmen shared the view.

"There was nowhere I'd rather be in combat than next to a Marine," said Adam Clayton, who stayed in the Navy, moving up through the enlisted ranks.

In a 2022 discussion, harkening back to his days in Ramadi, he gushed about the young men he fought with, sometimes searching for the right words.

"They're just the simplest, smartest—they're just good. The Marine Corps trains them to kill, and they do it very well."

"People think of the Marine Corps infantry as like all these buff guys and everything. They're not. It's this little skinny dude that looks like he's been on meth his whole life, from the Midwest somewhere, just grew up hunting and shooting guns."

Clayton talked about once seeing a Marine eat a bar of soap for five dollars; how another drew a knife across his palm to check the edge and needed stitches; and how a third jumped from a two-story ledge to practice a combat roll and broke a leg.

"They're these knuckle-dragging, brainwashed—" Clayton paused, searching for the right word.

"I just love them."

ACKNOWLEDGMENTS

To THE EXTENT this narrative brings to life the experience and sacrifice of combat in the city of Ramadi, Iraq, during the spring and summer of 2004, all credit must go to the men and women who graciously agreed to revisit very difficult wartime memories.

During time spent in their homes, in coffee shops, or on Zoom, they consented to deep-dive discussions of a pivotal moment in their lives. They were generous and kind and I'm forever grateful.

In some instances, they shared journals, diaries, logbooks, and letters that provided contemporaneous insight into what they endured. Among those who did so were Jodelle "Jody" Schroeder, Arthur "Buck" Connor Jr., Tim Weber, and Kyle Teamey. One of the most fascinating journals was kept by a rank-and-file Marine with Golf Company—Corporal Jonathan Embrey. Poured into those pages were the observations and emotions of a twenty-one-year-old Marine as he quickly evolved into a combat-hardened veteran. It was chock full of details, dates, and drama. Army Medic Colt Crutchfield displayed a gift for evocative prose in the letters he wrote home about the wounded at Charlie Med.

In May 2023, I visited Iraq with my youngest son, Noah Zoroya. We met an old friend of mine, Sabah Anbaki, who assisted my war coverage for *USA Today* years before and who today runs an international translation service with offices in the US and Baghdad. With Sabah's help, we spent a day in Ramadi visiting key battle sites where Golf and Echo Marines and sailors fought and

ACKNOWLEDGMENTS

died. It was a remarkable experience, particularly in the company of my son.

A special thanks goes to Chris MacIntosh, who was a lance corporal with First Platoon of Echo Company and endured, like many of his brethren, some of the most severe combat in Ramadi. I met and first interviewed Chris when I was an embedded journalist with 2nd Battalion, 4th Marines in June 2004. We stayed in contact down through the years. He always reminded me that there was a story to be told about the Magnificent Bastards. Chris was right.

Those in the Marines and the Navy to whom I owe a debt of gratitude for granting me interviews are Frank Aiza (formerly Frank Gutierrez), Manaia Alaimalo, Anthony Alegre, Jeff Andrade, Kevin Barger, James Baum (formerly James Buttrey), Jason L. Birmelin, Jim Booker, Christopher Bronzi, Derek Callaway, David Carbungco, Adam Clayton, Damien Coan, Greg Coats, Tom Cogan, Jarad Cole, Bernard Calvin Coleman, Aaron Cox, Joe Crane, Colin Crickard, Dean Cugliotta Jr., Tyrynn Dennis, Todd Desgrosseilliers, Dave Dobb, Ryan Downing, Joe Dunford, Rick Dunham, Jon Embrey, Miguel Escalera, Cameron Ferguson, Christopher Ferguson, Peter Flom, James "Jimmy" Gentile, Abe Guillen, Sean Gustavison, Sergio Gutierrez, Glenn Hamby, Jonathan Hancock, Dave "JD" Harrill, Dominic Harris, Joe Hayes, Joe Herscher, Amir Heydari, Reagan Hodges, Brandon Honeycutt, Paul Kennedy, Charles Kubic, Charles Lauersdorf, Brandon Lund, Chris MacIntosh, Victor Madrillejos, Michael Martley, Jim Mattis, Heath McKenzie, Dan McNaghten, Brian "Mack" McPherson and his wife Heather, Ryan Miller, Elias Monarez, Wilmer Munoz, Bill Nash, Stewart Navarre, Phil Nohren, Evan Null, Shane Nylin, Bruce Orner, Jason Rosman, Kelly Royer, Romeo Santiago, Sean Schickel, Matthew Scott, Nate Scott, Charles Sheldon, Zachary Shores, Eric Smith, Ted Stanton, Richard Stayskal, John "J.D." Stephens, Justin Tate, Brian Telinda, Jose Texidor Jr., Roy Thomas, Theophilus Tor, Wyeth

ACKNOWLEDGMENTS

Towle, Victor Urena, Jose Valerio, Justin Weaver, Tim Weber, Brian Weigelt, Rob Weiler, Lucas Wells, Curtis Winfree, Justin Woodall, and Mike Wylie.

Among those who spoke with me and who served (or are serving) in the Army, my thanks go to Nick Ayers, William "Dave" Brinkley, Irving "Ray" Bush, Richard "Mike" Cabrey, Arthur "Buck" Connor, Colt Crutchfied, Mike Elledge, Tyler Faulk, Kate Guttormsen (formerly Kate Pendry), Greg Huebbe, Marty Leners, Hector Mirabile, Shannon Morgan, Clint Murray, Tom Neemeyer, Randy Radmer, Ron Riling, Ranie Ruthig, Jodelle "Jody" Schroeder, Andre Soares, Justin Springer, Kyle Teamey, and Wade Welsh.

Still others who allowed me to ask them questions when I was in Ramadi in 2004 were Kenneth Conde Jr., Chris Conner, Anthony Crutcher, Travis Friedrichsen, Mike Green, Deshon Otey, Ryan Pape, Damien Rodriguez, Daniel Tapia, Vincent Valdes, and Marcus Waechter.

I'm extremely grateful to my assistant in this effort, Kim Habitch, who is an excellent journalist. Her tireless efforts to conduct research and analysis and endlessly find people with whom I needed to speak were foundational to this book's completion. Special thanks go to my agent, Jill Marr, who forever has my back. I'm grateful for the professionalism of my editors, Dan Ambrosio and Amar Deol. I wish to thank Rick Paddock for his photographic knowledge and support, and his wife, Dana Theus. For love, encouragement, and a willingness to always listen, special thanks go to my sons, Noah and Jackson Zoroya, and my close friend, Denise Kostbar. They never tired of whatever I had to say.

My North Star was Faye Fiore. She was my wife and my life. Her boundless love and support nourished and kept me whole. Her brilliance as a writer generated priceless insight and editing. I only wish with every fiber of my being that she had beaten cancer to see the book to its completion and, more than anything, to never leave me.

NOTES

PROLOGUE

1. *Encyclopaedia Britannica Online*, s.v. "James Mattis," by Michael Ray, accessed June 27, 2024, https://www.britannica.com/biography/James-Mattis.
2. Jason A. Rosman, *I Should Have Gone to College* (Middleton, DE: Rosman Publishing, 2018), 73.

CHAPTER 2: CITY

1. Gary W. Montgomery and Timothy S. McWilliams, eds., *Al-Anbar Awakening, Volume II: Iraqi Perspectives: From Insurgency to Counterinsurgency in Iraq, 2004–2009* (Quantico, VA: Marine Corps University Press, 2009), 6.

CHAPTER 3: PRELUDE

1. Associated Press, "Marine Lance Cpl. Andrew S. Dang," Honor the Fallen, *Military Times*, https://thefallen.militarytimes.com/marine-lance-cpl-andrew-s-dang/257092.
2. "Marine Death Comes After He Returns Home," *East Bay Times*, August 16, 2016.
3. "Marine LCPL Sean Carroll," YouTube video, 4:20, posted by Home for Our Troops, February 26, 2019, https://www.youtube.com/watch?v=_2ZAteRjVoM.
4. Pamela Hess, "Days Marked by Battles, Not Calendar," UPI, August 13, 2004.

CHAPTER 4: EVE OF BATTLE

1. Thomas E. Ricks, *Fiasco: The American Military Adventure in Iraq* (New York: Penguin, 2006), 331.

2. Timothy S. McWilliams and Kurtis P. Wheeler, eds., *Al-Anbar Awakening, Volume 1: American Perspectives: U.S. Marines and Counterinsurgency in Iraq, 2004–2009* (Quantico, VA: Marine Corps University Press, 2009), 7.
3. "U.S. Army: 'We Will Respond' to Contractor Killings," CNN, April 1, 2004.
4. Kenneth W. Estes, *U.S. Marines in Iraq, 2004–2005: Into the Fray* (Washington, DC: History Division United States Marine Corps, 2011), 33.
5. "Inside the Ambush Known as Black Sunday," ABC News, November 7, 2017, https://abcnews.go.com/US/inside-ambush-black-sunday/story?id=50962302.

CHAPTER 5: BATTLE, DAY 1: CITY CENTER

1. "Pam Hallal Mother of Deryk Hallal Marine Died in Battle at 9 11 2021 Event at Wolfies on Geist," YouTube video,3:27, posted by VoicesLiveOn, October 2, 2021, https://www.youtube.com/watch?v=vtE5OIH4tZs.
2. Donovan Campbell, *Joker One: A Marine Platoon's Story of Courage, Leadership, and Brotherhood* (New York: Random House, 2009), 167.

CHAPTER 6: BATTLE, DAY 1: SOFIA DISTRICT

1. Milo S. Afong, *HOGs in the Shadows: Combat Stories from Marine Snipers in Iraq* (New York: Penguin, 2007), 28.
2. "Pfc. Ryan M. Jerabek," Legacy.com, https://www.legacy.com/obituaries/name/ryan-m-jerabek-obituary?pid=3097641.
3. Brad Knickerbocker, "One Marine's Memorial: Day of Racing to Honor Veterans' Service," *Christian Science Monitor*, May 29, 2010.
4. "Fernando Mendez-Aceves (March 6, 1978–April 6, 2004)," City of Chula Vista Veterans Memorial Hall, https://www.chulavistaca.gov/home/showpublisheddocument/9157/636510751750670000.

CHAPTER 7: BATTLE, DAY 1: THE AMBUSH

1. David Swanson with Joseph L. Galloway, "Battle at Ramadi: An Embedded Photographer Talks of the Firefight Around Him, and of Those Who Died," *Philadelphia Inquirer*, April 13, 2004, https://www.inquirer.com/philly/news/nation_world/Battle_at_Ramadi.html.
2. David Stout, "Bush Firm on Iraq Policy, as Kennedy Assails Him for 'Deceit,'" *New York Times*, April 5, 2004, https://www.nytimes.com

/2004/04/05/international/middleeast/bush-firm-on-iraq-policy-as
-kennedy-assails-him-for.html.

3. Alissa J. Rubin, "12 Marines Are Killed as Violence Spreads in Iraq," *Los Angeles Times*, April 7, 2004, https://www.latimes.com/archives /la-xpm-2004-apr-07-fg-iraq7-story.html.

4. Joseph Schuman, "U.S. Struggles to Manage a Seemingly Resurgent War," *Wall Street Journal*, April 7, 2004, https://www.wsj.com /articles/SB108136029785776839.

CHAPTER 8: BATTLE, DAY 2

1. Gary Boyle, "The Road from Marja: Wounded in Afghanistan, Capt. Erik Quist '99, USMC, Sees Another Side of Combat," *Colby Magazine*, Winter 2012, 17, https://digitalcommons.colby.edu/cgi /viewcontent.cgi?article=1044&context=colbymagazine.

2. "Pfc. Christopher D. Mabry," Legacy.com, https://www.legacy.com /obituaries/name/christopher-d-mabry-obituary?pid=3097677.

3. Kenneth W. Estes, *U.S. Marines in Iraq, 2004–2005: Into the Fray* (Washington, DC: History Division United States Marine Corps, 2011), 36.

4. Thomas E. Ricks, *Fiasco: The American Military Adventure in Iraq* (New York: Penguin, 2006), 342.

5. Estes, *U.S. Marines in Iraq*, 42.

6. Estes, *U.S. Marines in Iraq*, 36.

7. "Things Fall Apart, April 2004," chapter 12 in *The U.S. Army in the Iraq War, Volume 1: Invasion—Insurgency—Civil War, 2003–2006*, eds. Joel D. Rayburn, Frank K. Sobchak, Jeanne F. Godfroy, Matthew D. Morton, James S. Powell, and Matthew M. Zais (Carlisle, PA: Strategic Studies Institute, 2019), 289.

8. "Things Fall Apart," 290.

9. "Transportation Corps in Operation Iraqi Freedom 2 April Uprising, Good Friday Ambushes," US Army Transportation Corps, https://transportation.army.mil/history/studies/april_uprising.html #sixth.

CHAPTER 9: BATTLE, DAY 3

1. Sara Lin, "California Marines Die in Fighting with Iraqi Insurgents," *Los Angeles Times*, April 18, 2004, https://www.latimes.com /archives/la-xpm-2004-apr-18-me-ayon18-story.html.

2. Bing West, *No True Glory: A Frontline Account of the Battle of Fallujah* (New York: Bantam, 2005), 346.

3. K. D. Royer, nonpunitive letter of caution, Staff Sergeant Jeffery R. Craig, Ramadi, Iraq, July 19, 2004, 1.

CHAPTER 10: LUNACY

1. *Encyclopaedia Britannica Online*, s.v. "First Battle of Fallujah," by John Swift, accessed March 28, 2024, https://www.britannica.com /event/First-Battle-of-Fallujah.
2. Michael E. O'Hanlon and Jason H. Campbell, *Iraq Index: Tracking Variables of Reconstruction & Security in Post-Saddam Iraq* (Washington, DC: Brookings, 2020), 15.
3. David Swanson and Thomas Ginsberg, "Anguish over Fallen Comrades," *Philadelphia Inquirer*, April 12, 2004.
4. Swanson and Ginsberg, "Anguish."
5. Donovan Campbell, *Joker One: A Marine Platoon's Story of Courage, Leadership, and Brotherhood* (New York: Random House, 2009), 203.
6. Leonard Greene, "WTH THS RNG I THEE WD—Iraq Marine Marries Calif. Gal by Cellphone," *New York Post*, September 16, 2004.

CHAPTER 11: PERSEVERANCE

1. Eric Barton, "The Deadliest Day," *Miami New Times*, December 30, 2004, https://www.miaminewtimes.com/news/the-deadliest-day -6342261.
2. Donovan Campbell, *Joker One: A Marine Platoon's Story of Courage, Leadership, and Brotherhood* (New York: Random House, 2009), 224.
3. "Remembering Area's Loved Ones Lost to War," *San Gabriel Valley Tribune*, updated August 30, 2017, https://www.sgvtribune.com /2007/03/18/remembering-areas-loved-ones-lost-to-war/.
4. Ryan Kim, "Santa Clara / Family Mourns Loss of Dutiful Marine in Iraq," SFGate, June 5, 2004, https://www.sfgate.com/bayarea/article /SANTA-CLARA-Family-mourns-loss-of-dutiful-2715688.php.
5. Summary of Action, for authorization of combat distinguishing device for Major Michael P. Wylie, 2/4 battalion executive officer.

CHAPTER 12: MISTAKES

1. "Commanding Officer 1st Battalion, 5th Marines, Lieutenant Colonel Mark E. Carlton," United States Marine Corps, https:

//www.1stmardiv.marines.mil/Leaders/Biography/Article/555499
/lieutenant-colonel-mark-e-carlton/.

2. David J. Danelo, *Blood Stripes: The Grunt's View of the War in Iraq* (Mechanicsville, PA: Stackpole), 204.

3. "Oral History Interview with Brandon A. Winneshiek," Wisconsin Veterans Museum, https://wisvetsmuseum.com/ohms-viewer/render .php?cachefile=OH_02244.xml.

4. Danelo, *Blood Stripes*, 207.

5. Mark Oliva, "Company Memorializes Two Fallen Marines," United States Marine Corps, May 11, 2004, https://www.1stmardiv.marines .mil/News/Article/Article/540618/company-memorializes-two-fallen -marines/.

6. Kevin Sullivan, "Mexicans Disrupt Marine's Funeral," *Washington Post*, July 6, 2004, https://www.washingtonpost.com/archive/politics /2004/07/06/mexicans-disrupt-marines-funeral/19b6efa3-3d62-4968 -bfe9-f8c365d65628/.

CHAPTER 13: WICKEDNESS

1. Ann Scott Tyson, "Fallujah Parallels in Ramadi," *Christian Science Monitor*, July 23, 2004.

2. John F. Burns and Eric Eckholm, "The Reach of War: Insurgency; in Western Iraq, Fundamentalists Hold U.S. at Bay," *New York Times*, August 29, 2004, https://www.nytimes.com/2004/08/29/world/the -reach-of-war-insurgency-in-western-iraq-fundamentalists-hold-us -at-bay.html.

3. Donovan Campbell, *Joker One: A Marine Platoon's Story of Courage, Leadership, and Brotherhood* (New York: Random House, 2009), 269.

4. Operational order for Operation Traveler, August 3, 2004, 17.

5. Campbell, *Joker One*, 257. Tyson, "Fallujah Parallels."

6. Tyson, "Fallujah Parallels."

7. Burns and Eckholm, "The Reach of War."

8. 2/4 Command Chronology for June 1 to June 30, 2004, II-9.

9. Burns and Eckholm, "The Reach of War."

10. Campbell, *Joker One*, 289.

CHAPTER 14: EXIT

1. Jason A. Rosman, *I Should Have Gone to College* (Middleton, DE: Rosman Publishing, 2018), 62–63.

NOTES

EPILOGUE

1. John Spencer, Jayson Geroux, and Liam Collins, "Urban Warfare Project Case Study Series: Case Study #7—Fallujah II," Modern War Institute at West Point, July 25, 2023, https://mwi.westpoint.edu/urban-warfare-case-study-7-second-battle-of-fallujah/.

2. Thomas E. Ricks, *Fiasco: The American Military Adventure in Iraq* (New York: Penguin, 2006), 399-400.

3. Bing West, *The Strongest Tribe: War, Politics, and the Endgame in Iraq* (New York: Random House, 2009), 60.

4. Joel D. Rayburn, Frank K. Sobchak, Jeanne F. Godfroy, Matthew D. Morton, James S. Powell, and Matthew M. Zais, eds., *The U.S. Army in the Iraq War, Volume 1: Invasion—Insurgency—Civil War, 2003–2006* (Carlisle, PA: US Army War College Press, 2019), 370.

5. "Darkhorse Snipers Kill Insurgent Sniper, Recover Stolen Marine Sniper Rifle," Defense Visual Information Distribution Service, June 22, 2006, https://www.dvidshub.net/news/6922/darkhorse-snipers-kill-insurgent-sniper-recover-stolen-marine-sniper-rifle.

6. Timothy S. McWilliams and Kurtis P. Wheeler, eds., *Al-Anbar Awakening, Volume 1: American Perspectives: U.S. Marines and Counterinsurgency in Iraq, 2004–2009* (Quantico, VA: Marine Corps University Press, 2009), 11.

7. Thomas E. Ricks, "Situation Called Dire in West Iraq," *Washington Post*, September 10, 2006, https://www.washingtonpost.com/archive/politics/2006/09/11/situation-called-dire-in-west-iraq-span-classbankheadanbar-is-lost-politically-marine-analyst-saysspan/0d815991-c7fe-4aee-97ec-ba95ca9a5c00/.

8. McWilliams and Wheeler, *Al-Anbar Awakening, Volume 1*, 135.

9. McWilliams and Wheeler, *Al-Anbar Awakening, Volume 1*, 12.

10. Jane Arraf, "After Years as a Battleground, Investment Boom Lifts Iraqi City," *New York Times*, July 10, 2021, https://www.nytimes.com/2021/07/10/world/middleeast/after-years-as-a-battleground-investment-boom-lifts-iraqi-city.html.

11. Gregg Zoroya, "Memo: Military Lacks a Plan to Deal with Brain Injuries," *USA TODAY*, March 9, 2007.

12. Terri Tanielian et al., *Invisible Wounds: Mental Health and Cognitive Care Needs of America's Returning Veterans* (Santa Monica, CA: RAND, 2008), 2.

13. Gregg Zoroya, "Military Focused on Brain Trauma: New Rule Pulls More Troops off Battlefield," *USA TODAY*, October 28, 2010.

NOTES

14. Rita Florez, "Short Film Based on Southeast Grad Unspools at Festival," *Daily Dalton Citizen*, updated October 18, 2014, https://www.dailycitizen.news/short-film-based-on-southeast-grad-unspools-at-festival/article_8f674a27-0125-5037-9102-6de6e1a6329c.html.

15. James Dao, "Learning to Heal, One Memorial Day at a Time," *New York Times*, May 28, 2012, https://www.nytimes.com/2012/05/29/us/2-4-marine-regiment-marks-ramadi-losses.html.

16. Julie Watson, "Human Errors, Mechanical Woes Caused Marine Tanks Sinking," Associated Press, March 25, 2021, https://apnews.com/article/us-news-accidents-california-san-diego-02638f3b00a049b0355799b1e0855fcb.

17. Michael Moss, "Bloodied Marines Sound Off About Want of Armor and Men," *New York Times*, April 25, 2005, https://www.nytimes.com/2005/04/25/world/middleeast/bloodied-marines-sound-off-about-want-of-armor-and-men.html.

18. Eric Tucker, "Once Tortured in Iranian Jail, Ex-Marine Fights Spy Claims," *Los Angeles Times*, March 16, 2021, https://www.latimes.com/world-nation/story/2021-03-16/once-tortured-in-iranian-jail-ex-marine-fights-spy-claims.

19. Ian Shapiro, "A Green Beret's Cancer Changed Military Malpractice Law. His Claim Still Got Denied," *Washington Post*, March 29, 2023.

20. Dave Philipps, "A Marine Attacked an Iraqi Restaurant. But Was It a Hate Crime or PTSD?," *New York Times*, October 18, 2017, https://www.nytimes.com/2017/10/18/us/damien-rodriguez-marine-portland.html.

21. Gregg Zoroya, "Military Playing Catch-Up on PTSD: Much Still to Be Learned in Treating Invisible War Wounds," *USA TODAY*, April 4, 2014.

22. Gregg Zoroya, "Marine Corps Suicides at Record High," *USA TODAY*, June 8, 2010.

23. Gregg Zoroya, "Experts Worry High Military Suicide Rates Are 'New Normal,'" *USA TODAY*, June 12, 2016.

24. Second Battalion, Fourth Marines Association, Facebook post, December 28, 2021, https://www.facebook.com/TheMagnificentBastardsAssociation/photos/i-hate-posting-these-more-than-anything-our-bastard-family-lost-yet-another-stud/2809837825981386/?_rdr.

25. "Marine Death Comes After He Returns Home," *East Bay Times*, August 16, 2016.

26. John D. Daigh Jr., *Health Care Inspection: Review of the Care and Death of a Veteran Patient, VA Medical Centers St. Cloud and Minneapolis, Minnesota* (Washington, DC: Department of Veterans Affairs, Office of Inspector General, 2007).

27. Dan Margolies, "Court Slaps VA with Damages After Finding It Liable in Suicide of Kansas City Veteran," KCUR, July 3, 2018, https://www.kcur.org/health/2018-07-03/court-slaps-va-with-damages-after-finding-it-liable-in-suicide-of-kansas-city-veteran.

28. Draughon v. United States, 309 F. Supp. 3d 934 (2015), 1274.

29. Scott A. Huesing, *Echo in Ramadi: The Firsthand Story of U.S. Marines in Iraq's Deadliest City* (Washington, DC: Regnery History, 2018), 222.

30. Huesing, *Echo in Ramadi*, 296–297.

31. "Madison Man Sentenced to 13 Years in Jail for Drunk Driving Death Three Minnesota Students," *Republican Eagle*, November 2, 2011, https://www.republicaneagle.com/news/madison-man-sentenced-to-13-years-in-jail-for-drunk-driving-death-three-minnesota-students/article_0f74eeba-d483-5988-add5-e6ad5033bda7.html.

32. Bessel van der Kolk, *The Body Keeps the Score: Brain, Mind, and Body in the Healing of Trauma* (New York: Penguin, 2014), 205.

33. "Drug Fact Sheet: Ecstasy/MDMA," US Drug Enforcement Agency, https://www.dea.gov/sites/default/files/2023-03/Ecstasy-MDMA%202022%20Drug%20Fact%20Sheet.pdf.

34. Paul Kennedy, "How the FDA Can Help American Veterans Suffering from PTSD," *The Hill*, July 2, 2024, https://thehill.com/opinion/healthcare/4750481-how-the-fda-can-help-american-veterans-su%EF%AC%80ering-from-ptsd/.

35. Van der Kolk, *The Body Keeps the Score*, 31.

36. Van der Kolk, *The Body Keeps the Score*, 12–14.

Combat experiences constituting much of this narrative were assembled in large part from interviews with more than 130 Marines, soldiers, and sailors who fought in Ramadi in 2004. In many cases, they were reinterviewed several times and, subsequently, patiently subjected themselves to further queries during fact-checking sessions to go over the final draft. Notes from my embed with the 2nd Battalion, 4th Marines in June 2004 as a

NOTES

reporter with *USA TODAY* contained twenty-five interviews that focused on events still fresh in the minds of the Marines. It included valuable observations and insights by two people who would not survive the deployment: Kenneth Conde and Deshon Otey. I will never forget the recurring nightmare Deshon shared with me following his narrow escape from death on April 6 and how the details of that dream tragically seemed to come true a few weeks later. In addition, audio recordings of additional interviews were graciously made available to me by retired Marine Lieutenant Colonel David Kelly, who visited the battalion in the summer of 2004 as a senior field historian for the Marine Field History Detachment to memorialize firsthand accounts by several members of the battalion.

This book would not have been possible without an extensive file of material graciously provided by Paul Kennedy. The paper and digital records he made available were a rich vein of sourcing that included after-action reports and summaries of enemy attacks, rife with photographs, maps, and diagrams. There were also PowerPoint presentations, color-coded maps tracking anti-coalition attitudes, photographic records of mosques, military centers, observation posts, and other key locations in the city. Most crucially, an almost hour-by-hour account of what the battalion experienced was recorded in a battalion register of significant actions, or "sigacts." This provided a framework for telling what happened to the Magnificent Bastards. Other material included a summary of a debriefing of senior leaders for the Florida National Guard unit that preceded 2/4 in Ramadi and that provided insight into that unit's experience and conclusions regarding the insurgency just prior to the arrival of the Magnificent Bastards. Paul also generously put me in touch with key leadership figures up to and including James Mattis and Joe Dunford.

Other valuable material obtained included a roster of 2/4 service members, spreadsheets documenting the battalion's casualties, and summaries of actions for crucial valor awards, all made available by Mike Wylie, the former battalion executive officer. Wyeth Towle, the ex–intel officer for 2/4, shared a detailed, minute-by-minute chronology with maps of the battles of April 6, 7, and 10. Chris Bronzi, the former commander of Golf Company, pointed me toward a published battlefield study he created of his men's actions on April 6 and 7.

An excellent photographic record of the fighting was possible because of the brave work of combat photojournalists David Swanson and Maurizio Gambarini, both of whom suffered grazing bullet wounds for their efforts. Also helpful was amazing footage of July combat captured by Fox News crews who accompanied retired Marine officer Oliver North during his reporting visits with 2/4.

Diaries, journals, logbooks, photographs, and letters home were crucial contributions by Marines, soldiers, sailors, and family members that also helped tell this story. I obtained a copy of the fitness report that documented reasons behind Kelly Royer being relieved of command of Echo Company. The report contained details on the results of a climate survey administered to gauge the company's sinking morale.

Psychiatrist and retired Navy Captain Bill Nash, a friend with whom I have worked for years on issues related to post-traumatic stress disorder, made available to me newsletters he wrote home from Ramadi in 2004 regarding battalion mental health issues.

Details about the raucous Valentine's Day brawl that preceded deployment were possible because of a fabulous essay on the event written a few years after the incident and shared with me by Lucas "Duke" Wells, former executive officer of Weapons Company.

Facts pertaining to the assassination of the Echo Company sniper team on June 21, 2004, were from a redacted Navy investigation report obtained through a Freedom of Information Act request.

The Historical Resources Branch for the Marine Corps History Division provided copies of 2/4 command chronologies—

NOTES

monthly summaries of events by battalion staff during the deployment.

Live quotes in the book were reconstructed from the memories of those who said or heard them, with the wording cross-checked whenever possible by others who were present. Other quotes were collected from after-action reports, where statements were cited with quotation marks.

I am extremely grateful for the generous assistance of Cynthia O. Smith, the deputy division chief of the Media Relations Division of US Army Public Affairs. Casualty data from the mortar attack on Camp Ramadi that killed or wounded Navy Seabees was contained in documents donated by Jodelle "Jody" Schroeder to the 1st Infantry Division Museum in Cantigny, Illinois. Additional details were from an after-action report on the event, an excerpt of which was provided by retired Rear Admiral Charles Kubic.

Fox Company veteran Amir Heydari alerted me to a valuable Google Earth Pro program containing historical satellite images of Ramadi from June and August 2004, which allowed me to track precise distances and get a thorough understanding of the terrain. I also traveled to Ramadi in May 2023 to visit battlefield sites for Golf and Echo companies from the April 6 fighting, many structures still showing the damages of war.

One of the difficult challenges was reconstructing, with as much precision as possible, the movements and actions of individual Marines, sailors, and soldiers during the fighting. I studied official written accounts, pored over maps and photographs, and interviewed—and frequently reinterviewed—participants, and then I went over with them my written account of their actions, all with an eye for getting as close to the truth as possible.

INDEX

Abbot, Elijah, 204

Abizaid, John, 37–38, 209

Abu Ghraib prison, 35, 240, 286, 311

Abu Risha, Sheik Abdul Sattar, 43, 343–344

AC/DC, 212, 215

agonal respiration, 182

Aguirre, Simon, 60–61

Ahlquist, Clinton, 342

air support

    Fallujah display of, 203–204

    Ramadi forces lacking, 203–204, 206, 233

    show-of-force limitation on, 103–104, 204

Akey, Eric, 2–3, 141–145, 150–154, 189, 309

Alaimalo, Manaia, 224–225, 266–267

alcohol use, PTSD and, 367

Aldrich, Nickalous, 291–292, 314–315

Alegre, Anthony, 267–269

Allawi, Ayad, 287

Amanpour, Christianne, 43

Amara, Shia attacks in, 87

Al Anbar Awakening, 343–344

Appel, Nathan, 58, 223–226

arches (eastern gateway), Day 1 action at, 114–115, 130–131

Arlington National Cemetery, 79, 350

armor, vehicle. *See* vehicle armor

armored personnel carriers (APCs), 131–132. *See also specific actions involving*

Army, tactics of Marines *vs.*, 49–50, 78–79. *See also* 1st Brigade, Army 1st Infantry Division

Army engineers, reinforcement and rescue by, 177–186, 233

Arneson, Gregg, 267–269

Arnold, Theresa, 250–251

AT4 recoilless anti-tank weapon, 102–103, 229

Atkins, Craig, 275–277

August, Matt, 41–42

August, Maureen, 42

Awakening (Iraqi movement), 343–344

Ayers, Nicholas, 84, 270

Ayon, Eric, 185, 212–213

Ba'ath Party, 29–31, 287

Badaa, Jassim Mohammed, 307–308, 311

Baghdad

    ambush of supply convoy traveling to, 208–209

    capture of, 1, 11

    Shia attacks in, 87, 208

    transfer of power in, 287–288

Barclay, Brandon, 302

Barger, Jacquelyn, 375

Barger, Kevin, 186, 223–226, 266–267, 375

Barron, Ramon, 222

Bastard, as command (Kennedy) call sign, 71

Bastards' Road (film), 371–372

Bastards' Road Project, 372

Battle of Fallujah. *See* Fallujah, First Battle of; Fallujah, Second Battle of

396   **INDEX**

Battle of Ramadi. *See* Ramadi, Battle of
"battleground character," 195
Bearded Guys (undercover unit), 242–246
Bennet, Jeremy, 173
Bernardino, Jose, 69
Biden, Joe, 360
Birmelin, Jason L., 75–76, 232, 265, 369
Blackwater USA contractors, killing of,
    77–78, 86, 116
Blue Diamond (Mattis headquarters),
    52, 59
The Body Keeps the Score (van der Kolk),
    367–370
Bohman, Jeremy, 321
Bolding, Todd, 262, 296
bombs, roadside. *see* IEDs
Booker, Carla, 356
Booker, Jim
    aggressive, retaliatory tactics of, 81–83
    assassination of sniper team and,
        282, 283
    background and legendary status of,
        5–7, 80
    clash with Weapons Company, 244,
        245–246
    Day 1 combat of, 112, 135
    Day 1 loss of communication with, 133
    Day 3 advance/attack on rooftop
        stronghold, 6–7, 225–226
    Day 3 Route Apple fighting of, 234
    Echo Company morale as issue for,
        326–327
    Kennedy protected by, 135
    Langhorst's helmet found by, 112,
        119
    nonregulation weapon of, 5
    post-Ramadi career of, 6, 354, 355
    reaction to 2/4 Marines' bulked-up
        swagger, 17
    realization of Day 1 losses, 190
    removal of dead Marines by, 5
    respect for adversary, 193
    Royer and, 70–71
    Ryan regarded as 2/4 Marine by, 298
    Silver Star awarded to, 241
    stroke suffered by, 6, 355–356
    undercover intel operation of, 80–81,
        88, 242

undercover unit created and led by,
    242–246
vigilance over troops, 5–7, 60, 320
"Wicked Wednesdays" and, 301
"boot drops," 20–21
Bradley Fighting Vehicles, 32, 84. *See also*
    specific actions involving
Bremer, Paul, 30–31, 87, 287–288
Brinkley, William "Dave," 33–34
Bronzi, Christopher J.
    background of, 94–95
    call sign for, 71, 246
    Day 1 ambushes of squads under,
        94–112, 118–119
    Day 1 hammer-and-anvil response of,
        119, 134–136
    Day 1 relief missions led by, 107–112,
        134–136
    Day 2 fighting of, 195–197, 202–206
    final Ramadi missions of, 332–333
    first life taken by, 109
    heat casualties as concern on, 293
    injury of, 85
    Leftwich Trophy awarded to, 356
    orientation in Ramadi, 44
    post-Ramadi career of, 356–358
    route clearance ended by, 270
    Silver Star awarded to, 119, 241
    training accident involving, 357–358
Bronzi, Mary, 94–95
Bryant, Todd, 39
Burgess, Abdul Kareem, 288, 304,
    307–308
Bush, George W.
    Abu Risha's handshake with, 344
    de-Ba'athification strategy of,
        30–31
    declaration of mission accomplished,
        1, 11, 17
    Fallujah ceasefire ordered by, 209
    insistence on retaliation in Fallujah,
        78–79
    low-profile during days of battle,
        191–192
    spray-painted insult of, 57
    Wroblewski Sr.'s meeting with,
        350
Bush, Irving "Ray," 180–181, 184

INDEX

397

Cabrey, Richard "Mike," 33–34, 36
Calavan, Cody, 162, 265–269
Call Sign Chaos (Mattis), 354
call signs, 71, 246, 278–279
Callaway, Derek, 185
cameras, phony, 84
Camp Pendleton (California)
  drunken clash during dinner at, 21–24
  Hancock's honor walk ending at,
    371–372
  as 2/4 Marines home base, 14–15
Camp Ramadi
  as Connor's headquarters, 32, 52
  medical facility at, 45–49 (*see also*
    Charlie Med)
  preparations for 2/4 Marine departure
    at, 331
  Seabee disaster at, 254–257
Camp Victory (Kuwait), 24–26, 99
Campbell, Donovan
  background of, 104, 314
  Bronze Star awarded to, 191, 262, 314
  care for injured Iraqi children, 262
  Day 1 fighting of, 104, 109, 112, 119
  heat casualties in platoon of, 293
  Marine run over by convoy of,
    314–315
  "poolside" memories of, 249
  school-visit attack on platoon of,
    261–262
  "Wicked Wednesdays" and, 302
Cantu, Richard V., Jr., 197, 199
car bombs. *See* vehicle-borne IEDs
Carlton, Mark, 274–277, 302–303,
  354–355
Carman, Benjamin, 128, 139, 167–168,
  209–210, 351
Carman, Marie, 210
Carman, Nelson, 210
Carroll, Sean, 65–66, 67, 75, 143
Carter, Adam, 142, 143, 154, 181, 187
casualties, insurgent, 11, 206, 317–318
casualties, US
  Battle of Ramadi, 1–2, 190, 206, 210,
    240, 241
  Embrey's tracking of, 67
  first killed, 1st Brigade, 38
  first killed, 2/4 Marines, 59–62

inadequate vehicle armor blamed for,
  13–14
medical (trauma) facilities for, 45–49
total, 2/4 Marines, 1, 11, 339
catfish, in water supply, 249
Catto, William, 38
Central Command (CENTCOM), 37,
  209, 353
Charlie Med, 45–49
  Connor treated at, 261
  contempt *vs.* medical care for enemy at,
    270–271
  Day 1 casualties at, 123–124, 168
  Day 2 casualties in, 200
  early 2/4 casualties at, 60–61
  post–Battle of Ramadi casualties at,
    256–257, 261–263
  Seabee mass casualties at, 256–257
  sniper-attack victims at, 312–313
Cherry, Andre, 129
Cherry, Marcus, 20, 127–129, 138, 139,
  140, 168
children, Iraqi
  absence of, as tip-off, 63
  challenge of dealing with, 33
  presumed innocence of, 56
  protection of, 95
  sniper team approached by, 116–117
  struck by insurgent fire, 262
city center (Ramadi)
  Bronzi's hammer-and-anvil response on,
    119, 134–136
  Day 1 East Cemetery ambush in, 92–96,
    103–104, 119, 134–136
  Day 1 fighting in, 91–119
  Day 1 Mukhabarat fighting in, 98–107,
    111–112, 118–119
  Day 2 battles in, 202–206
  Day 2 plan for, 195
  Day 2 psyops campaign in, 195–196
civic improvement projects, 32, 34–35, 270
civil affairs missions, Marines attacked
  during, 258–263
Clausewitz, Carl von, 83
Clayton, Adam, 227–228, 261, 269, 295,
  309, 377
climate survey, for Echo Company,
  327–330

398 INDEX

Coalition Provisional Authority (CPA), 30–31, 287
Coan, Damien
  "ass-chewing" from, 16
  background of, 25
  clash with Royer, 277–278
  Day 3 fighting of, 216, 227, 229–230
  discovery of assassinated sniper team, 282–285
  hydration as concern of, 293–294
  loss of Wroblewski and, 185, 216, 264
  new commander and, 264
  post-Ramadi life of, 374
  suicide of Marine disciplined by, 25–26
Cobb, Christopher, 156–157, 179, 184, 351
Cobras. See helicopters
Cogan, Tom
  background of, 76
  Day 1 arches (eastern gateway) actions of, 115, 130–131
  Day 1 Gypsum-Nova actions of, 172–173, 177–178, 182
  Day 3 assignment of, 216, 230–231
  Day 3 attack on sniper positions, 231–233
  Day 3 coordinated attacks by, 230
  dissatisfaction with company commander, 323–324
  grief over US casualties, 241–242
  marriage by proxy, 250–251
  post-Ramadi life of, 376
  reflections on Ramadi experience, 376–377
  relationship with Marines serving under, 76–77
  Silver Star awarded to, 241
Cole, Jarad, 127–129, 220–222
Coleman, Bernard C., 14, 129, 185, 316, 325–327, 358
Collins, Jonathan, 311–312
color-coded maps of Ramadi, 54–55
Combat Action Ribbon, 317–318
Combat Outpost (COP), 53–54
  car bomb victims sent to clinic at, 267–269
  catfish in water supply of, 249
  children playing near, 56
  Mattis's visit to, 273

memorial service at, 241–242
mortar crew attacking, elimination of, 67–71
nighttime ambush near, 64
personnel stripped from, 166
"Wicked Wednesday" attack on, 304
Conde, Kenneth, Jr.
  Bronze Star awarded to, 191, 290, 351–352
  building named in honor of, 351–352
  Day 1 reinforcements led by, 109–110
  death of, 290–291, 339
  demeanor and reputation of, 109–110
  psyops assignment of, 196
  respect for adversary, 193–194
  wounding of, 110, 339
Conde, Theresa, 110
Connable, Alfred "Ben," 343–344
Conner, Christopher
  ambush of forces trying to reach, 147–150
  attack on route-clearing patrol of, 140–145, 147, 150–154
  Day 3 Route Apple fighting of, 218
  desperate fight while cut off, 150–152, 169–170, 186–187
Connor, Arthur, Jr., "Buck," 31–42
  ambush targeting, 40–42
  background of, 31
  casualties in brigade under, 11, 38, 40–42, 79
  collection/care of human remains by, 5, 79, 111–112
  concern over patrols' vulnerability, 93
  congregating discouraged by, 255
  Day 1 combat action of, 108, 111–112, 133, 135–136, 168
  diary entries of, 213, 253, 260
  early Ramadi operations of, 32–37
  end of Ramadi tour, 331
  grief over lives lost, 42
  hearing loss of, 136
  IEDs striking, 8–9, 260–261, 298–299, 301
  IEDs threatening troops of, 37–42
  Iraqi headquarters of, 32, 52
  as Kennedy's superior, 273
  Marine bias against tactics of, 50

INDEX

medic's mistake in presence of, 251–252
Operation Traveler of, 309
Paladin howitzers of, 32, 35–36, 204
Parkinson's disease of, 7–9, 348–349
response to sniper team's
assassination, 283
sidelined at outset of Iraq War, 31–32
Sofia District action of, 136
traumatic brain injury of, 7–9, 260–261,
348–349
Contreras, Pedro, 129, 139, 225–226,
280–285, 296, 342
Conway, James, 78
cows, in battles areas, 153, 217, 219
Cox, Aaron, 110
Craig, Jeffrey, 218–222
Crane, Joe, 305–307
Crawford, Dan, 88
creativity, in 2/4 Marines, 83–84
Crickard, Colin, 86, 267–269, 295
cross-country walk, honoring veterans,
371–372
Crowley, Kyle, 20–21, 156–157, 184, 351
Crutcher, Anthony, 103–104, 107–108
Crutchfield, Colt, 124
Cruz, Omar Morel, 228
Cugliotta, Dean, Jr., "Marine Dean," 21,
60–61
cultural challenges, for US personnel,
54–57
Cummings, Marshall, 200
Cussans, Justin, 68–69
Cutchall, Christopher, 38

Dang, Andrew, 59–62, 76, 82, 89, 274, 275
Darkhorse Marines
drunken clash of 2/4 Marines with, 21–24
fighting and losses in Iraq, 340–342
DarSalam restaurant (Portland, Oregon),
3–5, 362–363
Davis, Brandon Lee, 79
Dawson, Brett, 143
Day 1, Battle of Ramadi, 91–194, 196–210
arches (eastern gateway) actions on,
114–115, 130–131
Bronzi's hammer-and-anvil response on,
119, 134–136
city center fighting on, 91–119

command challenges and confusion on,
132–134
East Cemetery ambush on, 92–96,
103–104, 119, 134–136
Gypsum-Nova intersection ambush on,
147–150, 155–164, 172–186
Headhunter 2 sniper team on, 115–117,
120–129, 137–140
insurgency's initiative and
sophistication on, 192–194
litany of Marine losses in, 190
medals awarded for valor and heroism
on, 191
media coverage of, 185, 191
Mukhabarat fighting on, 98–107,
111–112, 118–119
Route Apple ambush on, 136–137
route-clearing patrol attacked on,
140–145, 147, 150–154, 168–170
Sofia District engagements on, 114–118,
120–194
See also specific actions
Day 2, Battle of Ramadi, 195–210
ambush of Rainmaker on, 197–199
Bronzi's plan for, 195
casualties on, 206
city center fighting on, 202–206
cycle of ambush, reinforcement, and
counterattack on, 197
Mabry's death during, 202–203
Nova fighting on, 199–200
psyops campaign in, 195–196
Route Apple fighting on, 200–202
Day 3, Battle of Ramadi, 212–239
AC/DC song as accompaniment to,
212, 215
advances/attacks on insurgent
strongholds on, 6–7, 218–226
casualties on, 240
predawn raids and searches on,
213–216, 226, 230–231
pre-staged insurgent locations on, 217, 236
psyops and taunting on, 215, 236
Route Apple battles on, 216–218,
222, 225
sewage-ditch escape on, 226–229
US women engaged in direct combat on,
234–237, 364

400   **INDEX**

death letters, 77, 157
de-Ba'athification, 30–31
DeGoede, John IV, 282
Denman, Joseph, 205
Dennis, Tyrynn, 65–66, 128, 139, 213
Devil Brigade. *See* 1st Brigade, Army 1st Infantry Division
Devlin, Pete, 343
Diaz, Brad, 332
distraction trauma, 48
Dobb, David
  background of, 197, 198
  Day 1 actions of, 108, 187–189
  Day 2 ambush of Rainmaker platoon under, 197–199
  Day 3 Lionesses (women) fighting with, 234–237, 364
  Day 3 Route Apple fighting of, 222, 234–239
  Hodges defended by, 89
  IED striking platoon of, post-Battle of Ramadi, 258–260
  post-Ramadi life of, 376
  standby duties *vs.* sleep needs of men under, 245–246
  Weaver's service under, 373
Downing, Ryan
  cinder-block shed as shelter for, 160, 173–177
  death letter of, 77, 157
  Gypsum-Nova ambush of, 157–164, 172–186
  post-Ramadi police work of, 369
  rescue of, 172–186
  wounding and evacuation of, 159–160, 184
Draughon, William, 366
Dunford, Joe, 15–16, 19, 192–193, 329–330, 354
Dunham, Jason, 253–254, 343
Dunham, Rick, 335–338

East Cemetery
  Day 1 ambush in, 92–96, 103–104, 119, 134–136
  Day 2 fighting around, 202–206

Easy Street, fighting on, 98, 107–110, 202–206
Echo Company (2/4 Marines)
  ad hoc relief force from, 166, 167–168
  arches (eastern gateway) actions of, 114–115, 130–131
  call sign for (Porcupine/Porky), 71, 246
  car bomb attack on, 264–269
  casualty rate in, 11, 278
  climate survey of, 327–330
  Combat Outpost as home of, 53–54
  Day 1 engagements of, 114–118, 120–194
  Day 3 advances/attacks on insurgent strongholds, 6–7, 218–226
  Day 3 attack on sniper positions, 231–233
  Day 3 fighting of, 212–239
  Day 3 platoon assignments of, 216
  Day 3 Route Apple battles of, 216–218, 222, 225
  Day 3 sewage-ditch escape, 226–229
  final stages of Ramadi deployment for, 330–338
  Gypsum-Nova intersection ambush of, 147–150, 155–164
  harrying opening attacks on, 57–58
  horrific IED explosion in, 73–77
  morale/dislike of commander in, 228, 277–278, 322–330
  mortar crew targeted and eliminated by, 67–71
  patrols and territory of, 62
  platoon leaders of, 76–77
  rifle company of, 54
  route-clearing duties of, 63–67
  Royer fired as commander of, 327–330
  Royer's appointment as commander of, 23, 70
  second deployment to Iraq, 342
  sniper team of (*see* Headhunter 2 sniper team)
  See also specific individuals and actions
Echo in Ramadi (Huesing), 366–367
Edress, Shamel, 143

INDEX

Eggink, Eric, 92, 95–96
82nd Airborne Division, 49–50, 52, 77
Elkins, Ryan, 263–264
Elledge, Mike, 181
Ellis, Joe, 342
Embrey, Jonathan "Chaplain/Chaps," 67, 92, 95–96, 206, 318–319, 369, 375
Erickson, Bradley, 367
Erwin, Nicholas, 95
Escalera, Miguel, 68–69, 77, 157, 375

Fallujah
   Blackwater contractors slain in, 77–78, 86, 116
   coordinated ambushes in, 73
   as insurgent stronghold, 304
   measured response *vs.* retaliatory assault in, 78–79
   Ramadi compared with, 2, 28–29, 191–192
Fallujah, First Battle of, 86–87
   air support in, 203–204
   ceasefire in, 209, 253, 304
   progress of Marines in, 206–207
   US casualties of, 241
Fallujah, Second Battle of, 241, 339–341
Fallujah Brigade, 209, 254
"Fallujah model," 287
Farhan, Adnan Hassan, 88–89, 94, 134, 238
Farhan, Majeed Abdullah, 88, 94
Al Farouk water tower, 107–110, 206
Faulk, Tyler, 131–132, 182, 233
Fedayeen Saddam, 29
Ferguson, Cameron
   background of, 116
   Day 1 attack on, 120–129, 137–140, 166–168
   Day 1 counterattack of, 137–140
   Day 1 rescue of, 167–168
   Day 3 advance/attack on insurgent strongholds, 219–222
   Day 3 assignment of, 217
   Day 3 run away from cow, 219
   as member of sniper team, 116
   overwatch duty on Route Michigan, 280
   post-Ramadi police work of, 369

Fiasco: The American Military Adventure in Iraq (Ricks), 77–78
Fighting Fifth, 14–15
1st Brigade, Army 1st Infantry Division, 7–9, 31–42
   armored personnel carriers of, 131–132
   Connor as commander of, 31–32
   Day 1 command challenges in, 131–134
   early encounters with insurgents, 35–37
   equipment and vehicles of, 32, 35
   female teams (Lionesses) in, 33–34, 234–237, 364
   first casualty killed, 38
   IEDs as threat to, 37–42
   reconnaissance/patrol mission of, 32–35
1st Marine Division, 19
Fisher, Joseph R. "Bull," 15
Fishhook Lake, 214, 234
Flom, Pete, 98, 102, 105–107
Florida National Guard, 35, 43–44, 52, 57, 62
Flowers, Craig, 205
Fox Company (2/4 Marines)
   Day 2 engagements of, 199, 202, 205
   final Ramadi engagements of, 333–338
   first killed casualty of, 59–62, 274
   harrying opening attacks on, 57
   high-rise outpost of, bombing of, 310–311
   high-rise outpost of, Iraqi sniper attacks on, 311–314
   patrols and territory of, 62
   rifle company of, 54
   second deployment to Iraq, 342
   Snake Pit as home of, 53
   waterborne-assault tragedy in, 274–277
   "Wicked Wednesdays" and, 302–303
   See also specific individuals and actions
friendly fire, risk of, 111, 180, 203, 233
friends *vs.* foes, distinguishing between, 54–56

Gaeden, Kevin, 127–129, 292
Garcia, Felix, 237
gas attack, on Hurricane Point, 309
Gentile, James, 100–107, 118, 119, 123–124, 362

402 INDEX

Global Position Lightweight GPS receiver, 80–81

Golf Company (2/4 Marines)
call sign for (Joker), 71, 246
Combat Outpost as home of, 53–54
Day 1 attacks on, 92–112, 118–119
Day 1 hammer-and-anvil response of, 119, 134–136
Day 2 battles of, 196–197, 202–206
Day 2 plan for, 195
early actions involving, 64
East Cemetery ambush of, 92–96, 103–104, 119, 134–136
events leading up to battle and, 85
final Ramadi missions of, 332–333
Hayes's return to, 295–297
heat casualties in, 293–295
Marine run over by convoy of, 314–315
Mukhabarat ambush of, 98–107
outpost abandoned by, 314
patrols and territory of, 62
"poolside" recreation of, 249
religious militants' response to, 73
rifle company of, 54
rocket hitting operations center of, 249
route clearance ended for, 270
RPG fired at observation post of, 291–292
school-visit attack on, 261–263
"Wicked Wednesdays" for, 299–303
wounding of commander, 85
See also specific individuals and actions

Gonzalez, Benjamin, Jr., 266–269
Gonzalez, Christopher, 280–281
Good Friday attacks, 208–209, 212–214
GPS tracking, of personnel, 133
graveside reunions, of veterans, 352–353
Green, Jeffrey, 275–277
Greene, David, 305–307
Guillen, Abe, 334–338
Gustavison, Sean, 294–295, 349
Gutierrez, Frank, 183, 248, 267
Gutierrez, Sergio, 75–76, 163, 232–233
Guttormsen, Kate. *See* Pendry, Kate
Gypsum-Nova intersection
description of, 149
fatal Good Friday explosion at, 212–213
rebuilding of, 345

Gypsum-Nova intersection, Day 1
ambush at, 147–150, 155–164, 172–186
Army clearance of and rescue at, 177–186
casualties and human remains at, 181–186
cinder-block shed as Marine shelter in, 160, 173–177
fire on advance Humvees in, 157–161
insurgents' organization and tactics at, 149–150, 157, 159, 184, 193
Iraqi civilian used as test of enemy gunfire, 176–177
Marine gunners' heroics at, 158–159, 161–162
media coverage of, 185
nightmares about, 194
Otey's after-action report on, 158, 177
radio communications at, 161, 162–163, 172, 175, 182

Habbaniyah, 30, 36, 39, 341–342
Habbaniyah Lake, 30, 114, 280–281, 305, 320
Habeisi, Ja'ardon Mohammed, 80, 288, 310, 311
Hagee, Michael, 16
Hagee, Silke, 16
Hallal, Deryk, 100–107, 111–112, 118, 123
Hamby, Glenn, 332–333
Hancock, Jonathan, 310, 319, 333–334, 371–372
Hancock, Maura, 371
Hancock, Tiffany, 372
Al-Haq Mosque, 58, 73, 322–323
Harrill, Dave "JD"
background of, 18
company assignment of, 18
Day 1 loss of communication with, 133
dissatisfaction with Royer, 324, 327
interrogation by, 286
Kennedy alerted to bad news by, 272
post-Ramadi career of, 355

INDEX

reflections on Ramadi experience, 376

reservations about waterborne assault, 274–275

Silver Star awarded to, 18

tactics and creativity of, 81–85

Hassell, Kenneth, 227–228

Hawn, Michael, 127–128

Hayes, Joe

background of, 98–99

Bronze Star awarded to, 191, 295–296, 369

Mukhabarat ambush and fight of, 98–107, 111–112

PTSD and risky behavior of, 124, 369–370

rescue of, 118

return to Golf Company, 295–297

shock of McPherson's wounds affecting, 49

wounds and medical care of, 104–105, 124

Headhunter 2 sniper team

assassination of B members of, 281–285, 309, 342, 376

choreography of, 126

Day 1 ad hoc relief force for, 166, 167–168

Day 1 attack on, 120–129, 137–140, 166–168

Day 1 counterattack of, 137–140, 166–168

Day 1 exposed location of, 116–117

Day 1 mission of, 115–116

Day 1 reinforcements for, 123, 127–129, 130, 132, 136–137, 167–168

Day 1 rescue of, 167–168

Day 3 advances/attacks on insurgent strongholds, 218–222

Day 3 assignment of, 216–217

media coverage of deaths in, 283, 285

overwatch duty on Route Michigan, 279–280

regular Marines pulled to assist, 279–280

retribution for slayings in, 286–287

Santiago as leader of, 116

weapons of, 121, 342

heat casualties, 292–295, 303, 349

Hefley, Joel, 38

Hekmati, Amir, 242, 245, 360

helicopters

attack response of, 238–239, 299

deadly attack on, 304–307

lack of air support from, 103–104, 203–204, 206

"Hells Bells" (AC/DC song), 212, 215

Heredia, James, 332–333

Hernandez, Robert, 224, 316

Herscher, Joe, 238

Hesener, Jonathan

background of, 92

Day 1 ambushes of squads under, 92–112, 119

Day 1 positions held by, 134–136

Day 2 action of, 199, 203, 206

Heydari, Amir, 242, 335–336

Highway 1, IEDs on, 63, 84

Highway 10

IEDs on, 39, 40–42

main Ramadi road (*see* Route Michigan)

in privileged Ramadi enclave, 30

surveillance to prevent IEDs on, 84

in 2/4 Marine battle space, 51

"hillbilly armor," 13–14, 32, 68, 128, 258–259, 265

Hizo, Paul, 349–350

Hodges, Reagan, 61, 238, 258, 260

Hoffman, James, 41

Holt, Allen, 99–107

Honeycutt, Brandon, 336–337

Howell, Dustin, 263–264

Huerkamp, John, 231–233

Huesing, Scott, 366–367

Hueys. See helicopters

Hufstedler, Doyle, III, 79

human remains

Connor's collection/care of, 5, 79, 111–112

enemy, collection of, 201–202, 206

Gypsum-Nova intersection, 181–186

horror of Dang's death and, 60–62

horror of Wiscowiche's death and, 75–77

shocking findings of, 60–62, 75–77, 79

INDEX

Humvees
Connor's injuries in, 8–9
first casualty killed in, 1st Brigade, 38
first casualty killed in, 2/4 Marines,
59–62
improvised (hillbilly) armor on, 13–14,
32, 68, 128, 258–259, 265
inadequate armor of, 13–14, 149
mobile assault company of, 54
Royer as whistleblower about,
358–359
up-armored, 84, 196, 289, 291, 300,
320
vulnerability according to order of and
seat in, 265
See also specific actions involving
Hunter of Gunmen (HOG), 116
Hurricane battalion (Florida National
Guard), 35, 43–44, 52, 57, 62
Hurricane Point (base), 52–53
beginning of battle at, 89
Day 1 command challenges at, 132–133
Farhan held at, 89
gas attack on, 309
respite provided at, 320
rocket attacks on, 59
spray-painted insult of Bush at, 57
Husaybah, fighting in, 253–254
Hussein, Saddam, 29, 37, 52
hydration, importance of, 293–294

I Should Have Gone to College (Rosman),
6, 292
IEDs (improvised explosive devices)
Abu Risha killed by, 344
blast wave exposure from, 12
Connor struck by, 8–9, 260–261,
298–299, 301
Connor's soldiers killed by, 40–42
creative concepts for dealing with,
83–84
Day 1 attack on patrol clearing, 140–145
fatal Good Friday explosion of, 212–213
first casualty killed by, 1st Brigade, 38
horrific injuries in Echo Company from,
73–77
human remains from, care of, 5, 60–62,
75–77

hunting for, 63–67
insurgents' reliance on, 37–42, 66–67,
257–261
protocol for disposing of, 64, 141
trigger device for, 75, 257
trigger men for, 39, 64, 74–75, 257, 265
US media and political focus on, 38
vehicle-borne, 39, 189–190, 264–269,
302, 333–334
"Wicked Wednesdays" of, 297–307
insurgency, Iraqi
alliance of militants in, 37–38, 87
coordination and organization of, 72–73
curtailed US operations and, 287–288,
308–315
IEDs as weapon of choice, 66–67
initiative and sophistication of, 192–194
opening test attacks against 2/4
Marines, 57–67
ouster of US as goal of, 73
prisoner release and replenishment of,
240–241
resistance to and receding of, 343–344
roots and rise of, 11–12, 30–31, 35–44,
207–208
Rumsfeld's underestimation of, 19
See also specific actions
intelligence (intel)
bad, dated, or misleading, 88, 94
Booker's Bearded Guys for, 242–246
Booker's undercover operation for,
80–81, 88, 242
capture and interrogation of Farhan,
88–89
intercept on danger to sniper team, 282
signs of impending insurgent action in,
72–73, 87–88
Tactical Fusion Center for, 72
interim government, Iraqi, 35, 287–288
intravenous (IV) fluids, 294
Iran, Hekmati detained in, 360
Iraq War
Army *vs.* Marine tactics in, 49–50,
78–79
bloodiest months of, 241
conditions before arrival of 2/4 Marines,
28–44
cycle of violence in, 339–344

INDEX

declaration of mission accomplished in,
1, 11, 17
start of, 11
transfer of power in, 287–288
US withdrawal of forces in, 344
See also specific actions and individuals
Iraqi Unity (political organization), 299
Islamic State of Iraq and Syria (ISIL/
ISIS), 344

Jaugan, Winston, 85, 296–297
Al Jazeera, 209
JDAM (guided bomb), 50
Jerabek, Ryan
background of, 148
Bronze Star awarded to, 191
death and remains of, 159, 184–185
enemy seizure of weapon, 179
Gypsum-Nova ambush of, 148,
156–164
heroic manning of machine gun,
158–159
Joker (call sign), 71, 246
Joker One (Campbell), 314–315
Junction City, 32

Kaler, Benjamin, 64, 143
Karr, Michael G., 79, 181
Katz, Kyle, 143
Kellogg Brown & Root (defense
contractor), 208–209
Kelly, John, 50, 78, 213, 350–351, 354
Kelly, Mike, 341
Kelly, Nick, 199
Kennedy, Constance, 18
Kennedy, Paul
aggressive, retaliatory tactics of,
81–83
assassination of sniper team and, 283,
286–287
assignment as 2/4 Marines commander,
17–19
background of, 17–18
Bearded Guys monitored by, 245
Booker's undercover operation approved
by, 80–81
Bronzi nominated for trophy by, 356
burden of command on, 272–273

call signs chosen by, 71, 246, 278–279
concern over Ramadi as terrorist
haven, 307
congressional testimony of, 317
Day 1 combat of, 112, 133, 135
Day 3 provocative strategy of, 213–216
Day 3 Route Apple fighting of,
225, 234
deployment news disclosed to, 19
displeasure with Weiler, 239, 246
emotional trauma and marital troubles
of, 368
hand-over of operations to 2/5 Marines,
330–338
hurried preparations for deployment,
19–21
intel for, 44, 94
Iraqi headquarters of, 53
Langhorst's helmet found by, 112, 119
leadership style and tactics of, 5–6, 50,
60, 83, 104, 195
letters to families of slain Marines,
210, 212
as Mattis protégé, 17
MDMA for PTSD advocated by,
368–369
mobile assault company of, 54
nurse honored by, 373
Operation Traveler of, 309
post-Ramadi career of, 354–355
pride in conduct of Marines, 320
Purple Heart awarded to, 355
report of Snake Pit defense to, 338
respect for adversary, 192–193
Royer fired by, 327–330, 358–359
Royer's attitude and, 71, 278–279, 324
security detail of, 135
staff selected by, 18–19
suspicious vehicle spotted by, 265
tragic waterborne assault approved
by, 274
Valdes's punishment deferred by, 323
"Wicked Wednesdays" and, 298–303
Kennedy, Richard, 18
Kepler, Derrick, 352–353
Kerry, John, 360
Khalidiyah, 30, 36–37, 39, 300
kill shots, 2–3, 145

406 **INDEX**

killing
  accidental, 319–320
  Marines' feelings about, 318–320
  questionable, by Mattis's security force,
    320–321
  2/4 Marines weariness over, 338
  See also casualties
King, Genevieve, 129
King, James, 267–269
Kubic, Charles, 255
Kuwait
  ambush of supply convoy from, 208–209
  Camp Victory of, 24–26, 99

Landrus, Sean, 41–42
Landstuhl Regional Medical Center
    (Germany), 48
Lane, Shawn, 304, 305
Langhorst, Moisés
  adventure *vs.* reality of war for,
    25–26, 49
  death and remains of, 118–119, 124, 202
  hometown memorial for, 351
  loss of classmate to suicide, 25–26, 99
  missing and presumed dead, 106,
    112, 118
  Mukhabarat ambush and fight of,
    99–107
  Rodriguez's memories of, 362
  youth and background of, 20
Lauersdorf, Charles, 184, 227–228, 358
LAVs (Light Armored Vehicles), 320
Layfield, Travis, 77, 156–157,
    184–185, 223
Lee, Bumrock "Bum," 268–269
Leech, Wilson, III, 22–23
Leftwich Trophy, 356
Lens, Dirk, 61–62, 275–277
Lenz, Shaun, 162, 182
Letterman, Jeremiah, 92–96, 103–104,
    107, 118, 123–124
Light Armored Vehicles (LAVs), 320
Linares, Juan, 100–107
Lioness (film), 372
Lionesses (US military teams), 33–34,
    234–237, 364, 372
Litke, Simon, 366–367
Lloyd, David, 68–69

Lopez, Juan, 280–285, 342, 351
Lord, Richard "Ricky," 314
Lund, Brandon, 5, 128, 166, 168, 292

M1 Abram tanks, 32
M203 grenade launcher, 99–100, 102, 121,
    126, 165, 319
Mabry, Christopher, 202–203
MacIntosh, Chris
  anxiety over route-clearing duties of, 63
  attack on route-clearing patrol of,
    141–145, 150–154, 168–170
  cow's collaboration with, 153
  despair over sniper team's
    assassination, 285
  desperate fight while cut off, 143–145,
    150–154, 189
  feelings about taking lives, 319
  first aid provided by, 169
  kill shots fired by, 2–3, 145
  last days in Ramadi, 315–316
  naked dancing of, 249–250
  nickname of, 246–247
  platoon reputation of, 3
  PTSD of, 370–371
  relationship with mother, 315–316
  rescue for patrol, 187–190
  Tor and, 219
  troubled homecoming of, 353
  wounds suffered by, 66–67, 315–316
MacIntosh, Lauren, 67, 315–316, 353
Madrillejos, Victor "Shorty,"
    155–156, 246
Magee, Joseph, Jr., 226, 229
Magnificent Bastards, 1, 246. *See also* 2/4
    Marines
Mahdi Army, 87, 208–209
Majid, Samar, 374
Malaab District, 55, 308–309
Marine uniform, lure and appeal of,
    98–99, 142
marriage by proxy, 250–251
Martinez, Higinio, 102, 106
Martinez, Miguel, 128, 137, 139, 166, 168
Martley, Michael, 264–269
"mascal" (mass casualty event), 256
Mattis, James
  "All Hands" letter from, 50, 239

INDEX

career successes of, 353–354
Combat Outpost visit of, 273
Fallujah battle plans, advances, and
outcomes of, 86–87, 206–207,
209, 304
hygiene demanded by, 242–243
Kennedy as protégé of, 17
Kennedy informed of Iraq deployment
by, 19
Ramadi as "key terrain" for, 2
Ramadi headquarters of (Blue
Diamond), 52, 59
security force for, questionable behavior
of, 320–321
subordinates fired by, 273
tactics of (Marine *vs.* Army), 49–50, 78
testimony in whistleblower case, 359
2/4 Marines service of, 19
Maupin, Keith "Matt," 208–209
McKenzie, Heath, 110, 135, 199
McNaghten, Dan, 336
McPherson, Brian, Sr., 48–49, 76
McPherson, Brian "Mack," 45–49,
346–348
McPherson, Heather, 347
MDMA, for PTSD, 368–369
Medal of Honor, 254, 340, 343
medical (trauma) care, 45–49
Day 1 casualties requiring, 123–124, 168
Day 2 casualties requiring, 200
distraction trauma for personnel in, 48
monitoring for TBIs in, 67
ongoing, for veterans, 345–350
shortage of specialists for, 47
medical malpractice cases, against
military, 361–362
memorials and honors, 351–352
Mendez-Aceves, Fernando, 148–149,
156–164, 181, 183–184, 186, 223
mental health, 318–322
counseling from chaplain, 319–320
Hurricane Point respite, 320
inadequacy of services for, 12–13,
321–322, 361–367
Marines' feelings about killing, 318–329
Post-Deployment Health Assessment of,
321–322
See also post-traumatic stress disorder

Milczark, Matthew, 20, 25–26, 99
Miller, Kevin, Jr., 205–206
Miller, Ryan, 158, 161, 194
mine-resistant ambush-protected vehicles
(MRAPs), 13
"minutemen," 220
Mirabile, Hector, 43–44
"Mission accomplished," declaration of, 1
mistakes, 272–285. *See also specific
actions*
Mitchell, Sean Robert, 79
MK19 automatic grenade launchers, 111,
137, 165, 173, 180, 187, 199, 335
Mogadishu, Somalia, 78
Monarez, Elias, 63, 65
Moore, Alfred, 230
Moothart, Travis, 41–42
Morgan, Shannon, 234–237, 364
Morris, Geoff, 24, 85–86, 132, 137,
165, 374
Morrison, Brian, 371–372
motorcyclist's suicide charge, 165
Moudy, Vincent, 296
MRAPs, 13
Mukhabarat
Day 1 attack in, 98–107, 111–112,
118–119
description of neighborhood, 29
Mukhabarat intelligence service, 37
Murray, Clint, 256–257, 261, 263,
372–373
Murray, Jason, 74–75, 232
Musser, Benjamin, 229

Nackers, William, 289–290
Najaf, Shia attacks in, 87
Nash, Bill, 53–54, 321–322
Nasiriyah, Shia attacks in, 87
nasopharyngeal airway device, 46
National Suicide Hotline Designation
Act, 367
Natonski, Richard, 330
Navacastro, Fredi, 143, 154
Naval Criminal Investigative Services, 282
Navarre, Stewart, 21–24
Navarre, Yana, 22
Navy Seabees, disastrous attack on,
254–257

408   **INDEX**

Neighbors, Candace, 296
Neller, Robert, 342–343
Newman, Randy, 330–331, 339
nicknames and call signs, 71, 246–247, 278–279
Nieto, Misael, 164, 265–269
Nohren, Phil, 337
North, Oliver, 299, 302–303
Nova (Ramadi byway)
    Day 1 attack on route-clearing patrol, 140–145, 147, 150–154, 168–170, 186–190
    Day 1 attack on sniper team and reinforcements, 115–116, 120–129, 137–140, 166–168
    Day 2 battle on, 199–200
    Gypsum intersection with (*see* Gypsum-Nova intersection)
    IED striking Rainmaker platoon on, 258–260
    route clearance on, 63–67
"No-War 2/4," 14–19, 21
Null, Evan
    cinder-block shed as shelter for, 160, 173–177
    Cogan respected by, 76
    Gypsum-Nova ambush of, 160, 172–186
    post-Ramadi life of, 374
Nylin, Shane, 86, 165, 201

Obama, Barack, 354–355, 360
observation posts, 84, 270
    assassination of sniper team at, 281–285, 309
    Golf Company, RPG fired at, 291–292
    high-rise, bombing of, 310–311
    high-rise, Iraqi sniper attacks on, 311–314
    sniper team's overwatch duty at, 279–281
Oguin, Russell, 143
1/5 Marines, 341
OP Ghetto, 312, 334–338
Operation Bug Hunt, 213–216
Operation County Fair, 206
Operation Mend, 346–348
Operation Traveler, 309
Operation Treasure Island, 274–277

Operation Wildbunch, 88–89
Orner, Bruce, 305–307
Ortiz, Juan, 99–107, 123–124
Otey, Deshon
    after-action report of, 158, 177
    assassination of, 281–285, 296, 342
    assignment to sniper team, 280
    cinder-block shed as shelter for, 160, 173–177
    confrontation at arches, 114
    escape from deathtrap Humvee, 157–159
    Gypsum-Nova ambush of, 156–164, 172–186
    litany of losses listed by, 190
    nightmares of, 194, 284
    origins of MacIntosh's nickname and, 246–247
    rescue of, 172–186

Pacific deployment, of 2/4 Marines, 15–19
palaces, in Ramadi, 52–53
Paladin howitzers, 32, 35–36, 204, 214
palm groves, as Day 3 battlefield, 217
Parker, Tommy, Jr., 217, 280–285, 342, 376
Parkinson's disease, 7–9, 348–349
patrols. *See* reconnaissance/patrols
Patton, Gary, 339
Pendry, Kate, 33–34, 372
personal role radio (PRR), 105, 150–151, 153
Phelps, Chance, 213–214
plugger (GPS receiver), 80–81
"pocket pussy," 248–249
Poindexter, Jason, 334
police officers, Ramadi veterans as, 369–370
Porcupine/Porky (call sign), 71, 246, 278–279
Post-Deployment Health Assessment, 321–322
post-traumatic stress disorder (PTSD), 2–5, 361–372
    accidental killings and, 319
    alcohol use and, 367
    bond among veterans and, 365, 370–371
    collection of human remains and, 75

INDEX

inadequacy of services for, 12, 361–367
MDMA for, 368–369
post-deployment assessment for,
321–322
relationship toll of, 368
risky behavior in, 369–370
Rodriguez's restaurant rampage, 3–5,
362–363
signature traumas causing, 12
suicides linked to, 12–13, 364–367
symptoms of, 364
women combat veterans and, 364
Powers, Caleb, 313–314, 350
Powers, Rosanna, 314
Pretrick, Albert, 275–277
prisoner releases, 240–241
privacy, seeking on base, 247–249
psychiatrist, division's sole, 321–322
psychological operations unit (psyops),
195–196, 215, 236
PTSD. *See* post-traumatic stress disorder

al-Qaeda, 37, 304, 308, 343–344
Al-Qaim District, 253–254, 343
Quetglas, David, 127–128, 166–167
Quill, Richard, III, 352
Quist, Erik, 196–199, 202–206

Radmer, Randy, 136, 251–252, 261
Rainmaker platoon
Day 1 ambush of, 197–199
Day 3 Route Apple fighting of, 234–239
unrelenting attacks on, post-Battle of
Ramadi, 257–260
Ramadi
anticipated easy duty in, 43–44
as battle space, description of, 51–55
color-coded maps of, 54–55
conditions before arrival of 2/4 Marines
in, 28–44
coping with madness of, 247–252
cultural challenges for US personnel in,
54–57
cycle of violence in, 339–344
friends *vs.* foes in, distinguishing
between, 54–56
geography and history of, 28–29
ISIS control of, 344

as key terrain, 2
as privileged enclave, 29–30
rebuilding of, 344–345
Sunni Arab population of, 29–31
threatening posters in, 87–88
See also specific locations and actions
Ramadi, Battle of
air support lacking in, 203–204,
206, 233
citywide offensive beginning, 93–94
cycle of ambush, reinforcement, and
counterattack in, 197
Day 1, 91–194
Day 2, 196–210
Day 3, 212–239
events leading up to, 72–89
insurgents' initiative and tactics in, 1,
192–194
as life-altering experience, 372–377
media coverage of, 185, 191
overlooked status of, 2, 191–192
prelude to, 45–71
US casualties of, 1–2, 190, 206, 210,
240, 241
unrelenting violence after, 253–271
US cultural context for, 91–92
*See also specific combatants and
actions*
Ramirez, Jeremy, 231–233
Ramos, Ronnie, 172
Raney, Cleston, 79
Rapicault, Patrick, 297–298, 301, 331
ratlines, 29
reconnaissance/patrols, 32 35,
62–67
color-coded maps for, 54–55
Echo Company's horrific experience in,
73–77
finding IEDs during, 63–67
Harrill's objections and alternatives to,
83–85
Lionesses' work in, 33–34
Marine run over by US convoy during,
314–315
route clearance in, 62–67
vulnerability to attacks during, 93
*See also specific events occurring
during*

410   **INDEX**

Reigelsperger, David, Jr., 259

religious militants, 37–38, 52, 73, 87

reverse V formation, 64

Reynolds, Jeremy, 365

Reynolds, Joel, 46

Rezaian, Jason, 360

Ricks, Thomas E., 77–78, 343

Riling, Ron, 42, 112, 135–136, 168, 241, 377

roadside bombs. *See* IEDs

Roberts, Anthony, 156, 184

Robins, Christopher, 65–66, 67

rocket-propelled grenades (RPGs)

    Booker's retaliation on man firing, 82

    Dang's horrific death caused by, 59–62

    fired at East Cemetery reinforcements, 135

    fired at Golf Company observation post, 291–292

    fired at Gypsum-Nova intersection, 159–160

    fired at sniper team's location, 125, 167

    fired at Weapons Company, 85–86

    fired elementary school, 261–263

Rodriguez, Damien

    assignment during outbreak of battle, 93

    Hayes's return and, 296–297

    Mukhabarat ambush and fight of, 98–107, 112, 118–119

    PTSD and restaurant rampage of, 3–5, 362–363

Rommel, Erwin, 83, 325

Rosman, Jason, 6, 292, 319

Route Apple (Sofia District)

    Day 1 ambush on, 136–137, 165–166

    Day 2 battle on, 200–202

    Day 3 fighting on, 216–218, 222, 225, 234–239

route clearance, 62–67

    abandonment of, 270

    IED striking Weapons Company on, 263–264

route clearance, Echo Company patrol on

    Day 1 attack on, 140–145, 147, 150–154, 168–170, 186–190

    desperate fight of Marines cut off from, 143–145, 150–154, 169–170, 186–190

    missing-in-action personnel of, 187–189

reinforcements trying to reach, 147–150, 177–178, 181–182

    rescue of, 187–190

Route Michigan

    base locations on, 53

    car bomb attack on, 264–269

    Connor targeted on, 7–9, 50, 260–261, 298–299

    curtailed US operations and insurgent action on, 308–315

    Day 1 engagements on, 93, 114–118

    Day 2 fighting on, 202–206

    early 2/4 Marine action on, 73–74, 81–82, 84

    Echo Company's entry into mosque on, 322–323

    final missions of 2/4 Marines on, 330–338

    high-rise outpost on, bombing of, 310–311

    Iraqi police station on, 309–310

    Marine run over by US convoy on, 314–315

    path and description of, 51

    psyops campaign on, 195–196

    as route-clearance priority, 63

    sniper team assassinated in outpost near, 281–285

    sniper team's overwatch assignment on, 279–281

    surveillance to prevent IEDs on, 84

    Weapons Company struck by IED on, 289–291

    "Wicked Wednesdays" on, 297–307

Royer, Kelly

    AC/DC song's effect on, 215

    alienation of Marines serving under, 228, 277–278, 322–330

    appointed Echo Company commander, 23, 70

    assassination of sniper team under, 281–285, 309

    background of, 69–70

    as "Captain America," 228

    as "Captain Casualty," 278

    Day 1 arches (eastern gateway) actions of, 115, 130–131

    Day 1 decisions of, 115, 130, 147

INDEX

Day 1 Gypsum-Nova actions of, 155–156, 161, 163, 172–173, 177–178, 182, 184
Day 3 platoon assignments of, 216
Day 3 sewage-ditch escape by, 226–229
firing of, 327–330
Harrill's clash with, over patrols, 84–85
interceding for Cogan's marriage, 251
Iraqi adversaries and, 73, 193, 270–271
mortar crew eliminated by, 67–71
near-death experience of, 227–229
overwatch of Route Michigan, 279–281
post-Ramadi career of, 358–359
route-clearance mission of, 62, 63–67
stateside clash with rival Marines, 23–24, 70–71
superiors' opinion of, 70–71, 278–279
RPGs. *See* rocket-propelled grenades
rules of engagement, 221, 229, 342
Rumsfeld, Donald, 14, 19, 78–79, 192
Ruthig, Ranie, 234–237
Rutledge, Samuel, 223–226
Ryan, Marc, 297–298

Saddam Magnificent Mosque, 52, 108, 196, 202, 206
al-Sadr, Muqtada, 87
Sadr City (Baghdad slums), 87
Sanchez, Ricardo, 35, 78–79
Santiago, Romeo
assassination of B members of team, 281–285, 287, 309, 376
background of, 116
Day 1 counterattack of, 137–140
Day 1 engagements of, 116–118
Day 1 insurgents' attack on, 120–129, 137–140, 166–168
Day 1 rescue of, 167–168
Day 3 advances/attacks on insurgent strongholds, 218–222
Day 3 assignment of, 216–217
nickname of, 116, 246
nightmares of, 194
overwatch duty on Route Michigan, 279–281

Royer's reprimand of, 285
as sniper team leader, 115–116
SASO. *See* stability and security operations
satellite formation, for patrols, 62, 93, 196–197
Savage, Cassandra, 259, 350–351
Savage, Eva, 253, 259–260
Savage, Jeremiah, 198, 253, 259–260, 263, 373–374
SAW (squad automatic weapon), 100–101, 220–221, 229, 235
Scharnhorst, Gerhard von, 83
Schickel, Sean, 57, 278, 323–324, 329
schools visits, Marines attacked during, 258–263
Schrage, Dustin, 275–277, 351
Schroeder, Jodelle "Jody"
background of, 48
contempt *vs.* medical care for enemy, 270–271
as honored guest of Marine Corps ball, 372–373
medical care provided by, 45–49, 61
post-Ramadi career of, 373
school-visit victims treated by, 262–263
Seabees treated by, 256–257
sniper-attack victims cared for by, 312–313
Schulze, Jonathan, 62–63, 365–366
Schwarzenegger, Arnold, 251
Scott, Matt
background of, 148
cinder-block shed as shelter for, 160, 173–177
escape from deathtrap Humvee, 159
Gypsum-Nova ambush of, 148, 159–164, 172–186
rescue of, 172–186
Scott, Nate, 281. 284
Sergeant First Class Richard Stayskal Military Medical Accountability Act, 361–362
7 tons (trucks), 13
shaving, undercover unit and, 242–246
Sheldon, Chuck, 67–68
Shia Arabs, 29, 87, 208

INDEX

Shores, Zach
  bullet and shrapnel wounds of, 159, 174
  cinder-block shed as shelter for, 160, 173–177
  Gypsum-Nova ambush of, 156–164, 172–186
  medical evacuation of, 184
  rescue of, 172–186
Shoulder-Launched Multipurpose Assault Weapon (SMAW), 100, 336
show-of-force passes, by helicopters, 103–104, 204
silhouettes, as deceptive tactic, 193
Sims, John, Jr., 231–233, 240
Sledgehammer platoon, 197
sleep deprivation, 63–64, 245–246
SMAW (Shoulder-Launched Multipurpose Assault Weapon), 100, 336
Smith, Eric
  command and promotion of, 164, 216
  Crowley chosen as team leader by, 156
  Gypsum-Nova ambush of, 161–164, 172–186
  heat casualties in squad of, 294–295
  heroic actions of, 162–164
  IED striking, post-Battle of Ramadi, 261
  Navy Cross awarded to, 191, 261, 375
  PTSD and post-Ramadi life of, 375
  rescue of, 177–186
  response to horrific death scene, 75–76
  retrieval of fallen Marine, 232
Smith, Shelly, 375
Snake Pit (base), 53
  attack on, 334–338
  Day 1 command challenges at, 133–134
  first Marine killed near, 59–62
sniper team. *See* Headhunter 2 sniper team
snipers, Iraqi, 311–314
Soares, Andre, 179–180
Sofia District
  as battle space for 2/4 Marines, 51
  Day 1 arches (eastern gateway) actions in, 114–115, 130–131
  Day 1 engagements in, 114–118, 120–194
  Day 1 Gypsum-Nova ambush in, 147–150, 155–164, 172–186

  Day 1 Headhunter 2 sniper team in, 115–117, 120–129, 137–140, 166–168
  Day 1 north end of, route-clearing patrol in, 140–145, 147, 150–154, 168–170, 177, 181–182, 186–190
  Day 1 Route Apple ambush in, 136–137, 165–166
  Day 2 Route Apple battle in, 200–202
  Day 3 advances/attacks on insurgent strongholds in, 218–226
  Day 3 blocking of entry and egress in, 220
  Day 3 Route Apple fighting in, 216–218, 222, 225, 234–239
  Echo Company assigned to, 54
  finding IEDs in, 63–67
  as privileged enclave, 30
  rebuilding of, 345
  "soft cake," 57
Son, Kenneth, 267–269
Special Ops: Lioness (tv series), 372
Springer, Justin, 180–183, 189, 191
squad automatic weapon (SAW), 100–101, 106, 220–221, 229, 235
stability and security operations (SASO), 50, 78
Stanton, Ted
  background of, 116
  Day 1 attack on, 120–129, 137–140, 166–168
  Day 3 advances/attacks on insurgent strongholds, 219–222
  Day 3 assignment of, 217
  first lives taken by, 126–127
  as member of sniper team, 116
  overwatch duty on Route Michigan, 280
  rescue of, 167–168
  Royer's reprimand of, 285
  wounding of, 140, 217
Stayskal, Megan, 361–362
Stayskal, Richard
  background of, 116
  concern over exposed position of, 116–117
  counterattack of, 137–140
  insurgents' attack on, 120–129, 137–140, 166–168

INDEX

413

life-passing-before-your-eyes moment
for, 125
medical malpractice case of, 361–362
as member of sniper team, 116
rescue of, 167–168
wounds and medical evacuation of,
138–140, 216–217
Stephens, John "JD"
background of, 85
collection of enemy remains, 201–202
Day 1 rescue mission for sniper team,
132, 136–137
Day 1 rescue of route-clearing patrol,
187–190
Day 1 Route Apple ambush of, 136–137
Day 2 reinforcement for Rainmaker
platoon, 198–199
Day 2 Route Apple battle of, 200–202
insurgents pursued by, 137
Morris's death and, 85–86, 132, 137
nicknames bestowed by, 246
pre-deployment morale of, 16
shrapnel wound of, 201
Stewart, Michael, 161
stop-losses, 15–16, 19
Strohl, Michael, 213–214
Suarez, Rafael Reynosa, 266–268
suicide
alarming rate of, 364–365
disciplined Marine's, at Camp Victory,
25–26, 99
risk assessment for, 321–322
TBI and PTSD causing, 12–13,
364–367
suicide hotline, 367
Sullivan, Dan, 356
Sunni Arabs, 29–31, 72
supply convoy, Good Friday ambush of,
208–209
Swanson, David, 191, 213, 223, 226–229

Tactical Fusion Center, 72
Taking Chance (headline and movie),
213–214
tank graveyard, 116, 121, 129, 137–140,
166–168
Tapia, Daniel, ambush and fight of,
101–107

Al Taqaddum Air Base (TQ), 30, 48,
305–307, 313
Tate, Justin
background of, 160
cinder-block shed as shelter for, 160,
173–177
Gypsum-Nova ambush of, 160, 172–186
post-Ramadi police work of, 369
wounds and medical care of, 190
Teamey, Kyle, 37, 43, 88–89, 134, 241, 303
Telinda, Brian, 16, 127–128, 189,
220–222, 322–323
Texidor, Jose, Jr., "Tex"
background of, 58
Day 3 attack on insurgent stronghold,
6–7, 223–226
medical saga of, 345–346
nickname of, 6, 246
realization of insurgent's enemy
status, 58
wounding of, 6–7, 224, 266
Thao, Arnold
cinder-block shed as shelter for, 160,
173–177
Gypsum-Nova ambush of, 157, 172–186
rescue of, 172–186
Thomas, Melissa, 370–371
Thomas, Roy
ambush of forces trying to reach,
147–150
attack on route-clearing patrol of,
140–145, 147, 150–154, 168–170
Bronze Star awarded to, 191, 370
MacIntosh's bond with, 370–371
reaction to inadequate vehicle armor, 14
rescue of, 187–190
wounding of, 154, 168–170, 181, 187
Thompson, Kelsey "Kelly," 341
3/5 Marines
drunken clash of 2/4 Marines with,
21–24
fighting and losses in Iraq, 340–342
Tipton, John, 255–257
Tomich, Donna, 350
Tor, Theophilus, 3, 219, 223–226,
266–269
TOW (tube-launched, optically tracked,
wire-guided missile), 200–201, 302

414   **INDEX**

Towle, Wyeth, 18–19, 30, 57, 308
trash bags, for human remains, 75
trauma care. *See* medical (trauma) care
traumatic brain injury (TBI)
  Connor's, 7–9, 348–349
  military unprepared to deal with, 12
  monitoring protocols for, 67
  signature traumas causing, 12,
    66–67
  suicides linked to, 12–13
tribes, friendly *vs.* enemy, 54–55
trigger device, 75, 257
trigger men, for IEDs, 39, 64, 74–75,
  257, 265
Trump, Donald, 353–354
Tuberville, Tommy, 356
2/4 Marines
  aggressive, retaliatory tactics of,
    81–83, 270
  arrival and orientation in Ramadi, 44,
    50–51
  attachment to Army 1st Brigade, 8
  attrition in, 19, 292
  battle space for, 51–55
  "boot drops" into, 20–21
  bulked-up swagger of, 16–17
  casualties of, 1, 11, 339
  Combat Action Ribbons awarded to,
    317–318
  coping with madness of Ramadi,
    247–252
  creative solutions and tactics of, 83–84
  curtailed operations of, 287–288, 307
  dangerous reality confronted by,
    45–49
  deployment in Pacific, 15–19
  deployment to Iraq, 19–26
  drunken clash at Camp Pendleton
    dinner, 21–24
  duration of combat tour, 247
  enemy KIAs attributed to, 317–318
  fighting heritage of, 15
  final stages of Ramadi deployment,
    314–316, 330–338
  first killed casualty of, 59–62
  harrying opening attacks against,
    57–67
  insurgents' view of, as "soft cake," 57

  Iraqi bases and headquarters of,
    52–54
  Kennedy assigned as commander of,
    17–19
  Kennedy's staff selections for, 18–19
  as Magnificent Bastards, 1, 246
  Mattis's soft spot for, 19
  nicknames and call signs of, 71,
    246–247, 278–279
  platoon leaders of, 76–77
  primacy of small-unit leaders in, 83
  resentment over Hagee's
    "benchwarmer" tag, 16
  second deployment to Iraq, 342
  sidelined, at outset of Iraq War,
    14–19, 21
  stop-losses imposed on, 15–16, 19
  *See also specific individuals and
    actions*
2/5 Marines, 297–298, 330–339

UCLA, Operation Mend at,
  346–348
Una Causa Noble (A Noble Cause)
  (film), 351
United Nations Security Council, 35
University of Anbar, 36
up-armored Humvees, 84, 196, 289, 291,
  300, 320
urine checks, for hydration status,
  293–294

Valdes, Vincent
  background and reputation of, 117
  Day 1 counterattack in tank graveyard,
    139–140, 166–168
  Day 1 reinforcement of sniper team,
    123, 127–129, 139–140, 166–168
  Day 1 route-clearing patrol of, 117–118,
    140–145, 188–189
  Day 3 advance/attack on rooftop
    stronghold, 222–226
  Day 3 assignment of, 216
  Day 3 reinforcement of other
    platoons, 218
  fall into marsh, 58
  gun planted in mosque by, 322–323,
    328–329

INDEX

machine gun manned by, 139
wounding of, 224
van der Kolk, Bessel, 367–370
VBIEDs. *See* vehicle-borne IEDs
vehicle armor
  APC's inadequate, 132
  Humvee's inadequate, 13–14, 149
  improvised (hillbilly), 13–14, 32, 68,
    128, 258–259, 265
  MRAPs and improvement in, 13
  Rumsfeld's response to questions
    about, 14
  up-armored Humvees, 84, 196, 289,
    291, 300, 320
vehicle-borne IEDs, 39, 189–190,
  264–269, 302, 333–334
veterans
  access to health services as challenge
    for, 347
  ad hoc assemblages/reunions of,
    352–353
  medical sagas of, 345–350
  memorials and honors for, 351–352
  painful memories of, 2–5 (*see also*
    post-traumatic stress disorder)
  suicide of, 12–13, 364–367
  See also specific individuals

Waechter, Marcus
  arches (eastern gateway) actions of,
    130–131
  cinder-block shed as shelter for, 160,
    173–177
  Day 1 losses in squad, 190
  escape from deathtrap Humvee,
    159
  Gypsum-Nova ambush of, 147–150,
    156–164, 172–186
  inadequate vehicle armor of, 149
  post-Ramadi police work of, 369
  rescue of, 177–186
  shots fired at, 160
Wahhabis, 37
Walker, Allan
  arches assignment of, 131
  background of, 147–148
  death and remains of, 157,
    183–185

Gypsum-Nova ambush of, 147–150,
  156–164
inadequate vehicle armor of, 149
Walker, Kenneth, 148
Walter Reed Army Medical Center, 48
Warth, Clinton, 59
waterborne assault, tragedy in,
  274–277
WBGT (wet-bulb globe temperature),
  292–293
Weapons Company (2/4 Marines)
  Booker's clash with, 244, 245–246
  capture and interrogation of Farhan,
    88–89, 94
  collection of enemy remains, 201–202
  Day 1 reinforcement by, 103–104,
    107–110, 112
  Day 1 rescue of route-clearing patrol,
    187–190
  Day 1 Route Apple ambush of, 136–137,
    165–166
  Day 2 ambush of Rainmaker platoon,
    197–199
  Day 2 Nova battle of, 199–200
  Day 2 psyops assignment of, 196
  Day 2 Route Apple battle of, 200–
    202
  Day 3 Lionesses (women) fighting with,
    234–237, 364
  Day 3 Route Apple fighting of, 222,
    234–239
  final Ramadi missions of, 332
  harrying opening attacks on, 58–59
  IEDs striking, 258–260, 263–269,
    289–291
  mortar units of, 197–198
  pre-battle RPG attack on, 85–86
  as quick-reaction force, 54
  unrelenting attacks on, post-Battle of
    Ramadi, 257–260, 263–269
  weapons of, 165–166
  "Wicked Wednesdays" and, 298–303
  *See also specific individuals and
    actions*
Weaver, Justin, 21, 373–374
Weber, Tim, 60, 242, 275, 277, 312–313
Weigelt, Brian, 26, 170, 242, 277, 285,
  319–320

416   **INDEX**

Weiler, Rob
   Booker's clash with, 245–246
   collection of enemy remains, 201–202
   Conde and, 109–110, 351–352
   Day 1 rescue mission for sniper team, 132, 136–137
   Day 1 rescue of route-clearing patrol, 187–190
   Day 1 Route Apple ambush of, 136–137, 165–166
   Day 2 ambush of Rainmaker platoon under, 197–199
   Day 2 Route Apple battle of, 200–202
   Day 3 Route Apple fighting of, 225, 234–239
   Day 3 taunting by, 215
   final Ramadi missions of, 332
   friend *vs.* foe quandary for, 55–56
   IEDs striking company of, 258–260, 263–269, 289–291
   interrogation of Iraqi hospital workers, 239
   near-death by refrigerator, 250
   pessimism/fatalism of, 239, 246
   post-Ramadi career of, 356
   Silver Star awarded to, 241, 356
   stateside clash with rival Marines, 23–24
   "Wookie" nickname of, 246
Weldon, Curt, 359
Wells, Lucas "Duke"
   background of, 23
   Day 2 Nova battle of, 199–200
   detainees under control of, 89
   drunken, unruly behavior at dinner, 23–24
   IED striking platoon of, post-Battle of Ramadi, 258–260
   near-death by refrigerator, 250
   owning of bastards reputation, 17
   psyops assignment of, 196
Welsh, Wade, 178–186, 189, 191
West, Bing, 340
wet-bulb globe temperature (WBGT), 292–293
whistleblower, Royer as, 358–359
"Wicked Wednesdays," 297–307
Williams, Marcel, 200, 290

Winfree, Curtis, 324–327
Wiscowiche, Joseph, 74, 232
Wiscowiche, William, 73–77
women, Iraqi
   absence of, as tip-off, 63
   challenge of dealing with, 33–34
women, US military
   ban on combat operations for, 33, 235
   engaged in direct ground combat, 234–237, 364
   Lionesses, 33–34, 234–237, 364, 372
   PTSD of, 364
Woodall, Justin
   attack on route-clearing patrol of, 142–143, 150–154
   background of, 142
   desperate fight while cut off, 150–152, 169–170, 187–189
   listed as missing in action, 187
   rescue of, 188–189
   wounding of, 151
Wroblewski, John
   accessibility of, 76
   arches (eastern gateway) actions of, 115, 131
   background of, 26
   death of, 185, 216, 264, 277–278
   father's pilgrimages to Iraq, 350–351
   grave of, 350
   grief over young Marine's suicide, 26
   Gypsum-Nova ambush of, 147–150, 156–164, 172–186
   replacement for, 265
   rescue of forces by Army engineers, 177–186
   wounding of, 162–164, 172, 177, 232
Wroblewski, John, Sr., 350–351
Wroblewski, Shawn, 350–351
Wylie, Mike, 18, 104, 133, 283, 300–301, 324

Yansky, Chris, 64
Young, Ryan, 39
youth of 2/4 Marines, 20–21

al-Zarqawi, Abu Musab, 304, 308, 343
Zimmerman, Patrick, 45

ABOUT THE AUTHOR

Gregg Zoroya was a journalist for *USA TODAY* for twenty-five years and throughout his career has reported from Somalia, the West Bank, Gaza, Pakistan, Afghanistan, Iraq, and Liberia. For five years until retirement in early 2022, he was a member of the *USA TODAY* editorial board. He is the author of *The Chosen Few*.